4.

11+

WITHDRAWN

BANK CREDIT

BANK CREDIT

Edited by
Herbert V. Prochnow

HARPER & ROW, PUBLISHERS, New York
Cambridge, Philadelphia, San Francisco,
London, Mexico City, São Paulo, Sydney

1817

FIRST EDITION

Library of Congress Cataloging in Publication Data
Main entry under title:

Bank credit.

Includes index.
1. Bank loans—Addresses, essays, lectures.
I. Prochnow, Herbert Victor, 1897–
HG1641.B33   332.1′753   80–8883
ISBN 0–06–014857–8   AACR2

81 82 83 84 85 10 9 8 7 6 5 4 3 2 1

Contents

81-2474

Contributors

WILLIAM A. ADKINS, JR., *Senior Vice President*
First National Bank of Topeka
Topeka, Kansas

JOSEPH E. BANTA, *Vice President*
Morgan Guaranty Trust Company of New York
New York, New York

ROBERT N. BEE, *Managing Director and Chief Executive Officer*
London Interstate Bank Ltd.
London, England

WILLIAM G. BRANNEN, *President*
U.C.B. Leasing Corporation
(A subsidiary of United Central National Bancshares, Inc.)
Des Moines, Iowa

WILLIAM H. BRYAN, *Instructor, Credit and Financial Analysis*
Business Education Division, Dun & Bradstreet, Inc.
New York, New York

T. RONALD CASPER, *Vice President*
Mellon Bank N.A.
Pittsburgh, Pennsylvania

JAMES S. CUNNINGHAM, *Vice President*
The First National Bank of Chicago
Chicago, Illinois

JAMES KURT DEW, *Manager of Financial Research*
Chicago Mercantile Exchange
Chicago, Illinois

RALPH B. GILPATRICK, JR., *Vice Chairman of the Board*
Mellon Bank N.A.
Pittsburgh, Pennsylvania

R. W. GOGGIN, *Senior Vice President, World Banking Division*
Bank of America NT & SA
San Francisco, California

WILLIAM E. GOODMAN, *Senior Vice President*
First Tennessee Bank N.A.
Memphis, Tennessee

HENRY HARFIELD, *Partner*
Shearman & Sterling
New York, New York

WILLIAM P. JILEK, *President and Chief Executive Officer*
Richland Trust Company
Mansfield, Ohio

WILLIAM J. KORSVIK, *Senior Vice President*
Worldwide Banking Department
The First National Bank of Chicago
Chicago, Illinois

PHILIP M. LEWIN, *General Manager, Commercial Finance Division*
Continental Illinois National Bank & Trust Company of Chicago
Chicago, Illinois

JOHN B. MCCARTER, *Senior Vice President and Senior Loan
Administration Officer*
Central National Bank of Cleveland
Cleveland, Ohio

C. EDWARD MCCONNELL, *Senior Vice President*
Keefe, Bruyette & Woods, Inc.
New York, New York

GARY MRAZSKO, *Vice President and General Manager*
Central Commercial Finance Division
Walter E. Heller & Company
Chicago, Illinois

P. HENRY MUELLER, *Chairman, Credit Policy Committee*
    Citibank N.A.
    New York, New York

LEIF OLSON, *Chairman, Economic Policy Committee*
    Citibank N.A.
    New York, New York

JERRY H. PEARSON, *Vice President*
    Harris Trust and Savings Bank
    Chicago, Illinois

RICHARD PUZ, *Executive Vice President*
    Bank of America NT & SA
    San Francisco, California

HAROLD T. REDDING, *Senior Vice President*
    Dun & Bradstreet
    New York, New York

JACK W. ROBISON, *Vice President*
    First Tennessee Bank N.A.
    Memphis, Tennessee

MARVIN G. ROHN, *Vice President*
    The Omaha National Bank
    Omaha, Nebraska

PAUL E. SHAFFER, *President*
    Fort Wayne National Bank
    Fort Wayne, Indiana

THOMAS R. SMITH, *President*
    Fidelity Brenton Bank and Trust Company
    Marshalltown, Iowa

RICHARD P. SPENCER, *Vice President*
    Bank of America NT & SA
    Los Angeles, California

HARVEY B. STEPHENS, *Member*
    Brown, Hay & Stephens
    Springfield, Illinois

HERBERT G. SUMMERFIELD, JR., *Vice President*
    Pittsburgh National Bank
    Pittsburgh, Pennsylvania

GREGORY B. TOMLINSON, *Partner*
      Peat, Marwick, Mitchell & Co.
      San Antonio, Texas

FRIEDA WATSON, *Commercial Banking Representative*
      Harris Trust and Savings Bank
      Chicago, Illinois

MAYNARD I. WISHNER, *President*
      Walter E. Heller & Company
      Chicago, Illinois

CLAYTON YEUTTER, *President*
      Chicago Mercantile Exchange
      Chicago, Illinois

Introduction

No other single function that the banks of this country perform is more important than the extension of credit.

Bank credit plays a significant role in providing funds for the operation of business, industry, and economic activities of all kinds, as well as for the personal financial needs of millions of Americans. Some businesses borrow only occasionally from banks for special purposes. Many businesses, however, borrow regularly to take care of seasonal needs or to finance an increasing volume of business. In addition, with the use of installment credit, which enables individuals to buy many types of durable goods by borrowing from banks, the lending facilities of banks are being used by more and more individuals.

A number of principles of sound lending practice have been developed through decades of experience. No banker can manage his bank in the best interests of his stockholders, his depositors, and his community if he does not understand these principles and observe them in extending credit. Moreover, there is a practical need for an integrated study in one volume, such as this one, which covers the operation of a credit department; the sources of credit information; a critical analysis of balance sheets, profit and loss statements, surplus accounts, business budgets, and trial balances; unsecured and secured loans; term loans; letters of credit; certain legal aspects of bank loans; consumer credit; equipment leasing; credit and the business cycle; international loans; slow loans and workouts; and many other aspects of bank lending, together with a large number of practical illustrations. Changes in recent years in the types of bank loans and in the relative significance of the different kinds of loans make it desirable to have these trends analyzed and well understood.

The banker can serve the growing economic needs of his community by the sound extension of credit. At the same time he must earn an adequate return for his stockholders and provide safety for his depositors. These several responsibilities make it imperative that he understand thoroughly the principles he must observe if he is to extend credit safely and for the mutual benefit of the borrower and the bank.

The loan-making activities of banks represent one of the most significant phases of their operations. Earnings from loans and discounts constitute the largest single item in the profit and loss statements of most banking institutions.

The loan-making activities are the economic lifeblood not only of banking and financial institutions but, in many ways, of our whole system of free enterprise.

In view of these facts, it is strange that there has been a dearth of practical literature on loan operations. A number of volumes have been published on the general subject of financial statement analysis, but none of them has discussed the matter essentially from the point of view of the commercial banker and his loaning problems. Books likewise have been published analyzing sources of credit information and the work of the credit department, and studies have been made of principles of the loan-making process. However, the discussions have not been carried through to the practical application of the principles by those experienced in the extension of credit.

In this volume an effort has been made to present the subject of loan making in commercial banks in its entirety: the operation of the bank credit department; the analysis of all types of financial statements, including the trial balance; the consideration of all factors that enter into the granting of credit; and the various types of loans. In addition a number of loan illustrations are taken from the everyday experience of bankers in large and small banks in various parts of the United States.

Every effort has been made to present a thorough discussion of the theoretical aspects of the subject, as well as the practical application of the principles. In the everyday work of the banker, a comprehensive understanding of both theory and practice is imperative to intelligent banking.

The subject of bank credit is now so broad with so many different types of credit that no one person can be an authority on all aspects of bank lending. Consequently, bankers, business executives, and attorneys who are authorities in the many aspects of credit extension were invited to contribute chapters to this book. The contributing authors represent the largest banks, regional banks, and smaller banks in various areas of the country as well as other financial institutions. I should like to express appreciation to them for making possible this comprehensive discussion of bank credit.

It is hoped that this volume will appeal to students of banking, finance, accounting, economics, and business administration in our colleges and universities, to young men and women now in banking who earnestly desire a comprehensive grasp of all the fundamentals of loan making and financial statement analysis in order that they may become competent bankers, and to executives of business organizations who wish to conduct their banking relationships with a thorough background of knowledge. Finally, this book is meant to be useful to those persons who have spent years of their lives in banking but who would like an opportunity to refresh their thinking by a study of statement analysis, loan-making experiences of other bankers, and special phases of the subject of particular interest to them.

This book presents a comprehensive discussion of one of the most important responsibilities of bank management—the extension of credit. On this subject no banker can be too well informed.

I should like to express appreciation to Herbert V. Prochnow, Jr., for his helpfulness on many aspects of the book manuscript.

H.V.P.

BANK CREDIT

1

The Banker and the Credit Decision

As one who makes and administers loans, the bank loan officer must understand the significance of financial statements and be able to interpret and analyze them. This does not require the accountant's ability to put financial figures together but it does require an ability to read and understand the statement components and analyze their relationships.

Four separate financial statements are required by the Securities and Exchange Commission in the annual report of every corporation whose stock is publicly held. These four are the financial statements that the bank loan officer will commonly encounter and which must be understood as part of the loan decision. They are:

1. Balance sheet
2. Income (profit and loss) statement
3. Reconciliation of stockholders' investment or of the retained earnings account
4. Source and application of funds statement

In the pages which follow, these four financial statements will be described, item by item, starting with the basics and taking nothing for granted. We shall then describe the important financial ratios and how they contribute to an understanding of relationships in the form of internal and comparative financial analysis. Finally, we shall touch upon the importance of operating budgets and how, from operating budgets, it is possible to prepare projections of cash flow and future financial requirements.

The Promise to Pay

Credit is defined as the delivery of money, goods, or services today in exchange for a future promise to pay. A credit decision is concerned with the validity of the promise to pay, what the chances are that it will be lived up to.

Banks deliver money today, in the form of loans, in exchange for a promise to pay at a specified future date. In their extension of credit, bankers must, generally, be more conservative than trade suppliers because they lend not their own money or that of the bank's stockholders but money which has been placed in their safekeeping by depositors for whom funds must be available for withdrawal on demand or when a certificate of deposit falls due.

Like other credit grantors, the banker must evaluate the likelihood that the borrower will repay as promised. The risk that the loan will not be repaid must be balanced against its profitability. The possibility of future profit in the case of a new business making an initial loan must be a part of the decision just as surely as future profitability must be a factor in the decision of a merchant considering a first order from a newly established business enterprise.

The banker is a dealer in a commodity and the commodity is money. A bank loan is a "sale" of this commodity on credit. The banker is involved in a credit decision which requires the marshaling of facts and their evaluation.

The Three C's of Credit

Those who deal regularly with the credit decision are familiar with the three C's of credit. They are Character, Capacity, and Capital. It gets to be a game to add other C's, such as Conditions and Coverage (insurance), but Character, Capacity, and Capital are basic.

Character, combining integrity with fortitude, is placed by many at the head of the line. This is on the theory that a determination to pay will see the credit transaction through to a successful conclusion even in the face of difficult problems not of the borrower's making. But, lacking character, there will be little determination to pay. Experienced credit grantors agree there is no way to protect with legal safeguards from one whose intention is to welsh on a commitment.

Character is an inner quality and not something worn as a visible garment. Despite the ability some claim to size up the other fellow in a brief face-to-face encounter, character as such is not easily read. The astute credit grantor looks instead at reputation, which is what others think, and background, which is an evidence of character traits as past actions have displayed them.

Capacity is the ability of those who manage a business to manage it successfully. Once again, the record of past experience is the key. The background of owners and managers should be appropriate for a sound management of the enterprise. If the business is well established and its management represents a balanced set of abilities, prospects for the future are good.

If the business is new, then the experience of owners and managers becomes important. If previously in business, what has been the record? Lack of past success, in the absence of extenuating circumstances, does not bode well for the future. If a record of previous business ownership or general management is lacking, then the employment record of the principals becomes important. Unbalanced work experience—all sales or all production—will not bridge the gap between the two. Too often we see some variant on the classic situation of the super salesperson and red-hot production manager joining forces to make for themselves the money they had been making for others, forgetting that general management in the form of administration and finance is an essential ingredient for success.

Capital refers to the finances available for the operation of a business. Entrepreneurs possessing character and capacity will see to it that at least minimal capital is available before starting a new enterprise; those lacking character and capacity may well dissipate quickly what capital they do bring into the venture.

Few businesses have the capital to operate entirely on their own without ever using some sort of outside financial support. Some businesses are highly seasonal, and it would be an unwise and unprofitable use of capital to have enough money invested to take care of peak requirements. The clothing industry, for example, has heavy spring and heavy fall seasons. Dresses are made up in advance of heavy seasonal shipments to retailers. After shipments are made, receivables are collected, suppliers' bills are paid off, and the manufacturer is practically out of business until the next season approaches and the cycle is repeated. Outside seasonal financing in the form of short-term bank loans is normal, and there will be a payout period between seasons.

Some banks have entered a field that used to be the private prerogative of the more costly finance company. This is financing secured by accounts receivable or inventory and used by less adequately capitalized companies on a more or less permanent basis.

Finally, there are many companies which use longer-term financing in the form of mortgage loans or bonds held by insurance companies, institutional investors, or the general investing public. These can be due over a period of years and provide capital on a more permanent basis. There are some few large national concerns which borrow on a long-term basis without giving any security, but these are exceptions.

The proportion of owners' investment to capital obtained on the outside from lenders is an important factor in considering the adequacy of capital. Generally speaking, the owners' equity in the assets owned should be equal to or more than the equity of outside creditors. But much will depend on the line of business. The tremendous investment of an electric utility will be financed largely by bonds greatly exceeding the dollar amount of the stockholders' investment.

The best illustration of the relativity between stockholders' investment and the claims of outsiders is the bank itself. Banks originated as places where people could put their money and valuables for safekeeping. Somebody discovered that the level of such deposits was steady and the funds could be loaned profitably at interest. So a bank's own capital represented by stockholders' investment will at all times be small compared to the amounts it owes its depositors.

An analysis of financial statements provides an indication of all three C's of the credit decision, Character, Capacity, and Capital. Much of what we read in financial statements is an indication of their presence or absence.

The Importance of Backgrounds

Before the bank loan officer gets around to analyzing financial statements, he or she ought to know something about the history of the borrower and its method of operation. It is impossible to read financial figures intelligently without supplemental information. A meat-packer selling on weekly terms presents a different financial picture from an encyclopedia publisher selling on terms of a year or more.

Background information is the first order of business. How long in operation? The first five years are the hardest. Have there been repeated changes in management? Sometimes it's a struggle to get the right combination. Does management represent a well-rounded diversity of skills? Does the company or its principals have a clear business record or are there questionable failures and fires which reflect upon character or capacity? Is there a good balance in the management between youth and maturity? A preponderance of either can lead, on the one hand, to rashness of judgment or to ultraconservatism on the other.

The line of business can be important. Some lines of activity are the wave of the future, with growth almost assured. Others represent receding opportunities, with stagnation if not financial difficulties ahead.

Meaningful financial analysis is impossible without knowledge of the method of operation. What are the products sold and what is the competition? What is the customer mix—is there concentration of sales in a few accounts? What are terms of sale and is a cash discount offered? What are purchase terms and are suppliers many or few? Is manufacturing involved and, if so, what is its complexity? What indication is there of the nature of employee and union relations? What is the relationship with the bank, favorable or just so-so? Finally, what is the magnitude of the plant investment? How is the plant financed? If on a long-term basis, is there any problem meeting each year's debt maturities?

Questions like these should be answered before any financial analysis begins.

Credit and Financial Analysis

When a bank acts as lender, someone in the bank makes the decision and someone is the point of contact with the borrower. Sometimes the decision maker and the point of contact are the same; sometimes not; sometimes partly.

Banks are limited by law as to the size of loan they make. If a local borrower requires more than the local bank's legal limit, the excess may be taken by a larger correspondent bank in a neighboring city. If the local bank is small enough, it may be its president who makes the decision and contacts the borrower, having, in most cases, the benefit of close personal acquaintance.

In areas where branch banking is legal, local managers have authority to lend up to a certain limit. Beyond that they seek the approval of a regional office, which may involve the decision of a regional loan committee. Much of the financial analysis may be done at the regional office.

In large banking institutions in major cities, the setup is more complex. The commercial loan officer is, herself or himself, a person knowledgeable in financial matters who will know the borrower's situation through study and through periodic visits, both in the bank and at the customer's location.

The loan officer of the large bank must understand credit and financial analysis but will not always do the mechanical work involved. In the bank's credit department or in a separate department are credit and financial analysts who interpret financial data and keep information up to date for the benefit of the loan officer handling the account.

The credit and financial analysis section in today's large city bank is often a training ground for future loan officers. Those engaged in this work are often recent MBA graduates in finance who provide invaluable backup.

The Computer—A Helpful Ally

Financial statement analysis involves setting up figures in columnar form and the computation of numerous ratios and averages. At one time the setting up was done by hand and the computations were made with a calculator or slide rule. No more!

Today the computer is a helpful ally. Figures from the latest statement are fed into the computer which prints out a columnar comparative, computes and prints the ratios and industry comparisons, and computes the percentage of various balance sheet items against totals and against the industry.

Dun & Bradstreet offers a "Financial Profile" service under which an individual company can present its own financial figures for a three-year comparison and get back a computation of percentages against totals and against industry norms.

Whatever help the bank loan officer receives from the credit and financial analysts, he or she still must understand financial statements and how to interpret them in terms of what they say about the validity of the borrower's promise to pay. The final decision on a large loan may go to a loan committee for a yes or no, but the loan officer's recommendation will be an important factor in that decision.

The next chapter will describe the four important financial statements with which the bank loan officer must deal.

2

The Four Financial Statements

The four main financial statements with which the bank loan officer works are (1) balance sheet, (2) profit and loss statement, (3) reconciliation of changes in net worth, and (4) reconciliation of changes in working capital.

Types of Statements

Each of the financial statements may be one of the following types:

Fiscal Statement. A statement drawn off at the close of a fiscal (financial) period, which is usually one year. The close of the fiscal year may be the close of the calendar year, or it may be any other date, which is then called the fiscal closing. Fiscal closing dates are chosen to coincide, in the case of a seasonal business, with a between-season time of year when the financial condition is liquid.

Interim Statement. A statement drawn off between fiscal closings— monthly, quarterly, or at the close of any four-week accounting period.

Individual Statement. In the case of a corporation, a statement of the finances of one individual corporation only. If stock is owned in another corporation, it is shown as a noncurrent investment asset.

Consolidated Statement. A statement consolidating assets and liabilities of one corporation, the parent, with those of a subsidiary corporation (or more than one) in which it owns more than 50 percent of the capital stock. Assets and liabilities of the two companies are combined except for intercompany offsetting transactions which wash out. If there are outside stockholders who own stock in the subsidiary, then the subsidiary's capital stock owned by the outsiders is shown as a noncurrent liability—minority stock interest—and will thus be deducted from the consolidated net worth.

Pro Forma Statement. A statement giving effect to proposed changes which have not yet taken place. A pro forma statement, for example, will show the financial condition if a $3 million bond issue, which is offered for sale, is actually sold and the cash proceeds invested in the business.

ACCOUNTANT'S CERTIFICATION

Virtually all financial statements bankers work with are prepared by outside accountants. It is important to know the qualifications of the accountant and whether the accountant is a certified public accountant.

The auditors' report, otherwise known as certification, at the end of the financial statements reports the extent of the audit and expresses an opinion, if there is no qualification, that "the financial statements . . . present fairly the financial position . . . and the results of operations and the sources of funds . . . in conformity with generally accepted accounting principles applied on a consistent basis."

If the outside accountants do have a qualification, it will be clearly stated. Example: "Subject to the effect, if any, of the litigation referred to in the preceding paragraph, the financial statements . . . present fairly the financial position. . . ."

The Balance Sheet

The balance sheet is the first of the four financial statements which the analyst must understand. It is not necessary to know how to put figures together in order to understand them, though it may help. Furthermore, knowing how to prepare the financial statement does not necessarily enable a person to interpret its meaning.

What follows is a step-by-step description of the components of a balance sheet. Some will find it no better than a review of basics; others will find some of the concepts new and necessary for what follows.

THE BALANCE SHEET EQUATION

A balance sheet consists of two vertical columns of figures which must balance. The left-hand column lists everything the business (or the individual) owns. These are called assets. The right-hand column lists all claims against those assets, claims of those to whom money is owed, and claims against the assets by the owner or owners. The claims of outside creditors are called liabilities, those of the owners are called net worth.

Another way of thinking about the balance sheet is to think of a listing of all assets in the left-hand column and a listing, in the right-hand column, of all those who have an equity in those assets. This is like a $50,000 home we own. We have a $25,000 equity in the home and the mortgage company has a $25,000 equity. In the same way, a business "owns" certain assets, and a combination of equities in those assets equals their total.

Outsiders having an equity in the assets are creditors and the debts owing them are liabilities. After deducting the total of liabilities from the total of assets, then what is left is the equity of owners. This equity is called net worth.

The accounting or balance sheet equation looks like this:

$$\text{Assets} = \text{Liabilities} + \text{Net worth}$$

or

$$\text{Assets} = \text{Creditors' equity} + \text{Owners' equity.}$$

CURRENT ASSETS

Assets listed in the left-hand column are divided into current and noncurrent assets. Current assets are those used in normal day-to-day operation. Current assets are converted into cash and used to pay bills in much less than a year and they should never include items which it is not expected will turn into cash within 365 days.

The current assets we see on almost every balance sheet are Cash, Accounts Receivable, and Inventory. Other current assets less frequently encountered are Government or Marketable Securities, Prepaid Expenses, and Advances or Prepayments to contractors or suppliers.

Cash may be broken down into Cash on Hand, which would include office cash in the petty cash drawer, and Cash in Bank. Only in the rare case where cash is held in escrow for a future debt payment is it not immediately available, and then it should be so marked.

Government or Marketable Securities are the next thing to cash because they can be converted overnight to cash. Marketable Securities must be securities listed on a major stock exchange so that a call to the broker will produce an immediate sale and its cash proceeds.

Accounts receivable, which are amounts due from customers for merchandise sold, may include notes receivable taken to close out an old account or due from customers sold on note. The important thing is that accounts receivable should be due from customers for merchandise sold. Other accounts receivable—an amount due from an officer of the company, or from salespeople for travel advances, or from a related company—should be included under noncurrent assets rather than current assets.

Accounts receivable are the total of all unpaid bills or invoices which have been issued to customers. When it becomes clear that one of these unpaid customer invoices is not going to be paid—is uncollectable—it should immediately be charged off and no longer carried as an account receivable. Furthermore, it is reasonable to assume that not all of the accounts we now consider collectable will actually be collected. It is proper, therefore, to set up a Reserve for Uncollectable Accounts and to deduct this reserve from the total of unpaid customer invoices to arrive at a conservative collectable amount. This Reserve for Uncollectable Accounts will run in the neighborhood of 3 percent of gross accounts receivable. The reserve is deducted from the gross to arrive at net accounts receivable like this:

Accounts Receivable	$103,000
Less Reserve for Doubtful Accounts	3,000
Accounts Receivable (net)	$100,000

Inventory is the amount of merchandise on hand and, while it may sound simple, it is far from that. There is nothing—certainly nothing among the current assets—which can vary so much in dollar value. As we will see when we study the makeup of the statement of earnings, or profit and loss statement, there is nothing that has more to do with the amount of profit we show ourselves to have earned than the way we value inventory.

The first step in valuing inventory is to make a physical count in the warehouse. A long tabulating sheet is used to mark down a figure representing the number of each inventory item on hand. Once this physical count has been made, a value is assigned to each of the items counted.

The two most common methods of valuing inventory are first in, first out (FIFO) and last in, first out (LIFO). Under FIFO we assume that inventory items bought first are the first to go out. What we have left, therefore, is what was bought last. In a rising market this means a higher inventory valuation and, as we will see, a lower cost of goods sold, and a higher gross and net profit.

Somebody discovered that a different method of valuing inventory would lower the dollar valuation and, therefore—as we will see when we consider the profit and loss statement—lower the net profit upon which corporate income tax is paid. Many businesses, within a few years after the discovery, changed from FIFO to this method of valuing inventory, called LIFO.

LIFO assumes that the last item brought into the inventory is the first to go out. The rationalization is that the cost of the item we sell today is truly reflected in the cost of the item we buy to replace it.

Under LIFO, if items in the warehouse have been bought at progressively higher prices, inventory is valued at lower and older prices, which gives a lower inventory valuation, possibly substantially lower. When a company changes its method of valuing inventory from FIFO to LIFO, as many have done in recent years, the Internal Revenue Service and the Securities and Exchange Commission both have something to say because a switch from FIFO to LIFO changes not only the value assigned to Inventory but the final net profit upon which income tax is paid.

All this makes clear how important it is, when looking at Inventory on a balance sheet, to know how it has been valued. Nothing is more important for the credit analyst to look into.

Prepaid Expenses can best be illustrated by Prepaid Rent and Prepaid Insurance. Rent and insurance are usually paid in advance. When we prepare a balance sheet at an interim date during the lease or insurance year, the amount of occupancy or coverage we have already paid for but not yet used is set up as Prepaid Expense and as a current asset.

Advances, or Prepayments on Merchandise (or on Contracts) are amounts paid to a supplier or contractor for goods not yet delivered or work not yet done. This often happens in the case of a plant construction job or a major equipment installation running into millions of dollars. The contractor or the equipment manufacturer is not expected to finance such a major project without money up front. The amount advanced under the terms of the contract will show up as a current asset on the balance sheet.

Up to this point the balance sheet looks like this:

Cash		$40,000
Marketable Securities		25,000
Accounts Receivable	$72,000	
Less Reserve for Doubtful Accounts	2,000	
Net Accounts Receivable		70,000
Inventory		85,000
Total Current Assets		$220,000

After listing each of the current assets in order we draw a line and enter the total.

NONCURRENT ASSETS

Below the line we begin our noncurrent asset listing with Fixed Assets. In the case of a retailer this is the store in which business is done; in the case of a wholesaler, the warehouse and office. Fixed assets for the manufacturer comprise the plant property—real estate, buildings, factory equipment, and office furniture and equipment.

Real estate (land) is not depreciated; its value on the balance sheet—its book value—is always the price paid. Buildings and machinery and equipment, on the other hand, are depreciated to reflect current value. On the theory that they wear out slowly, buildings are depreciated over as much as 40 years. Machinery and equipment are depreciated over a shorter period and automotive equipment over as little as five years.

Depreciation means that each year we mark down the book value of fixed assets. Actually, we add the current year's depreciation to a Reserve for Depreciation, which we then deduct as a book entry from the aquisition cost of the asset. Our Fixed Assets section looks like this:

Land	$10,000	
Buildings	30,000	
Machinery and Equipment	50,000	
Total	90,000	
Less Reserve for Depreciation	40,000	
Total Fixed Assets		$50,000

There are other assets in the noncurrent category. First, receivables not due from customers. Such receivables might include amounts due from corporate officers or employees for advances, or sales people for travel advances. There might also be loans to subsidiary or affiliated companies. (A subsidiary is a company more than 50 percent of whose capital stock is owned by the parent; an affiliate is a company less than 50 percent of whose stock is owned or whose stock is owned by the same individuals.)

Miscellaneous investments are also noncurrent assets. In addition to unlisted stocks, these would include stock ownership in a subsidiary or affiliated company.

Cash Surrender Value of Life Insurance is generally listed as a noncurrent asset unless it has been borrowed against. Many companies carry life insurance on principal officers. As premiums are paid a portion goes to build up a cash surrender value in the policy, which can be borrowed against. Most accountants show CSVLI as noncurrent on the theory that it is not normally used as a working asset. But if the loan has been made and shows up as a current liability, then the loan collateral in the form of the CSVLI is shown as a current asset.

Intangible assets include (1) goodwill, (2) patents, (3) copyrights, (4) mailing lists, (5) catalogues, (6) trademarks, and (7) organization expense. Some of these can represent real cash outlay and have substantial value. But conservative financial appraisal considers them to be without realizable value for the payment of debts and they are considered intangible.

Larger and more financially sound concerns probably will value such intangible assets at a nominal figure of perhaps one dollar, if at all.

Tangible net worth is the figure which is used in the computation of financial ratios. It is essential to recognize the intangible assets from among other assets in the noncurrent category and then deduct the total of intangible assets from Net Worth to arrive at tangible net worth on the basis of which ratios are figured.

Once we have listed assets, current and noncurrent, we draw a line at the bottom and enter the total. The bottom half of the left-hand side of the balance sheet now looks like this:

Total Current Assets		$220,000
Land	$10,000	
Buildings	30,000	
Machinery and Equipment	50,000	
Total	$90,000	
Less Reserve for Depreciation	40,000	
Total Fixed Assets		50,000
Notes Due from Officers		5,000
Advances to Salespersons		2,000
Capital Stock in Related Company		10,000
Cash Surrender Value of Life Insurance		5,000
Copyrights and Trademarks		3,000
Total Assets		$295,000

CURRENT LIABILITIES

Now we are ready to list in the right-hand column of the balance sheet all claims against assets. These claims include claims of outsiders (liabilities) and those of owners (net worth). The total of liabilities and net worth at the bottom of the right-hand column must equal the total of assets at the bottom of the left-hand column. That's what makes it a balance sheet.

First among the claims of outside creditors are current liabilities. These are debts due for payment within one year, within 365 days or less. If a debt is due over a period of years payable so much a year, then the amount due for payment within 365 days is shown as a current liability and labeled Current Maturity on Long-term Debt.

Usually heading up Current Liabilities at the top of the right-hand column is Accounts Payable. These are amounts owed suppliers for merchandise or services which have been delivered and billed. Accounts payable are the reverse of accounts receivable. They represent invoices issued to us by our suppliers and held in their unpaid invoice file.

Notes payable to bank are generally on a 90-day or other short-term payment basis to provide seasonal financial requirements. There may also be notes payable to a finance company due within one year. If the bank or finance company notes are secured by assets such as accounts receivable or inventory, then the notes payable and the asset pledged as security should be keyed and footnoted. The loan should never be shown as a deduction from the pledged asset on the left-hand side of the balance sheet. Both should be shown separately, the pledged asset on the left and the secured note on the right.

There may be other notes due within one year, to an officer, perhaps, or to a related company. A demand note is payable at the pleasure of the lender and therefore considered due within one year. A note which has no definite due date ("That's owing my father and I'm to pay it when I can") is presumed to be payable on demand and is a current liability.

Next among the current liabilities we find accruals. These are expenses that have accrued but are not yet paid. They may be lumped as accruals or they may be shown separately: Accrued Wages and Salaries or Accrued Taxes. Example: We make up payroll at the close of each two-week period. If we prepare a balance sheet at a date which falls in the middle of the two-week period, then, though we will not write payroll checks for another week, we already owe for the week which has been worked. This week's pay becomes Accrued Payroll. The same is true of Accrued Taxes already due but not yet payable.

Next we may find Customers' Advances or Customers' Credit Balances. These are amounts advanced to us by our customers for work we are yet to perform or merchandise we are yet to deliver. Credit balances are amounts we have credited to customers' accounts—perhaps an allowance for faulty goods delivered—and which have not yet been deducted by customers from payments made to us.

Current Maturity on Long-term Debt is that portion of debt due over a period of years that is payable within 365 days. For example, a $100,000 mortgage is to be paid in ten equal annual installments. Of the $100,000 total, $10,000 is due within one year and is therefore a current liability: Current Year's Mortgage Maturity.

Having listed all liabilities due within 365 days, we draw a line and show total current liabilities. It looks like this:

Accounts Payable	$50,000
Notes Payable to Bank	25,000
Accrued Wages and Taxes	10,000
Customers' Credit Balances	5,000
Current Year's Mortgage Maturity	10,000
Total Current Liabilities	$100,000

NONCURRENT LIABILITIES

Below the line there are still more claims of outside creditors to list before going to owners' equity in the assets of the business. Liabilities still to be listed are those due for payment beyond one year, known as noncurrent liabilities —deferred debts, or long-term liabilities. Having already shown the portion of long-term debt due within one year as a current liability, we are concerned now with the portion of debt due beyond one year.

Noncurrent liabilities include mortgages, notes, debentures, or bonds maturing beyond one year. All are nothing more than IOUs indicating a certain amount of money due and when. What we need to know about a deferred debt is when it's due; how it's payable; whether or not it's secured, and, if so, by what assets; to whom it's owed; rate of interest; and any provisions under the indenture. The indenture is, in effect, a memorandum that goes with the IOU and contains certain promises on the part of the borrower. They may include no dividends if earnings fall below a certain amount, no investment in fixed assets without authorization of the lender, or a commitment to maintain working capital above a certain level. If the provisions of the indenture are not lived up to, then the entire amount of the long-term debt becomes immediately due.

Some debts may be subordinated, which means a signed document promises that nothing will be paid on the subordinated debt as long as anything is unpaid on certain other debt. A subordination may be in favor of one particular creditor such as a bank, or may be given to subordinate one particular debt to amounts due all other creditors. In the case of a general subordination, we consider the subordinated debt pretty close to net worth because all other liabilities are paid before anything goes to the holder of the subordinated debt, usually the owner.

NET WORTH

Now, having listed all liabilities current and noncurrent, having provided for all outsiders' equity in the assets of the business, we are ready to talk about the equity of the owners in those assets. This equity we calculate by subtracting the total of liabilities from the total of assets. What remains is the equity of owners, or net worth. When we add Net Worth to Liabilities at the bottom of the right-hand column, we arrive at a total which equals the total at the bottom of the left-hand column. If it doesn't, we don't have a balance sheet.

So, after deducting the equity of outside creditors in the business, we have arrived at the owners' equity, or net worth. If the business is owned by a single proprietor—a proprietorship—the net worth is shown as Net Worth, or, possibly, Owner's Equity. Partnership Net Worth will be shown as just that, or, possibly, Partnership Equity. Or the equities of the partners may be shown individually: John Jones Equity, $50,000; Tom Smith Equity, $25,000.

In the case of a corporation, the way net worth is shown is more complex. To understand it, we need to go into the way a corporation comes into being. You and I are forming a corporation and apply to the secretary of state for a charter. The charter authorizes us to engage in a certain line of business and authorizes us to issue, say, 10,000 shares of capital stock at $5 par value. (Some corporation stock has no par value, in which case a stated value may be arbitrarily assigned.)

Now we sell part of the stock we have been authorized to issue. At first we sell 5,000 shares at $5 par, which brings in $25,000 of capital. On our balance sheet this is shown as Outstanding Capital Stock, $25,000. Two years later our corporation is doing well and we need more capital. We sell the remaining 5,000 shares of $5 par stock. But now, our business having prospered, investors are willing to pay us $10 for each share rather than its $5 par value. Of the $50,000 the sale of these 5,000 shares brings in, we add $25,000 to Outstanding Capital Stock and the remaining $25,000 becomes Paid-in Capital.

Our corporation is profitable. Each year, after paying corporate income tax and after paying a dividend to stockholders out of our net profit after tax, we keep what's left in the business for expansion. Profit retained in the corporation accumulates to become an $86,000 Retained Earnings account. So far, we have Outstanding Capital Stock, $50,000; Paid-in Capital, $25,000; and Retained Earnings, $86,000.

Now, after several years, Aunt Susie, who bought 300 shares of our stock to begin with, wants to take a trip around the world. We tell her we'll buy her stock back and pay her what it has become worth, which is $20 a share. So we pay Aunt Susie $6,000 for her 300 shares of stock and lock it up in the vault to hold for the treasury. We do this rather than cancel it because it will be easier to sell again than to reissue the same number of shares.

We have a deduction from our corporate net worth representing the $6,000 we took out of our cash account to buy Aunt Susie's stock. This $6,000 we show as a minus figure under the caption Less Treasury Stock.

Net worth now looks like this:

Outstanding Capital Stock	$50,000
Paid-in Capital	25,000
Retained Earnings	86,000
Less Treasury Stock	−6,000
Shareholders' Equity	$155,000

Now, dropping three zeros to show the figures in thousands, our completed balance sheet looks like this:

Cash		$ 40	Accounts Payable		$ 50
Marketable Securities		25	Notes Bank		25
Accounts Receivable	$72		Accrued Wages and Taxes		10
Less Reserve	2				
Net Accounts Receivable		70	Customers' Credit Balances		5
Inventory		85	Current Mortgage Maturity		10
Total Current Assets		$220	Total Current Liabilities		$100
			Mortgage		40
Land	$10				
Buildings	30				
Machinery, Equipment	50				
Total	$90				
Less Depreciation	40				
Total Fixed Assets		50			
Notes of Officers		5	Capital Stock		50
Advances to Salespersons		2	Paid-In Capital		25
Stock of Related Companies		10	Retained Earnings		86
Cash Surrender Value of					
Life Insurance		5	Treasury Stock		−6
Copyrights and Trademarks		3			
Total Assets		$295	Total Liabilities		$295

This has not been intended as an all-inclusive classification of every item which may appear as an asset or liability or a component of net worth on a balance sheet. There are such all-inclusive lists. One is made available by Robert Morris Associates. Another is included in the *Dun & Bradstreet Handbook of Credits and Collections* by Harold T. Redding and Guyon H. Knight, published by Thomas Y. Crowell Company, a division of Harper & Row, Publishers, Inc., New York.

Statement of Profit and Loss

Store managers, department managers, and plant managers may not know all the ins and outs of the balance sheet but most of them have a pretty good acquaintance with the profit and loss, or P & L, statement. The bottom line, which has become almost a household word, has real meaning for managers because it may be a prime factor in their compensation. They are well aware of what affects that bottom line.

The income, or profit and loss, statement may be visualized as a chipping-away process. We start with Gross Sales, the total of everything we bill, and end up, after everything has been chipped away, with the bottom line, Net Profit After Tax.

The profit and loss statement is also known as the statement of income, or the earnings statement. Here is a thumbnail review:

GROSS SALES: Chip away Returns, Allowances, and Discounts and you have—
NET SALES: Chip away Cost of Goods Sold and you have—
GROSS PROFIT: Chip away Selling and Administrative Expense and you have—
OPERATING PROFIT: Chip away Other Expense and add Other Income and you have—
NET PROFIT BEFORE TAX: Chip away Income Tax and you have—
NET PROFIT AFTER TAX

GROSS AND NET SALES

If a shipment leaves the shipping dock of a manufacturing plant today, a corresponding invoice or bill should be prepared and mailed to the customer no later than tomorrow. When a shopper in the grocery store comes to the checkout counter and purchases are bagged, a total bill is rung up on the cash register. Each invoice prepared by the manufacturing plant and each cash register sales slip represents a sale. Their total for a given period—week, month, or year—represents gross sales for that period.

Gross Sales are what we start with. We have deductions to make before arriving at net sales, which is what we work with in interpreting the profit and loss statement. These deductions are: (1) Discounts, (2) Returns, and (3) Allowances.

Cash discounts are an incentive given for early payment. Example: Selling terms call for payment of our invoice within 30 days from billing date. If our customer is willing to pay in 10 days rather than 30, we offer a 1 percent or a 2 percent discount to be deducted from the face amount of the bill. We tell our customer to deduct 1 percent or 2 percent in the payment of the bill 20 days earlier than terms of sale require. Because the customer can do this 18 times a year (360 divided by 20), we are offering 18 percent per annum to have our money 20 days faster. If the discount we offer is 2 percent, the 18 percent per annum inducement becomes 36 percent.

When our customer pays in ten days and deducts the cash discount, Gross sales are reduced by the amount of the discount. This is the first deduction from gross sales.

Now, unfortunately, it turns out that we have printed our customer's boxes upside down. The fault is ours but our customer understands that we will have a complete loss if the boxes are returned, and offers to use them if we will stand the cost of the extra labor. We accept the offer gratefully and say we will compensate with a 50 percent credit on the bill. This, too, must be deducted from gross sales as an allowance.

The next time we print boxes upside down, we're not so lucky. It's a first order and the customer doesn't want to make do. The order is returned and we have a bill to cancel out in total. In this case we have a return to deduct from gross sales. Now, having chipped three times from Gross Sales, our Net Sales look like this:

Gross Sales		$1,029,500
Less Discounts	$9,500	
Less Allowances	8,000	
Less Returns	12,000	
	$29,500	
Net Sales		$1,000,000

COST OF GOODS SOLD

The next chipping away is to calculate what it costs to produce the goods we have sold and then to subtract this Cost of Goods Sold from our Net Sales to arrive at a Gross Profit. This Gross Profit, we hope, will cover our selling and general administrative expense and leave us, after paying income tax, a Net Profit After Tax as a return on the money we have invested in the business.

To arrive at Cost of Goods Sold, we start with what we had on hand at the beginning of the period, our Opening Inventory. To this we add Purchases during the period, and what we spent in the form of Labor and Factory Overhead to make the raw material we purchased into a finished product. (This is in the case of a manufacturer; a retailer and a wholesaler may simply buy a product for resale without doing anything to it.)

Adding the cost of producing a finished product to the cost of what we purchased gives us Cost of Goods Available for Sale. But not everything available for sale is actually sold. We have some items left—our Closing Inventory—and this Closing Inventory must be subtracted from the Cost of Goods Available for Sale to arrive at Cost of Goods Sold. It looks like this on the profit and loss statement:

Opening Inventory	$160,000
Purchases	500,000
Labor and Factory Overhead	200,000
Cost of Goods Available for Sale	$860,000
Less Closing Inventory	− 160,000
Cost of Goods Sold	$700,000

It is this Cost of Goods Sold which we subtract from Net Sales to give us Gross Profit, out of which must come expenses, to leave an Operating Profit.

It can be readily seen how the method of inventory valuation has everything to do with the Cost of Goods Sold and, therefore, with the Gross Profit and Net Profit. If the closing inventory is lower, as it would be using LIFO (last in, first out), there is less to subtract from Cost of Goods Available for Sale, and, therefore, a higher Cost of Goods Sold and lower Gross and Net Profit. If we used FIFO (first in, first out), and valued inventory at the latest and highest purchase price, then the Closing Inventory would be higher, the Cost of Goods lower, and the Gross and Net Profit figures higher.

This is why it is so important when reading a profit and loss statement to inquire closely about inventory valuation.

SELLING AND ADMINISTRATIVE EXPENSES

Having chipped away Returns and Allowances and Discounts from Gross Sales to arrive at Net Sales, and having chipped away Cost of Goods Sold to arrive at Gross Profit, we are ready for the final chipping away of expenses to arrive at Operating Profit.

First we have Selling Expenses: Sales Commissions, Travel and Entertainment, Advertising, and other Sales Expenses. (Sometimes shipping expense is included under Selling Expenses, sometimes as a factory cost under Cost of Goods Sold.)

General and Administrative Expense can be combined with Selling Expense as Selling and Administrative Expense; sometimes it is shown separately. Administrative Expense will include Officers' Salaries, Office Salaries, Office Expense, and, perhaps, Depreciation and Interest.

OPERATING AND NET PROFIT

After we have chipped away Selling Expense and Administrative Expense from Gross Profit, what we have left is Operating Profit, the profit made on the operation itself. From the Operating Profit, there must still be deducted Other Expense and to it must be added Other Income in order to arrive at Net Profit Before Tax.

Other Income and Other Expense are usually small amounts but they can, in isolated cases, be extremely large. Interest may be included in Other Expense or it may be included in Administrative Expense if the line of business is one where seasonal loans and their interest would be normal procedure. Other Expense may include the sale of an asset at below book value or it may include expense involved in the sale of new capital stock or the issuance of bonds. Other expense in the form of a loss taken in the sale of an asset below book value can run into millions of dollars when a major company disposes of substantial unprofitable operations.

What we now have is almost the bottom line, but not quite. We have arrived at Net Profit, but out of this net profit we must pay corporate Income Tax. Once this is done, we are, indeed, at the bottom line. Our constant chipping away from Gross Sales at the top of the profit and loss statement has now produced a Net Profit After Tax. If our chipping away leaves us a minus figure when we deduct Selling Expense and Administrative Expense from Gross Profit, we have a Net Loss.

Our completed profit and loss statement now looks like this (again, we will drop three zeros):

Gross Sales		$1,029
Less Discounts	$9	
Less Returns	12	
Less Allowances	8	
	$29	
Net Sales		1,000
Opening Inventory	160	
Purchases	500	
Labor and Factory Overhead	200	
Cost of Goods Available for Sale	$860	
Less Closing Inventory	160	
Cost of Goods Sold		700
Gross Profit		$300
Less Selling Expense		120
Less Administrative Expense		130
Operating Profit		$50
Less Interest		10
Profit Before Tax		$40
Income Tax		20
Net Profit After Tax		$20

Three figures in the profit and loss statement stand out. They are Net Sales, Gross Profit, and Net Profit After Tax. If Net Profit is too small—or nonexistent—as a percentage of Net Sales, then we look at Gross Profit. If Gross Profit is too small, then we are selling too low or paying too much for what we are selling. If Gross Profit looks in line, compared with the line of business or industry, then we look at Selling and Administrative Expense for the trouble.

It all starts with what we sell, Net Sales, and ends up with the bottom line, what we have left after paying income tax, Net Profit After Tax. The relationship of Net Profit to Net Sales represents the efficiency of the operation. The relationship of Net Profit to Tangible Net Worth measures the Return on Investment.

Net Worth Reconciliation

A third financial statement included in annual reports of publicly listed companies and included in most accountants' audits is the reconciliation of changes in net worth, called a statement of stockholders' investment, or a statement of retained earnings.

In an examination of the balance sheet, we recognize that owners' equity in the assets of a business is what remains after subtracting the equity of outside creditors in the form of liabilities. In the case of a corporation, this Net Worth is represented by Capital Stock issued and outstanding, Paid-in Capital in the form of money paid for capital stock in excess of its par value, Retained Earnings accumulated over the years, minus Treasury Stock at the price paid for stock held in the treasury. Net worth of a corporation is also called Shareholders' Equity, or Shareholders' Investment.

Changes in net worth and what causes them are significant in reading financial statements. We have seen that the bottom line on the profit and loss statement is Net Profit After Tax. This is the money made on the year's operation now available for dividends to stockholders on their investment or for reinvestment in the business to finance growth. Some companies pay no dividends at all, retaining all earnings to finance growth. On the other hand, some companies pay almost all earnings out in the form of dividends in order to keep the return on capital stock at a level to attract investment. Somewhere between the two is the ideal situation.

That portion of earnings retained in the business is added to the Retained Earnings account to increase it from one year to the next. Retained earnings are thus a part of corporate net worth.

The same thing happens in a proprietorship or partnership when earnings are reinvested in the business. On the other hand, if withdrawals on the part of the owner or partners are in excess of earnings, or if dividends to a corporation's stockholders are in excess of earnings, then net worth is reduced.

Profits retained in the business increase net worth; losses reduce it.

Net worth also changes as the investment of the owners is increased or reduced. When Aunt Susie wanted to take a trip around the world and we agreed to buy her stock for the treasury for $6,000, we used $6,000 from the cash drawer to do it and reduced our net worth by that amount. But if we issue and sell 1,000 additional shares of unissued capital stock at $10 a share, we have $10,000 added to our investment. Capital stock is increased by that amount, and so is net worth.

Likewise, if the owner or partners in a business, recognizing the need for additional investment to finance growth, put $10,000 more into the business, they have increased their net worth by that amount. But if family illness develops which requires heavy medical expenses and the owner or partners withdraw $10,000, then net worth is reduced by that amount.

Here is how a statement of retained earnings might look:

Retained Earnings at Beginning of Year	$56,907,251
Net Income for the Year	3,652,901
Cash Dividends	684,214
Retained Earnings at Year End	$59,875,938

Working Capital Reconciliation

One item essential to the operation of any business is not even mentioned by name in either the balance sheet, profit and loss statement, or net worth reconciliation. This unmentioned item is working capital.

Working capital, without which it would be impossible to operate, is made up of the net current assets with which to operate on a day-to-day basis. Working capital is capital available to finance current requirements and is arrived at by subtracting Current Liabilities from Current Assets.

SOURCE AND APPLICATION OF FUNDS

Working capital reconciliation traces changes which take place in working capital from one year to the next. A working capital reconciliation statement is also known as a source and application of funds statement, and sometimes appears in an annual financial report as statement of changes in financial condition.

A source and application of funds statement, as the name indicates, tells us where money came from to increase working capital, where it was spent to decrease working capital, and what changes took place in the current assets and current liabilities which make up working capital. This information is important in any financial analysis because adequate working capital is essential to the successful operation of business. It is crucial to know what factors are causing it to increase or decrease.

To repeat, working capital is the excess of current assets over current liabilities; it is the figure arrived at by subtracting the second from the first. Anything which changes current assets and current liabilities equally will not change the amount of working capital. For example, if current assets last year were $200,000 and current liabilities were $100,000, then the difference between the two was $100,000 and that was working capital. Now current assets have increased by $50,000 to $250,000 and current liabilities by the same amount to $150,000. The difference between the two is still $100,000, so there has been no change in the amount of working capital.

There may have been changes in various current asset and current liability items and these changes in composition of working capital are important. We will touch on them shortly but right now we are concerned with changes in working capital itself.

Changes in working capital can only take place as a result of changes in noncurrent balance sheet items. There are three such categories: (1) Net Worth, (2) Noncurrent Assets, and (3) Noncurrent Liabilities. When there is a change in one of these categories (and nothing else changes on the balance sheet), a change in working capital results.

A change in net worth is directly reflected in an identical change in working capital. When net worth goes up, working capital goes up; when net worth goes down, working capital goes down.

EXAMPLE: We earn a $50,000 profit, pay $10,000 dividends, add the remaining $40,000 to the Retained Earnings account, increasing Net Worth by that amount. This $40,000 goes into our cash drawer, increasing Current Assets without changing Current Liabilities. Working capital, being the difference between the two, is increased by $40,000, directly reflecting the net worth change. The same would have happened had we increased net worth by $40,000 by investing that amount in additional capital stock and had then put the $40,000 in the cash drawer.

There would have been the same $40,000 increase in working capital if, in either case, we had not put the $40,000 in the cash drawer but had used it to reduce current bank loans. Current Assets would have remained unchanged but Current Liabilities would have been reduced by $40,000 and working capital increased by that amount.

A change in noncurrent liabilities is likewise directly reflected in a similar change in working capital. When noncurrent liabilities go up, working capital goes up; when noncurrent liabilities go down, working capital goes down.

EXAMPLE: We issue $10 million of long-term debentures none of which is due for payment within the next year. We add $10 million to our Cash account, increase Current Assets by that amount, do nothing to change Current Liabilities, increase the difference between Current Assets and Current Liabilities by $10 million, and thereby increase working capital by that amount.

If we had used the $10 million to pay off short-term bank loans, the result would have been the same. A $10 million increase in working capital would have resulted from a decrease in Current Liabilities without any change in Current Assets.

Finally, a change in Noncurrent Assets is inversely reflected in a change in working capital. If Noncurrent Assets go up (and nothing else happens), working capital goes down. If Noncurrent Assets go down, working capital goes up.

EXAMPLE: We buy a new metal stamping press for $50,000, financing the purchase with a 90-day bank loan, pending the arrangement of long-term equipment financing. The $50,000 we borrow from the bank increases current liabilities by that amount and reduces working capital. The working capital reduction would have been the same had we bought the $50,000 press for cash because that would have reduced current assets and, therefore, working capital by the same amount.

ANOTHER SITUATION: We finally sell an old, long vacated plant we formerly used before moving to our new location. We had depreciated the old plant down to $100,000 and the sale is for that amount in cash. The $100,000 proceeds from the sale are added to our cash account, increasing current assets by that amount, without changing current liabilities. The result is a $100,000 increase in working capital.

The examples we have used are, of course, oversimplified. In real life a single below-the-line change affecting working capital does not happen all by itself. A $50,000 increase in net worth and a $50,000 increase in noncurrent assets cancel each other out; there will be no change in working capital. A $500,000 plant expansion financed entirely with long-term debt will result in offsetting increases in noncurrent assets and noncurrent liabilities, and there will be *no* change in working capital.

Here are a couple of cases from the recent history of business in the United States: A major corporation embarks upon a $20 million plant expansion. Construction is well advanced before long-term financing is brought into the picture. In the meantime, short-term bank loans reach $15 million. There is serious concern on the part of the bank and trade suppliers. Finally a 20-year $20 million loan is arranged through a major insurance company to finance the program. Working capital, which had been reduced to the danger point, is now restored to a level adequate to support operations.

One of Detroit's Big three suffers operating losses running into the hundreds of millions, seriously depleting net worth and working capital. Long-term unsecured bank loans carry provisions which place the loans in default if working capital is reduced below a certain point. This point is reached and passed. In an effort to raise cash and bolster working capital, the company attempts to sell off a number of related activities, including a finance company, which had been used to finance auto sales.

CHANGES IN WORKING CAPITAL COMPOSITION

Changes in current assets and current liabilities above the line do not affect the amount of working capital from one year to the next as long as the difference between the total of current assets and current liabilities remains unchanged. A working capital reconciliation or an application of funds statement is concerned only with changes occurring below the line: changes in net worth, noncurrent assets, and noncurrent liabilities.

But we are concerned with changes in the composition of working capital even if the amount of working capital remains constant. In the following examples the amount of working capital is the same but there is a world of difference in the current assets and current liabilities which make up working capital:

Cash	$100,000	Accounts Payable	$ 25,000
Accounts Receivable	25,000		
Inventory	50,000		
Total Current Assets	$175,000	Total Current Liabilities	$ 25,000
Working Capital	$150,000		

Cash	$ 10,000	Accounts Payable	$150,000
Accounts Receivable	150,000	Bank Loan	60,000
Inventory	200,000		
Total Current Assets	$360,000	Total Current Liabilitites	$210,000
Working Capital	$150,000		

Surely these must be two different concerns. One is extremely liquid with four times as much cash as it owes; the other owes more than its working capital and its current ratio (current assets divided by current liabilities) is less than two to one.

And yet, these figures may very well be one concern. The first condition is at the highly liquid time between seasons. The second is at the height of the season, when working capital is represented by heavy accounts receivable and inventory supported by amounts due suppliers and borrowings from the bank.

What are some of the things we seek to learn from a study of the changes in the composition of working capital? First of all, if accounts receivable and inventory have doubled, has this expansion been financed by an increase in working capital, in which case current liabilities would not have increased? If working capital has remained stationary, then the increase in accounts receivable and inventory must have been financed by a corresponding increase in current liabilities. If so, has the increase in current liabilities been in the form of additional bank loans, or larger accounts payable to suppliers, or has there been some other form of financing such as a seasonal loan from one of the owners?

In comparative financial analysis we follow trends in sales, profits, working capital, and individual asset items. With a healthy growth in sales, we expect a corresponding growth in accounts receivable and inventory, and it is important how this growth is financed. It is desirable for sales expansion to be supported by working capital growth rather than an increase in current liabilities in the face of stagnant working capital.

Working capital—current assets minus current liabilities—is an important factor in the financial health of a business enterprise. It must be maintained at a level sufficient to support the scope of operations.

3

Financial Analysis and the Key Business Ratios

Financial analysis requires an understanding and interpretation of figures contained in the four financial statements which have been described in the previous chapter. The first step is to compare certain items on the balance sheet and the profit and loss statement one with another. These relationships are expressed as a percentage (%) or as times ($\times$). The second step is to compare these relationships with similar relationship figures for the line of business in which the subject of the analysis is operating. Finally, one single ratio may tell an incomplete story; it is only as various ratios are related one to another that a broad picture unfolds.

This process can be meaningless without a clear understanding of how the subject operates. It would be bizarre to compare the figures of a retailer selling for cash, for example, with an electric utility whose plant investment and long-term financing dwarf the working capital used in the normal course of operation. Financial analysis begins with detailed information concerning the method of operation.

Standard Industrial Classification (SIC)

The Standard Industrial Classification code is a method developed by the U.S. Department of Commerce to provide a precise classification of all lines of business. The SIC number contains four digits, the first two of which designate the major industry group. The third and fourth digits provide information as to the products within an industry or line of trade. There are ten major industry groups: (1) agriculture, forestry, and fishing; (2) mining; (3) construction; (4) manufacturing; (5) transportation, communications, electric, gas, and sanitary services; (6) wholesale trade; (7) retail trade; (8) finance, insurance, and real estate; (9) services; and (10) public administration. Retail SIC numbers are from 5211 to 5999, wholesale from 5012 to 5199, and manufacturing from 2011 to 3999.

The key business ratios are published by SIC number. Balance sheets and profit and loss statements from a number of businesses within the same standard industrial classification are grouped to come up with the upper quartile, the median, and the lower quartile for each ratio within each SIC number grouping.

Median, Upper, and Lower Quartile

The median concept has replaced the concept of average in many statistical tabulations as statisticians discover how badly averages can be thrown off by a drastic deviation from the norm at either the top or bottom. For instance, with a group of ten individuals, nine aged 20 to 25 and one 80, it hardly gives a meaningful picture to say that the average age is 29. The statistician points out that it is more meaningful to say that the median age—that of the person whose age is midway between top and bottom—is, say, 23.

Business ratios are published by line of business as indicated by SIC number and, within each SIC code, by upper quartile, median, and lower quartile. The median ratio is exactly midway from top to bottom, the upper quartile is midway between the top and the middle, and the lower quartile is midway between the middle and the bottom. In financial analysis each ratio of the subject is compared with median, upper, and lower quartile for the line. If the precise method of operation of the subject has been determined, finding the SIC number is easy by referring to the Standard Industrial Classification listing. It is found, among other places, in the front of the *Dun & Bradstreet Reference Book.*

Where to Find Financial Ratios

There are two major sources of financial ratios for the broad range of business. Robert Morris Associates, the national association of bank loan and credit officers, with a membership representing about 87 percent of all U.S. commercial banking resources, publishes each year its Annual Statement Studies, including various asset and liability items as a percentage of total assets and liabilities, operating items as a percentage of sales, and the financial ratios most commonly used in financial analysis. This information is shown for each industry group as designated by SIC number. It is broken down into four asset size categories. The ratios are shown for median, upper, and lower quartile.

The Business Economics Division of Dun & Bradstreet, the commercial credit information organization, publishes each year its Key Business Ratios, a listing, by SIC classification, of the 14 most commonly used financial ratios in over 800 lines of business. These figures, in each line of business, are broken down into three net worth size categories, and use the median, upper, and lower quartile method of presentation.

Now that we know how the business ratios are used in financial analysis and where the industry figures can be obtained, we are ready to take a look at each of the ratios, how it is computed, and its significance.

The Financial Ratios

NET PROFIT ON NET SALES

Formula:

$$\frac{\text{Net profit after tax}}{\text{Net sales}} \times 100 = \%$$

This ratio is also known as profit margin, or rate of return on sales. It is what is left of net sales after subtracting cost of goods sold, selling, administrative, and general expenses, and income tax. It reveals the profit earned on every dollar of sales and is, therefore, a measure of the overall efficiency of the business. It should be considered in close conjunction with the second following ratio, net profit on tangible net worth.

GROSS PROFIT ON NET SALES

Formula:

$$\frac{\text{Gross profit}}{\text{Net sales}} \times 100 = \%$$

This is the gross margin after subtracting cost of goods sold from net sales and out of which all expenses must be paid to produce a profit. Gross profit can range all the way from 20 percent for grocery stores to 40 percent for apparel and accessory stores. If, in a particular case, it is too low for the line, then selling prices must be too low or the cost of what is being sold too high. This is an obvious conclusion because only net sales and cost of goods are involved in the comparison.

NET PROFIT ON TANGIBLE NET WORTH

Formula:

$$\frac{\text{Net profit after tax}}{\text{Net worth} - \text{Intangible Assets}} \times 100 = \%$$

This ratio is also known as return on investment, or ROI. It represents the financial return on the owner's investment in the business, and is generally considered an important measure of management efficiency. Generally, a return on investment of 10 percent or more is looked upon as a desirable objective. After all, money invested in a government security may earn this much and, presumably, without the risk business takes.

An illustration will demonstrate how important it is to look at this ratio in relation to the ratio net profit on net sales. The median rate of return on sales for all grocery stores in a recent year was 1.79 percent, less than $2 of profit on every $100 of sales. Women's ready-to-wear stores, on the other hand, earned 5 percent net profit on net sales, two and a half times as much. The return on investment picture differs. The grocers earned a median net profit of 20.17 percent on tangible net worth, meaning they earned that $1.79 on every $100 of sales almost ten times a year. The women's apparel store owners earned slightly less—18.77 percent—on their investment despite the higher profit on every dollar sold because they turned their investment less than three and half times a year against the grocers' ten.

NET SALES TO TANGIBLE NET WORTH

Formula:

$$\frac{\text{Annual net sales}}{\text{Tangible net worth}} = \text{Rate of investment turnover}$$

This is the turnover of owner's investment, which we have just looked at in connection with the grocery and women's apparel stores. Dividing tangible net worth into net sales gives us the number of times we turn over the money invested in the business, how many times we repeat each year the process of selling a dollar's worth of goods and earning a profit on the sale.

It might appear to the businessman that the higher the rate of investment turnover the better, in order to earn more on a fixed rate of return on sales. But this can lead to overtrading, and many businesses have run into trouble by overtrading. Each dollar of increased sales requires an increase in accounts receivable and inventory. Unless the increase in sales is somehow accompanied by a proportionate increase in working capital, the larger accounts receivable and inventory will have to be financed by larger debt. As long as everything goes smoothly and money keeps turning, it's all right, but if anything happens to interrupt the flow—a plant shutdown for any reason, a customer in financial trouble, or business dropping off in an economic slowdown—overtrading catches up and financial problems can loom quickly. What some investors like in the form of leverage—a small investment upon which to earn a return—credit grantors, including bank loan officers, are inclined to look upon with alarm.

For this reason the upper and lower quartiles in this ratio are often reversed. The lower turnover of tangible net worth is shown as the upper quartile and the higher (overtrading?) as the lower. This is also true of the next ratio.

NET SALES TO NET WORKING CAPITAL

Formula:

$$\frac{\text{Annual net sales}}{\text{Net working capital}} = \text{Rate of working capital turnover}$$

This ratio is also known as the turnover of working capital. It measures whether or not working capital used in the normal conduct of business is adequate to support the scope of operations. As in the turnover of tangible net worth, a too rapid turnover of working capital can indicate overtrading, with the heavy debt which usually goes with it. Once again, the upper and lower quartiles in this ratio are reversed, the lower turnover of working capital shown as upper quartile and the higher turnover rate as lower quartile.

Even if the turnover of tangible net worth is not too heavy, there can still be a too rapid turnover of net working capital. This can happen when too great a portion of the total investment is represented by plant and other noncurrent assets. In the absence of long-term financing in the form of noncurrent debt, this can leave too little of the total investment available for normal operation, and thus produce a too rapid turnover of working capital. We have seen in Chapter 2 what it is that adds to and subtracts from working capital.

CURRENT ASSETS TO CURRENT DEBT—THE CURRENT RATIO

Formula:

$$\frac{\text{Current assets}}{\text{Current debt}}$$

Years ago financial analysis emphasized this ratio much more than it does now. If the current ratio was as much as 2 to 1, it was thought to be an indication that all was well. Today it is recognized that the current ratio must be considered in conjunction with an examination of the quality of the current assets upon which it depends. If current assets include heavy, slow-moving inventory with obsolete items which will have to be written off, then the current ratio can be better than two to one and the concern still will be unable to pay its bills. The same would be true of uncollectable receivables which swell current assets without providing funds for meeting obligations. If we want to consider the current ratio as an indication of liquidity and paying ability, we must look into what current assets provide coverage for current liabilities.

LIQUID (OR QUICK) RATIO

Formula:

$$\frac{\text{Cash and equivalent } + \text{ Net trade receivables}}{\text{Current liabilities}}$$

This ratio is also known as the acid test. It attempts to arrive at a measure of business liquidity by determining if current liabilities are covered by assets considered to be liquid, namely, cash and its equivalent plus accounts and notes receivable from customers, on the theory that they will soon become cash with which bills can be paid. "And its equivalent" would normally comprise government or listed and marketable securities immediately convertible into cash. Another way to arrive at these liquid assets for purposes of computing the liquid ratio is to subtract from the total of current assets those which by definition are not liquid, namely, inventory and prepaid and deferred assets.

Any time the liquid ratio is as much as 1 to 1 we think of the business as being in a liquid condition. This is a very arbitrary measure of liquidity though surely better than the current ratio. It is particularly arbitrary to label a business not liquid just because the liquid ratio is less than 1 to 1. Consider a business selling entirely for cash. In this case there are no accounts receivable to add to cash and its equivalent as a part of liquid assets against which to compare current liabilities. The liquid ratio might well be below 1 to 1 and there still might be more than enough cash produced by inventory in the form of cash sales to provide for the prompt payment of bills. Here again the method of operation is important.

COLLECTION PERIOD—DAYS SALES OUTSTANDING

Formula:

$$\frac{\text{Trade accounts and notes receivable (net)}}{\dfrac{\text{Net credit sales for the period}}{\text{Number of days in period}}} = \text{Days sales outstanding}$$

This ratio relates the dollars tied up in customer accounts and notes receivable to the volume of business being done. No one would object if receivables doubled in the face of a tripling of sales. Yet there would be plenty to object to if the situation were reversed and receivables tripled while sales doubled. For people involved in finance and the management of accounts receivable, collection period, or days sales outstanding, or DSO is a daily working tool.

The first step is to find the average day's credit sales by dividing credit sales for the period by the number of days in the period. Calendar days are used—365 for a year, 30 for a month. Then the average day's credit sales are divided into the customer accounts and notes receivable. The result is the number of average day's credit sales represented by the receivables.

DSO is in general use and has the virtue of being easily understood but it does have limitations. Seasonal variations, if allowance is not made, can distort days sales outstanding figures. Consider a department store's DSO at December 31, when most customers still owe for Christmas purchases. Then consider the same DSO two months later, when Christmas accounts have been paid.

Most businesses close the fiscal year and prepare the fiscal statement when the peak season has ended, and, as long as we are comparing one concern with another in the same line, we will not be badly misled.

Generally, the collection period should approximate terms of sale plus 10 or 15 days to allow for mail time and the occasional delinquency. Much beyond that, there may be excessively slow or uncollectable accounts included in accounts receivable which will affect liquidity and the ability to pay bills.

INVENTORY TURNOVER

Formula:

$$\frac{\text{Cost of goods sold}}{\text{Inventory}} = \text{Rate of inventory turnover}$$

This is the method used to compute this ratio in the preparation of the Robert Morris Associates Annual Statement Studies. It provides an actual physical turnover of inventory on hand by comparing inventory with the cost of goods sold, before adding profit or overhead expense. The bank loan officer will normally have access to detailed profit and loss information, of which cost of goods sold is a part. The RMA ratio studies make this assumption by furnishing inventory turnover ratio figures to which the bank loan officer will be able to relate.

The Dun & Bradstreet Key Business Ratios, prepared for the use of banks but also for commercial credit executives who may not have access to detailed profit and loss information, use a different method of computing Inventory, as follows:

Formula:

$$\frac{\text{Annual net sales}}{\text{Inventory}} = \text{Rate of inventory turnover}$$

This ratio compares inventory, which does not include profit and overhead expense, with sales, which do, and is therefore not a true physical inventory turn. Technically, it is an indicated rather than an actual inventory turnover. It does provide a means of comparison for those who may know sales and profit but not the details of the profit and loss statement. For comparative purposes, the ratio serves a useful purpose as long as we know its basis and we are comparing similar entities.

INVENTORY TO NET WORKING CAPITAL

Formula:

$$\frac{\text{Inventory}}{\text{Net working capital}} \times 100 = \%$$

Like the preceding inventory turnover ratio, inventory to net working capital is another indication of inventory size, this time in relation to the working capital of which it is a part. This ratio measures the adequacy of working capital to support the inventory. If this ratio is over 100 percent, inventory is too large or working capital too small, and we turn to other ratios to determine which.

If a combination of the inventory turnover ratio and the inventory to working capital ratio shows inventory to be too large, then there may be obsolete or slow-moving items in stock which tie up money needed elsewhere. Sometimes a vigorous inventory management program to bring inventory down to median levels will make thousands of dollars available for the payment of bills or bank loans and thereby eliminate costly loan carrying charges.

FIXED ASSETS TO TANGIBLE NET WORTH

Formula:

$$\frac{\text{Fixed assets (net)}}{\text{Tangible net worth}} \times 100 = \%$$

This ratio indicates the proportion of owner's capital invested in fixed assets; that is, land, buildings, machinery and equipment, furniture and fixtures, and net of reserve for depreciation. Dollars invested in fixed assets, unless they are financed by long-term, noncurrent liabilities, are not available for working capital purposes. We have seen in Chapter 2 how a too rapid expansion in plant and equipment may strip working capital. If this takes place in the face of rising sales, financial problems arise. In order to compete, a business must keep its plant modern and efficient, but funds necessary for plant expansion and modernization should be supplied by increases in tangible net worth through retained profits or additional investment, or by long-term financing—not by stripping working capital.

In the case of a manufacturer, a fixed asset to tangible net worth ratio of as much as 100 percent should prompt questions. In the case of a retailer or wholesaler, the danger point might be 75 percent but the important thing, in this as in all other ratios, is the comparison with others in the same line.

CURRENT DEBT TO TANGIBLE NET WORTH

Formula:

$$\frac{\text{Current liabilities}}{\text{Tangible net worth}} \times 100 = \%$$

This ratio compares the investment in the business of current, short-term creditors with that of the owners. The higher the ratio between liabilities payable within one year and tangible net worth, the larger the risk being taken by short-term creditors and the smaller the margin of safety provided by the owners. It should be a cause for concern when current liabilities approach 100 percent of tangible net worth. There are instances when this ratio seems to be in good shape but an examination of the ratio which comes next may show that the liquid current position is made possible by heavy long-term borrowings.

TOTAL DEBT TO TANGIBLE NET WORTH

Formula:

$$\frac{\text{Total liabilities}}{\text{Tangible net worth}} \times 100 = \%$$

This ratio shows what percentage of assets belongs to outside creditors and what percentage to the owners of the business. When this percentage is over 100 percent, then creditors' equity exceeds that of the owners. As the percentage grows, creditors have less and less protection in the event of liquidation. Debt can grow to the point where it is the creditors who actually own the business and have a greater stake in the outcome of business decisions than the owners. This is a situation to be avoided by creditors and owners alike. Most business failures are preceded by excessive growth in debt.

Some businesses—some entire industries—operate regularly with total debt well in excess of tangible net worth. Electric utilities and banks themselves are examples. The key to the situation is whether the debt can be managed without causing trouble. Can interest be paid and still allow for a profit? Can annual principal payments be made out of cash flow without cutting into working capital?

LONG-TERM DEBT PAYBACK

Formula:

$$\frac{\text{Net profit} + \text{Noncash operating expense}}{\text{Current portion of long-term debt}} \times 100 = \%$$

This ratio tells whether or not cash flow is sufficient to cover annual payments on long-term debt. If the ratio percentage is over 100 percent, then the current year's debt payment can be made out of current cash flow without dipping into working capital. If the percentage is less than 100 percent, then working capital will be stripped to meet the current long-term debt payment. The result can be disastrous.

For purposes of this ratio computation, cash flow includes profits plus operating expenses that reduce profit but do not require an outlay of cash. Depreciation is the most common such noncash operating expense. When we depreciate the value of a piece of equipment each year to reflect its true depreciated value, we make a bookkeeping entry to arrive at the depreciated figure. This is an operating cost just as much as the light bill, but, unlike the light bill, it does not require our writing a check. Therefore, such noncash expense items as depreciation, depletion, and amortization are combined with net profit to arrive at cash flow.

Subtracting the current year's payment for long-term debt from cash flow will give us in dollars the margin with which we have to work. If the current payment for long-term debt exceeds cash flow, working capital suffers.

ACCOUNTS PAYABLE TURNOVER

Formula:

$$\frac{\text{Accounts payable}}{\dfrac{\text{Purchases for the period}}{\text{Days in the period}}} = \text{Days for payment}$$

This is the reverse of the collection period by which we determined the number of average days sales represented by accounts receivable. Now we determine the number of days purchases represented by accounts payable. This gives us the manner of payment of suppliers' bills—how many days, on the average, does it take to pay. This can be compared with terms of purchase to find out if payments are being made promptly.

For this calculation to be meaningful, we must know purchase terms in detail. If 50 percent of purchases are made on 60-day terms and the other half for cash, we use half the total purchases in the computation to avoid distortion.

Internal Analysis

One single balance sheet and profit and loss statement reveals the financial condition of a business at a particular instant. Theoretically, each asset and each liability is valued at the same moment. It is like an instantaneous photo taken with a high-speed camera. By implication, something of the past and a glimpse of the future may be derived from one financial statement, but basically it is a static record.

Internal financial analysis involves interpretation and analysis of a single financial statement. As the name implies, the object is to learn about the finances of the business internally, not what has happened and what is going to happen so much as what is going on right now.

COMPUTING AND COMPARING THE RATIOS

The first step in internal analysis is to compute each of the ratios we have discussed. Next, the ratios should be compared against the upper quartile, median, and lower quartile for the line of business in which the subject operates. Here is where the SIC number comes in handy; it appears at the top of the Dun & Bradstreet report or it can be determined by reference to a Standard Industrial Classification list.

The significance of the ratio—in general and without any specific reference to the case being analyzed—should be reviewed. Then, as the subject's ratio is compared with the ratios for the line, note should be taken of the way the subject lines up with the industry. For instance, if a manufacturer of paperboard containers and boxes has a net profit on net sales ratio of 6 percent and the upper quartile for the line is 4 percent, we can conclude that our subject operates efficiently, earning a profit margin exceeding the upper quartile for the line.

If, as we next compute the ratio of Net Profit on Net Worth, we find it to be 10 percent, slightly lower than the industry median of 12 percent, we know that, although the return on sales is good, the return on investment is not so good. Some of the capital invested in the business is not being productively employed. An examination of subsequent ratios would tell us where the poorly employed capital is.

RELATING THE RATIOS TO EACH OTHER

A single financial ratio compares one item on the balance sheet or profit and loss statement with another. If the ratio is out of line, what it tells us is that one or the other of the two items being compared—or both—is out of line. What the ratio does not tell us is which of the items is the culprit. One ratio related to another may give us a more precise picture.

For example, our manufacturer of paperboard containers and boxes has an inventory to working capital ratio of 75 percent against an industry median of 45 percent. This tells us one of two things: inventory is too high or working capital too low; we cannot tell which. We turn then to other ratios which compare inventory and working capital with other items. One of these is inventory to cost of goods (inventory turnover). Now we find our manufacturer of folding paperboard boxes has an inventory turnover nine times, which compares with an industry upper quartile of eight. Inventory, apparently, is not the culprit.

Now we turn to another ratio having to do with working capital, the ratio of net sales to working capital. Here we find our subject has a working capital turnover of 20 times a year. The lower quartile for the industry is 23.4, this being one of the two ratios where the upper and lower quartiles are reversed, so our manufacturer of paperboard boxes is close to the worst. By looking at the three ratios in tandem, we reach at least a tentative conclusion that inventory is well controlled but that working capital is inadequate to support operations.

Trend or Comparative Analysis

This is analysis which involves comparing a succession of balance sheets and profit and loss statements to learn trends over a period of years. The first step is to set up three or more balance sheets and profit and loss statements in columnar form on a spread sheet. Next the ratios for each of the three years are computed and entered on the spread sheet, as are the industry upper quartile, median, and lower quartile figures. This provides an easy comparison from one year to the next for each of the balance sheet and profit and loss items as well as the financial ratios. The mechanics of setting up the figures in columnar form is performed by computer in some larger banks but it is still a process accomplished by hand in many others.

What the analyst looks for in the successive years' figures are trends from one year to the next. It is desirable, first of all, that sales follow an upward trend or, at least, a trend in line with that for the general economy and the particular industry involved. For instance, a 5 percent sales growth in the computer industry even in recessionary times might not be favorable, but a similar trend in the automobile industry under adverse economic conditions might be an accomplishment.

The trend in after-tax profits should follow the sales trend. Depending on dividend policy, earnings retained in the business will bring about a steady increase in net worth. Unless there has been a drastic increase in fixed assets, the net worth upward trend will be mirrored in a working capital increase, which is what we want to see to support the sales growth. The increase in working capital will finance the growth in accounts receivable and inventory brought about by the sales expansion. This will allow for an increase in current liabilities at a rate no greater than that of sales. In other words, we are looking for a trend in balance sheet items to match the trend in sales.

In the situation just suggested, all ratios will remain fairly constant in the face of an upward sales trend as profits build up net worth and working capital to finance an expansion in working assets without a disporportionate increase in debt. This is the ideal. It is when, from one year to another, ratio distortions occur that we should be alerted to possible trouble. If the net profit on net sales ratio, after maintaining a satisfactory level, drops off to nothing, we detect a problem. Referring to the gross profit on net sales ratio, we find that it has held up, so the problem must be elsewhere. What we discover is that administrative expenses, as a percentage of sales, have risen abruptly. When we inquire, the write-off of a large bankrupt customer account receivable is the story which explains the drop in profit. We can only tell this by computing each ratio for the years involved, comparing against the norms for the line, and then following trends from one year to another.

EYEBALL ANALYSIS

An occasional case will be so good or so bad that a detailed analysis is not necessary to reach a conclusion. Such cases can be "eyeballed," which means that a visual examination of the figures will be sufficient. A mental calculation of debt to net worth may reveal such an outstandingly favorable relationship, or such a heavy one, as to make detailed analysis unnecessary. Furthermore, there are occasions when the bank loan officer must make preliminary appraisal of financial figures before a full-scale analysis is undertaken.

Eyeball financial analysis requires an ability to make rough mental calculations and to know which balance sheet and profit and loss relationships to look for first. The percentage of profit on sales and net worth, the proportion of debt to net worth, the current ratio, or a quick look at fixed assets along with a mental calculation of inventory and account receivable turnover may tell quite a story. If sales are $365,000 a year and accounts receivable are $50,000, we ought not need a calculator to compute days sales outstanding at 50 days. If the owner of a specialty shop shows us profit and loss figures with a $20,000 gross profit on sales of $100,000, we ought not need a computer to ask if selling price is too low or cost of goods too high.

Financial analysis, whether of the most exhaustive or of the eyeball variety, often raises more questions than it provides answers. The analyst should avoid final conclusions based upon the figures alone. But analysis will suggest a wealth of questions to ask in direct conversation. "Mr. Jones, why did your net and gross profit drop off so badly this year? Did it have anything to do with the heavy inventory you had on hand a year ago?" "Yes, it did. A style change caught me with old inventory. I had to take terrific write-downs to unload."

The most important factors in business are still human factors. Financial analysis helps us zero in on financial problems, but we have to know the character and capacity of the people grappling with them to know what the outcome is likely to be.

4

Budgets and Cash Forecasts

In the preceding chapters we have examined the four financial statements: balance sheet, profit and loss statement, reconciliation of changes in net worth, and reconciliation of changes in working capital. These four financial statements provide a picture of past trends and the present financial condition, but only by implication do they give any inkling of what the future holds.

A financial budget, on the other hand, whether for an individual or a business, is a tool to be used in planning the future. By forecasting income and outgo for a period of time, and then, by measuring performance against budget, it is possible to keep a constant watch on what is happening and to take corrective action when things go wrong.

Business budgets are commonly prepared for a month, a year, or a five-year period, and are revised as changing conditions require. Actual results are compared against the budget each month and at the close of each year. In effect, an operating budget is a profit and loss statement projected into the future; if "actual" is "on budget" at the year's close, then the year's net profit is that which had been budgeted.

People in accounting positions labor under tight requirements to prepare operating figures for each month probably no more than five working days after the month's close. Astute management will require month-end figures promptly in order to take immediate corrective action where there is a budget deviation to be dealt with. It is sloppy management to receive month-end figures toward the end of the following month, by which time the budget deviation has been allowed to continue for another month. There have been tragic cases where, for some reason or another, financial figures were delayed for a matter of months, by which time the business had become insolvent without any knowledge of the problem or how it might have been corrected.

Preparing the Operating Budget

SALES BUDGET

The sales budget, a forecast of goods to be sold and revenue to be derived from sales, is the starting point in the budgeting procedure. A sales estimate is based upon forecasting a number of factors, among them: general economic conditions, competitive conditions in the industry, relative market position, production capacity, advertising projections, sales programs, and strength of sales staff. In many businesses the sales budgeting process begins with a customer-by-customer sales projection on the part of each sales representative. Such projections may also serve as sales goals. Yet, while individual goal stretching may provide stimulus for accomplishment, it is not realistic budgeting. A good sales budget is one that can be achieved consistently within a very few percentage points—one way or the other.

Sales projection must start at the top of the profit and loss statement with gross sales. From gross sales a deduction must be projected for returns, allowances, and cash discount to arrive at net sales. In arriving at these estimates, experience serves as a guide, but only if known condition changes—the elimination of a cash discount from terms of sale, for example—are recognized and provided for.

FACTORY COST BUDGET

Sales budgets are based upon the sale of an estimated number of units at a projected price per unit. The next step in the budgeting process is determining an estimated cost of producing each of these units. In other words, we now come to a projection for the next section of the profit and loss statement, cost of goods sold. This calls for an estimate of each of the elements in the cost of production: material, labor, and factory overhead.

The cost of material going into each unit of production must first be estimated. Then, through previous experience or, perhaps, time and motion studies on a new product, the time required to produce each unit multiplied by the rate of pay, provides a budgeted labor figure. Finally, there are fixed factory costs which remain the same month in and month out regardless of the number of units produced. These fixed costs include factory rent, depreciation on machinery, and supervisory salaries.

STANDARD COSTS

These are costs that should be incurred under normal conditions in producing the product. A standard material and a standard labor cost per unit can be projected. Where there are deviations from this standard cost figure, the deviation is called a variance. Cost variances can be plus or minus, and they are a ready means of placing responsibility and correcting a problem.

Standard unit fixed costs must be based upon a fixed number of units to be produced. This fixed number of units is one which will utilize plant and equipment at a reasonably full level and produce a profit. Standard unit fixed costs are sometimes known as the hourly burden rate, which means that a piece of equipment will cost a certain amount in standard fixed costs each hour of the day whether it is operated continuously or not at all.

Plants with heavy fixed costs are under pressure to keep equipment running without interruption in order to absorb these costs which do not change. If unit standard fixed costs are calculated on the basis of a certain number of units to be produced and only half that number are actually produced, then there is an unfavorable variance equal to half the amount of the fixed costs. On the other hand, if standard fixed costs of one dollar per unit are budgeted on the basis of spreading monthly fixed costs of $10,000 among 10,000 units budgeted for production, and actual production is then 20,000 units, we have a favorable fixed cost variance of $10,000. It is not difficult to see how much pressure there is to keep the plant operating without downtime.

Standard costs are also used for pricing. It might be comfortable to avoid the pressure to run full by spreading fixed costs over a smaller number of units budgeted for production. But this will raise selling prices, and our competitors will keep us from adopting this course by underselling us. On the other hand, if we try to keep selling prices down by budgeting an unrealistically high rate of plant utilization under all conditions, then our sales efforts in the form of giveaway prices or loose credit practices may court trouble.

Budgeting of fixed and variable factory costs requires a high degree of skill and, above all, realism.

EXPENSE BUDGET

Budgeting selling expense is pretty much a matter of arithmetic. We know the number of sales representatives needed to sell the product we have budgeted to sell and produce. We then project, on the basis of travel cost estimates, what these costs will be. Finally, on the basis of a planned approach to marketing the product, we arrive at an advertising budget and a budget for special promotion planned for the year.

General administrative expense comes next. Here we budget salaries for officers of the corporation, office salaries, telephone, postage, office equipment rental, and all other expenses which have not been budgeted as a part of producing the product and selling it. This would include interest on borrowed money unless this item is to be shown separately under other expense. In either case, interest must be budgeted.

NET PROFIT BUDGET

Finally we come to the budgeted bottom line. Having already budgeted sales income and all the costs to be subtracted from that income, what is left is budgeted net profit. Knowing our income tax bracket, we budget that item as well, which leaves a budgeted net profit after tax for the year ahead. All we need now for a complete financial projection for the year ahead is a projection of dividends to be paid to stockholders. What remains of earnings will be reinvested in the business as an addition to net worth.

Operating budgets are prepared on a monthly, quarterly, and annual basis. Each department involved must make its contribution in order to come up with a useful over-all budget for the business as a whole. Then, at the close of each month, quarter, and year actual profit and loss figures are compared with budget figures and variations noted. Corrective steps are taken where necessary.

A comparison of actual profit and loss figures against budget might look like this:

	Current Period Budget	Actual
Units	16,000	14,000
Sales	$96,000	$84,000
Cost of Goods		
Material	32,000	28,000
Labor	19,200	16,800
Fixed Overhead	16,000	14,000
Variance Overhead		2,000
Total	$67,200	$60,800

	Current Period Budget	Actual
Gross Profit	$28,800	$23,200
Selling Expense	9,600	9,400
General and Administrative	10,000	10,000
Interest	2,000	2,000
Total Expense	21,600	21,400
Before-Tax Profit	7,200	1,800
Income Tax	3,500	880
Net Profit After Tax	$3,700	$920

In this case, corrective action needs to be taken!

Preparing the Cash Forecast

Most businessmen are familiar with and use operating budgets. Not so many are equally familiar with cash budgets. Yet cash forecasting is important to the financial health of any business. It should provide sufficient cash to meet operating needs but not too much. It also contributes substantially to the banking relationship by allowing the business person to know in advance what loan funds are needed to meet requirements.

The cash budget starts with the present cash balance. To this is added anticipated cash receipts to arrive at available cash. From this is subtracted anticipated cash outlays in order to arrive at the estimated cash balance at the end of the period. It looks like this:

Cash balance at beginning of period		$25,000
Add cash receipts		
Cash sales	$15,000	
Collections on accounts receivable	50,000	
Bank interest	2,000	
Available cash		67,000
Deduct cash disbursements		
Payroll	$20,000	
Accounts payable	30,000	
Taxes	5,000	
Dividends	10,000	
Miscellaneous	5,000	
Total disbursements		70,000
Estimated cash balance—close of period		$22,000

PROJECTING CASH NEEDS FROM THE SHORTFALL

A sales estimate is the starting point for all budgeting. This is certainly true for the cash budget because sales are the point from which all cash is received. It is possible to use the cash budget we have just examined as a means of arriving at a projection of future cash borrowing requirements. What we do is prepare the cash budget without using any starting cash balance at all. This assumes that the existing cash balance is already at the figure we consider minimal from an operating standpoint. Or, if we do not already have on hand a minimal cash balance, then we use a one-time disbursement in our calculations to bring it up to the required level.

Now, with operating cash at a steady level, we list cash receipts and cash disbursements to compare the two each month and on a cumulative basis. If in the first month, projected cash disbursements exceed projected cash receipts by $10,000, we have a shortfall of that amount. Cash of $10,000 must be obtained from some outside source, presumably the bank on a short-term loan. If the second month produces a similar $10,000 shortfall between cash receipts and disbursements, the cumulative loan requirement becomes $20,000. After six months the cumulative loan requirement may have become $100,000, and not until the seventh month will the trend begin to reverse. Then, for three or four months, cash receipts are budgeted to exceed disbursements by $20,000 each month so that, at year's end, the cash shortfall has been eliminated entirely and the need for outside funds completely gone.

What has been described is not unlike the cash flow picture of the typical manufacturer of promotional toys. Sixty to 75 percent of annual sales in this line are typically transacted in the last three months of the year. But production begins early in the year and continues steadily as inventory is built up in preparation for Christmas orders. In each of the first nine months of the year, very little cash is coming in and a great deal is going out. Successive monthly cash deficiencies pile up to add to the amount required in bank loans until a peak in September. Now orders, which had been received beginning in July, begin to ship out, and in November the cash starts rolling in. Production is shut down in December and January, accounts receivable are collected, and, as receipts of cash heavily outweigh disbursements, bank loans are paid down rapidly and finally paid out completely.

USING A PRO FORMA BALANCE SHEET TO PROJECT CASH

Another way to budget cash requirements is to project a succession of pro forma balance sheets complete except for the bank loan needed to balance. Once again, we use the operating budget as a starting point. Knowing each month's sales and expense projections, we use assumptions based upon historical experience to calculate each balance sheet item. The next step is to total all projected asset items on the left-hand side of the balance sheet and all projected liability items on the right-hand side along with the projected net worth, but excluding any projection for a short-term bank loan. If the total of net worth and liabilities on the right-hand side falls short of the total of assets on the left, then the amount of the deficiency represents the bank loan needed to provide necessary funds. Of course, if the asset total is greater than the total of liabilities plus net worth, there is a cash surplus.

In a typical situation here is how the balance sheet items might be arrived at:

- Cash. Month in and month out an arbitrary figure selected as the minimum cash required for comfortable operation.
- Accounts Receivable. With an historical collection period of 45 days and nothing expected to change that figure, we project accounts receivable to comprise all of the current month's sales plus half those of the preceding month.
- Inventory. This item on the balance sheet relates to cost of goods sold on the operating budget. If we require inventory on hand to provide for

the next two months' sales budget, we project inventory by combining cost of goods sold for the two following months.

- Prepaid Expenses. These are operating expenses which have been paid in advance. On the basis of experience, we know that one-third of each month's operating expense will be prepaid. One-third of the following month's budgeted operating expense therefore becomes our prepaid expense projection.
- Fixed Assets. Budgeted depreciation must be deducted from net fixed assets and budgeted capital expenditures added in order to arrive at a month by month projection of fixed assets.

Other assets will be projected according to the special situation of each. For example, if marketable securities appear among the current assets, they should be adjusted upward or downward in line with budgeted liquidation or additional investment.

Now we turn to liabilities and net worth:

- Accounts Payable. Purchase terms are 10th prox. (10th of the month following delivery), so we owe at the end of each month for materials delivered to us that month. Materials delivered this month will be used in production next month, to be included in the sales budget the month following. Therefore, this month's accounts payable will equal materials budgeted for the month after next.
- Accrued Expenses. Like prepaid expense, this is an arbitrary assumption based upon experience. Each month certain expenses are accrued though not yet paid and, if we know this is 25 percent of budgeted operating expense, this will form the basis for our projection.
- Income Tax. A computation based upon budgeted net profit.
- Current Year's Long-term Debt Maturity. This is a known figure based upon the terms of—
- Long-term Debt. This is the total of debt due over a period of years minus the portion due in the current year.
- Net Worth. This is the net worth figure with which we begin the period covered by the operating budget plus the profit after tax which has been budgeted for each succeeding month. Net worth projection will also be adjusted to provide for any known, anticipated change in capital investment through the addition or withdrawal of funds.

We have now extracted from the operating budget a pro forma balance sheet which should contain all items on both sides—assets, liabilities, and net worth—except one. The one item intentionally omitted from the liability side of the balance sheet is the current bank loan necessary to support operations. The required bank loan is the amount by which available liabilities plus net worth fail to equal and therefore fail to provide funds for the support of budgeted operations.

BALANCE SHEET ITEMS AS A PERCENTAGE OF SALES

Another way of projecting cash—and working capital requirements—is to compute each of the items on the balance sheet as a percentage of sales. Once this has been done for the already prepared current balance sheet, a pro forma balance sheet can be projected by calculating balance sheet items in dollars on the basis of their percentage relationship to the budgeted sales volume for the period to come. This is on the assumption that no changes are expected to occur which would significantly alter the relationship of balance sheet items to sales.

For example, if accounts receivable of $150,000 are this year 15 percent of $1 million sales, and sales for next year are budgeted for a 50 percent increase to $1,500,000, then accounts receivable next year, if they remain at 15 percent of sales, will be $225,000. Likewise, if accounts payable this year are 8 percent of sales and remain so, they will be $120,000 on the balance sheet one year hence. The same can be done for each asset and liability on the balance sheet.

Net worth should then be adjusted for the amount of profit to be retained in the business after the payment of dividends consistent with previous practice. This projected net worth can then be compared with the net worth arrived at by subtracting projected liabilities from projected assets based upon their percentage relationship to budgeted sales. What we arrive at is an estimate of additional capital required to finance the budgeted sales growth. The next question comes naturally: Where is it going to come from?

Many business people—particularly in small business—project rosy increases in sales without planning for the required growth in capital. The bank loan officer, the outside accountant, or the commercial credit manager can render invaluable service by assisting in the process of projecting cash flow requirements. The alternative can be financial chaos, starting with a tendency to lean on suppliers for financing and a developing sloppiness in meeting short-term bank loan commitments. The situation becomes even more serious if the growth in sales also requires additional investment in plant assets, thereby aggravating the working capital deficiency.

Operating budgets and cash flow projections provide the credit analyst with a glimpse into the future, just as internal and comparative financial analysis provide insights into the present condition and what has led up to it. Character, capacity, and capital are all integral parts of the financial picture and combine to determine the probable success or failure of the enterprise under review.

5

Sources of Credit Information for Bank Credit Departments

A small bank in a rural community will ordinarily have correspondent banks in several larger cities. In contrast, a large bank in New York or Chicago may have several *hundred* and occasionally several *thousand* correspondent banks located throughout the United States and in scores of foreign countries. Each of these hundreds or thousands of banks compiles and exchanges credit information with many others.

In addition, every business enterprise is a potential source of credit information regarding the individuals and the businesses with which it has relationships.

The gathering, compiling, recording, and interpreting of credit information is thus a dominant influence in American business life, and the thoroughness, intelligence, and accuracy with which credit investigations and analyses are made today have assumed the proportions of a practical science. The result has been a steadily increasing number of well-organized, fully equipped, and competently managed bank credit departments.

Bankers are occasionally credited with uncanny accuracy of judgment in detecting poor credit risks without using extensive credit information. Even with this unusual gift, if it does exist, bankers find it profitable to base their credit decisions upon exact facts. Insufficient investigations and inadequate facts are thin soil from which to expect sound loan policies to spring and grow.

Equipped with extensive credit information gathered from all available sources, however, the banker will avoid hasty loan decisions and bring to his task an intelligent comprehension of the borrower's request, a sympathetic understanding of the debtor's business and its operations, and a willingness to give every reasonable consideration to the borrower's credit requirements. Only an inadequate appreciation of the significant role of the credit department in the successful operation and management of a commercial bank could account for the failure to develop these credit facilities adequately.

Bankers obtain credit information directly from the executives of the business concerned. Indirect information comes from those in a position to be familiar with the various factors that make up the credit responsibility of the subject business enterprise or the individual.

Direct Information from Borrowers

Direct information may be obtained through the following four complementary approaches:

1. *Personal interviews.* Those take place generally in conferences at the bank or at the borrower's place of business.

2. *Investigations by the bank.* These may take a variety of forms, depending upon what information is sought, but will go beyond an interview. The banker may call upon the borrower at his place of business; make a careful investigation of the plant, the equipment, the farm, or other assets; and personally examine the accounting records. In large banks a staff of accountants may specialize in making detailed independent audits of the financial condition of borrowers.

3. *Correspondence with the borrower.* The correspondence may relate to such matters as general and specific business conditions, explanations of items in the balance sheet and the income statement, price trends, inventory problems, competition, expansion policies, estimates of credit requirements, and the borrower's program of retiring obligations. If the borrower is located nearby, this information may be obtained in personal interviews. When the borrower is located at some distance, however, correspondence generally is necessary.

4. *Financial and operating statements.* Financial statements may be prepared by the borrower's own bookkeeper or staff of accountants, by independent accounting firms, or by the bank's own accountants. The value of the information depends to a large degree upon the source. An unqualified statement prepared by a certified public accountant is preferred.

PERSONAL INTERVIEWS

A superior type of information may frequently be obtained by contact with the subject. In discussing inventory, labor, sales and managerial problems, and future plans, the borrower gives the banker an unusual opportunity to size up the credit risk. However, interviews are expensive and should be well planned. These steps should help:

1. Write out the specific things you wish to learn.

2. Eliminate those items you already know unless clarification or verification is needed.

3. Use alternative sources; for example, an agency report may suffice for much of the information.

4. Make certain you talk to the right person or persons; for example, sometimes the financial officer is more appropriate than the chief executive.

5. Make your interview positive in the sense that you convey an interest in the business and at the same time an expectation of cooperation in providing you necessary information.

A brief record of the interview should be prepared and you might take notes. In this way there is gradually built up in the file an excellent case history. This record will enable the banker to determine whether the management has demonstrated its ability to discharge its responsibilities adequately over a period of years.

A personal conference permits the banker to discuss with the borrower the various aspects of his financial statement, particularly increases or decreases in important items between the last two statement dates, and items that may not be fully understood by the banker.

The statements may, for example, show a large amount due from officers. The banker should ascertain the origin, trend, and liquidity of such an item. Certain officers may be living beyond their means and borrowing from the business for that purpose. The banker should also learn what possibility there is, if any, that such loans will be repaid in the near or distant future.

INVESTIGATIONS BY THE BANK

An idea of what a bank can accomplish in investigating a credit risk for itself, for a correspondent bank, or for one of its commercial customers may be obtained by examining actual reports of investigations made by the trained employees of an efficient credit department. Two such reports are presented below in the approximate form in which they would appear in the credit file. In the typical credit file, there would be a wide margin on the left-hand side of the page, and in that margin would appear the initials of the investigator and the date on which each call or interview was made. Sometimes an entire investigation is started and completed in less than a single day by one member of the credit department. At other times several members of the department may work several days on an investigation. As in the typical credit file, most of the following information is written in the first person, in the words used by the individual being interviewed.

The first illustration of a typical investigation made by the credit department of a bank deals with an individual who was establishing a new business enterprise. The Safe Trust and Savings Bank of Anko, Iowa, wrote the Traders National Bank of Chicago on February 28 requesting information regarding the general reputation and financial responsibility of Raymond U. Metcalf, 7642 West Kilman Avenue, Chicago, Illinois, explaining that one of their customers expected to enter into business dealings with him. The name did not appear in either the current telephone directory or the city directory. The following investigation was then conducted:

Credit Agency A: "We have no information on this individual."

Credit Agency B: "We have had no occasion to compile a report on this name."

Telephone information operator: "This individual does not appear to be one of our subscribers."

Elton Light Company: "This person is not a user of our electric service. We have no information regarding him."

Northern Gas Company: "This individual, as far as our records indicate, is not a user of our service. We are unable to be of any assistance."

INVESTIGATOR'S REPORT

Upon referring to the numerical street and avenue guide, which was several years old, I [the credit investigator] learned that, at the time the book was compiled, the property at 7642 West Kilman Avenue was vacant. However, according to the guide, the property at 7640 was occupied by Samuel Easton and his name appeared in the telephone directory. I called Mr. Easton on the telephone, and he stated that Martin Roberts resided at 7642 West Kilman Avenue. Mr. Easton was not acquainted with Mr. Metcalf. I telephoned the home of Mr. Roberts, and he said that Mr. Metcalf had been boarding with his family for the past month. He further stated that Mr. Metcalf was contemplating going into business for himself and he promised to have him get in touch with me.

Mr. Metcalf came in to see me today [one day later]. He indicated that he intended to engage in business for himself and would operate strictly on a commission basis, selling bottled and canned fruits, vegetables, pickles and condiments in behalf of several out-of-town fruit and vegetable packers. He stated that he was 35 years of age, and had been born and raised in Ohio. This would be the first business venture on his own account, and he had formerly been employed by the Smith Food Products Co., Inc., as sales manager for twelve years, and before that for about five years had been employed as a salesman for the Best Corporation, both companies being located at Cleveland, Ohio. He claimed that he would seek no credit, but would operate strictly on a commission basis, merely obtaining orders. Shipments would be made direct to his customers by the companies he represented. In addition to representing the two companies by which he had formerly been employed, he believed that in the very near future he would be able to make additional connections.

When questioned as to the extent of his resources, he stated that he owned no real estate, stocks, or bonds, but believed that he had sufficient capital to enable him to live comfortably until his business was fully established. At the present time he maintained no bank account, but would form a connection with one of the neighborhood banks within a month or two. He formerly carried a small savings account with the National Bank of Cleveland (Ohio), the account number being 136942.

His business would be operated from the above address temporarily. If the venture is successful, an office would be opened in the central manufacturing district. Mr. Metcalf indicated that he had severed his connection with the Smith Food Products because he felt that there was little prospect for him to go higher in an organization which was more or less a family concern. He was still a young man, and he believed that, with the experience and the contacts he had acquired, he should be able to make a success of this business. Mr. Metcalf was single, made a very good appearance, and impressed me favorably.

I telephoned the Chicago offices of each of the two corporations by which he had formerly been employed. The managers of each of these offices confirmed the information submitted by Mr. Metcalf. They also explained that he had left their services voluntarily. They believed him to be a gentleman of good character and reputation, and that, with the experience acquired through his connections with them, he should be successful in his operations.

I also communicated with his former bank, and they replied that he had carried a small three-figure savings account, but that he had never requested any loans. In our behalf they made several inquiries in Cleveland, and the information developed there was of a uniformly complimentary nature. Mr. Metcalf's record is apparently clear of suits and judgments. He has the reputation of meeting his obligations promptly.

The report on Mr. Metcalf is relatively simple but is typical of the investigations of individuals who are comparatively unknown and who have decided to start in business on their own account. The first reports, which indicated the inability to locate Mr. Metcalf, might have led a less experienced investigator to draw hasty and erroneous conclusions.

If the investigator had ceased to search for information after having failed to obtain any leads from the first five sources, his report would have been of no value to the bank nor to Mr. Metcalf. When the credit investigator had completed his inquiries, he was able to make an intelligent report which was helpful to both the inquiring customer of the Iowa bank and Mr. Metcalf himself.

A Typical Bank Investigation of an Established Enterprise. The second illustration is representative of investigations which are made of successfully operated business enterprises and which indicate no particularly unusual hazards. The Federal National Bank of New York City wrote the Manufacturers Trust of Akron, Ohio, on March 14, requesting credit information concerning the Arlan Distributing Co., 502½ North Central Avenue, Akron. One of the bank's depositors had been selling to that concern in substantial amounts and was contemplating a significant increase in its line of credit. The following investigation was then made by the credit department of Manufacturers Trust:

Credit Agency A. Key information from the report is as follows: Comparative statements for the most recent three fiscal years were prepared by a CPA, and attested without qualification. They reflected continued retention of profit, with a most recent tangible net worth of $161,600, a good financial condition, and a CB2 rating with Dun & Bradstreet ("good" composite credit appraisal with a tangible net worth between $125,000 and $200,000). Eight suppliers reported paying experience with subject, with all but one either discount or prompt. The remaining one was slow 15 days with nothing past due. Their account at the Safe Trust & Savings Bank was reported as satisfactory.

Mr. King, Credit Department, Safe Trust & Savings Bank: "We have been favored with a very satisfactory account from this concern since the inception of the business in 1930. Prior to that time the principal was a partner in another business which had maintained an account with us for a good many years. The account is satisfactory and averages in low five figures, balances last year having been better than $15,000. In recent months balances have been slightly under that amount. We have loaned the concern in liberal amounts on an unsecured basis, supported by the endorsement of the president of the company, whose outside worth is sizable. Last year our loans reached a peak of $50,000, and the account owes us $10,000 at this time. Borrowings were liquidated in full for three or four months last year. The principals have demonstrated their ability to operate the business profitably, even under adverse business conditions. Our last trade investigation was made a year ago and was very satisfactory. We believe that the concern is fully responsible for credit for its regular trade requirements. We have been furnished with their complete audit as of last December 31, which showed a tangible net worth of $161,600, consisting of capital stock, $120,000, and surplus, $41,600. Current assets amounted to $216,400, including cash of $14,000, accounts receivable of $132,800, and inventory of $69,600, to pay current liabilities of $61,400, of which $50,000 was due to us. Comparative financial statements reveal consistent increases in tangible net worth and net working capital. Operations last year were conducted at a profit (after income taxes) of approximately $25,000 on a sales volume of $956,000. The concern was started with a modest capital and earnings, for the most part, have been retained in the business. In the event you should care to consult several of their suppliers, they are doing business with the attached list of concerns."

Trade Reference A: "We have been doing business with this concern for several years and have not hesitated to grant credit up to $20,000 on 60-day terms. Bills have invariably been discounted in ten days. We consider the account one of the best on our books. The principals are capable and are highly regarded in trade circles."

Trade Reference B: "We have been selling this account for the past two years, the highest credit extended being about $15,000, and invoices have been paid promptly on 60-day terms. At the present time $6,000 is owing, none of which is due. The account has been a very desirable one."

Trade Reference C: "This enterprise is well known in the trade and has no trouble in securing credit for its reasonable requirements. Our account has never run over $5,000, although we would gladly go higher. All invoices have been retired on discount terms."

Trade Reference D: "This is a splendid account because bills are always discounted. The principals, in our opinion, are aggressive and know their line. They never miss a discount with us."

Trade Reference E: "We have a very high regard for the management of this business and do not hesitate to sell them up to $10,000. Invoices are discounted."

Trade Reference F: "This is a very small account with us, never running over $1,000, and bills invariably have been discounted."

Trade Reference G: "Overall we regard them as a good account. We have granted up to $5,000 with payments prompt to slow 30 days on N30 terms. There may have been some problem in the one instance of slowness but our records show no dispute."

Most bank investigations are similar to these two cases. They reveal the nature of the business, financial condition, and banking record of the borrower. Using the facts obtained, together with such information as the bank may already have, the banker then makes the decision. In making the decision the banker is not concerned with the out-of-pattern instances of slowness in the trade check and in the agency report. The banker knows that such instances occur in any business and may be caused by the supplier as well as the debtor.

The credit executives would have failed to discharge their responsibilities properly if they had not made thorough and complete investigations. In the first illustration the inability of an Iowa business concern to evaluate a credit risk in Chicago might have resulted in a loss of profitable business. In the second illustration the initial information obtained from the credit reporting agency tied in with the information obtained directly from the bank and from suppliers. However, a significant increase in an already substantial line requires a thorough investigation.

CORRESPONDENCE WITH THE BORROWER

As a worthwhile source of credit information, correspondence with the borrower ranks close to a personal interview. In a small community where all accounts are local depositors, there is little need for correspondence. However, as soon as a bank begins to accept accounts from depositors located at a distance, correspondence becomes an important means of obtaining information.

In a larger city the conditions are often different, and correspondence may be carried on with local depositors who are some distance away. The correspondence may cover explanations of various items on the balance sheet, income statement, or supplementary figures, reasons for changes in important items since the date of the last balance sheet, current progress of the business, problems confronting the management, and information regarding credit lines with other banking institutions.

There are three principal conditions under which a bank ordinarily will correspond directly with a borrower: (1) To ascertain the amount of total confirmed lines of credit; (2) to obtain an explanation of one or several items in the balance sheet; and (3) to obtain interim financial or operating information.

For purposes of illustration, typical letters requesting information on each of these three points are presented.

Total Confirmed Lines of Credit. In the case of a depositor who borrows at several banks, a loan officer needs exact data regarding his total confirmed lines of credit. Each bank with which the customer does business quite naturally might request the same information. The following three paragraphs are extracts from a letter written by the president of a successful corporation to the vice president of a depository who was seeking information of this nature from the former:

In order to complete your records, we are pleased to inform you that we have credit lines of $250,000 each, confirmed by the following three banks, on our plain unsecured note:

> Reliable National Bank, Minneapolis
> Old National Bank, Chicago
> Safe National Bank, New York

These lines, totaling $750,000, are the same as we had last year and, we believe, will be ample for our needs for the coming year.

If we find that additional loans are required, we shall be pleased to take the matter up with you again, as you have suggested.

Explanation of Balance Sheet Items. When the meaning of a particular item in the balance sheet or in the supplementary figures of a borrower is not clear, the banker often writes for further information. At times, a written explanation is desirable, particularly if it is complicated, so that there is no misunderstanding. Information of this nature is, however, often obtained in direct interviews, then summarized and placed in the credit file. The following four paragraphs are extracts from a letter written by the treasurer of a wholesale grocery house in answer to a letter requesting an explanation of the item Commitments, carried at $75,000 in the auditor's certificate attached to a recent balance sheet:

In response to your letter of June 25, relative to the item Commitments appearing in the certificate attached to our balance sheet for $75,000, we are pleased to give you the following schedule representing the items which make up this amount:

Flour	$5,000
Coffee	15,000
Sugar	10,000
Canned vegetables	35,000
Canned fruit	10,000

Under our contracts, we are permitted to take out merchandise as we need it. As a matter of fact, a substantial portion of the canned goods contracts runs for ten months.

You are familiar with our business, and know that contracts are entered into prior to the packing season. We feel the contracts we now have are very advantageous, in view of present market conditions.

We trust this explanation is satisfactory. If there are any other questions, please write us.

Interim Financial Information. In addition to the customary yearly balance sheet and income statement, the banker may wish to obtain information from time to time during the year regarding the progress of a business, especially one that is not in a particularly strong financial position. The following three paragraphs are extracts from a letter written by the president of a canning company to a banker who was anxious to ascertain the condition of the business after the first six months of its fiscal year:

We are pleased to enclose our balance sheet and six-month income figures, as of November 30.

You will note that our current position shows further improvement. Collections are good and sales are to be ahead of a year ago. The drought which prevailed in some sections of the Middle West reduced the corn pack considerably, so that we are experiencing a strong demand.

We expect to be out of debt to our banks not later than March 15.

FINANCIAL AND OPERATING STATEMENTS

The significance of exact information in the form of balance sheets and income statements cannot be overstressed. The detailed explanations and the interpretations of the figures are discussed in other chapters of this book. At this point we desire merely to emphasize the extreme importance of reliable, comprehensive figures relative to balance sheets, income statements, surplus accounts, budgets, and trial balances.

Information from Outside Sources

No less important than the information obtained directly from the borrower is that obtained from those who have had actual business relations with the borrower or who have had occasion to prepare a report on that business. Important facts regarding the establishment, the growth, and the business dealings of many concerns are also reported in newspapers, magazines, and public records. The following are eight important outside sources of supplementary information:

1. *Bank check.* Investigations made with other banks, particularly with those that share an account.

2. *Trade check.* Investigations with concerns that sell to the borrower.

3. *Public records.* Records such as judgments entered, suits pending in the courts, real estate transfers, and mortgages are available in the records of the various courts. Financial statements on corporations are available in some states.

4. *Newspapers, periodicals, and directories.* Information is available in the daily press, financial journals, trade papers, trade association directories, gov-

ernment bulletins and pamphlets, and the studies of local Better Business Bureaus.

5. *Reports from attorneys.* Services of attorneys located in the same community as the borrower may be utilized.

6. *Investment manuals.* Publishing companies prepare a mass of information regarding the earnings and the financial condition of corporations, particularly those with securities held by the public.

7. *Brokerage houses and rating agencies.* Reports are available from brokerage houses and ratings are provided by the rating agencies.

8. *Commercial credit reporting agencies.* Agency reports are used by almost every bank credit department. There are general agencies which prepare reports on all types of businesses and specialized agencies which confine their activity to one line of business or a limited number of lines.

Each of these sources is of assistance to the banker in evaluating a credit risk. The resourceful banker will determine the most suitable combination of these sources to use in a particular case.

BANK CHECK

The two most frequently used outside sources of credit information are other banks and mercantile concerns. If two or more banking institutions do business with the same customer, exchange of information and experiences is of mutual benefit. In such circumstances, progressive banks will ordinarily give complete information to each other. The information exchanged will include the history of the account since the bank has had it and a full report of its deposit and borrowing relationships.

Robert Morris Associates (RMA), an association of 2,100 commercial bank loan and credit officers, representing about 87 percent of United States commercial banking resources, has a Code of Ethics for the Exchange of Commercial Credit Information (*see* Chapter 6, pages 73–4). Adherence to this Code of Ethics is essential. Upon joining RMA, members acknowledge and agree to abide by these principals, and they expect others with whom information is exchanged to respect them also. This Code has been designed for commercial transactions, and its use is subject to applicable Federal and state laws.

Checking with other banks for the purpose of obtaining their full experience on accounts and then soliciting their accounts is regarded as unethical (unless the purpose is given as covered by Article 4). The inquiring bank would expect only general information, certainly nothing with regard to the amount of balances or the lending arrangement with the customer. If any information of substance is obtained from the prospect's bank in connection with the solicitation, it is generally considered appropriate that the bank cease active solicitation of the relationship for six months. This has not been a formal part of the RMA Code, but it is practiced in a number of cities.

A mutual revision is a credit investigation conducted between two or several banks that mutually have accounts from the same company. It is important in a mutual revision not to discuss compensating balances since this information is considered competitive. Normal procedure in a mutual revision is that the inquiring bank states its story first and that the replying bank replies in kind. Specifically, if the inquiring bank gives a very brief description of its relationship with the subject, the bank called upon to provide this information will give a similarly brief story.

TRADE CHECK

In larger central reserve cities, the bank credit departments maintain staffs of investigators to make direct personal or telephone calls upon other banks and also upon trade creditors. Many banks in small cities have no investigators and carry on most of their investigations by mail or by telephone. Form letters are often, sometimes too often, used by banking institutions for this same purpose.

The exchange of information between trade creditors of a business and banks must be governed by good sense and should be fair to the business being reported.

Robert Morris Associates and The National Association of Credit Management have a codified Statement of Principles in the Exchange of Credit Information Between Banks and Mercantile Creditors. It was adopted in 1955 and amended in 1971, as follows:

STATEMENT OF PRINCIPLES IN THE EXCHANGE OF INFORMATION
BETWEEN BANKS AND MERCANTILE CREDITORS

1. The first and cardinal principle in the exchange of credit information is absolute respect for the confidential nature and accuracy of inquiries and replies, and of the identities of inquirers and sources.

2. Written inquiries should be by direct communication, manually and responsibly signed, and should correctly give name and address of the subject of inquiry. When an inquiry is made in person or by telephone, the inquirer should satisfactorily identify himself.

3. Every inquiry should indicate specifically: amount involved, reason, terms, availability of other background information and whether source was given as reference. If inquirer's bank is used, the subject's bank of account should be named if known. When multiple bank inquiries are made, it should be so stated, and if two banks are in the same locality, their names given.

4. File revisions should be undertaken only when necessary, and such inquiries should contain an expression of experience if appropriate, and in compliance with Federal and state statutes.

5. When inquiries are made on behalf of third parties, it should be clearly stated

but the identity of the other party must not be disclosed without permission.

6. Replies should be prompt. If written, they should be manually and responsibly signed and as complete as possible, consistent, however, with the amount and nature of the inquiry. Specific questions should be answered if practicable, and in compliance with Federal and state statutes.

7. If the confidential nature of the relationship with the subject prevents disclosure of desired information, answers should so state.

PUBLIC RECORDS

A vast amount of credit information is available in Federal, state, and county courts and records. The typical bank credit department seldom uses these comprehensive records. Often information originating at these sources is utilized only when it has found its way into the press.

The principal source of record information regarding business transactions is probably the office of the county clerk, although Uniform Commercial Code filings are usually at the state level. The type of information available at these sources is concerned with the ownership, pledge, and transfer of real and personal property, including deeds, mortgages, liens, and wills; assessed valuations for tax purposes; corporate charters; registration of trade styles and assumed names; suits, judgments, and all judicial proceedings, civil and criminal, within the jurisdiction of the state courts. Federal cases, criminal and civil, including bankruptcy proceedings, are recorded in the Federal district courts.

Financial information of a most extensive nature must be filed with the Securities and Exchange Commission at Washington, D.C., and to a lesser extent at New York and Chicago, at periodic intervals by every corporation (except railroads, common and contract carriers by motor vehicles, and commercial banking institutions) whose securities are traded on a national stock exchange, and by substantially every corporation (except railroads, common and contract carriers by motor vehicles, and commercial banking institutions) that sells an issue of securities to the public with an aggregate offering price of $300,000 or more.

A duplicate copy of all information filed with the Securities and Exchange Commission by a corporation whose securities are listed on a national stock exchange is also filed for public inspection at the office of the particular exchange where the security is traded.

Reports filed with the Securities and Exchange Commission contain detailed individual and consolidated balance sheets, income statements and reconciliation of surplus; breakdowns and changes during the year in relevant balance sheet items, such as marketable securities and other security investments; amounts due from directors, officers, and principal holders of the equity security; investments in securities of affiliates and indebtedness of affiliates;

property, plant, and equipment; reserves for depreciation, depletion, and amortization of property, plant, and equipment; intangible assets; and details of any outstanding funded debts.*

The SEC also makes running statistical studies of numerous types, including the tabulation of combined balance sheets and combined profit and loss statements by individual lines of industry and commerce.

Comprehensive financial information and data must be filed at least annually with the Interstate Commerce Commission, Washington, D.C., by all public carriers, pipelines (other than those for water and gas), and freight forwarders engaged in interstate or foreign commerce. Class I motor carriers,† for example, must file an exhaustive annual report on specially prepared forms totaling about 70 pages. This most comprehensive schedule covers full details of organization and control, such as names of partners and, in the case of corporations, the names of officers and directors with the amount of their individual interests in the business; type of service rendered, whether carriers of general freight, household goods, or any one of 15 other distinct classifications; a detailed balance sheet with full explanation of every relevant item; an unusually complete profit and loss statement; breakdown of operating property; schedule of equipment obligations showing changes during the year; and list of routes in operation. This extensive information is open for public inspection.

Information similar to that filed with the Interstate Commerce Commission must also be filed with the Federal Communications Commission, Washington, D.C., by all radio and television broadcasting stations. Business enterprises in this line operate under a public license which stipulates the frequencies to be used, the power of transmitters, and the hours of broadcast. Detailed reports concerning ownership, financial condition, and extensive technical data must be filed *(a)* when an application is made for the original construction permit, *(b)* when an application is made for the renewal of the license every three years, *(c)* when an application is made for transfer of control (assignment of license), and *(d)* when an application is made for a construction permit for changes in station equipment. (On existing stations a construction permit must be applied for whenever there are substantial changes in equipment, usually in connection with changes in frequency, power, or location, or if there is modernization; usually this is required only on changes amounting to over $5,000.)

Financial information only must be filed with every application for a broadcasting license. Whenever an original or modifying construction permit

---

*Regulation S-X, Form and Content of Financial Statement, published by the Securities and Exchange Commission, contains detailed instructions and forms for registrant commercial and industrial corporations, management investment companies, unit investment trusts, insurance companies other than life and title insurance companies, committees issuing certificates of deposit, bank holding companies and banks, and natural persons.

†A Class I motor carrier is defined by the ICC as any interstate motor carrier of property whose average gross operating revenue from interstate and intrastate operations combined is $5 million or more annually.

is applied for, all information must be given. When the work is completed, a new license must be applied for. At this time the new financial statement showing the expenditures and financial condition of the business at the completion are submitted. All of this information is available for public inspection. The operators of radio and television broadcasting stations are also required to file annual operating figures, but these are not available for public inspection.

Similar extensive reports and financial information must also be filed with the Civil Aeronautics Administration by all civil airlines and with the Federal Power Commission by all producers and distributors of electric power and by all gas pipeline companies.

The Federal and state governments also publish numerous reports on prices, sales, production, inventory position, and supplementary facts in leading industries. For example, the following six bureaus of the Federal government are widely known and utilized by businessmen in obtaining reliable periodic figures and indexes for specific purposes:

The Bureau of the Census, in cooperation with state and local governments, has made available the census of population and of manufacturers since about 1800, the census of distribution and service trades since 1929, continuous monthly figures on important trades and industries by cooperation arrangements with trade associations, and continuous monthly figures on vital statistics and expenditures.

The Bureau of Agricultural Economics makes available data on agricultural commodity prices, volume of shipments, and special subjects such as farm values and mortgage financing.

The Bureau of Foreign and Domestic Commerce makes available monthly indexes on trade and industry, and special studies of operating costs in various lines of business activity.

The Bureau of Labor Statistics makes available monthly indexes of employment, payrolls, wholesale prices, and quarterly figures on the cost of living.

The Board of Governors of the Federal Reserve System makes available weekly and monthly figures of member banks and of the Federal Reserve Banks, bank debits to individual accounts, monthly figures on department store sales and collections, and various monthly figures on wholesale trades in certain Federal Reserve districts.

The Internal Revenue Service makes available annual data on statistics of income for corporations and individuals, including information on balance sheets and operating figures.

Numerous other departments, bureaus, agencies and instrumentalities of the Federal government carry on statistical studies varying in quantity and importance.* In seven states—Arizona, Colorado, Hawaii, Kansas, Michigan,

---

*Supplementing the original source material as issued, three principal publications of the Federal government contain extensive statistical data. These are *Survey of Current Business,* a

New Hampshire, and Vermont—financial information in the form of a balance sheet (in some cases highly condensed) and, in certain cases, some operating information is filed by every business corporation operating in those states and is open for public inspection.

There are government sources of valuable information which require contact by mail or phone for specific information. The Small Business Administration, the Department of Commerce, the Farm Loan Bank, and the Bank for Cooperatives are examples of these.

NEWSPAPERS, PERIODICALS, AND DIRECTORIES

In this category are included financial journals, trade magazines and papers, trade association directories, and investigations of local Better Business Bureaus. The newspapers and trade magazines, in particular, contain helpful information for the credit department. Reports on such subjects as plant expansion, development of new inventions and models, production and sales in various industries, commodity price trends, refinancing plans, changes in ownership and management, and death notices are all news items of importance to the efficient bank credit department.

For general economic and business information, a banker will profit by reading one or several periodicals which provide economic and financial data.

Bank libraries often have business magazines with articles about specific companies, industries, regional economic conditions, and interviews with members of companies in which the banks might have an interest.

Many types of trade directories are helpful as supplementary sources of information. Directories of attorneys, doctors, officers and directors in business corporations, and accountants may give brief reports regarding the personal history, educational background, and length of time an individual has been in his present location, and in some cases information regarding his financial standing. *Who's Who in America* gives biographical information about men who have become publicly prominent. *The Dun & Bradstreet Reference Book of Corporate Managements* provides background information on the officers of major businesses in the United States. There are numerous other directories available of a similar nature which can prove useful. Some of these include *Polk's World Bank Directory, Rand McNally Bank Directory, Trinc Directories of Motor Carriers, Thomas Register—American Manufacturers,* and such Dun & Bradstreet directories as *Reference Book of Manufacturers, Metalworking Directory, Million Dollar Directory, Middle Market Directory,* and *Principal International Businesses.*

---

monthly publication, and *Business Statistics, A Supplement to the Survey of Current Business,* a biennial publication, both published by the Office of Business Economics of the Department of Commerce; and *Statistical Abstract of the United States,* a yearly publication of the Bureau of the Census of the Department of Commerce.

There are numerous sources of statistical data for use in analyzing financial statements. Robert Morris Associates publishes *Annual Statement Studies.* *Key Business Ratios* is published by Dun & Bradstreet. Many trade associations publish such data on specific industries.

BETTER BUSINESS BUREAUS

There are local Better Business Bureaus in the principal cities of the United States and Canada. Each Better Business Bureau is a separate and completely independent nonprofit corporation, separately governed and separately financed. These bureaus maintain an organization known as the National Association of Better Business Bureaus, Inc., in Cleveland, a nonoperating organization which holds an annual conference to provide for the discussion of matters of mutual interest. In addition there is also the National Better Business Bureau, Inc., in New York City, similar in form to the local bureaus, but financed by cooperating concerns whose interests are national in scope. Its activities are similar to those of the local bureaus, but confined chiefly to the fields of national advertising and selling.

The eight main aims of Better Business Bureaus are:

1. To increase public confidence in advertising, salesmanship and business generally by assisting in the elimination of unfair and deceptive advertising
2. To promote accuracy in advertising, through the cooperation of advertisers themselves, advertising media, advertising agencies, and properly constituted authorities
3. To aid in the elimination of unfair competition through promulgation of ethical standards
4. To provide an unbiased medium for the settlement of disputes between competitors and between business concerns and their customers involving alleged false or misleading advertising
5. To expose fake promotions and to aid in the prosecution of fake promoters
6. To warn the public against the endless easy-money schemes which divert hard-earned dollars from the channels of legitimate investment and trade
7. To encourage the public to "investigate before investing"
8. To furnish dependable, disinterested information on offerings of securities, business opportunities, or services—thus not only protecting the public, but also removing unjustified suspicion from legitimate enterprises

ATTORNEYS

In special cases a bank may obtain credit information from an attorney residing in the same community as the individual or concern under investigation. Some banks make it a practice to use an attorney as a source of information only in towns of less than, for example, 12,000 people, where he might be acquainted with most of the businesses of the town, or be able to obtain information without too great difficulty. On the other hand, occasional law firms in larger cities have found this source of revenue sufficiently great to warrant opening up a commercial department to specialize in collecting and disseminating credit information.

INVESTMENT MANUALS

The facilities of an efficiently operated bank credit department may be rounded out by the use of one or more investment manuals on industrial, public utility, railroad, financial, and insurance corporations. Two well-known such services are Moody's Investors Service, Inc., and Standard and Poor's Corporation. Alfred M. Best Co., Inc., a third concern, specializes in the compilation and interpretation of somewhat similar information on insurance companies of all kinds.

BROKERAGE HOUSES AND RATING AGENCIES

Brokerage houses sometimes have research departments which prepare reports on businesses to which you may be contemplating granting loans.

There are rating agencies that provide ratings on bonds and commercial paper. Moody's and Standard and Poor's are the best known. Alex Sheshanoff provides ratings on domestic banks, and the firm of Keefe, Bruyette & Woods, Inc., provides similar information. Often it is important to look at a bank's strength in connection with letters of credit that they are issuing.

COMMERCIAL CREDIT REPORTING AGENCIES

Of all sources of credit information available to the banker, the most extensive are the reports of the general and specialized mercantile credit agencies. Dun & Bradstreet, Inc., disseminates information on more than four million business establishments. It does not provide credit reports on individual consumers. This general agency provides information for business-to-business credit transactions, as well as other business decisions. Information about each business includes name, address, *Duns* number, finances, history, operation, management, branches, subsidiaries, banking relationships, public record information, and bill-paying practices.

In 1976 the National Association of Credit Management and TRW Credit Data became operational with a service called NACIS, which provides trade payment information on businesses and operates as a general agency.

There are also investigative agencies which are better known for consumer reports that do commercial credit reporting. These agencies do intensive investigations on a business or on principals in a business and sometimes both. Bishop's, Fidelifacts, and Proudfoot are illustrations of that type of agency. Although some small banks are sometimes unaware of these sources and some are wary of using them because of their misunderstanding of the Fair Credit Reporting Act, they are useful sources when a loan is being considered for business purposes, and in such instances the Fair Credit Reporting Act is not applicable although it is well to have advice of bank counsel as to how the service is utilized.

THE DUN & BRADSTREET BUSINESS INFORMATION REPORT

Dun & Bradstreet reports are designed to provide information needed by a variety of business decision makers, including bankers. While the bankers must make the ultimate decision, agency reports can provide important information as a part of the banker's data collection process. The report on a particular business is updated on a regular basis through personal calls by reporters at the business premises, by telephone calls and by mail. The latter provides the business the opportunity to keep key information up-to-date and accurate. While the business itself is the primary source of the data, reporters use banks, trade creditors, and public records, not only to supplement the information provided directly, but also to serve as a cross-check as to its reliability. Also, reporters are trained to look at relationships of certain data to see that they are in line with industry norms and, if they are not, to try to learn why. Finally, users of the information are encouraged to ask questions if they do not understand something about the report or if they have information in their possession which raises a question as to the accuracy of any part of the report.

Various sections of the report will reflect information obtained at various dates, and for that reason there are dates in the left-hand margin which indicate when the particular information was obtained. The date at the top of the report is merely the date it was printed. While there are certain information sections that will appear in virtually every report, there are some such as "Special Events" or "Public Filings" which will not.

Report Content. In the report's heading, starting at the top left, is the DUNS number. Dun & Bradstreet assigns every business its own exclusive identification number, which, among other uses, greatly simplifies the computerization of business records. Immediately below the DUNS number appears: the business name, full headquarters address, ZIP code, and phone number. If a proprietorship, the owner's name will also be shown. (On partnerships and corporations, only one name will appear in the heading; the other principals are fully identified under "history.") In the center portion, the heading identifies the type of operation being conducted along with the appropriate Standard Industrial Classification (SIC) number, which reflects the business activity in numerical terms. (SIC classifications are assigned by the U.S. government.)

At the top right of the report is the summary. Starting with the Dun & Bradstreet Rating, this section provides a capsule view of the entire report and for the most part is understandable at a glance. Some captions, however, require a further word: "Started" represents either the year the business was founded or the date it came under present control; "Sales" is either an exact yearly total or an annualized figure based on partial results; "Worth" is listed net of goodwill, patents, or other intangibles; and "Trend" describes the overall direction of the business after considering profits and net worth as well as sales.

The "Payments" section presents the paying habits of the business by reporting the experiences of those sources selling the account on credit terms. Each line is dated and represents the experience of a particular supplier. Reading left to right, manner of payment (discount, prompt, or slow) is noted and followed by the amount of high credit extended, amounts currently owing or past due, selling terms, and an indication of how recently the account was sold. In using the payment information one should recognize the following:

1. The date of the particular line of trade is important, not simply so that one can see when it was reported to Dun & Bradstreet, but also as a means of spotting trends. Over a period of months, payments may be improving, staying the same, or retrogressing.

2. The paying record provides an overall measure of how bills are paid. Where there has been just one transaction, the evaluation is simple. When there is more than one description in one line of the paying record, that is, prompt to slow 60 days, the reader will know that there not only has been more than one transaction but that the payments have differed. For instance, there could have been a prompt payment of an invoice, slow 30 days on another, and slow 60 on still another. For that reason it is sometimes useful, when evaluating payments, to count such experiences in two halves, one half as prompt and one half as slow.

3. "High credit" indicates the highest amount owed recently at any one time. This is useful in totaling up all the high credits and comparing that total to accounts payable or to sales to see how representative the payment information is. However, one must be careful to avoid misinterpreting this figure. For instance, a very small amount from a particular supplier may simply mean that

requirements for that material or service is limited and not any restriction of credit. Also, the slow payment of an invoice combined with an additional current transaction will actually drive up the amount of high credit being granted, without necessarily indicating added confidence on the part of the supplier. Of course, credit executives try to avoid excessive exposure on weak risks.

4. "Now owes" is of even greater value in the aforementioned comparison with financial statements. In addition, it can be quickly seen whether the amount presently owed is approaching the recent high credit, which could be an indication that available credit is being exhausted if a number of the individual lines of experience read this way.

5. "Past due" is useful in several ways. One can see whether a slowness being reported exists at the present time. In addition, that amount compared with the total owed can give an indication of the respective portions paid promptly or slowly. When a relatively small percentage of the total is past due, this is often an indication that there is a dispute, skipped invoice, or some other reason which would indicate there is an explanation for the particular slowness being reported.

6. The "terms of sale" are useful to a credit executive in relating particular payments to one's own situation, in that one may find that most of those reporting slowness grant the same terms or perhaps not.

7. "Last sale within" indicates how recent the information is likely to be.

8. The dollar amounts are often reported to Dun & Bradstreet in ranges and are not necessarily exact amounts.

9. With the volume of credit transactions that take place in businesses of any significant size, there are bound to be some situations when bills are not paid within terms. The evaluation of the payment record of a business should be made in relation to experience with other businesses. Credit executives can do this by looking at their own experience with other accounts, as well as by reviewing on a comparative basis the paying records an agency reports on its various accounts.

The Dun & Bradstreet Reference Book is not intended as a substitute for detailed credit reports but as an auxiliary facility to be used for ready reference where light risk is involved and for other convenient and useful purposes. Each subscriber uses this service in a way that fits its own circumstance and situation. A banker may find it a useful tool, but would rarely make a loaning decision on this information alone.

Delivery of Services. In recognition of the varying needs of its subscribers, Dun & Bradstreet provides various types of services, as well as a choice in the method of delivery.

Special handling can be obtained when time is at a premium. Two-Way Priority Service takes the inquiry out of routine, and a response is usually made by telephone the same day unless there are delays in contacting the business being reported. One-Way Priority Service also takes the inquiry out of routine but does not include calling the information back.

The subscriber has a wide choice as to the delivery of the reports and ratings. For those who need full reports immediately, on-the-premises Dun Sprint terminals provide instant access. The report may also be requested by mail or by telephone with the response sent by mail.

For those who desire flexibility when ordering the report, Duns Dial is available. By dialing a toll-free number, the user can speak to an operator who calls up information on the screen of a cathode-ray tube (CRT). As information is read from a CRT, the user makes the decision as to the extent of the data to be read and whether a full report is to be mailed. Another alternative is Duns-Vue. This service, introduced on a test basis in 1980, provides ratings and summary data. It operates by means of an ordinary telephone and provides the information in print form or on a small desk-top CRT terminal. It provides instant access on an economical basis for those who require only summary data.

Dun's Financial Profiles is a customized service which provides the last two to three years' financial statements on a given business presented with uniform balance sheet and profit and loss classifications. It reflects year-to-year percentages of change for each item for trend analysis and provides industry norms for comparative analysis. All the key business ratios are also provided so that an in-depth comparison can be made to other businesses in the industry.

Key Account Report Service provides an in-depth custom report, exclusively for the inquiring subscriber. The inquiry is discussed prior to the investigation to insure coverage of the specific needs of the subscriber.

Change Notification Service is normally used by business credit executives. They register the names of their customers annually, and as significant changes take place, that information is brought to the subscriber's attention. These changes include rating changes, special changes such as reorganizations, bankruptcies and relocations, and successor changes. This service can also be obtained on computer tape for those with automated accounts receivable systems and that service is known as *Exception Credit Update Service.*

Dun & Bradstreet International Services provide Business Information Reports in 23 foreign countries. This report is quite similar to the domestic report and provides data on history, finances, operation, and payments. International also provides ratings on businesses and numerous directories for business.

Credit Clearing House is a specialized division of Dun & Bradstreet providing a line of credit services for the apparel and allied fields. Analysts who are experts in the apparel field provide recommended guidelines including dollar amounts. Subscribers can telephone CCH operators who use cathode-ray tubes to give instant responses. In many instances credit approvals can be made immediately. In those instances where no guideline can be provided, the Dun & Bradstreet Report is available for further consideration.

NATIONAL CREDIT INFORMATION SERVICES (NACIS).

This computerized business credit reporting service operates as a general agency, reporting on all types of businesses. It specializes in the sense that it provides credit data showing the paying habits of specific firms. This information is extracted from tapes from the accounts receivable files of contributors, who provide the tapes every 90 days.

The report may be obtained by means of a print terminal on the premises of the subscriber, which provides instant access, or by ordering it through a local chapter of NACM. For example, the report could include:

- *Payment experience.* Ledger-type information, including the industry in which the seller operates, date the information was reported, date of last sale, terms of sale, recent high credit, specific comments, and account balances stated in current and aged categories, reflecting the percentage of the open balance which is current and slow, with the latter shown in ranges.
- *Payment trends.* A month-by-month display of total reported payment performances over each of the prior six months.
- *Bank information.* Name and address of bank and banking relationships, i.e., the "borrower" where it is a borrowing account.
- *Inquiries.* All inquiries made within the last 90 days classified by business category and type of inquiry.

In some reports information is provided regarding such areas as number of employees, sales, and, in the case of certain publicly owned companies, financial statements.

SPECIALIZED AGENCIES

There are numerous specialized agencies. They are a diverse group, most of them small. In some lines of business there are several competing agencies and in other lines there are none. Some information on two of them is provided to indicate the nature of such services, although it should be kept in mind that the services rendered by other specialized agencies may not be identical or even similar to these. Other bankers can be helpful in providing details as to the availability and the usefulness of such services.

The National Credit Office (NCO) is a division of Dun & Bradstreet. It provides specialized information on the apparel, automotive, metals, electronics, and chemical industries. Its services include reports that are similar to the

Dun & Bradstreet Report with two major exceptions. NCO provides suggested dollar lines of credit and gives a list of the subject's major suppliers and banks. The report is divided into three sections: financial and trade information, with a credit suggestion in those instances where one can be made; data on the management and the operation of the business; and a complete financial statement when obtained. Among its other services are a consulting service in which line specialists provide answers to specific credit inquiries, group meetings primarily for an interchange of credit experience, special lines services, and specialized guides and directories.

The Lyon Furniture Mercantile Agency specializes in contract furnishings, the furniture trade, interior decorating, lumber, major home appliances, mobile home trailers, and stores (mainly department stores and general stores).

Its services include the *Lyon Red Book,* tracer sheets, credit reports, and collection. The *Lyon Red Book* is published semiannually in January and July and is a rating book covering the firms reported on by the agency. The format is similar to the *Dun & Bradstreet Reference Book* but the ratings are different. There is a capital rating, a payments rating, and, in contrast to Dun & Bradstreet, a rating for special conditions.

Tracer sheets are distributed weekly to cooperating subscribers soliciting information on a number of accounts of particular credit interest. Responses provide a customer's payment habits, amount owing, and amount past due. The nationwide results are compiled in *Result of Tracer,* which is available to all participating subscribers.

Credit reports provide the business name, address, and telephone number, management and management antecedents, general information, financial information, analysis including ratio analysis, bank information, trade information, summary, and Lyon rating.

CREDIT INTERCHANGES

One of the functions of the local chapters of the National Association of Credit Management is that of the credit interchange bureaus. There are 58 credit interchange bureaus which make up the National Credit Interchange System. Each bureau operates autonomously but cooperates with the others in the exchange of credit information. Each member company furnishes information on its accounts, such as how long the account has been sold, date of last sale, highest recent credit, amount owing, amount past due, terms of sale, and how payments are met (prompt, slow, etc.).

When a member needs such information on a customer, it sends a request for a report to the local bureau. The bureau responds by sending any report it has on file and circulates that request to its members to solicit responses from other suppliers. The responses are tabulated, issued, and placed on file.

A successful interchange requires a high degree of support and cooperation from its members, calling for prompt and complete responses to requests for experience with an account, providing names of known suppliers to the business being inquired upon, and, in some cases, providing the names and addresses of customers. Some bureaus ask their members to provide data on a periodic basis on all accounts. Some bureaus work with NACIS and incorporate their information into NACM Business Credit Experience Reports.

6

The Bank Credit Department

The two essential principles of good banking are safety and profits. The operations of a commercial bank must be sufficiently profitable to meet operating expenses and normal losses, provide a reasonable amount for reserves against future contingencies, and assure a fair return to the stockholders. On the other hand, operations must be carried on safely if the bank is to merit public confidence and to continue in business. To safeguard depositors, to serve the community properly, and to make a fair profit for stockholders, a banker must assume risks in the extension of credit, but these risks must be held to a safe minimum. Knowing how far he may go in assuming credit risks is a serious responsibility of the banker. The unpardonable sin in bank lending is to grant a loan with an inadequate background of essential credit data. The only sound basis for the extension of credit is complete and accurate information on every detail pertinent to a borrower's credit standing. Moreover, with constant changes in the financial condition of a bank's customers, credit data must be kept current if it is to be helpful in the granting of loans. Credit data can be collected and maintained most efficiently by a credit department or, at least, by one or more individuals who specialize in credit work.

INFORMATION MANAGEMENT

One of the major roles of the bank credit department is information management. This includes conducting investigations and exchanging and retaining information. The investigation function is to assist bank loan officers, trade creditors, correspondent banks, and others in their attempts to make sound credit decisions. The knowledge gained through proper investigation minimizes risk.

Areas of interest to the investigator include such items as status of the borrower's banking relationship, the experience of trade creditors, whether signatures are authentic, and whether there are prior liens against collateral or judgments against the customer. Many sources of information are available to the investigator, including newspapers, journals, trade periodicals and publications, research agencies, state and local governments, credit reporting agencies, other banks, trade creditors of the applicant, and the credit applicant himself. The frequency of interpersonal contact and the difficulty of obtaining some information require that the investigator possess good communication skills, resourcefulness, and a general understanding of commerce and industry.

The exchange of credit information is an important function that takes place between either two banks or a bank and a trade supplier. Bank credit departments need to establish uniform policies governing the release of credit information on such topics as credit commitments, loan experience, deposit information, customer recommendations, nonpublic information on publicly held firms, unfavorable information, and information regarding litigation. Promptness of reply and accuracy of information are essential. The person in charge of the information exchange function needs to distinguish the legitimate inquiries from the self-serving ones. The significant factor in making this distinction is the purpose of the request. A legitimate inquirer needs information to assist in a credit determination, but a firm merely seeking information about a competitor is making a self-serving inquiry. Credit departments seek to assist inquirers by providing information; however, the confidentiality of relationships must also be respected. Employees responsible for this important and often delicate function need good communication skills and an understanding of commerce and industry.

Robert Morris Associates recently revised its Statement of Principles and Code of Ethics for the Exchange of Commercial Credit Information Between Banks. (For international credits, they have developed Guidelines for the Exchange of Foreign Credit Information.) These guidelines have helped promote cooperation and understanding throughout the industry. The text is reprinted here, with the permission of RMA.

Principle 1. Confidentiality is the cardinal principle in the exchange of credit information. The identity of inquirers and sources should not be disclosed without permission.

Principle 2. All parties involved in the exchange of credit information must base inquiries and replies on fact.

Principle 3. The purpose of the inquiry and the amount involved should be clearly stated.

Principle 4. If the purpose of an inquiry involves actual or contemplated litigation, the inquirer should clearly disclose this fact.

Principle 5. The inquirer should make every effort to determine the subject's bank(s) of account before placing an inquiry, and indicate the extent of information already in file.

Principle 6. Proper identification should be provided in all credit communications.

Principle 7. Replies should be prompt and contain sufficient facts commensurate with the purpose and amount of the inquiry. If specific questions cannot be answered, the reasons should be clearly stated.

CODE OF ETHICS

Article 1. There are two cardinal principles in the exchange of credit information: confidentiality and accuracy of inquiries and replies. This includes the identity of inquirers and sources which cannot be disclosed without their permission. Adherence to these and the other principles embodied in this Code is essential, since offenders jeopardize their privilege to participate further in the exchange of credit information.

Article 2. Each inquiry should specifically indicate its purpose and the amount involved.

Article 3. Responses should be prompt and disclose sufficient material facts commensurate with the purpose and amount of the inquiry. Specific questions should be given careful and frank replies.

Article 4. It is not permissible when soliciting an account to make an inquiry to a competitor without frankly disclosing that the subject of the inquiry is a prospect. Reply is at the discretion of the bank of account.

Article 5. A request for information based on actual or contemplated litigation shall be clearly identified as such. Reply is at the discretion of the bank of account.

Article 6. All credit correspondence, including form letters, should bear the manual signature of a responsible party.

Article 7. The sharing of credit information on a mutual customer should not be more frequent than annually, unless a significant change in the relationship requires an earlier revision.

Article 8. When multiple inquiries are made simultaneously on the same subject, the inquirer should clearly state that information from the bank's own files is sufficient.

The most essential record in the credit department of a banking institution is the credit file, which contains all the pertinent information needed by a loan officer to evaluate a credit risk. This information is also needed to provide for continuity and a smooth transition if there are changes in bank personnel who handle relationships. Probably no two bank credit departments prepare their credit files or their auxiliary records on exactly the same basis.

There is no such thing as a model filing and record system suitable for all banks in all situations. The officer in charge of the credit department invariably modifies the system of filing and keeping records from time to time to meet the ever-changing needs of his particular bank. The active credit file must, however, be kept up to date, complete in every respect, and readily accessible. No situation is so exasperating to either a depositor or a bank officer as to have the processing of an application for a line of credit delayed because of a misplaced credit file.

The contents of the credit file include these sections:

1. Commitment sheets—documents indicating formal approval of a loan commitment that bear initials of members of the loan committee(s). Commitment sheets typically describe the transaction's amount, rate, due date, collateral, and other significant terms and conditions.

2. Financial statements. Many banks like to translate financial statements into their own individual format; this provides uniformity and comparability. These spread sheets are lodged in the credit file whereas the audited statements usually are placed in an audit file.

3. Correspondence with company.

4. Credit checkings/inquiries—documentation of the results of investigations and exchanges of information.

5. Revolving/term loan agreement synopsis. The loan synopsis summarizes the major terms and conditions of the arrangement. It often contains a chart for checking off compliance with certain provisions at various time intervals.

6. Credit analysis—a written evaluation of the risks involved in extending credit to a particular customer. The financial condition of the firm, the quality of management, the market the customer operates in, and the state of the economy are important considerations.

7. Memoranda. Reports from bank officers about significant items pertaining to the credit or recent contact with the company's management.

Other sections are added as needed.

The physical features of credit files may vary from manila folders to booklike files or entire file drawers. Books are generally looseleaf and will typically contain 8½ by 11 inch or 13 by 11 inch documents. With modern technology, it is now possible for all or part of the credit file to be recorded on microfilm. In maintaining credit files, consideration must be given to adequate security. The facilities should be waterproof, fireproof, and able to accommodate growth in number and size.

The need often arises to store information which is important but infrequently used. Instead of the credit file, this information may be lodged in other files. Examples include files that contain the company's published financial statements (audit files), legal files of executed loan agreements (loan agreement files), and files of general correspondence.

QUALITY CONTROL–ANALYTIC FUNCTION

Another major role of the credit department is its quality control–analytic function, which is the analysis and evaluation of the risk(s) associated in extending credit. It includes spreading financial statements, analysis of credit risk, loan review, and compliance review. One of the major issues in statement spreading and credit analysis centers upon who will do it: the credit analyst, the loan officer, or a trainee. The loan officer is qualified for this task because he is aware of events and trends which have a direct bearing on financial statement items and the subsequent evaluation of risks. But statement spreading and credit analysis are time-consuming, reducing the amount of time the loan officer spends on generating new business. The credit officer also is qualified for statement spreading and credit analysis, but the number of the bank's account relationships may impose restraints on his time as well. An advantage of the credit officer as statement spreader and credit analyst is that the account officer is freed to pursue business development. Another advantage is that the credit analyst is likely to possess a greater level of objectivity. Statement spreading and credit analysis provide excellent training for the commercial loan or credit department trainee. The simpler statements and easier analyses tend to be challenging and interesting for the trainee, but may be dull and routine for the experienced credit officer. The use of a trainee for those tasks frees the loan officer and credit officer for more important duties. Today, in larger banks, a reduction in personnel is possible through the use of computerized statement spreading. A clerk keypunches the accounts according to a preset classification system and the computer produces an income statement, a balance sheet, a statement of changes in financial position, and selected operating and financial ratios. The major advantages of computerized spreading are its speed, consistency, and ability to process large volumes of data.

The loan review function is designed to provide a continuing evaluation of the bank's loan portfolio. It helps identify potential problem loans before they reach a critical stage. It involves classifying loans when they are initially made (as well as at periodic intervals) on a scale from the most to the least risky. It is important to keep this function independent of the banking department, since objectivity is essential. It is the responsibility of the loan review officer to monitor compliance with internal lending policies, to classify loans, and to make recommendations for corrective action. This information can be used by management to assess overall loan quality and the adequacy of loan loss reserves and capital.

Monitoring compliance with laws and regulations imposed by external agencies is a necessary and important function. The size of the compliance staff may vary from one person in small banks to whole sections or divisions in larger banks. The compliance staff needs to be familiar with the laws and regulations of the various governing agencies. Ideally, the compliance staff will include an attorney; however, legal training and an association with a bank's legal counsel may be sufficient. Its duties are to see that external laws are complied with and that compliance procedures are appropriately documented.

Training credit personnel and future loan officers is a significant responsibility of the credit department of many banks. Many of the larger banks which have established separate training programs manned by full-time staffs require that their trainees spend a portion of their training period in the credit department. The credit department provides the trainee with exposure to firms and individuals of various net worths across a broad spectrum of industries and occupations. The relationship between the credit department and the trainee can be a mutually beneficial one. Since some principles and techniques are easily learned, the trainee can become productive in a short time. Investigations, easier spreads, and less complicated analyses provide good experience to the trainee while freeing the credit analyst for more difficult tasks. In addition to its role of initial training, the credit department can play a vital role in providing refresher courses for experienced officers. This retraining is especially important in insuring that the older staff is familiar with new laws and regulations.

The structure and organization of bank credit departments may vary widely. However, it is important for the credit department to report to a member of senior management who is not responsible for commercial loan activities. This is necessary to maintain objectivity and eliminate undue influences on the conclusions and recommendations of credit department personnel. Some banks achieve this separation by organizing the credit department so that it reports directly to the chief executive officer.

This chapter does not deal in depth with many of the functions of a bank credit department, although it presents the more significant items. For a more detailed presentation of credit department activities, the reader is referred to *Credit Department Management,* by Margaret A. Hoffman and Gerald C. Fischer and published by Robert Morris Associates. This book provides detailed coverage of credit department activities.

7

Credit and the Business Cycle

"Those who cannot remember the past are doomed to repeat it."
SANTAYANA

Lending money successfully is dependent upon obtaining and correctly interpreting timely information about borrowers. The ability to perceive what the risks are in making a loan distinguishes the successful lender from the saver or supplier of funds. If it were always easy and simple to determine such risks, many more suppliers of funds would lend directly instead of placing their funds at the disposal of banks and other intermediaries.

If information is important, what kind counts most? It is our purpose to go beyond the traditional credit information and deal with information about changes in economic conditions and their likely effect on the ability of business borrowers to service and repay their short-term debts.

The local banker in a small town is likely to possess a long-standing personal acquaintance with his customers and often their families. His knowledge of their integrity and competence is characteristically so thorough that the information in their financial statements reduces to secondary importance.

Far at the other end of the credit market spectrum is the highly impersonal market for commercial paper. Because borrowers who issue commercial paper are able to provide standard financial information and assurances of ability to repay—including, in many instances, backup credit lines with banks—corporate treasurers lend to them directly. But the commercial paper market is relatively restricted because not many borrowers can supply the kind of security that would give them quick and direct access to the excess funds of other corporations.

Basic to all lending, as bank credit officers know, is information about the borrower's past and present financial position, the expected use of funds, and the likely success of the venture that's to be financed. When we move to an examination of this last point, an important question usually receives less attention than it should or could: namely, how will changes in economic conditions affect the borrower's business?

Credit judgment is so tightly bound up with the recurrence of recessions and recoveries, boom and bust, that the behavior of both borrowers and lenders is predictable for any given phase of the business cycle. As illustrated in the accompanying chart, there are basic economic "givens"—verifiable propositions that enable us to anticipate the risks likely to arise when economic signals change.

Economic Forecasts

When the credit inquiry addresses the question of what's likely to happen to the borrower's industry and the market in which he sells, the lending officer is led to make either an explicit or implicit economic forecast. Most of the time it is the latter and typically it implies a blue-skies forecast of no trouble ahead.

But in point of fact it would be far better if lending officers would make an explicit economic forecast—however rudimentary—when they make business loans. Why? One good reason is that loan losses are common when an accelerating inflation is followed by a recession. Furthermore, the standard literature on credit largely ignores this link between loan losses and the business cycle. Yet in the last 30 years, loan losses of Federal Reserve member banks charged to reserves increased from 0.1 percent of loans outstanding in 1948 to 0.8 percent in 1977.

There were $21 billion of loan losses charged to reserves by these banks from 1948 to 1977, and it's reasonable to assume a sizable portion was associated with business cycles.

But even this may understate the influence of economic change on the success or failure of loans to business. Consider, for example, the loan that is made in the midst of a boom when the economy is close to a cyclical peak and the expectations of both the borrower and the lending officer are rosy. There is a recession and the business activity for which the loan was extended is impaired. The loan may, however, remain viable for another two or three years before it is written off. But it is nonetheless tied to the business cycle since the decision to lend was influenced by the abnormally strong, albeit transitory, demand that prevailed at the time.

How Borrowers and Lenders Behave Over the Cycle

Stage of Business Cycle	Behavior of Borrower	Behavior of Lender
Recession—unemployment and idle capacity	Liquidation in the case of marginal borrowers	Repairs liquidity
	Faced with melting backlogs and order cancelations, repairs balance sheet liquidity; pares inventory and cuts production; receivables run off; cost-cutting programs undertaken	Excess liquidity erodes loan prices; push for market share; irrational tendency to accept "caps" and fixed-rate deals
	Reduces bank borrowing; eligible borrowers turn to bond market; greater overall reliance on internal financing	Cautious on credit quality; security conscious
	Defers nonessential capital needs	
Recovery and expansion, commencing with pickup in consumer spending	Continues to repair balance sheet liquidity	Loan volume shows signs of pickup in the face of excess bank liquidity
	Inventory and receivables build	Intense competition tends to push bankers into unsound deals
	Increases productivity and earnings	Rates rise, and business borrowers turn to banks rather than to bond market
	Updates plant and equipment; considers future capital needs	
	More liberal on wage settlements	
	Overtime payments grow	
	Introduces new products, and new ventures appear	
	Large borrowers turn extensively to commercial paper market	
Boom—production of goods and services outruns the economy's long-term growth potential; result is an accelerating inflation	Optimism mounts; orders and prices soar above historic norms, often to unsustainable levels	Optimism mounts
	Reluctance to use long-term financing; substitution of short and intermediate credits	Increasing amounts loaned against rising cash flow; lenders overly generous; in some instances liquidity supplied by bank is all that keeps the borrower afloat
	Fears credit controls; anticipatory buying of supplies and raw materials; increases prices wherever possible; wages increased in anticipation of a freeze	Susceptibility to euphoria and loss of judgment of what constitutes good credit; mania for growth and going
	Limits of physical capacity bumped; uses less productive facilities and workers; productivity declines	

Crunch and recession; restrictive monetary policy, with the slowing of the growth of bank reserves; tight credit conditions and general frustration with inflation spawn proposals for credit allocation by government fiat; business activity contracts as economy slips further into recession

Profit margins narrowing; growth of internally generated funds slows; demand for short-term credit up

Backlogs increase as expansion ages; inventories rise

Costs of replacing depreciated capital equipment as well as those of stocks of materials all rising; acquisitions and tender offers more attractive

Working capital needs rise to accommodate rising unit costs

Total profits swelled by windfall inventory gains; profitable lines mask weak lines

Corporate liquidity declines; increasing instances of excessive leverage

Large borrowers return to banks from commercial paper market for short-term cash; anticipating a credit squeeze, revolving and other forms of committed credit are negotiated

Marginal borrowers find it difficult to hold on

Production is cut as backlogged orders fall

Borrowing is limited by high costs and other supply-side constraints, even though demand for credit is very strong

Pressure on working capital affects debt servicing ability

Attempts to improve collection of receivables as payments slow

Large write-downs taken in recognition that assets are inflated; this could precipitate further problems, depending upon how the marketplace interprets action

To the extent possible, limits borrowing as credit restraint takes hold, although inflation usually accentuates demand for credit

down market to get it

High dependence on cash flow for collectability

Demand for short-term funds increasingly strengthens

Lending for capital spending grows as upswing matures

Acquisition loans rise

Banks tend to become proxies for the equity and long-term debt markets

Wise lenders exercise caution—stress avoidance of exposure to weakening borrowers

Cautious and selective

Rations funds to fulfill basic needs of established customers

Discourages loans for:
—Purely financial activities—acquisitions, purchases of own shares
—Speculation
—Use outside domestic economy but funded domestically
—Deferred spending

Disposed to be less flexible on moratorium or grace periods but more flexible on repayments

Raises interest rates and hardens fee structure

What counts in ascribing causes to loan losses is not when a loan is written off but whether the lending officers considered the likely effect of economic change on the borrower's ability to pay interest and repay principal. In other words, cyclical changes are part of the risk and should not be disregarded as imponderable (see preceeding table).

Economists have been analyzing and forecasting business cycles for nearly 200 years. And the well-publicized differences in economic forecasts testify to the rich variety of theories and opinions relating to business cycles. It is not our purpose to deal with the history or the theory of business cycles. Instead, we shall look at the movements of various sectors of the economy that provide useful clues to where we are in the cycle—how far or near we are to full utilization of resources. Economists agree about the usefulness of asking where we are in the business cycle. But that agreement typically falls apart when they are pressed to be specific about where they think the economy is at any given point in time in relation to its capacity to produce goods and services. For example, during much of 1977 the administration's economists believed that there was an ample cushion of slack or idle resources while other economists believed that the economy was much closer to pressing its capacity ceiling and pointed to accelerating inflation as evidence to support that view.

Causes of Recession

Another point about which there is spirited disagreement among economists is the cause or causes of recessions. What is it that suddenly causes income to grow less rapidly, forcing consumers to spend less, followed by production cutbacks and worker layoffs? Many economists believe each recession has a different cause and that they occur at random, making them difficult if not impossible to predict.

But the differences that separate economists at any time are no greater— and probably less—than those that divide businessmen and investors who meet in the marketplace. A portfolio manager who sells equities and builds cash assets clearly has a different forecast from the investor to whom he sells. The borrower who seeks a fixed-rate loan has different expectations about the future than the lender who makes it. And, the manager who trims his inventories in the face of rising prices takes a very different view of the future than his competitor, who aggressively increases his inventory.

But almost all economists believe that accelerating inflation raises the probability of a recession. And a growing number lean to the view that economic expansions and contractions—business cycles—are primarily caused by sharp changes in monetary policy and, to a lesser degree, changes in fiscal policy. Efforts to damp inflation by markedly slowing the growth of the money stock push the economy into recession. Subsequent attempts to speed recovery and cut unemployment rekindle the fires of inflation. What's suggested, in short, is a stop-and-go mechanism that generates business cycles. Its validity is assumed in what follows.

Most of the time the economy is expanding, not contracting. For this reason, decisions based on an implicit assumption of business as usual, on average, work out reasonably well. Yet, as the old adage goes, a six-foot man can drown while crossing a river with an *average* depth of only four feet! There are times—and they may be occurring with greater frequency of late—when the inability to forecast a business recession is very costly to both lenders and borrowers. So it clearly pays to recognize some of the general signs of an impending recession.

PATTERNS OF BEHAVIOR

Economic series—the numbers on outstanding consumer credit, on business loans, on interest rates, industrial production, housing starts, capital investment or capacity utilization—all follow regular patterns of cyclical behavior. If you examine this rhythmic repetition of events as a cryptologist looks at the same letter in a sequentially coded message, you may gain insights into the recurring changes that have come to be known as the business cycle.

If large segments of the economy usually moved in an erratic or random fashion, there would be some validity to the popular notion that efforts to forecast are futile. This is not the case, however. There are, to be sure, events which impinge on the economy that are difficult if not impossible to predict —such as the oil embargo, the OPEC price increase, the introduction of price-wage controls, and tax changes. Still, even these factors do not alter fundamentally the broad contours of change once they have been shaped by the monetary and fiscal policy of governments as well as by the preferences of the consuming public. Accordingly, national income, durable goods production, housing starts, total employment, consumer credit, total business loan demand, and even Federal budget deficits can be forecast with tolerable accuracy.

THE NUB OF THE PROBLEM

Let's now turn to the nub of the problem, which is the predictability of business cycle turning points—especially turns into recessions.

If it is assumed that the economy is not at full employment—if there are idle people and idle machines—growth can proceed without a significant acceleration of inflation. There may be short bursts of price increases due to the volatility of food and other agricultural prices, for example, despite a steady underlying trend of inflation. Once the economic slack is largely taken up, however, the growth of the economy in real or physical terms is limited by the size of the labor force and its willingness to work extra hours and by increases in productive capacity. This potential growth rate is estimated to be about 3½ percent per year. If monetary and fiscal policies through their impact on total spending induce a faster rate of growth, inflation accelerates. The economy can be—and in fact has been—hoisted above its long-term potential path, which involves harnessing less efficient or obsolete production facilities and the hiring of less skilled and less productive workers. As a consequence, productivity declines and inflation accelerates, sometimes sharply, as the economy strains to respond to the larger and larger demands created by the rapid growth of money income, which, in turn, is caused by excessive monetary and fiscal policies. Finally, during this period monetary demand is pressing hardest against the limits of physical capacity, thus rendering the economy most vulnerable to recession.

Identifying the stage at which the economy reaches its potential—the full-capacity or full-employment level beyond which inflation worsens—is fraught with difficulties. The statistical tools and theoretical concepts are crude and the estimates of "full" employment or potential GNP are highly controversial. It is possible, however, to determine the likelihood that the economy is moving close to full capacity utilization and accelerating inflation. For example, as the economy contracted in the severe recession of 1973–75, a large number of people became unemployed and factories and machinery were idled. Once production was in better alignment with the reduced real demand, the decline ended and recovery began in the spring of 1975. At that time, however, the economy was clearly a long way from full capacity utilization. It was a matter not only of reemploying idle workers and idle machines but also of absorbing new people entering the labor force and utilizing the new industrial capacity that was under construction prior to the recession. This took time— and, in the opinion of many people, too much time.

In response to demands for a quick return to full employment, the government pursued highly stimulative fiscal and monetary policies that pushed the economy along at rates well above its long-term potential. The risks of that strategy weren't so great so long as there was a comfortable cushion of excess capacity to damp upward price pressures. By 1978, however, the size of the GNP gap—the difference between actual GNP and potential GNP—had so narrowed as to cause alarm.

Federal Reserve Policy

If the Federal Reserve, by influencing the growth of the money stock, is still seeking to achieve a 10 to 11 percent growth of nominal GNP, then inflation will run to at least as high as the difference between the 3.5 percent potential rate of income growth and the actual rate—namely, 6.5 to 7.5 percent. The situation can be compounded by the speed at which monetary and fiscal policies push the economy toward its potential. If the economy is moving fast, inflation may erupt well before potential is reached, in part because those making price and wage decisions form expectations about the future inflation implications of current monetary and fiscal policies—that is, their current decisions are based on their forecasts of the future. It's like a car heading toward a sharp curve. If it is going at a speed that leads the occupants to believe it will leave the road, they will take whatever precautions they can to minimize injuries.

When inflation accelerates to a level the public deems unacceptable, the Federal Reserve responds to political and public pressures, the demands that something—anything!—be done to slow the erosion of purchasing power. The monetary authorities may act with haste or they may delay severe actions to wait and see if the inflation is transitory, or they may expect government to adopt tighter fiscal policies or possibly direct intervention to influence price and wage decisions. Eventually, however, monetary policy reins are tightened, and as the growth of the nation's money supply slows, so too does the growth of the nominal GNP. Yet before there is any impact on prices, real GNP first declines so as to create excess capacity. At this point the economy has come full circle. The consequent increase in unemployment results in a great public clamor for a shift to stimulative monetary and fiscal policies. Real growth accelerates as inflation levels off and the economy begins moving back toward its potential growth path.

Determining Economic Recovery

The duration of the economic recovery is largely determined by the amount of excess capacity that is created by the recession and the speed at which the economy is driven to close the gap and overtake potential. If the recession is shallow, the recovery will be relatively brief and the next period of instability and possible recession will come sooner than it would if the recession were deep and the economy were stimulated with moderation. Under such circumstances, the recovery can be quite long-lived.

In either case, it is basically wrong to use the average length of previous recoveries as a guide to forecasting the duration of a current expansion because the instability that pervades the economy at cyclical peaks varies considerably. For example, strong expectations of even higher inflation in the foreseeable future can make matters worse than if inflation expectations cool off promptly in response to the government's anti-inflation policies. In addition, as already mentioned, the speed at which the economy is driven as it approaches its potential growth rate can also accentuate imbalances in labor and product markets. In short, there is greater uncertainty, greater stress in the financial markets, and greater strains on productive facilities once the economy has reached its potential growth rate than when there is a significant cushion of idle resources.

Because changes in industries during an economic recovery or recession take place somewhat sequentially, the perception of just where the economy is will vary with the vantage point of the observer. Auto manufacturers, for example, are likely to be a bit concerned about their sales beginning to top out while managements in the capital goods industries and some of the basic materials industries are still wondering when the recovery will begin. While these are simple illustrations, the error in making an implicit judgment about the state of the general economy from what is happening in a single industry or an individual company occurs in small- and medium-sized firms as well as large ones.

There is a natural tendency for corporate managements to suffer from tunnel vision as they view the economy largely, if not exclusively, in terms of their company and industry experience. For this reason business confidence is prone toward improvement if not exuberance, as the economy enters that period of one to two years prior to its peak when capacity limitations in force increase order backlogs. This does not mean that trouble lies immediately ahead in every instance of growing backlogs. However, an unusually sharp acceleration in unfilled orders—against the background of other evidence that demand is pressing hard against capacity and that inflation is accelerating—should be taken as a clear warning of trouble with outstanding loans to weak borrowers or those whose business is highly sensitive to cyclical contractions.

CAUSES OF A SUDDEN SURGE

Whenever the orders and output or prices for a particular product or service suddenly accelerate far above some long-term historic norm, the business should be carefully reviewed to determine the causes of the sudden surge. Here are some of the questions that should be answered:

- Is aggregative demand for goods and services generally strong?
- Is the sudden rise in output or prices sustainable? Or does it stem from special factors that are transitory?
- Are the price increases so large that they may cause instability in markets?
- Will demand decline abruptly because price increases have exceeded— albeit temporarily—that equilibrium level at which the market clears supply and demand in an orderly fashion? Have prices suddenly climbed so high that the balance of supply and demand for competing or alternative materials will shift, causing supply of the higher-priced products to become excessive, thus forcing cutbacks in production and prices in the effort to adjust inventories?

In hindsight such a list of questions would have been particularly useful in 1973, when raw commodity prices increased significantly faster than the prices of finished goods. Such a relative increase in commodity prices is rather unusual. And those firms involved in the production and processing of a single commodity, say copper, may have been persuaded that the sudden increase in copper prices far above any previous level was due to a sudden powerful surge in the underlying world demand for copper; and as a consequence, both borrowers and lenders would conclude that higher prices signaled a permanent change in the fortune of the copper industry, and an upward tilting of the long-term trend of the world demand for copper.

But even a cursory consideration of what happens to commodity prices, both for food and nonfoods, raises serious questions about the viability of the boom in copper prices. It suggests a worldwide force that was not affecting copper alone but caused *all* commodity prices to soar. And what should be borne in mind is that every movement of commodity prices to levels far above those of finished goods has proven transitory.

The real estate boom in the years prior to the deep recession of 1973–74 illustrates the importance of questioning the viability of sudden surges in output. Increased construction of multifamily homes, condominiums, commercial buildings, and hotels was far above both historic norms and the usual relationship among construction, household formation, and income. And the fact that these boomlets occur in real estate, commodities, and other markets testifies to the ease with which borrowers and lenders can be persuaded to ignore basic economic principles. Those who can successfully identify the short-run booms and avoid being swept up in them will, on average, be more successful.

CYCLICAL MOVEMENTS

The cyclical movement of the economy—moving from the nadir of a recession, through a period of recovery, and into another round of accelerating inflation and strained capacity—is neatly mirrored by interest rates.

Since the end of World War II, economic contractions, the swings from peaks to troughs, have run from 8 to 16 months. As sales and shipments diminish, the production of goods and services declines. At some point during the cycle, inventories are reduced—sometimes before the economy actually contracts, sometimes after. There is no fixed timing. The decline in output reduces short-term cash needs and business incomes as well. Yet the liquidation of inventories will have the added effect of enabling companies to cover more of their financing needs with internally generated cash flow, thus reducing the need to borrow externally.

For many firms the resulting cash flow exceeds their need for short-term working capital, and the excess funds are invested in Treasury bills or commercial paper, or used to repay bank loans, which increases the liquidity of commercial banks.

Short-term interest rates decline as liquidity mounts. If the recession is deep enough, short-term rates will fall below the rate of inflation, inflicting a negative real rate of return on the lender. At times when the demand for nonfinancial assets is depressed, however, cash may be invested in short-term money market instruments at the prevailing rate.

Economic contractions may generate increases in overall corporate liquidity, but not evenly among all companies. Corporate profits also decline. Fixed costs cannot be trimmed to offset the effects of declining volume. Even variable costs may not be cut fast enough if managements do not recognize the onset of recession in time. Confidence diminishes as order backlogs melt—at times literally overnight—and corporate managements become concerned about liquidity. As a consequence, there is a marked acceleration in the volume of new long-term bond issues. The proceeds are principally used to reduce short-term debt. This heavy bond issuance, which begins during the recession and does not begin to taper off until after the first year of recovery, thus catches the long-term bond rate at approximately its cyclical peak. Despite the fact that every recession has been followed by a gradual reduction in long-term rates for the next few years, preferences for liquidity—conditioned by the sudden and unexpected contraction of economic activity—override the effects of the decline in borrowing costs.

Once the economy begins to grow in real terms, corporate demand for short-term funds begins to rise as more inventories are required and more short-term working capital is needed.

As the economy recovers, credit demand accelerates in the household sector. Concomitantly, the volume of consumer credit and mortgage borrowings increases, and both are phenomena normally associated with a cyclical recovery. This revival of credit demand also plays a role in bringing about a rise of interest rates. In the business sector, the initial shift in short-term credit demand begins with decisions by corporate finance officers to buy marginally fewer short-term, marketable securities and instead to use a slightly larger amount of cash flow to finance inventory requirements or other short-term internal needs. Gradually, as the economic recovery widens, operating rates rise and real growth stimulates the demand for short-term funds. Long-term bond financing declines as a proportion of total funds raised by nonfinancial corporations. Corporate liquidity resumes its long-term decline. Then, a year or two before the economy reaches full capacity, inflation begins to accelerate and the demand for short-term credit picks up sharply and corporate liquidity drops faster. When aggregate demand—as reflected by the growth of real GNP —begins to grow faster than physical capacity, backlogs develop. And as the backlogs swell, management confidence rises once again.

The first half of 1974 provided a classic illustration of the strong correlation between confidence and backlogs of orders in manufacturing industries. Backlogs were so large that a fashionable rejoinder to the suggestion that the economy was in a cyclical decline was: "If this is a recession, I hope it will never end." It is when orders are pouring in, capacity is pressed, and confidence is running high that there is a touch of giddy apprehension that things may be too good to last. That's when the Federal Reserve decides, in the words of former chairman William Martin, "to take the punchbowl away." By this time, in the cold light of risk exposure, loan loss hangovers may be unavoidable, and yet credit demand, particularly bank loan demand, is likely to be stronger than at any other stage of the cycle.

Recognizing the cyclical features of credit flows can be critical for lending decisions and managing credits. Obviously, loans to borrowers who face difficulties in a general credit crunch because they are too heavily leveraged with short-term funds are much more risky than loans to borrowers with less short-term leverage.

Industries in which output and cash flow are highly volatile will require larger amounts of liquidity and/or ready access to bank credit or other short-term financing than more stable ones. This can be an element in determining overall creditworthiness.

VOLATILITY IN OUTPUT

Volatility in output—swings above and below the long-run growth path for a product—may stem from forces on the demand side. For example, the output of such industries as aircraft engines, equipment, and parts, trailer coaches, optical and ophthalmic goods, and communications equipment is more volatile than the average for all manufacturers and a relatively small part of that volatility is explained by business cycles. The demand for aircraft engines is subject to replacement cycles that are independent of fluctuations in general business activity. On the other hand, volatility of output in such industries as steel, building materials, wholesale trade, to mention only a few, is in large part explained by the business cycle.

The cause of volatility can be important. Companies whose output and sales fluctuate more widely than the overall industry average probably plan their financing needs accordingly, though this should not always be assumed. Companies experiencing a volatility that is external in origin—stemming from cyclical fluctuations in the economy as a whole, or changes in the position of an economic region—may be more prone to live dangerously unless they possess the rare faculty of knowing exactly when to start building liquidity or getting their bank lines cleared in anticipation of a credit crunch.

Inflation

Inflation, as we all know, is the source of a great deal of mischief, one piece of which is its effect on the distribution of credit in the open market. As inflation accelerates above its previous trend, those businesses that turn over inventories rapidly find that they need more short-term money to finance the same physical quantity of goods. They also are in a stronger position to bid for available funds than borrowers with longer time horizons who do not benefit quickly from the upsurge of prices. Furthermore, a surge of inflation —unless it is strong and persistent—is not likely to cause long-term borrowers to adjust their expectations of the future rate of inflation over, say, the next five, ten, or twenty years. Consequently, borrowers concerned with the more distant future are reluctant to bid against short-term users of credit and many withdraw from the marketplace. This phenomenon may produce an inverted yield curve—where short-term interest rates are higher than rates for longer maturities—that is not the product of restrictive monetary policy. In any event, once the Federal Reserve applies the brakes to credit growth, short-term rates will shoot even higher for a time and this crunch can create many difficulties for borrowers and lenders alike.

Classified loans and subsequent credit losses typically rise during recessions. Still, violations of prudent standards in the extension of credit can result in losses that are independent of economic conditions. The real estate investment trust losses, for example, were not primarily induced by the 1973–75 recession; they could well have occurred in the absence of that cyclical downturn. The point is that industries or managements prone to exuberances or speculative excesses are more likely to get carried away at times of accelerating inflation than during periods of stability, whereas basically weak credits are clearly going to be tested even in times of general prosperity. The Florida land boom and crash of 1924–26 is one such case that occurred in a period of overall price stability.

Economic and Market Forces

Both borrowers and lenders are very largely captives of the economic and market forces in which they operate. It is therefore difficult to swim against the tide of general corporate financing strategies. It can be rewarding if you have exceptionally good timing, but it is on timing where essentially correct forecasts can go awry. The forecast of the direction of change may be right, and for the right reasons, while the timing—let's say the forecast of a sharp increase in the demand for some durable good—can be premature. And six months or a year can make huge differences in maintaining a share of the market or earning high profits. But decisions based on such errors in timing are often irreversible. Bank lenders cannot withdraw from the marketplace at the very time when loan demand is unusually strong. By the same token, borrowers cannot build excess liquidity at the very time when inventory requirements are high and short-term working capital needs are strong. Nevertheless, lenders can be more prudent in examining loan applications when the economy has entered the cyclical zone of great instability and uncertainty.

And, of course, never to be ignored are the fluctuations other than the business cycle that invite trouble—new-product cycles, industry cycles, and, in the case of offshore lending, country cycles.

8

Lending Officers and Lending

"The tools to him that can handle them."
Napoleon

Since the late sixties, banks have become increasingly marketing and profit center oriented, and transaction volume is high. There is a bias in the direction of more difficult term lending areas. Bankers are undertaking transactions they would not have considered a few years ago. Managing risk is thus the central nature of things. George Moore, retired chairman of Citibank, said it best: "You can get into trouble in banking faster than in any other line of business." Banks succeed when the risks they assume are reasonable, controlled, and commensurate with their resources and credit competence. Lending officers, in turn, must accurately identify, measure, and manage risk if their banks are to succeed. What, then, does it take to excel as a lending officer?

This question could be asked about men and women in most endeavors, for differences in abilities can be subtle, not immediately apparent. But top performers in any field know more, possess an integrative intelligence, and instinctively fuse and energize whatever it takes to produce superior results. They perceive the moment and seize it, are good in the clutches, and have an acute intuitive "touch," the electricity, which even when recognized is not easily defined.

The lending officer's role reflects the cumulative impact of a variety of lending patterns, the nature and shape of banking competition, and the industry's growth, complexity, and organizational response to the economic and regulatory environment. Gone are the roll-top desk days, when the borrowers came to the lenders and when most commercial bank loans were for the purpose of filling in seasonal shortfalls of working capital. Traditionally, a strong credit culture has pervaded the industry. Lending officers were proven in the farm system. Until the seventies talent was usually developed and tested through tutoring and matured by the osmosis of experience. Personnel turnover was low and titles were slow to come by: only a generation ago, becoming a vice president by 40 or 41 was considered "fast track." By then the lending officer was seasoned. When he signed his work, whether he had originated it or not, he had taken great pains to understand it thoroughly. He knew that his reputation and advancement were linked to the way he used his initials. This sensitivity seemed temporarily skewed in the late sixties and early seventies, when the industry grew rapidly and the stress was on asset growth. Personnel turnover was high and some lenders' eyes were clouded to credit basics. However, the onset of the 1973–75 recession served to restore a heightened awareness of accountability.

Today's lending officers have often had considerable training in business subjects before joining the bank. Apprenticeship has been displaced by an MBA culture. Few trainees would tolerate a lengthy and tedious tutorial regime. Instead, they are exposed to varied levels of seminars and training, combined with on-the-job exposure. Some bring a quantitative orientation from their business school. They become mesmerized by figures and financial statements and emerge with a machinelike, technocratic quality which is troubling if left unbalanced. Unfortunately in banking, the seasoned middle cadre of lending officers that is needed to leaven the bread has largely retired from the scene. Nonetheless, the basic mission remains: to make loans that will be repaid as originally agreed upon.

Organizational homogeneity in banking and industry has declined, and management layering as well as decentralization have increased as organizations have attempted to respond to changes in scale and types of businesses they have undertaken. In larger banks, the generalists of earlier years have been giving ground to specialists. The same changes have taken place in the borrowers. The personal touch has become institutionalized, and development of the ability to follow and appraise strategies and actions of borrowers is more difficult. Yet, when lending money, one is basically looking to management. Money is borrowed and repaid by people—as individuals or as principals of corporate entities. Character and management capacity come first. It is only after a lender is satisfied on these points that he proceeds with his evaluation of such things as the business itself, plant, operations, liquidity, leverage, and other aspects of the balance sheet and income statement.

While information received from borrowers is more current and complete than it ever has been, getting to know borrowers as managers and individuals in a volume-oriented, impersonal environment of shifting values is not easy, except in small communities. With a more fluid, rather than a traditional fixed customer base, the time frame of familiarity has been compressed, sometimes to the point where banks find they do not know the borrower until a loan is in trouble. Superficial analysis of management—as was the case of many real estate deals in the early seventies—has been a primary cause of credit problems, ranking second to the influence of the business cycle on the fortunes of borrowers and, in due course, a bank's portfolio. Credit officers must delve deeply into the quality, integrity, reputation and image, and skills of the management team. There is danger in taking the borrower's word for too many things and not spending sufficient time in and out of the borrower's office getting to know the business and its management completely. Less experienced lending officers, however, must safeguard their objectivity from overly close personal involvement to avoid "clientism," that is, a tendency to over-emphasize the interests of the borrower. Failing to maintain some distance, they may find it difficult to shift the tone of their relationship when problems arise.

Loan officers now "sell" a host of credit "products"—for example, leases, syndicated credits, commercial paper backstop facilities, and standby letters of credit. Sometimes overlooked is the fact that, unlike soap, bank "products" are for the most part loaned, not sold. As they progress in their careers, loan officers do more market, budget and other planning, and supervise larger numbers of people. They are managers as well as bankers. Depending upon individual abilities and style, this could seriously impinge upon time that should otherwise be devoted to credit evaluation; when a loan officer is managing people and budgets, he isn't managing his credits. If officers perceive they are rewarded for being managers or, for that matter, marketers rather than loan officers, bank managements face not only a problem in motivating talented people to pursue seriously the credit function but also potential credit problems.

In reconnoitering the qualities required of loan officers—a many-sided topic—some starting points suggest themselves: (1) what a bank expects; (2) what a borrower expects; (3) personal traits that seem to exist in successful lending officers; (4) knowledge required; and (5) skills needed.

The Bank's Expectations

A bank's assets, primarily its loans, must be managed to provide the liquidity to meet deposit withdrawals, cover all expenses including losses, and still earn a profit large enough to make the return to the stockholder competitive with all other investments of comparable risk. These objectives set the framework for a bank's policies, rules, and guidelines for good risk-taking. Within the bank each lending unit's policies and procedures should conform to this overall policy objective, and each lending officer, wherever located, must speak a common credit language. Credit officers are expected to (1) balance the quality and quantity of the loan portfolio to achieve earnings objectives while also meeting appropriate credit needs, (2) maintain proper credit standards, (3) hold risk to reasonable limits, (4) avoid losses, (5) evaluate new business opportunities, (6) adjust to changes in the regulatory environment, and (7) ensure adequate liquidity in the portfolio.

Lending looks easier than it is, especially in periods of recovery, expansion, and boom. History says that bad loans are made in good times—credit extended to W. T. Grant and to the CB radio industry are fairly recent instances. Loans should be as defect-free as possible because there always exists the chance of unexpected loss caused by the business cycle and other external influences, or by factors related to the credit or its administration. To quote a colleague, "You can never earn in interest what you can write off in principal."

Credit decisions obviously cannot be based entirely on any set of credit guidelines or analytic technique. Each officer is expected to exercise sound, practical sense and good judgment, and to be scrupulously provident. A good many losses can be avoided by using common sense. The officer must grasp the qualitative and quantitative details of each transaction, analyze its future variables, and make adequate allowance for their impacts. His job or hers is to see that risks that should not be taken are avoided.

Borrower Expectations

What the borrower should expect is that (1) the price he pays for a loan is fair and competitive; (2) the credit officer will have a thorough grasp of the borrower's business and industry and their interactions; (3) he will receive wise and highly professional financial counsel (for example, when a loan is in trouble, officers should have the guts to discuss the problem with the borrower); (4) his legitimate bank financing needs will be met; (5) he will not have to deal with a fair weather banker; and (6) turnover of lending personnel will be minimal. There are subsidiary expectations, such as introduction to bank services and products which will reduce cost and improve financial effectiveness, but credit facilities when and where needed override.

Personal Attributes

There are common traits to be observed in successful loan officers which play their part according to individual temperament:

- *Integrity.* They must be honest of opinion, straightforward, and objective, and not manipulate information, openly recognize upside and downside risk, and divorce intrinsic credit decisions from profitability considerations. They must retain these traits even under pressure, in the face of profit center earnings targets, for example.

- *An educated mind.* They think independently, have good conceptual abilities, are analytical, but do not miss the forest for the trees. They are also quick studies, with sharp mental reflexes, and they marshall facts well. They are highly observant, can measure and weigh alternatives well, possess good learning capacity, and are capable of "zero base" thinking. They have the knack of getting off on the right track immediately, never allowing themselves to become intellectually "stiff in the joints," but willing to adapt and adjust for soundly based reasons or as new information emerges.

- *Good common sense and judgment.* These cardinal qualities are needed when problems walk off the pages of the textbook—and most credit problems do. The characteristics cannot be taught, even in the best schools, and intelligence does not assure their presence or substitute for them. They must be combined with a sound value system, a mature and balanced view of problems taken in perspective. "Street smarts" and perceptiveness, getting to the heart of a problem instantly and accurately—the *coup d'oeil*—count for much. Abilities to choose the best way to accomplish tasks and to know when it is necessary and from whom to seek advice is essential, as well as capacity to choose the best options in decision-making. Much is to be learned from discussion with others: opposite views can be weighed, new information adduced, ideas tested, impacts evaluated.

- *Physical strength.* Stamina, not being easily worn down, combined with resiliency and a reserve store of energy are offsets to what can be the agony of decision-making. Capacity to cope with the frustrations of problems that have "outcomes" rather than solutions is needed, while also bearing in mind H. L. Mencken's point that "there are some questions on which there are not two sides."

- *Emotional stability.* There is nothing like a cool head in difficult circumstances. A top credit officer feels comfortable with responsibility, like a clutch player toward the end of a close game who is put in to handle critical plays with assurance and control.

- *Achievement orientation.* Soundly based success in most endeavors is hard to come by except through dedication combined with consistent application of high standards, tenacity, drive, and mental toughness. To find meaning and satisfaction as a loan officer, one must appreciate the banker's constructive—in fact, creative—economic role, believe in its importance, and enjoy it as a way of life.

- *Creativity.* This translates into resourcefulness, imagination, and the ability to contribute new or different ideas in solving problems. The solution to the Equity Funding problem is an example of this in a workout situation, and large project financing illustrates another application of this quality.

- *Decisiveness.* Good leadership abilities are always assets. A measured sense of when to say yes or no is indispensable. Loan officers are exposed to the breezes of contending opinions. Taking and articulating unpopular decisions are often the warp and woof of what they do. A mature and able loan officer trusts his or her own judgment and conviction in the face of disagreement, yet is not so inflexible that sound reasoning of knowledgeable associates cannot be recognized.
- *Ability to coach.* One of the most common attributes of good lending officers is their talent for developing, teaching, and encouraging juniors.
- *Image.* This quality is important and useful in most professions. Poise, bearing, tact, and a friendly personality are especially critical in banking because it is so people-oriented. Even brilliant undertakings can fail if they are clumsily or tactlessly executed. The respect of subordinates, peers, and seniors is also never to be overlooked; they are part of every good loan officer's image.
- *Humility.* It takes modesty to be clear-sighted, according to Freud, and the best loan officers are those who always realize that they still have much to learn. In credit, one never knows all of the answers. Arrogance is especially fatal. One should never take such pride in his or her ability to make good loans that he or she refuses to recognize adverse developments that can and may occur, or fully to evaluate considerations offered by associates. The marketplace will not tolerate foolhardy cockiness.
- *A searching mind.* A willingness to ask questions, especially when in doubt, is a given with top lending officers. In credit, there is no such thing as a dumb question. Implicit is the loan officer's tenacity to demand and get answers he or she needs. Good lenders do not fool themselves by wishful thinking or by winking at important points.
- *Application.* This means being able to apply one's knowledge, common sense, and experience effectively to actual credit situations and to communicate findings, both orally and in writing, lucidly and in a balanced manner. There is no substitute for doing one's homework well. More than that, a credit mistake stemming from failure to do one's homework is a cardinal lending sin. This often happened in lending to the real estate industry during the early seventies and, on occasion, has occurred in lending into the "middle market."
- *Good instincts and timing.* As in the case of top internists, the passage of time upgrades the knowledge and experience of loan officers, provided that they are not stifled along the way. Habitual practice develops instincts. Financial statements are read like librettos and the loan officer hears the music as he or she reads. Such factors as liquidity, the use of debt, profitability, and asset use can tell quite a bit about the quality

of management, unless a new management has just assumed command. Maturity usually sharpens one's feel for credit pressure points. And, in the case of existing credits, one invariably heeds "itches," sensing changes and variables that could adversely alter the situation. There is a saying that every loan is good when it's made—at least it is usually well represented to be. An experienced lending officer may feel otherwise, even though the reasons for making the loan seem plausible and are persuasively presented. Yet it is hard at the time to prove one's instinct that a deal is flawed. Waiting for proof could be too late. This is often the position in which harbor pilots in a fog find themselves. Such situations usually arise when someone is reaching or stretching to make a loan.

The Knowledge Base

Banking is a knowledge business. The profession of lending will absorb all that anyone can give it in the way of knowledge, training, experience, and reflectiveness. This is a lifelong sequential pursuit which combines experience and chalk-talk, and matches other professions in its demands for breadth of understanding and analysis. A variety of subjects is needed to develop even the basic skills required to be an effective lender. A broad background in the humanities, history, and economics is best in most fields, including banking. Further schooling and training can develop whatever else is needed. With respect to one's own bank, one must start by understanding the bank's organization and how it relates to the banking system, the credit and account management process of the institution, the bank's business strategies in the face of a changing regulatory environment, the bank's operating procedures, and, most importantly, what is expected of the lending officer.

The minimum level of knowledge relevant to a specific credit assignment is related to the level of authority involved—entry, intermediate, senior—and the knowledge criteria established for each. Prerequisites at the entry level would be a knowledge of accounting, corporate finance, business strategies, and economics, including money markets; following this, principles of credit, credit analysis techniques, loan structuring, specialized lending—such as real estate and asset-based lending, legal instruments and documentation, problem credits, plus credit and portfolio policy. Succeeding levels move into more advanced aspects of these subjects, plus supplementary courses, some of which might be further specialized lending topics.

A word should be said about international lending. To some, it implies a mystique, but lending principles are the same in Des Moines and in Timbuktu—understanding the transaction, adequate knowledge and understanding of the borrower, risk definition, and a clear indication that the loan will be repaid. Foreign credit markets may have more moving parts and differ in detail, but not in basics.

Skill is the amalgam of intuition and other personal attributes, knowledge and experience.

Lending is not episodic. The anatomy of credit analysis can be described by three concentric circles. The core is the credit in intrinsic terms—its purpose, how it will be repaid, its appropriateness from the standpoint of the bank and the borrower, and what analysis reveals about its financial characteristics. Knowledge of management—character, capacity, financial and administrative controls, ability to manage as the business grows—is of critical importance. Surrounding the core is knowledge of the industry, the position of the company in its industry, and, in turn, of the industry in the national economy. The outer ring encompasses political, technological, and regulatory considerations as well as other exogenous factors which have the potential of affecting a credit over the period of the bank's exposure. This configuration is not static and must be viewed in a time dimension in which the parts interact. The fact that they hang together at the outset of the analysis is no assurance that they will continue to do so. In a moving state, they have the potential for change. This may be decisive and must be taken into account.

The implicit skills required to prepare and use the analysis of a credit are: expertise in the areas of information gathering, business and industry dynamics, financial and credit analysis and evaluation of variables, sensitivity analysis, loan structuring, lending procedures, and documentation. Negotiating ability—stepping back occasionally to review the bidding—counts for much, especially in difficult and demanding credits, as does working with different lenders, lawyers, and others. Sensitivity to the business cycle (and other species) and their impacts are part of the equation. Finally, precision and scrupulous attention to detail are the hallmarks of a pro, just as they are in any demanding activity. Imagine a top surgeon, musician, or athlete being indifferent to these!

Aside from technical skills and a willingness to utilize the wisdom of associates, instead of going it alone, one must be proficient in interpersonal skills and possess an ability to operate smoothly and effectively within his or her own institution. Ignoring or not recalling the past has sometimes proven costly. This is why history repeats itself. Unlike older cultures, which revere age and experience, and then heed them, few red kimonos in recognition of seniority are awarded in U.S. banking or business. It has been said that taking advice is something in the nature of getting experience without going through events. Yet each generation, with occasional refreshing exception, seems bent on learning for itself. As Oliver Wendell Holmes pointed out, "The young man knows the rules, the old man knows the exceptions."

The Lending Officer's Expanding Job Description

With the impact of change on jobs such as the loan officer's, it would be wise for banks to review hiring practices and job criteria periodically, much the same as President Bok caused Harvard to review its own curriculum.

Growth in the size of individual banks, their organizational complexity and fragmentation, and competitive shifts in the industry have broadened the compass of many lending officers beyond credit evaluation per se. As they progress, lending officers become more involved in marketing and administrative matters such as budgeting and profit center management. What was once exclusively credit training tends to be melded with subjects—marketing, selling skills, people management, business planning, budgeting—that identify with what might be called an overall account management process. This integrated overview, a unity of process, is designed to maximize profitability by the cultivation and development of the customer relationship institution-wide, rather than only on an individual account basis. It requires analysis of customer and prospect needs, introduction to the appropriate services and products, and provision of credit facilities tailored to the needs of the individual borrower.

But the center of gravity in commercial banking must always be credit. Lending is outstandingly an intellectual task which needs to be combined with skills, experience and instinct. In an era of mass higher education, it is often practiced by the unlikely; over the years, some of the ablest loan officers have been self-taught. In a world where talent is often long but experience short, there is a danger of slipping into the notion that loan officers can be stamped out and credit extended on a factory system. At the same time, one could reflect that a bank, or any institution, is as old as the experience of its people. Commercial bank lending is as much a craft as a science.

Nevertheless, clear training objectives and plans for their implementation are called for. In determining training needs, criteria should be set for each level of credit authority. Lending personnel should be reviewed in terms of education, training, and experience to avoid gaps in individual development. Matching criteria with human resources will uncover gaps, should they exist.

Loans go awry when good judgment is not exercised in the original instance, when there is a defect in structuring, follow-through, documentation, or other elements of the bank's credit process, or when unanticipated external factors intervene even though the credit may have been intrinsically sound when booked. Under pressure to develop lending personnel, bank managements have occasionally delegated lending responsibility too early. Many past credit errors have been made by otherwise able people who had picked up a superficial understanding of lending. Instead of learning how to avoid making bum loans and managing delinquency, they were given the idea that there is no mystery to lending—just go ahead and build assets. Brainpower by itself is not the answer. Nature cannot be forced. There is a natural order in an individual's development, ignored at peril to the individual and the institution. A leading winery "will sell no wine before its time." A parallel thought suggests itself for lending talent.

The "Whole" Credit Person

The significant loan officer is the one who can synthesize. The best new-business officer is often also a top lender. If he or she is an analyst only, the bank may lose customers; if he or she is primarily a salesperson, he or she can lose the bank.

Because he or she conjugates the lending scene, dealing with the interaction of many varied elements, a loan officer's job description is less bound by precise qualifications than are many others. More than a compendium or sum of the parts, the job is not described merely by looking at its pieces; this does not provide solutions to problems. Credit has a projective thrust which calls for unusual competence, practicality, sensitivity, and timing. The lending officer's challenge, like that of the symphony orchestra leader, is to pull together and project multiple components so as to optimize performance.

The best bankers rise above specialties which they may have acquired along the way, and achieve greater perspective. It is difficult to be a well-rounded person inside a bank without being a broad-gauged person generally. Being technically proficient is not enough. What Churchill said at Copenhagen University about narrow technical training has some bearing: "The first duty of a university is to teach wisdom, not a trade; character, not technicalities. We want a lot of engineers in the modern world, but we do not want a world of engineers." Skills are temporal, and narrow specialization in any profession can stifle. Wisdom, on the other hand, endures. Broad perspective of the social, economic, legal, and political forces which influence judgment and of the principles and problems related to the management of varied enterprises, great and small, is essential. Loan officers deal both in broad diversity and in specifics. They must constantly place a litmus to their own judgment. Is the deal good for the bank as well as the borrower? Would I put my own money into it? If the plan does not work, where does that leave the bank? What is the first, second, and, if possible, the third way out? While credit losses draw attention at senior supervisory levels, the unsung hero is the loan officer who keeps the bank from taking a loss. This usually goes unnoticed and unrecorded; losses avoided are rarely quantified.

The best credit officers have had wide lending exposure. They are concerned with substance over form, are restrained in making big bets, eschew concentration in loan transactions, and are also mindful that diversification reduces the *beta* of the loan portfolio. They go behind the figures, weigh risk/reward with care, and are not diverted by profit center considerations.

They realize that not every event that occurs or every situation in which they involve their banks will lend itself to being managed and controlled. They know that the future has a way of fast becoming the present, and are highly perceptive and forward-looking, anticipating rather than reacting. In taking steps one and two, they have taken into account the steps that could follow, knowing that change is a master key. Well informed on industry generally and on names within an industry, they know the risk of extrapolation, that banking reflects both the economy and the fortunes of its borrowers. We live in an era of economic, social, and political discontinuity. Rather than advancing in a straight line, banking ebbs and flows, pulsating with the marketplace. This has behavioral implications for the portfolio and for involvement in specific borrowing relationships, whether to be aggressive or defensive.

For those who would succeed in credit, one's own efforts at self-improvement are critical. The stuff of credit can be mastered over time with guidance, but one's mind must be open constantly to new knowledge, curious, and exposed to the changing lending scene. It is a matter of concentration, getting it straight, so that one can deal instinctively, following sound fundamentals without being conscious of them. Since each situation is unique, computers and checklists are useful only as tools. This is where art comes in, for good credit decisions are tailor-made. This is also what gives the craft high marks for stimulation and interest. Self-focus is something to be minimized, since carrying it to excess is dangerous for both individuals and institutions. At the same time, a realistic sense of one's own worth obviously helps in coping with the ups and downs of a career.

By now the reader may feel that there are no such officers. Indeed, someone like a Diogenes would have a hard time finding one. Ingredients—the accessories to lending—can be enumerated and measured, but writing about the qualities required of an ideal loan officer must be approached with humility. Winners in any field are hard-pressed to articulate the reasons why they succeed. Mozart was asked by an aspiring composer how to write symphonies. "I didn't ask how," was the reply.

What top loan officers know and do is cumulative. Dedication, tenacity, and determination play parts, as do alertness, attitude, knowledge and application of the necessary tools, and application and practice of proven rules and principles. Aptitude, or a natural bent, is critical, just as it is in sports, music, and engineering, or in most fields. Homer pointed out some 2,700 years ago that "to one man a god has given deeds of war, and to another dance, to another the lyre and song, and in another wide-sounding Zeus puts a good mind." Some have the knack, others do not. Top loan officers probably have a minimum number of the laundry list of desired qualities, but their strengths may vary in combination. There are many paths to stardom. Common sense and good instincts are essentially what are at stake for, like able generals in the field, top lenders integrate varied data and then select and engage whatever elements are needed to view and interpret problems in their entirety.

For all of this, D. A. Forward, a lending doyen of his day, suggested a point of departure: "It takes a loan officer of only average intelligence to make the right decision on a loan if he has all the facts. The difference between a smart lending officer and one who is not is that the former has the intelligence and takes the time to obtain all the pertinent facts before he reaches his decision." This, plus experience, expert application, a sound knowledge of the marketplace, and the intuitive grasp of what makes sense and what does not must certainly move one closer to the *sine qua non* of successful practice. Loan officers will always be tested to lend intelligently. It is their interplay with circumstance that produces good or bad decisions.

9

Bank Credit Policy

From Development to Implementation

A bank's credit policy must establish the broad framework of its worldwide lending activities and at the same time define day-to-day operating procedures to insure that the lending strategy and procedures are communicated and understood throughout the organization. Credit policy should strive to maximize the profitability of the lending activities within the risk contraints acceptable to the bank.

The first and most obvious risk in lending is a borrower's inability or unwillingness to repay a loan in accordance with its terms. Management of the default risk requires the bank to understand the risk profile of its loan portfolio and to have procedures in place to identify weakening credits as quickly as possible. Portfolio management models have shown that default risk can be effectively managed and controlled by procedures which assure portfolio diversification. Diversification must include not only avoidance of significant concentration with a single borrower but limit concentration in, for instance, a single industry, country, or geographic region. Finally, although most banks have significantly increased the average maturity of their loan portfolios, there is a recognition of the need to provide reasonable maturity distributions in order to provide liquidity.

However, there are at least two other major risks which are more subtle and often neglected in the development of credit policy and lending strategy.

The first risk arises primarily from the fact that commercial lending, particularly corporate lending, normally involves the approval and extension of a commitment which is a willingness to lend to the borrower at some future date. Specifically, the corporate customer is generally asking his bank for a commitment to lend rather than making a specific loan request which will be borrowed on a known date. The bank's arrangements to lend may be as informal as an uncommitted line of credit, or as formal as a firm commitment under a revolving or standby credit agreement. Whether the commitment is informal or formal, the bank is under a strong moral, or even legal, obligation to lend under the commitment when the customer wants to borrow even though the timing of the request may not suit the funding and lending capacity of the bank. Therefore, it is important that the development of a bank's credit policy include a comprehensive analysis of the commitment position of the bank and a simulation of the bank's ability to meet the potential funding requirements if its customers were to increase the utilization rate of their commitments. In other words, a bank must assess its capability to fund a surge in outstanding loans.

The second risk has been made painfully obvious to many banks with the increased volatility of interest rates. This volatility requires that credit policy recognize the risk inherent in a fixed-rate loan which can result in a funding mismatch; that is, fixed-rate assets supported by floating-rate liabilities. Therefore, unless all fixed-rate lending is eliminated, an effective credit policy requires that the asset managers work closely with the liability managers in the formulation of credit policy and funding strategy.

The Development Process

Development of credit policy requires a bank to assess the compatability of its marketing and lending strategies and corporate objectives. Since the loan portfolio is typically the single largest asset category in a commercial bank, it is obvious that lending strategy must be consistent with the corporate objectives. In fact, it could be argued that corporate objectives need to be developed and analyzed for reasonableness within the parameters of the bank's lending strategy. For example, it is probably unrealistic for most banks to establish an objective of a 20 percent increase in annual earnings with modest increases in staff expense without an increase in losses as a percent of average loans outstanding.

It is also important to assess the capability and availability of the lending officers and lending support staff in order to insure that acceptable loan portfolio quality and loan loss levels can be maintained with growth in loan assets. Specifically, a high rate of loan growth may require the bank to lend to weaker credits, enter new or unfamiliar lending markets, or develop specialized lending expertise. The bank's senior management must insure that experienced personnel are available to service and manage the risk present in the loan growth or specialized lending situations. Accounts receivable and inventory financing, factoring, project financing, and other lending activities offer the opportunity for asset growth at attractive returns, but if not properly controlled may introduce unreasonable risk and subsequent loan losses into the bank's loan portfolio.

Credit Approval

A bank's credit policy is implemented on a day-to-day basis through its credit approval system. Therefore, the credit approval system must be as carefully developed as the credit policy objectives. The delegation of credit approval authority must consider:

1. The experience of the lending staff
2. The need to provide a timely response to the customer's request
3. The size of the loan request relative to the size of the bank
4. The financial strength of the borrower
5. The consistency of the loan structure and pricing to the bank's portfolio objectives
6. The quality of internal control systems and their ability to provide early identification of weakening or problem loan situations
7. The nature of the request, that is, extension of a new facility, renewal or increase of an existing facility, or a change in maturity or pricing of an existing facility

It is likely that the decision to establish a centralized or decentralized credit approval system will be determined by the general operating and management philosophy of the bank. Nonetheless, it is an important principle in any credit approval system to provide a review of each credit by more than one responsible bank officer, and to insure that procedures and systems in place provide an ongoing review of the quality of the loan assets and commitments.

Loan Administration

It is essential that the bank's credit policy recognize the importance of sound loan documentation and administration. Careful analysis of a credit to determine appropriate terms and conditions of a loan is a wasted effort if the documentation and ongoing administration of the loan and/or collateral are haphazard and unprofessional.

The most common administration failure is not requiring current financial statements from business and personal borrowers. The failure to prepare and furnish timely financial statements has proven to be an excellent warning signal that there is something amiss with the credit. Although the lender may prefer audited financial statements, for many smaller borrowers the cost of preparing these statements is prohibitive. In these instances, it is important that the unaudited financial statements be subject to rigorous scrutiny by the credit analyst and lending officer to insure that the financial trends and position are fairly presented.

Secured lending arrangements obviously require that the bank carefully document its security position and file financing statements or take other action as required in order to perfect its security interest. It is equally important that reasonable control and testing of the collateral be performed on a continuing basis in order to insure that the collateral is adequate and available in the event that it must be relied upon to liquidate the loan.

Loan Workout and Collection

All bank lending requires an ability to assess and a willingness to assume risk. Clearly, all banks and most lending officers occasionally make loans which the borrower is unable to pay in accordance with the original understanding. In some banks the workout and collection function remains the responsibility of the lending officers. Other banks have centralized this function in specialists who are responsible for nonperforming assets and managment and renegotiation of problem assets. Industry loan loss recoveries range between 20 and 40 percent of gross loan losses. While the recovery ratio can be influenced substantially by the bank's charge-off policies, the actual net loan loss performance is often a function of the bank's effectiveness in managing and collecting problem loans. An important element in any loan workout or collection effort, whether centralized or decentralized, is the learning experience. The experience with each problem loan should be analyzed to determine whether there was an error in procedures or judgment which can be avoided in the future. Are there other assets in the portfolio which have similar characteristics, where remedial action may prevent future problems or loss? Are there aspects of the administration or control procedures which if corrected could prevent recurrence of the problem? In short, the workout group, properly structured, is the ultimate learning and feedback agency for the effectiveness of credit policy, procedures, and staff.

Commitment Management and Credit Rating Systems

In an effort to gain a better understanding and effective control of their commitment portfolios, many banks actively monitor the dollar amount and utilization of commitments outstanding by type of credit facility. While this approach can be helpful in forecasting potential asset levels, this simplified analysis may be less than satisfactory as a bank increases in size and complexity. Many banks have found it necessary to develop more detailed and sophisticated commitment control systems in order to understand and manage the potential fluctuations in loan demand which may occur in periods of tight money or economic uncertainty. Since the size and credit quality of the borrower normally determines its access to alternative financial markets, there has been increased interest in the development of credit rating systems. Experience with credit rating systems has shown that companies of higher credit quality and larger size are able to satisfy a major portion of their financing requirements in alternative debt markets. Conversely, the borrower of lesser quality and smaller size is forced to rely upon its banks for a major portion of its financing requirements, particularly when there is instability in the financial markets. The borrower's reliance on its banks is a key issue. Commitment portfolios of identical size can result in substantially different loan volumes as a result of utilization, which is a function of the credit rating distribution.

It is the volatility in loan demand that is often of even greater concern than the absolute level of loan demand. Experience has shown that it is the average-quality borrower which causes much of the volatility in a loan portfolio. In periods of economic stability, alternative financial markets may satisfy a significant portion of the average-quality borrower's financial needs. In periods of economic adversity, these alternative markets are often available only to the strongest borrowers and, therefore, the average-quality borrower must rely on banks to satisfy an increasing share of its financing needs.

The introduction of this volatility into the portfolio highlights the need to insure that commitment pricing recognizes that backup facilities do require a resource allocation, as they are likely to be used at the time when loan demand is high and bank funding is most difficult.

In an effort to recapture a portion of the short-term loan demand, which has been lost during the last decade to the commercial paper market and foreign banks, many domestic banks have developed special lending programs priced at rates which are intended to be competitive with alternative money market rates. These programs have provided substantial incremental assets and earnings, albeit at reduced margins, to many larger banks. Importantly, some banks believe that the transaction nature of these programs can be used to reduce the volatility of their loan demand since an increase in the rate will cause the borrower to refinance. However, given the substantial increase in money market loan assets by the banking system, this assumption may prove to be false, since the aggregate increase in demand in the alternative financial markets would probably be excessive. Nonetheless, a credit rating system does provide a useful guideline for pricing differentials within these special lending programs and may assist in the identification of borrowers which are likely to have refinancing difficulties.

The effective use of the credit rating system and the management of the commitment portfolio requires that a bank place increased emphasis on the development of internal systems which are intended to monitor and identify unusual changes in the commitment portfolio. It is essential that all commitments to lend, whether informal or formal, be identified and included in the commitment system of the bank. Active commitment management requires that each commitment be appropriately identified as to dollar amount and maturity, and that all borrowings by the customer under that commitment be posted to the commitment record so that outstandings, availability, and utilization of the commitment can be monitored on a timely basis. The development of a reliable and useful commitment system requires that the lending, credit policy, and executive management of the bank be actively involved in the design and the development of the system and that the work not be delegated to systems analysts who lack lending experience and expertise.

International Considerations

Historically, international lending in significant amounts was limited to a few banks. In 1970, foreign assets of the U.S. banking system were roughly $40 billion; by the end of 1979, they had risen to $310 billion. Not surprisingly, this growing involvement of the U.S. banking system with foreign lending activities has increased interest in the attention paid to "country risk" and international credit policy not only by bankers but by regulators, the Congress, and the general public.

By "country risk" we mean the possibility that some economic or political event will interfere with the ability or willingness of borrowers in one or more countries to service their debt. Under the general heading of country risk, a distinction is frequently made between "cross-border" and "total country" risk. The former refers to exposure in currencies other than the local currency, and thus cross-border risk is primarily a question of the availability of foreign exchange, or the willingness of governmental authorities to release it for the servicing of externally held debt. Total country risk, on the other hand, generally includes local currency assets, and most banks tend to include all in-country exposure, even if there are guarantors in other countries, as in the case of a branch of a bank headquartered elsewhere.

There are three distinct challenges in designing and implementing effective credit policies to deal with the overall problem of country risk:

1. The design of management information systems
2. The development of useful approaches to risk analysis
3. The internal management system which weighs the variety of factors involved in actually setting lending limits

First, management information systems must be developed to measure the country risk to which the bank is exposed as a result of its lending activities. This means that an analyst must review and continuously monitor all the myriad forms of existing or potential exposure that can arise in the normal course of customer operations in any commercial bank. For example, exposure can include term-loan outstandings, confirmation of letters of credit, short-term interbank deposits, contractor performance bonds, underwriting commitments in a large syndicated loan, Federal funds transactions with a New York branch of a foreign bank, bond purchases, or foreign exchange contracts.

One of the most difficult areas for defining "exposure" is in the case of short-term facilities that have never been formally advised but which are heavily used, perhaps to the extent that the maximum limit of the facility is clearly understood by the borrower. Eliminating or reducing availability due to assessments of deteriorating country risk can be extremely difficult without damaging relationships. Consequently, it would seem appropriate to include such facilities as part of a bank's overall country risk exposure. In general, although practices vary widely, a conservative approach toward measuring exposure is highly recommended, so that if difficulties should arise maximum potential exposure can be quickly determined.

Even though the regulatory authorities have instituted a semiannual country exposure report,* anyone familiar with that report will recognize that there are several types of exposure which are not included in the survey. However, the report is probably a good starting point for the design of any country risk management system.

Ideally, the reporting system should include an ability to list expected repayments so that the maturity profile of exposure in any one country is available to management. Difficult questions regarding the timeliness of data, responsibility for data maintenance, report frequency, and the need to review the system periodically to handle new forms of exposure arise frequently. As a general rule, all good reporting systems for managing country risk will always be undergoing modification to adapt to changing requirements.

The second set of challenges in designing appropriate credit policies for managing country risk is in establishing a procedure for assessing risk. Until very recently, emphasis in risk assessment focused heavily on current and prospective economic conditions in a given country. Since most attention was focused on cross-border (that is, foreign exchange availability) risk, analysis of current and forecasted balance of payments positions, exchange rate policies, and debt servicing requirements were presumed to be the key factors. Accordingly, many country risk assessment systems were designed, staffed, and managed by economists. Although this approach was helpful in monitoring such countries as Turkey and Peru, both of whom experienced severe debt servicing crises, it was not particularly successful in anticipating problems in Iran and Nicaragua, where political factors were the precipitating elements in the collapse of foreign debt servicing. Furthermore, some of the earlier economic-oriented approaches relied too heavily on data which were out of date and incomplete, and thus were not very useful in monitoring fast-breaking situations.

*Comptroller of the Currency, form CC 7610-08; Federal Reserve System, form FR 2036; and Federal Deposit Insurance Corporation, form FDIC 6502/03.

Consequently, increased emphasis is being placed today on political risk assessments in order to assess not only capacity but also willingness to service debt when it is due. Since solid data and expertise in the area of political risk are in considerably shorter supply than international financial statistics, the tendency at the larger commercial banks has been to make lending officers and country risk assessment specialists more sensitive to key political questions in the countries under review and to look to outside consultants and services for assistance.

At this point, a word on scoring-type risk assessment systems is in order. The evidence to date is that although such systems may be helpful, they cannot be relied upon to any substantial degree. A number of systems have been developed and tested in recent years, using financial and economic data or panels of "experts" for a wide sample of countries. They are probably most useful for alerting those responsible for risk assessment to the need for a deeper look at a country which begins to show fairly rapid changes in its scoring. Such a look, of course, may mean that favorable as well as unfavorable developments are taking place, which might argue for either upward or downward adjustments in the country limit.

The third critical element in overall credit policy for managing country risk is the design of a system for establishing and changing individual country limits. The design of the system is important because, although risk assessment may well be the single most important factor in setting lending limits in a particular country, it is usually not the only factor that should be considered. For example, diversification, exposure as a percentage of capital, important customer relationships, and market share are additional factors that should be considered. All of these can be relevant considerations in many cases, arguing for either smaller or somewhat larger limits than would be called for if risk were the sole criterion. Thus, the composition of the country limit committee and associated reviewing system should be designed in such a manner that all factors can be explicitly recognized and included in the limit setting process.

This need for balancing various factors requires that the limit-setting process have a substantial degree of independence from the lending function. No matter how objective lending officers try to be, pressure to accommodate customers and to reach departmental profit objectives are serious impediments to a careful balancing of the factors which should go into the limit-setting process.

Finally, any system should not be excessively complex, since it could interfere with the ability of lending officers to make fast decisions. Limits should be set so that in normal circumstances reviews need take place no more than once a year. Lending divisions should be encouraged to develop realistic marketing plans designed to fit into an appropriate country limit, so that neither the plan nor the limit need to be altered if there are no unexpected developments.

Public Sector Risk

International lenders have long shown a preference for public sector risk over that of the private sector. This has been evidenced by the more generous terms generally offered to public sector borrowers in a particular country.

This may have been caused partly by the greater bargaining power of government entities. But the overwhelming reason is the assessment by most lenders that public sector borrowers represent a lower risk than those in the private sector. This assessment is usually based on one or more of the following three assumptions:

1. Governments have better access to funding sources than private sector borrowers. In the case of domestic currency debt, the government can simply resort to the expansion of money supply to service debt. As for foreign currency debt, a government generally controls a high proportion of a country's foreign assets through the central bank's management of foreign exchange reserves.

2. Governments will behave more responsibly than private sector borrowers. This is based on the belief that all countries must import certain goods and that most countries must have access to foreign financing in order to import.

3. Governments are better long-term risks since countries cannot be liquidated like private sector corporations. Since countries are almost always continuing entities, lenders are unlikely to suffer losses in the long term because the sovereign borrowers cannot evade repayment by going through bankruptcy proceedings.

Each of these assumptions has weaknesses.

1. Governments certainly have better access to domestic funding than private sector corporations, but there is a constraint on domestic monetary growth. If governments are limited in issuing additional currency by inflationary pressures, their ability to service debts may be affected. Furthermore, it is not always true that a government has good control of its country's foreign exchange resources, particularly in the case of countries with balance of payments problems. The usual result of a weak external position, particularly if there is exchange rate inflexibility, is the creation of an unofficial market for currency. As a country's balance of payments deteriorates, a greater proportion of its external earnings will be routed through the unofficial market— which is, of course, out of the control of the central bank. In some countries unofficial market currency holdings are several times larger than official international reserves. The government can regain control of these gray market funds by appropriate exchange-rate policy, but this is seldom an attractive policy option for domestic budgetary reasons.

2. In the past, governments have not all behaved responsibly. Some have

decided that it is better to do without import credit than to repay debts. They may either cut themselves off from imports from Western sources—as did Cuba—or they can pay for imports in cash—as did Uganda under Amin. There is even a possibility that debtor countries will repudiate debt maliciously —that is, for political purposes. An example is the repudiation by Egypt of military debts to the Soviets.

3. Although countries are usually continuing entities, governments are not. There have been several cases of successor governments repudiating, or attempting to repudiate, the debt incurred by their predecessors. Since many governments spend borrowed money defending themselves from potential usurpers of their power, repudiation risk is significant in some public sector loans.

Overall, there are clearly differences between public and private sector risk, although these differences are sometimes exaggerated in the market. Having established this, it is necessary to define public sector. It can be measured in terms of ownership; control; or the importance of the entity to the economy.

Ownership by a government is the usual measure used. However, it can be confusing since governments can retain interests in corporations for commercial reasons. An example is venture capital injections in start-up operations by several governments in less developed countries. Since shareholders are not normally called on to pay the debts of the limited liability companies they own, it may be unrealistic to expect a government to rescue a company in which it has a commercial shareholding.

For this reason, it is also helpful to look at the degree of control which the government exerts over a public sector company. Does it appoint the management, have veto power, or take an active part in the day-to-day running of the company? The closer the government's control, the greater is the likelihood that the government may support the company in times of trouble.

Similarly, the greater the importance of the company to the economy in terms of employment, or the quantity or nature of its output (either a major necessity or a major export), the more likely it is to be supported by the government. However, it must be said that the fact that an enterprise is government owned, employs a substantial labor force, and produces an important product is not enough to ensure the government's support.

Municipal Lending

The domestic equivalent of public sector risk is municipal lending. Inherent in municipal lending are many of the risks present in international public sector lending, and an additional risk is that the municipal borrower cannot print currency to repay its local currency debt.

Municipal lending is particularly difficult in the more mature areas of the country where a stable or declining and often aging population may result in an erosion of the tax base in the face of rapidly increasing operating costs, large unfunded pension liabilities, and the need to undertake significant capital expenditures in order to maintain the existing infrastructure.

While municipal bankruptcy is rare, the risk in lending to municipalities is one of cash inadequacy. Municipalities derive a substantial amount of their revenues from local taxes. Therefore, it is difficult for a municipality to build a large cash reserve without taxpayer complaints of overtaxation. Without a cash reserve a municipality can experience temporary cash shortages due to an unexpected reduction in revenues or an increase in expenditures. Chronic budgeting problems result in longer-term financial difficulties.

The primary source of revenues for most municipalities is taxes, although some municpalities provide water, sewer, or electric service for which they charge a fee. Major taxes levied are the property tax, sales tax, and wage or income tax. While it is desirable to have revenues coming from a diversification of taxes, many states limit the kinds of taxes which a municipality is permitted to levy and also the rate of taxation. Other major sources of revenues are intergovernmental assistance programs (Federal Revenue Sharing, CETA, anti-recession, state aid). Dependence on these revenue sources leaves the municipality vulnerable to cash flow difficulties should any of these revenues be reduced or eliminated.

Since the major expenditure for municipalities is salaries, inflation has a tremendous impact on expenditures. The ability of a municipality to reduce expenditures is limited, as it requires an elimination or reduction of services to the voter. In some cases the state or Federal government has mandated services which the municipality is obligated to provide. A declining ability to pay does not always precede a decline in expenditures. For instance, a population decline has little impact on the expenditures required to support a police force or an effective highway maintenance program. Similarly, a decline in school enrollment will not cause an immediate decrease in school teachers or school buildings.

Finally, a municipality's fiscal health is a function of its economic health. A persistent decline in population and assessed value, stagnant per capita income, or high unemployment rates can all lead to a reduction in revenues without a corresponding reduction in expenditures. In a municipality greatly dependent on one manufacturing concern for its fiscal health, a closing of the firm or a reduction of capacity could reduce revenues substantially.

In addition to being able to analyze adequately the above factors to determine the municipality's ability to pay, the bank may face several additional problems:

1. Current financial statements are frequently not available or incomplete. Audited statements are normally unavailable and accounting standards are, at best, incomplete.

2. Municipal officials are normally more responsive to taxpayer and voter pressure than the need to preserve financial strength.

3. Proper documentation for a loan is often complex and requires knowledgeable lenders to insure that the municipality is authorized to borrow, does not go over its borrowing limit, and is not improperly arbitraging, and that any security interests are properly perfected and collateral is correctly administered.

4. As a primary depository, a bank may feel a responsibility to lend to the muncipality even when there is a substantial credit risk.

5. Adverse publicity is likely to result from any action by the bank against a municipality in an attempt to protect or collect outstanding loans.

6. Physical presence of a bank (or branch office) within the geographic area of the municipal body limits the bank in its dealings with the municipality.

In addition to a legal position which provides few rights and remedies to the lender, the bank also has the problem that financial and accounting standards are limited and the quality of financial information varies greatly among municipalities. Furthermore, in smaller political subdivisions, the management and financial controls can be the responsibility of part-time employees or elected officials who often lack sophistication in management, financial control techniques, and reporting systems. As a result the bank is often called upon to be the advisor and financial consultant to the municipality and at the same time lender of last resort. Finally, the location of a bank or branch office within a municipality creates a "Catch-22" situation. Many of the economic factors which will influence the financial condition of the municipality will also influence the strength of the bank. Therefore, it is likely that the bank will be asked to support the municipality when the performance of the bank (or branch) is weakening.

CONCLUSION

An effective credit policy should recognize that:

1. Successful management of the commercial lending activities requires management of not only a loan but also a commitment portfolio.

2. Volatility of interest rates and the increased dependence on purchased funds requires integration of the asset and liability management strategies.

3. Credit approval and loan administration systems must be as carefully developed, implemented, and monitored as the credit policy.

Perhaps most importantly, the guiding principle should be that credit policy is never static but is always evolving to take advantage of market opportunities and the ongoing learning experience of the organization.

10

Secured Lending

As time changes both the Federal Bankruptcy Act, legal decisions based thereon, and documentation formats, primarily the Uniform Commercial Code, this discussion will be limited to concepts of secured lending.

The American banking system has long considered the plain-note, seasonal borrower to be the mainstay of its lending portfolio. These loans represent advances to top-rated credits for working capital purposes, where there is no doubt as to the repayment of the obligation. Over the years, three things have happened to make this type of credit a rarity. First, other financial intermediaries (primarily the commercial paper market) have assumed a large part of the financing of top-rated names. Second, inflation and heavy capital investment requirements have largely eliminated the seasonality of credit. Third, fluctuations in the economy, foreign competition, and technological changes have caused some "fine names" to be unable to pay their debts as they mature.

With regard to this last point, the banking system has attempted to monitor long-term unsecured involvements with borrowers by frequent receipt of financial statements and review of various ratios. Theoretically, the banker will be given a call on the company's note should one of these ratios or a convenant arising from the loan agreement not be met. Unfortunately, the banker is then often faced with an adversary position by the company's management, heavy legal expenses, and a claim that is only equal in asset distribution to the unsecured trade debt or, in some cases, secondary to other obligations such as payroll taxes, wage claims, and a myriad of lessors and possibly bona fide lien holders. I have used the words "theoretically" in describing the bank's ability to monitor an unsecured loan because interim statements are most frequently prepared by management, while even the annual statement prepared and certified by independent accountants may be suspect as to thoroughness in writing off aged accounts or slow-turning inventories.

A truism in banking states that the only things we really know about a customer is the collected balance position and the amount owing to us—everything else is conjecture. However, we will spend much time analyzing balance sheet ratios, trends, and debt coverage performance, with the hope that somehow our knowledge of the customer's business will create a better loan. Obviously, such analysis has great value, but it is tied heavily to the once-a-year report of examination by an independent certified public accountant and, in the interim, company-prepared figures. In most instances an unsecured loan does not call for a pre-loan examination, but only the interview of company management by an account officer who will handle the relationship. Good secured lending practices call not only for the initial physical evaluation of collateral but also for constant onsight monitoring to determine changes in the value of such assets (dilution or market price, both to be discussed later). Free cash flow is, obviously, the most desirable way to have a loan repaid, although, as the life cycle of a business or industry evolves and as the economy goes through its many fluctuations, the ability to realize against assets becomes an increasingly important loan collection alternative.

While the subject of secured lending covers numerous forms of collateral other than business assets, I would like to concentrate on an analysis of those most frequently used by asset-based lenders to secure their loan positions.

Accounts Receivable

An account receivable should be defined as a record of the customer which evidences items shipped to and received (signed bill of lading) by a credit-worthy account debtor pursuant, in most instances, to a written bona fide purchase order with no dispute as to quality, quantity, style, or other description of the items covered and not subject to setoffs (warranties), performance claims under a continuing contract, or contra sales. The valuation of an accounts receivable portfolio begins with the analysis of the aging. Bankers often stop at a statistical analysis without looking deeply into the components of the borrower's relationship with his account debtor. The lender should not focus on the statistical analysis of the receivables alone, but, rather on the potential "dilution" of the accounts receivable. Dilution represents those events which would cause the secured party to realize less than par against the stated invoice amount at the time of payment.

The following represent some aspects of the secured lending situation to be viewed by the loan officer whether he takes an assignment of the accounts receivable or is preparing monitoring systems for an unsecured arrangement.

Aging. The aging spread provides three inputs to the lender. Initially, it is a comment upon the quality of the accounts with the thought that poor credits pay slowly. In this regard, necessary bank checkings should be made to determine creditworthiness of the account debtors. Second, it indicates a problem when good credits are paying slowly because of (1) disputes over prices, compliance to purchase orders, or imperfection in the goods shipped and/or (2) return items not recorded (unposted credit memos) on the aging but representing items shipped that will not be paid for because of quality, quantity, or price disputes. Third, the aging provides the basic means by which the lender can independently verify the status of the account with the debtor. This can be done either with the customer's knowledge or by the creation of a monitoring organization that will test-check the genuineness of the receivable list.

Terms. Terms should reflect the common practices (both as to trade and cash discounts) of our customer's industry and may thus be extended to adjust for seasonal needs of the account debtor. However, extended terms can also be indicative of hidden discounts (an effective loss of interest), showing a marketing weakness in the merchandise shipped. It must be remembered that extended terms represent a potentially long collection cycle, which puts the lender at greater risk because there should be some relationship between the size of the loan and the monthly cash collection. Obviously, the loan against receivables which represent only 30 days' collections or less allows the secured lender to get out of the credit rapidly without the trade being aware of a lengthening in payments into an additional 30-day category.

Credit Memos and Adjustments. Past due amounts from well-rated account debtors should be investigated for items not being paid on a timely basis as the situation may reflect credit memos not posted. Two items that impact the collectibility of the full amount of the account receivable and result in dilution are disputed discounts, both trade and industry, and credits for items returned for a multitude of reasons ranging anywhere from goods not made or delivered pursuant to a purchase order to defective merchandise. The former situation could portend a fraud upon the lender as it could mean that goods were shipped on an understanding not reflected in the purchase order or the invoice, while the latter raises questions as to the quality of other receivables, the unsold inventory specifically, and the credibility of management in general. A borrower may dishonestly issue a credit memo to remove an aged item due from an account debtor so that the lender will not disqualify the total account under the often used "10 percent crossage rule." This rule renders an entire account ineligible for advance if 10 percent or more of the amount owing is past due beyond terms. Admittedly, 10 percent represents stringent control of the borrower's availability and often this number is raised to 25 percent or, unfortunately, the rule is waived altogether.

Warranties. The bank often finances the sale of goods which require high technical competence or long-term performance and thus are sold under warranty. The user will pay currently for the merchandise if he believes the seller will be in business at least for the length of the warranty. The moment a secured lender begins action against the warrantor, there is a strong likelihood that merchandise under a warranty will either not be paid for or returned on the pretext that the seller (the warrantor, our borrower) has or will default on his contract pursuant to the warranty. The sale of automobile batteries is a case in point, as is the sale of those other high-technology products which have become so common. The subject of warranties brings up the whole matter of service receivables, contractor receivables, and other types of sales that represent contractual relationships between our customer and the account debtor. A bank may finance shipments of coal mined and delivered to a user sold under contract for a specific tonnage to be delivered over a period of time. Although there are legitimate invoices, purchase orders, and bills of lading evidencing delivery, the user of the coal might not pay these receivables if the seller (our customer) goes out of business under the theory that the user will have to obtain coal elsewhere at a price that may be higher than that quoted in our borrower's contact with him or on less favorable terms as to quality or timely delivery.

Contra Items. Often our customer will sell to account debtors who are in turn selling to him. The situation frequently occurs where our borrower is processing inventory for others or is dealing with a large conglomerate operation where he is performing services for one division of the conglomerate while buying goods from another division.

Purchase Orders. As previously stated, the two critical aspects of an account receivable are evidence of shipment (consideration for a receivable being on the books of our customer) and the fact that goods have been made pursuant to a bona fide purchase. Obviously, improper purchase orders will result in return items and/or price adjustments and, of course, like the credit memos which they will cause, evidence either poor management or potential fraud.

Consignment Sales. Again it is important to review the purchase order carefully. In some cases this documentation is a result of a telephone order and is not on the purchaser's stationery. Verbal purchase orders may be suspect and should lend themselves to telephone verification by the secured lender. Consignment sales are common in a number of industries; rack-jobbing is a foremost example of consignment sales, where the consignee-purchaser may extinguish his obligation and, unfortunately, the receivable upon which the loan is predicated by return of the merchandise. Consignment terms should be spelled out on the purchase orders, but, if not, the banker should be aware of various industry trade practices and/or the numerous side deals that take place between buyer and seller in an effort to move merchandise.

The above concepts should be used as a basis to determine proper the maximum advance against the borrower's accounts so that the lender is not subject to dilution in liquidation greater than the lending margin.

Inventory

Over the years both secured and unsecured lenders have attempted to measure inventory values by a concept of turnover. Annual cost of goods sold would be divided by average inventory during the year, most often half the sum of two consecutive annual inventories, to arrive at an inventory turnover figure. Obviously, a denominator based upon monthly inventory accounting would give a better statistical turnover. However, such turnover is an average and does not cover the situation that would arise if half the inventory were obsolete and not turning over while the other half of the inventory were quality goods having excellent marketability with a better-than-average turnover. Thus, a turnover of eight times a year on half the inventory with a zero turnover on the other half of the inventory could result in a four times turnover average, thus lulling the banker into some general level of confidence as to the quality of the inventory. The truth of the matter could well be that half the inventory should be charged off against net worth. In secured lending, the banker looks at the inventories in two ways: first as a commodity value fluctuating daily, and second as a total of various stockkeeping units where the turnover of each unit is analyzed separately to determine the statistical obsolescence of the inventory as a whole.

ANALYSIS OF TURNOVER

The secured lender must have a good understanding of his borrower's business, not only as to the terms upon which he sells goods, but also the nature of the stock itself. Inventories lend themselves to two types of statistical analysis: first, the relative breakdown between raw materials, work in process, and finished goods; and second, the analysis of the finished components in the various stockkeeping units or other differentiating measures. Too many times the borrower will have large quantities of inventory, but unless the basic components of such inventory have a commodity value themselves, the inventory may consist of relatively little finished and saleable product.

It is important that the borrower have the computer or manual bookkeeping capability to record inventory both as to price and date of entry into the records. Unless there is a massive technological change, inventory agings are still the best way for a banker to determine that his customer is selling what he is buying.

COMMODITY EVALUATIONS

A secured lender has to be prepared at all times to dispose of inventory under a lien in a rapid fashion, obtaining a price at least equal to his advance against a particular type of goods. Obviously, raw materials or finished goods having a stated commodity value are most desirable. Work in process generally takes the expense of further labor to make a finished good, and the labor applied, factory burden, and material content of the finished good may be less than the commodity value of the original raw material. The banker should have the ability constantly to price the inventory components either by using published prices (for items such as plywood, liner board, plastic resin, or other "commodity components") or by being close enough to the market place so that he is aware of diminution or, for that matter, appreciation in value of the pledged inventory. Furthermore, the banker, through his field examination staff, should be able frequently to test-check inventory quantities to make sure that the lien assets are physically present as to quantity and quality between independent audit dates.

An inventory lender should only view inventories as component commodities, not as a whole. A company that manufactures products requiring high technological and/or intensive skilled labor to complete the conversion of the raw materials into the finished goods may not be the most desirable candidate for an inventory loan. Such inventory often carries with it product warranty that makes it difficult to dispose of the product without a significant discount or continued involvement by the lender.

It is hard to generalize, but often those companies which have the lowest gross profit margins (resulting from normal trading markups rather than inefficiencies buried in the cost of goods sold) will be dealing in products that by their nature are "standard" in value and, thus, can be disposed of quite easily. High-margin businesses often reflect unique products, and such products will not always have a ready market.

Lastly, two concepts which intertwine and should be reviewed by an asset-based lender before making inventory advances are, first, that the borrower has proper title to the inventory, and second, the use of a field warehouse. Often a supplier may provide the bank's borrower with finished goods on consignment. If the lender has knowledge of this practice, even though no lien on specific goods has been filed against the borrower by the supplier, the lender might not have liquidating rights to these goods located on premise. This situation can be corrected by a subordination agreement signed by the supplier for the benefit of the lender. Another problem arises when an account debtor ships raw or in-process inventory to our borrower for conversion to finished goods. This situation not only provides title problems but creates a natural offset to monies owed our borrower and assigned to us from the account debtor. Substantial dilution in liquidation can occur in the accounts receivable from this practice.

Once clear title to the inventory has been established, the question arises as to the use of a field warehouse. It is always desirable to have a bonded third party control the physical presence of the inventory. Unfortunately, the competitive climate among lenders is such that the borrower often does not have to go through the expense of a field warehouse, much to the possible eventual detriment of the lender.

Chattel Mortgages

Some years ago an aggressive chattel mortgage loan represented a 66⅔ percent advance against a knockdown appraisal value on a piece of equipment with a payment schedule not exceeding five years. The banker attempted to limit his advances to general purpose equipment and avoided customized items or those built with restrictive modifications. Furthermore, he attempted to take into account the cost of removal from the premises. In recent years, when banks have attempted to shelter their pretax earnings with losses arising from depreciation, leasing has become the vogue. The yield to the bank has become a function of the rental payments, the value of the depreciated loss for tax purposes, the investment tax credit, and the residual value of the equipment financed. In consideration of all these "future benefits," the banking industry has made 100 percent advances on the laid-down value of machinery. Such value includes the cost of installation and special modifications and does not take into account, in many instances, cost of removal. The term of the lease is often ten years or more. Obviously, such "loans" are predicated upon the creditworthiness of the lessee as opposed to the real value of the equipment at any given date.

In inflationary times, equipment may well appreciate in market value or at least not depreciate as rapidly. However, specific market demand, general business cycles, or technical obsolescence can rapidly destroy these chattel values. The banker must remember that unless assets liquidate themselves to cash in the normal course of business (such as receivables and, to a lesser extent, inventories), advances should be subject to the most rapid reduction that the borrower's cash flow allows. Pretax earnings before interest and depreciation should be sufficient to service the above equipment debt (exclusive of all other debt being serviced by such earnings) in an amount equal to one and a half to two times the required principal and interest. Assuming adequate coverage, the advance itself should be predicated upon experienced machinery appraisers who are able to render a professional opinion as to the knockdown value of the equipment after cost of removal and auctioneer's expenses.

In some instances, good machinery can be sold as rapidly as good inventory. Many lenders prefer machinery loans to inventory advances because of the general durability of the collateral. Still, the secured lender should realize that machinery is a slower asset than receivables or inventory, and is often subject to obsolescence. Also, legal problems often arise when an attempt is made to remove machinery from the premises and an unfriendly landlord claims such equipment to be a fixture or leasehold improvement subject to protective covenants of our borrower's lease.

Real Estate

Real estate lending, in a formal sense, is discussed in Chapter 15 of this book but, suffice it to say, equity values in excess of the first mortgage on the borrower's real estate (owned corporately or by management) may prove extremely valuable in the ultimate collection of a loan. Furthermore, a strong lien position or control of the equity by assignment of title allows the lender to house his collateral (records of accounts receivable, inventories, machinery and equipment, and leasehold improvements of value, among other assets) should the company default in its rental or mortgage payments. Although real estate can appreciate dramatically in times of inflation, the asset-based lender should never be lulled into a false sense of security by presumably strong equity values in such collateral. Unlike receivables and inventory, where there is a sense of self-liquidation, or machinery, which may take little upkeep, real estate must be maintained (mortgage payments, taxes, repairs and maintenance, insurance and security, for example). It is most desirable to take real estate equity as an abundance of collateral and leave purchase money advances to other lenders who are willing to rely on the borrower's long-term ability to service debt. The asset-based lender should be primarily interested in comparable real estate values in the area in case of the need to force a rapid liquidation of the property. When the situation arises where our borrower does not own its premises, but leases from a third party, the assignment of the leaseright would be of value, first, to insure control of the facility and, second, to collateralize the value of the leaseright. (Differential between contracted rent and present market.)

Aside from corporate real estate, it is often desirable to take a second lien on personal residences to supplement the value of personal guarantees. In many situations, the guarantor could have considerable value in his personal real estate after his first mortgage. Aside from enhancing the overall collateral position, the pledge of a personal residence tends strongly to encourage the cooperation of the guarantor in the liquidation of corporate debt.

Other Considerations

In recent years the banker has learned the all too painful lesson that an unamortized blanket lien on company assets gives little assistance in the timely and ultimate liquidation of a loan. The only way to assure timeliness in liquidation is by constant audit systems in the form of frequent and detailed field examinations. A good secured lending bank ought to have developed an audit staff that is thorough and perceptive. It is sometimes more important for the auditor to spend a week with the company's bookkeeper than for the account officer to interview and entertain the borrower's management. This does not mean undervaluing the important judgment to be made as to competency of management, its track record, or its plans for the future. However, daily monitoring of the borrower's accounts receivable, supplemented by frequent field examinations, will tell the lender more about the borrower's customer, product quality, and the way in which it conducts business, in general, than any other single accounting or interviewing tool. Obviously, the careful review of the independent auditor's annual statement as well as company-prepared interims is helpful in gauging broad trends. Perhaps the best signals to the lender as to when to begin cutting back on advances to the borrower to achieve a timely and total liquidation of the debt will come from the results of daily receivable analysis, account debtor balance verifications, the work papers of the field examiners, and all the other testing techniques set up by a competent asset-based lender.

Events outside the control of the banker or the borrower often strongly impact on the liquidation value of the collateral. Adequate insurance is, of course, crucial to the maintenance of these values in particular and the performance of the borrower in general. Coverage should include casualty, business interruption, key-man life insurance, and product liability insurance. Proceeds from the first three categories should be assigned to the lender. It is helpful to have an independent insurance expert rate the quality and value the quantity of these coverages.

The law provides for public notice of many types of claims against a corporation or, for that matter, an individual (the guarantor). Before credit is granted and on a regular basis afterward, the lender should check for other asset liens, law suits (both as plaintiff and defendant), and subsequent judgments and tax liens of all types. These searches will give indications of the company's formal involvements with other creditors, its disputes with customers and suppliers, the adequacy of its bookkeeping procedures, cash flow problems, and integrity of management in general.

An asset-based lender should also have the ability to monitor the trends of his customer's industry in general and inventory collateral values in particular. Reviewing trade journals and daily commodity prices and, most importantly, frequent contact with close-out liquidators can help to ensure proper inventory advances being quoted when a loan is made. Recently, banks specializing in asset-based lending have followed the lead of their counterparts in the commercial finance industry and have quoted advances on both accounts receivable and inventory in terms of "up to ____ percent" as opposed to a fixed percentage. Thus, it behooves the lender constantly to stay abreast of the market value of the assets being financed, including decreased values of machinery and equipment caused by technical obsolescence.

The political and legal atmosphere in which a company operates can also be important to a secured lender. Will the labor union with which our borrower deals be cooperative with the company and bank during liquidation? Work in process (and, in some cases, raw materials) must be finished off with additional labor to provide for maximum collateral realization. Environmental agencies may require machinery modifications or diminish the market value of the borrower's finished products by their decisions.

CONCLUSIONS

A bank makes loans secured by assets other than those mentioned in this chapter. These assets range from savings passbooks to works of art, from collateral with relatively fixed value and requiring little or no monitoring of market price to collateral which can fluctuate dramatically in value and requires constant and sophisticated monitoring (often through the use of professional appraisers) to determine compliance with agreed upon margins for the loan granted. In between lie pledgeable assets such as bonds of all types, cash surrender value of life insurance, preferred and common stocks, bullion receipts, numismatic coins, and jewelry. The lender should obviously consult legal counsel to ensure proper lien rights and compliance with applicable government regulations as regards large possessory forms of collateral. Advances may range from 100 percent on government bonds due within 90 days to 75 percent on listed securities to less than 50 percent on the book value of privately held common stocks or the appraisals on works of art. Valuation sources can range from a bank's money market desk to the above-mentioned employment of expert appraisers.

An individual will often build a secondary level of liquidity in the form of marketable stocks, municipal bonds, or government securities. From time to time, a need arises to borrow against these investments for reasons that may range from the physical improvement of a residence to the purchase of other investment assets. The banker should be aware that the government regulates loans collateralized by equity securities through the amount of margin (down payment) required to be given to the lender for security purposes. This limitation is an important fiscal tool of the United States government in controlling stock market speculation, as it applies when the purpose of the loan is purchase of publicly traded securities but has the residual affect of giving the lender a generally substantial collateral cushion. Margin regulations vary from time to time, and the lender should guard against violation of such laws regarding borrowings against equity securities. Stock price fluctuations and the resulting margin adequacy are impacted by many things such as the volume of shares traded, the insider status of the borrower, amount of "float stock" outstanding, the exchange upon which the trade takes place, and, of course, the general fortunes of the company as viewed by the public and as evidenced by the bid-ask differential for a given number of shares. In my experience, a pledged stock has never been sold at the right time as far as the borrower is concerned. In a down market, the borrower will feel that the stock will eventually go up in price and, consequently, the banker should be patient. In an up market, the borrower may wish to hold on to the security longer than the agreed-upon term under which the borrowing was made. If the lender forces sale of the collateral security and the market subsequently rises, we may have bad feelings between the bank and the borrower. To avoid misunderstandings, it is wise to have a schedule of debt amortization agreed to before the loan is made regardless of the apparent goodness of the collateral at the time credit is granted.

Whether the asset be of high and unquestioned value and in the possession of the lender or of questionable value (evidenced by a thin market subject to depreciation, obsolescence, or deterioration) and on the premises of the borrower, the lender hopes to avoid enforcing his security interest through legal remedies. This risk can be lessened through written understandings as to maintained margins, payment of interest, and debt amortization on the loan portion secured by the least liquid part of the collateral.

The prime question to be asked by the banker after he determines the value of collateral to be pledged is, assuming a break-even operation or a maintenance of lifestyle in the case of individuals, are the advances* adequate to take care of the borrower's needs? Considering the business situation only, the banker should be satisfied that all trade debt, employee payroll and other benefits (including applicable taxes), rental payments, present debt amortizations, and other accruals can be maintained without additions to net worth through earnings or other capital or debt infusions. A careful analysis of trade payables including turnover and further slowness which would be tolerated before suppliers cease shipping is critical to the credit judgment.

Secured lending differs from the extension of plain note accommodations primarily in shifting the main responsibility of monitoring the borrower's performance from the independent accountant to the collateral manager and the field examination staff of the bank. (The banking industry must recognize in regard to both salary levels and career paths the importance of collateral managers and field examiners.) For example, a traumatic event affecting credit may occur just after the issuance of the independent CPA's statement. The lender could be exposed to inadequate collateral coverage and a deteriorating situation for many months without being aware of it. Constant monitoring, as described above, or even an interim field examination by trained professionals may well make the difference between a substantial charge-off and a timely liquidation or the chance to be paid off by another lender.

---

*That is, going concern asset valuation less margin for dilution and depreciation made under forced sale.

Unsecured Bank Loans

Unsecured loans to business enterprises require careful and thorough analysis since their repayment depends solely upon the financial strength of the borrower. Since there is no specific collateral to look to as an alternative source of repayment, the lending officer must analyze the financial condition and trends of the applicant in order to assure himself that the capability to repay the loan is and will remain present.

There are a variety of ways to approach unsecured loans, but they all cover essentially the same principles. Regardless of the particular approach, the character and ability of management, the past operating record of the enterprise, and the nature and economics of the industry must be understood and reviewed in order to make an informed lending decision.

Financial analysis is a cornerstone in the unsecured lending process. However, it is important that the lender not place undue emphasis on numbers, but rather look beyond the numbers to understand what they say about the business and its operations. Financial statements are merely a means of communicating information about a business and its operations. Although considerable attention is paid to financial analysis in making loan decisions, it is important continually to remember that loans are made to and repaid by people. The financial statements are only a medium by which the capability of people can be evaluated.

Types of Unsecured Loans

Unsecured loans are made for a variety of purposes and in a number of ways. Short-term unsecured loans may be made via 30-, 60-, or 90-day notes or by demand notes. Unsecured term loans may be made through renewable 90-day notes with reductions at each maturity, by demand notes with periodic reductions, or through notes requiring monthly or quarterly amortization to an ultimate maturity several years in the future.

Regardless of the type of note and repayment schedule used, there are only two basic types of unsecured loans: (1) temporary asset acquisition; and (2) permanent asset acquisition.

Temporary asset acquisition includes the conventional seasonal working capital loan, which is discussed in Chapter 12. Other temporary asset acquisitions include such things as a special order, a temporary nonseasonal increase in sales volume, or some types of project loans. The important point is that the loan is used to acquire an asset which will not be permanently retained by the business and the loan will be repaid from the proceeds of the asset sale.

Permanent acquisition loans are for the purpose of funding assets which will be retained by the business. Additional fixed assets, such as plant or equipment, are common examples of this type of loan. Not so commonly recognized as asset acquisition loans are those to acquire increased levels of accounts receivable or inventory to support sales growth. Permanent increases in receivables and inventory levels are inherent to steady sales growth over the years and represent permanent assets just as necessary to the continued operation of the business as additional machinery or other fixed assets. These loans are not intended to be repaid by disposition of the assets, but rather from the profits which these assets are expected to produce for the enterprise.

There are only three ways in which any loan can be repaid: (1) disposition of assets; (2) transfer to another lender; or (3) increase in equity capital either by new investment or retention of earnings. Unsecured loans are normally repaid by each of these three means depending upon the purpose of the loan. Seasonal working capital loans are commonly paid by disposition of temporary assets acquired. Unsecured loans to fund permanent asset expansion are normally paid from the increased equity resulting from retention of the earnings generated. For some companies and particular industries, unsecured loans may be paid by rotation of borrowings among lenders. This is particularly common among larger companies who have multiple bank line relationships so that short-term unsecured borrowings are never paid in full by the company, but each individual bank is paid out for a period of time each year.

An important element of loan analysis is to determine the primary source of repayment as well as to have a secondary source available in the event the primary source does not work out. For example, an unsecured loan may be expected to be repaid from liquidation of seasonal inventory, but in a period of economic slowdown, sales volume may temporarily fall off and the lending bank may be repaid by borrowing from another bank under an existing line of credit.

The purpose of the loan generally indicates the primary source of repayment. A loan for a temporary asset acquisition can be expected to be repaid from the disposal of that asset. General earnings produced by the business could be a secondary source of repayment if the asset disposition does not work out as planned. Loans for permanent asset acquisitions can be expected to be repaid from the earnings produced by the assets, but may also be repaid from general earnings if the anticipated volume does not materialize or could be repaid by disposition of the acquired assets in a deteriorating situation.

Sometimes the applicant for an unsecured business loan will not recognize the true purpose for which funds are needed. It is very common for a businessman to approach his bank for a short-term loan for working capital purposes because he needs to purchase inventory, carry receivables, or make payment to his suppliers. The real need may be to replenish working capital which has previously been used to acquire additional machinery and equipment. The businessman realized his need for working capital, but may not always recognize that the need results from the diversion of funds from working capital to fixed assets. In this situation the true purpose is to finance the assets previously paid for, and the astute lender will recognize this purpose and structure his loan accordingly.

Nature of the Business

In order fully to understand the flow of funds through a business enterprise, it is necessary to understand the nature of the enterprise. There are an infinite number of types of businesses depending not only upon the product sold or service rendered but also upon the markets being serviced. A few general examples will be outlined to indicate the analysis required, but they will be by no means all-inclusive.

Trading companies may operate either as retailers selling products direct to consumers or as wholesalers serving as middlemen in the movement of products from manufacturers to retailers. These companies are distinguished by the fact that receivables and inventory are usually their primary assets, and their function is to purchase a completed product and make it available to their customers. Style and perishability may be important elements in the products, which increases the risk that obsolete or nonsaleable items may build up in inventory.

Service companies do not provide a product and consequently have little inventory. They may need substantial fixed assets, such as a telephone company, or limited fixed assets with service provided as a result of the knowledge of professional people, such as an engineering or law firm.

Assembly companies produce a product by putting together components purchased from manufacturing or other firms. They may do some manufacturing work, but purchase a significant number of specific components. Automobile assemblers and appliance companies are general examples of this type of firm.

Manufacturing companies generally take raw materials and bend, shape, cut, mill, or otherwise produce products from raw materials, plastics, or other materials. Their primary distinguishing characteristic is that significant changes take place in their raw materials in the manufacturing process.

Mining companies are engaged in the extraction of material resources from the earth or the manufacture of materials by chemical process. Their products are the raw materials for manufacturers and other users. In many cases, their principal asset is the supply of ore in the ground, which is difficult to measure precisely. Heavy expenditures for exploration and development of coal or ore fields or deposits of oil and natural gas are common for this type of business.

It should be apparent from the above capsuled descriptions that the need for funds and the means of repayment can differ widely among various types of businesses. It is important to be aware of the specific nature of a borrower's business in analyzing an unsecured loan request.

Financial Statements

The easiest and most tangible segment of loan analysis is the financial area. Financial statements are provided with precise numbers which can be evaluated in a number of ways. Complete financial statements consist of a balance sheet, a statement of profit and loss, a reconciliation of net worth, and a source and application of funds statement, along with explanatory footnotes. Anything less is not a complete financial statement.

Financial statements may be provided directly by the borrower or they may be prepared by an independent accountant. If the statements have been reviewed by a certified public accountant, they may be audited, unaudited, or prepared on a compilation or review basis. Audited statements are based upon examination of the financial records in accordance with generally accepted auditing principles and will contain an opinion of the auditor either unqualified or qualified as to some specific item, or rarely with a disclaimer of opinion because the statements do not comply with generally accepted accounting principles. When an opinion is expressed, the auditor assumes responsibility for the accuracy of the statements. Unaudited statements do not have the same high degree of reliability since they have not been subjected to an independent objective review.

In order to make an intelligent appraisal of the financial strength of a borrower, it is mandatory that more than one financial statement be reviewed.

A minimum of three fiscal years is necessary to have any indication of trends, and five years is much to be preferred. Interim statements for periods less than a fiscal year are valuable not only to provide current information between fiscal year ends, but also to indicate seasonal patterns in the statements.

Balance Sheet Analysis

The balance sheet provides a still picture of the assets, liabilities, and equity of a business enterprise at a specific moment in time. Changes in the balance sheet over a period of time are generally more important than the proportions in a single balance sheet. Generally, balance sheet analysis is devoted to the two areas of liquidity and structure.

Liquidity is generally measured by the relationship of current assets to current liabilities and the quality of the current assets. The excess of current assets over current liabilities indicates the working capital or amount of current assets being funded by equity and long-term liabilities.

Inventory and receivable turnover give an indication of the time within which these assets convert to cash. The trading cycle, consisting of the number of days of sales in receivables and inventory less the number of days of sales in trade payables, indicates the amount of working capital necessary to support a given sales volume.

It is important not to let the numeric magnitude of ratios, such as the current ratio, overly influence a loan decision. A small department store may well have a current ratio (that is, current assets to current liabilities) well in excess of two to one but have limited true liquidity, since there is usually a long trading cycle and limited fluctuations in the magnitude of inventory and receivables. A small trucking company, on the other hand, may have a current ratio of less than one to one due to significant maturities of equipment financing being included in current liabilities, but have a short trading cycle resulting in rapid turnover and significant cash flow to meet debt requirements.

Balance sheet structure deals with the overall funding of the enterprise, the relationship of total liabilities to net worth, as well as the relationship of net worth to fixed assets as the important areas. Net worth and long-term debt should fully fund fixed assets and provide some working capital for the business. As short-term debt is being used to fund fixed assets, an imbalance in financial structure exists.

The more total debt there is in relationship to net worth, the higher the company is leveraged. The degree of leverage acceptable in a particular firm depends in large part upon the nature and quality of the assets. The more volatile the assets, the less leverage that should be permitted. As leverage moves above two or three to one, there is a tendency by most lenders to think in terms of collateral for their loans. However, it is not uncommon to provide unsecured short-term financing where significant long-term financing exists covering the fixed assets. It is axiomatic that if any short-term lender is secured, an unsecured loan to the same borrower requires extremely thorough analysis and evaluation.

A quick and easy means of testing the maximum leverage that should be available to a given company is to list the assets and the normal amount that could be borrowed against each of the assets on a secured basis with the sum of these borrowings being the maximum borrowings the firm could be expected to sustain. If the aggregate of unsecured loans exceeds this amount, leverage is probably excessive and the risk is beyond the parameters for unsecured lending.

Cash Flow Analysis

The strongest support of unsecured lending is the ability of the borrower to earn profits consistently and generate cash to finance both interim needs of the business and retire debt. The primary source of cash is profits. The income statement should be scrutinized to determine that margins are adequate, that there are not excessive returns and allowances indicating potential customer dissatisfaction with product quality, and that operating expenses are reasonable. Industry comparisons are universally valuable in evaluating income statements. Robert Morris Associates, the national association of bank loan and credit officers, provides annual statement studies giving industry comparisons for a wide variety of businesses of varying sizes.

Cash, however, is produced from operations not only by profits but also by noncash expense charges such as depreciation. Net profit plus depreciation is a common definition of gross cash flow. However, it must be recognized that in periods of inflation, depreciation charges may not be adequate to replace worn-out equipment and, therefore, while earned depreciation is a source of cash flow, it may not be available for debt repayment. In looking at cash flow, it is important to recognize management's access to available cash. While dividends to shareholders may be discretionary, they cannot be long reduced or eliminated without impacting the company's ability to acquire capital. Dividend reductions or eliminations by publicly held companies are not easily accomplished. Therefore, dividend requirements frequently reduce cash flow available for other purposes.

A continuing business must regularly modernize and expand its fixed assets. Deferring of these requirements can lead to serious operational problems and, therefore, the astute lender makes a deduction from available cash flow for fixed asset replacement before determining the net amount available to repay debt.

In most businesses there is a relationship between the amount of receivables and inventory necessary to support sales. If sales grow, the dollar requirements for receivables and inventory grow. A portion of the growth may be financed by increased trade payables, but additional working capital is required to support sales growth. These funds also must be provided from gross cash flow before making debt repayments.

In addition to cash produced from operations, a firm may have additional cash flow from the disposition of unnecessary assets. There also may be additional funds available from additional borrowings. The point is that there are a multiplicity of claims for whatever cash the business produces and the lender must evaluate all of these claims in order adequately to determine what may be available to repay debt.

Knowledge of Customer

The more the lender knows about the customer and his affairs, the better the lender can prescribe proper financial solutions to the borrower's problems. Knowledge is to a large extent a function of time. It is impossible ever to obtain 100 percent knowledge about the affairs of a borrower. However, the longer the period of time over which a relationship extends, the more each party will know about the other.

There is a minimum level of knowledge which a lender must have to make an intelligent loan decision. By the mere passage of time, the lender may approach, reach, or surpass this minimum level. However, unlimited time is not always available to provide this natural route to knowledge of a borrower's affairs. The lender must take conscious steps to get to this minimum knowledge level as quickly as possible. This can be done by seeking specific information from the borrower and other sources. By obtaining adequate information, the lender is able to render the best service to his customers.

The basic data a lender needs to have about a borrower are essentially contained in the answers to three questions: (1) Who is the borrower? (2) What is the borrower's business? (3) Where has the borrower been?

Who is the borrower? What type of business entity is the borrower? Is it a sole proprietorship with one individual operating personally? Is it a partnership in which two or more individuals have joined together in a venture? Are there limited or silent partners? Is it a corporation, a legal entity established under statute? Who owns the corporation? individuals? another corporation? It is important to understand parent-subsidiary or affiliated corporate relationships. The answers to these questions pin down the fundamental question of who this borrower is.

What is the borrower's business? It is important to know whether the borrower is a retailer, wholesaler, manufacturer, or a service business. Each type of business has somewhat different characteristics and financial requirements. The source of materials and labor as well as the markets in which products are sold both bear importantly upon the financial and operating needs of a business enterprise. In order to have adequate knowledge about a borrower, the lender must understand the borrower's business.

Where has the borrower been? In order to understand the present, it is necessary to examine the past. How long the firm has been in existence and what progress has been made to date are important indicators of what can be expected in the future. The competitive status of the firm and its standing in its industry are measures of the capacity of management.

In order to project into the future, it is essential that the lender know with whom he is dealing, what the business is, where it has been, and where it is now. With this understanding it is more likely that a sound estimate can be made of where the business is going.

Fundamental Factors of Credit

The fundamental basis for extending credit is the lender's confidence in the borrower. This confidence must be developed in three areas which make up the traditional three C's of credit—Character, Capacity, and Capital. We repeat these requirements to emphasize their importance.

Character deals with the integrity of the borrower, his reputation, and his record for meeting obligations. Character is best tested by adversity. It is not difficult to avoid temptation when there is no need to stray. However, under pressure, weak character may be swayed and unethical or dishonest practices may be resorted to in a futile attempt to prevent financial difficulties.

Capacity deals with the ability of the borrower wisely to utilize the borrowed funds. Are the borrowed funds being used for a worthwhile purpose? Will the use of the borrowed funds produce future funds with which to repay the loan? Capacity includes the management ability of the borrower as reflected in his earnings record and standing in the industry in which he is engaged.

Capital strength is represented by the equity invested in the enterprise. Is it sufficient in relation to present and proposed debt? Have the owners demonstrated their confidence in the success of the enterprise by committing adequate funds of their own before seeking to borrow? Capital serves as a buffer against adversity for the lender and should be adequate in relation to the risks of the business.

Sometimes inadequacies in the equity protection for creditors can be somewhat improved by assignment of collateral. Collateral provides a specific asset or group of assets which the lender can liquidate to obtain repayment if necessary. Collateral is not a substitute for credit analysis. If a loan can only be repaid by sale of the collateral, it is better to sell the collateral at once for funds rather than borrow and have to sell the collateral in a possible adverse market at a later date.

In evaluating these credit factors, it is important to take into account the *conditions* under which the borrower is operating. Economic conditions have a direct bearing on the financial strength of business enterprises. In good times, prosperity tends to provide additional support, making it somewhat easier to meet financial obligations. The pattern of prosperity helps overcome lending mistakes. When the economy slumps, management is more critical and lending mistakes are easier to make.

The position of the individual firm and its own industry are also important. There are differences between industries. Some industries are stable, some volatile; some are growing, some are stagnant or declining. The individual firm may be well entrenched or it may be a marginal operation. All of these factors influence the conditions under which a borrower operates and have a direct bearing on the three basic credit factors.

Sources of Information

Required information can be obtained from several sources, the most important of which is the borrower. The borrower will submit financial statements and will provide considerable information about himself and his operations. As our primary source of information, the borrower will also indicate the sources from which additional data can be obtained and sources which can verify or confirm information provided by the borrower.

Obviously the loan applicant is desirous of obtaining funds and can be expected to present his situation in the most favorable light. Thus it is prudent to check and verify data provided by the borrower with others.

Bank files provide considerable data about present and past customers. Deposit activity, past borrowing record, and other information can be obtained from the bank's own records. By reviewing deposits and paid checks, it is possible to determine who the major customers and suppliers are. The bank's files may contain industrial or regional data which may be applicable to the borrower.

Other sources of information include (1) credit agencies, (2) other lenders, (3) customers, (4) suppliers, and (5) competitors. These sources can provide valuable insight into past and present performances of the borrower. They should be fully utilized to obtain important information to assist in credit analysis.

Once the information has been collected, the analytical task commences. The lender must apply his analytical skill, knowledge, and experience to the data. Important matters must be isolated from less important items. As the analysis progresses, questions may develop which should be answered by seeking additional material.

An essential trait for sound analysis is innate curiosity. The lender must constantly ask himself, why? when? where? how? An inquiring attitude is essential for an adequate understanding of the situation. With this approach, the lender demonstrates an interest in the people that the bank is serving.

Loan Agreements

An important tool in administering some loans is the loan agreement. This legal document outlines the obligations of the lender and the borrower. So long as the borrower complies with the terms, the lender is obligated to provide loans under the agreement. Such agreements may be simple or complex as the credit situation requires. Legal assistance is essential in the preparation of loan agreements.

The purpose of placing limitations on the borrower in a loan agreement is to provide some degree of control by the lender. Obviously the borrower has sufficient financial strength to support the loan at the outset. Otherwise it would not be made. However, financial strength can change. In a term loan, conditions may change before all the payments are due and payable. Therefore, the lender should have some assurance that present financial strength will be maintained.

Common loan agreement provisions will create limits within which the borrower has absolute freedom to operate. Restrictions can be exceeded with the lender's consent. Thus, if circumstances warrant, the lender, upon being consulted, can waive loan agreement provisions for specific, desirable actions. Common loan agreement provisions limit the total indebtedness the borrower may incur, limit dividends or withdrawals of equity, limit acquisitions, limit disposal or pledging of assets, require minimum net worth and working capital, and control owner-management compensation. Each loan agreement is drawn for a specific situation. Its terms and conditions should be tailored to the specific credit involved.

Through a well-drawn loan agreement a bank lender can keep informed of the borrower's progress. Submission of periodic financial statements is a basic agreement provision. In administering a loan agreement the lender can control the borrower's rate of expansion, permitting proper digestion of volume increases. At the same time, control can be exercised over dissipation of resources in side ventures. The loan agreement is a valuable administrative tool.

SUMMARY

Unsecured lending rests on the faith and understanding between the lender and borrower. A significant percentage of bank loans are made on an unsecured basis, attesting to the knowledge and confidence bankers have in their customers. No amount of desk analysis can substitute for direct personal contact with the borrower and his business. An onsight view of the premises and operations provides significant insights into the operation.

Lending money is essentially the business of taking risks. No one can consistently predict the future with certainty. Careful evaluation of the past and present can help provide a vision of the future, but it is by no means precise. Unsecured loans rest in large part upon the capacity of management to make future events work out as projected. There should always be some margin for error. Very frequently anticipations are not always fully realized.

However, careful analysis will provide an understanding of the borrower's business, and the external factors which might influence the business either positively or negatively. The bank loan officer then can make unsecured loans which will produce earnings for the bank and contribute to the economic progress of the community.

12

Seasonal Lending

Seasonal loans were the principal type of obligation that banks extended to their customers early in the nineteenth century. Most of our customers were farmers, and the seasonality of farming dictated a need for short-term loans during the planting, growing, and harvesting seasons. As banks expanded and as industries sprang up, many of the characteristics of the seasonal loan were retained in bankers' relationships with their commercial customers.

Today the seasonal loan plays a much smaller role in the overall total lending activity of banking, but it is an important one because it does affect virtually every customer who borrows from a bank.

A seasonal, or short-term, loan is one written for a specific period of time, usually less than one year. It is made to support a specific transaction and is paid from the proceeds of that transaction.

The seasonal loan that assists a customer through the trading cycle of inventory accumulation, production, sale, and the collection of receivables is the type of short-term loan bankers most frequently encounter and will be discussed in this chapter.

We should understand why the need for seasonal funds has lessened. Change has taken place in customers and banking. Industrial customers in particular have expanded their operations and invested capital in permanent facilities and have established assembly lines to take advantage of cost savings with mass production. It is difficult for manufacturing managements to justify idle capacity. As a result, most industrial and commercial customers have added product lines to take up the slack during the seasonal times of their basic manufacturing processes. And with improved transportation, better storage facilities, and modern technology, agricultural borrowers have tended to use fewer of the seasonal lines available to them.

Banks also have changed. Today commitments for mortgage loans, term loans, and revolving credit loans are heavier, in an attempt to stabilize the base of loans outstanding.

In spite of these basic changes, the short-term, seasonal loan is still an important part of the day-to-day activities of commercial banks. The short-term, seasonal loan is perhaps one of the safest loans a banker can make because its repayment comes from the liquidation of the asset that is, for example, being processed or manufactured. Nevertheless, seasonal loans are not without risk, and it is important that a bank have a full understanding of all aspects of seasonal lending to be successful at it.

Characteristics of a Seasonal Business Cycle

Let us take a look at the characteristics of a seasonal business cycle and how a bank supports it. As an example, we shall be using a manufacturer of Christmas cards, located in the upper New England states. The typical business cycle would involve the following schedules:

Task	Date
Design line	Midsummer
Freeze line, start production	February
Annual financial statements reviewed	March
Arrange for loan	March
Full production	March-November
Sample cards out	September
Reorder start	Thanksgiving
Season completed	Christmas
Collect receivables	February
Liquidation of loan	February

By midsummer each year the manufacturer must start designing his line of cards for the following year. In doing so, he and his artist must guess what people will be buying during the pre-Christmas season 18 months later.

By January or February a decision must be made to freeze the line and start production. The most important decision at this time is what products will be produced and in what quantity.

In late March financial statements are received from the accountant (year end, February 28) and the owner makes his annual visit to his banker for a seasonal loan to get him through the next manufacturing cycle.

From March through November, paper supplies are ordered, the manufacturing process begins, and the inventory accumulation begins, in anticipation of the Christmas selling season.

In September the owner begins his rounds with his samples to take orders from the various small retail stores he deals with in the New England area. Between September and Thanksgiving, orders roll in and reorders start as sales are generated throughout the retail outlets.

Christmas finally arrives and the cycle of our manufacturer has almost reached the full swing. Actually, it is not quite over, as all of the merchandise is sold on a dated basis, meaning that all receivables are due January 30, regardless of when the cards were purchased by the retail outlet.

Most of February is spent cleaning up accounts receivable, and the seasonal loan is paid back at the bank.

We have just described a standard yet somewhat short seasonal business cycle that sees a borrower purchase merchandise, produce a finished product, sell it in the market place, and collect the proceeds.

In reviewing a seasonal credit, one of the considerations is the customer's balance sheet. It is most important to remember that the balance sheet represents a single point in the business cycle, and that point may or may not be the high or low point. It is important as a lender to understand what point in the business cycle the balance sheet represents. Many financial statements are prepared when assets have shrunk or the business cycle is at its low point. Inventory taking and other accounting techniques cost less and are more accurate, and perhaps a borrower feels the balance sheet proportions may look a bit better to the banker and other creditors on that date.

In our customer's case, the fixed assets remain fairly constant, as no major purchase of equipment or expansion of plant is contemplated during the next year.

Cash balances begin to shrink as raw materials are purchased. During the period from February through December 31, inventory builds, expenses increase, and the line of credit is gradually taken down. Between December and February the inventory is turned into accounts receivable, which, at the end of the cycle, it is hoped, are turned back into cash, and the line of credit is paid down.

There are several conclusions we can draw concerning a seasonal loan: Repayment requires a successful completion of the production cycle. The source of liquidation is from the assets which are produced. If our customer can get through one season, our loan can be paid, even if the company makes no profit or sustains some losses.

Several other conclusions can be reached concerning seasonal lending: If the assets produced cannot be sold, the banker will have difficulty getting the loan paid. If the loan customer fails during the production cycle, it may be difficult or impossible to liquidate inventory in process but not completed.

Once a customer starts the annual business cycle, you will probably have to see him through it. A final point: Never agree to lend a customer a little money with the idea that you will see how he does, and then decide later whether or not you are going to lend him the rest of the money.

Analysis of a Seasonal Credit

In analyzing a seasonal loan request, it is important that we identify certain basic areas that must be covered completely before the loan request is granted. The loan officer should completely understand the operation and project of his loan customer. One should evaluate the character and ability of management. As part of the review, the loan officer should consider the financial and nonfinancial trends of the past as a basis for predicting the future of his customer. Any other seasonal considerations should be evaluated. If possible, the loan officer should identify any factors that could make the future vary from past history.

Some of the nonfinancial considerations would be: What product is going to be manufactured? Is the customer producing the same basic product line as in the past? Is he rapidly increasing production and/or introducing a new line of merchandise? A major increase in production and/or a swing into a new product line should be reviewed with caution. Can the product which is being manufactured be sold? We can make a good guess based on past performance and an analysis of the economy and the competition; however, some immediate change in the economy or the competition could have an effect on our customer.

If this is an old-line customer, we have a history of what he can and cannot do. If the customer is new in the marketplace, the loan officer must make some careful judgments concerning management and the ability to produce. Once the product is sold, will the buyer pay for the merchandise received? A review of the larger customers of our client could indicate some strengths or weaknesses and the ability of those people to pay.

Note that important parts of our analysis precede a look at the financial statement, and that awareness of the history of our customers combined with our understanding of how new events will affect the future are primary.

The most important element is the management. A banker cannot really judge the best product mix, but he can judge people by evaluating their best performance, plans for the future, and response to questions.

In order to be as thorough as possible, it might be well for the loan officer to work from a check list. Pertinent items to be considered are the *nature of the request,* for instance, a line of credit to be paid in full at the end of the customer's business cycle, and the *purpose of the loan,* which might be to carry a seasonal build-up of inventory and the receivables with the understanding that the source of repayment will be the liquidation of the assets produced.

The banker should know what his customer manufactures, how he sells his product, and whether he is capable of producing it. A thorough understanding of management is vital; bankers make loans to people, not to financial statements. Careful consideration should be given to the reliability of the information on which we are basing our decisions. For this reason, an unqualified opinion from an accountant whose work is known to the bank is important and should be mandatory if a loan represents a significant amount in relationship to the bank's capital.

If sales increase, the borrower will need more inventory to support them, and there will be more receivables to collect. At some point a customer may outgrow his plant and more fixed assets will be required. Thus, more sales will eventually require more assets. If net worth does not grow in proportion, it means that the banker will be lending more in proportion to net worth as sales volume grows.

It may be important to request quarterly and maybe even monthly financial statements, depending upon the size of the customer. A financial statement at the end of the business cycle presents a picture that will change drastically through the cycle. A quarterly statement will give information regarding progress as your customer moves through the business cycle.

The borrower's assets are your source of repayment and you should spend considerable time evaluating their quality. In a seasonal credit, two areas would be paramount to review: inventory and accounts receivable. The relationship of fixed assets to capital and planned expansions will determine how much time is necessary to spend reviewing those assets. First, let us check inventory; if it is stale or contains a poor mix of products, it will not sell and you will not get paid. Certainly, a review of ratios such as inventory to cost of goods sold will help. However, a walk through the shop and warehouse, with some experience, will tell a surprising amount about a company's inventory. Accounts receivable ought to be reviewed in detail. Here again, a balance sheet ratio of receivables to sales could give you a clue. However, a copy of receivables aging would allow you to spot delinquencies and concentrations. Additional credit checks could be made on these particular customers if there is a concern regarding payment.

Management must be questioned concerning accounts payable and any other debt. The flexibility that accounts payable play in the average business is significant. The banker should be assured that relationships with suppliers are good and that credit is available. A review of terms and covenants of any other obligations would be in order.

Next, we should turn our attention to profits. If we are interested in a long-term relationship, the banker should spend some time reviewing profitability, even though the customer could pay the loan in a loss year. The banker should be interested in companies with good earnings records, and loans to companies with spotty earnings records should be approached with caution.

How to Make the Loan

We now proceed to structure a loan that is satisfactory to the borrower and the bank. As indicated earlier, we must approve a line of credit that covers our customer's maximum requirements rather than just a portion of those requirements. Typically, we might lend on a revolving credit, a demand note, or a 90-day note, depending on the convenience and needs of both parties. A 90-day note would force the banker and the customer to meet on a quarterly basis to review the current situation and any major changes that have occurred since the line was approved.

Whether or not you take collateral depends on the risk you see in the credit. A loan of this type would generally be secured by inventory, accounts receivable, and a personal guarantee of the owner.

During the life of the loan it is important for the banker to recognize what kind of collateral he really has. Inventory and work in process probably could not readily be turned into cash. If you get stuck halfway through the season, it is difficult to rely on the value of this collateral to liquidate the loan. On the other hand, inventory will normally turn into receivables and those receivables into cash over a relatively short period of time. Toward the end of the business cycle, the loan outstanding should be comfortably secured by accounts receivable and you would have an excellent chance of a payoff if there is a deterioration in the company then. The time to get out of a credit is at the seasonal low, when the collateral value is at its maximum.

Following the Credit

The degree of control required on a seasonal loan varies with the degree of risk. A few loans are put on the books and left unattended for twelve months. A few credits will require substantial reviews of inventory and accounts receivable on a monthly basis. Some loan officers believe that interim information is a waste of time, since you can never really gauge how the borrower is doing until the season is over. In any event, you do want to keep track of asset and liability build-ups, and quarterly figures help. In more sensitive cases, we like to look at monthly data on receivables, inventory, bank debts, payables, and sales. This information is particularly useful when it is compared with either the prior years' performance, or better yet, your customer's projections. Such study takes only a small amount of time and can help you anticipate and prevent serious problems in the future.

It is valuable to remember that many things happen in a business that do not show up on the balance sheet: production problems, lack of sales, and other problems of this nature would be difficult to discover from a balance sheet. It is desirable for the loan officer to call on his customer several times during the year to see for himself if plans are progressing as anticipated.

What to Do When It Does Not Work

There are two basic ways that the seasonal short-term loan can go wrong: first, the customer requires more money to complete the cycle or, in rare instances, he cannot finish it at all; second, the customer finishes the cycle, but cannot make a payout at the seasonal low point.

The first problem is a difficult one. It is not easy to say no to a request for more funds to finish goods, since they are basically worthless to both the borrower and the lender until they are in a finished state. Nevertheless, look over this request carefully before you decide. There is no point in throwing good money after bad. Your decision may depend on where the customer is in the manufacturing cycle. It may be that if he is beginning the manufacturing cycle, other difficulties or problems are on the horizon, and you are better off to pull the plug and liquidate. It is also possible that your customer is close to finishing the product, has a ready market, and is just a short step from turning raw materials into sales, accounts receivable, and cash.

We said that a source of credit is accounts payable. Theoretically, our customer could let the payment of his payables slide from 30 days to 90 days, thus tripling the funds available from this source.

Several other options are available. If fixed assets are of sufficient value, additional funds could be lent, secured by those fixed assets. Additional capital may also be injected by the owner, if available. It is also possible that another banker or a commercial financial company would be willing to bail you out. At the high point, it usually makes sense to help the customer finish the cycle. Make sure the borrower is honest. Do not worry if the customer cannot clear the line of credit for the right reasons. Worry a great deal if the customer cannot clear the line of credit for the wrong reasons. If you do wish to get out of the credit, be a tiger at the low point. Be willing to send your customer to another lender if you feel you do not wish to continue the credit.

CONCLUSION

We have seen the importance for a seasonal loan of those items which show up on the balance sheet, as well as those that do not. We have seen how the mechanics of repayment, that is, asset liquidation, can make this one of the safest loans if we are careful. However, we need to understand how saleable our customer's product is and what his statement will look like at the high point, because it might worry us a great deal when first reviewed. And, we have seen that once you take off on the seasonal flight with a customer, it is rather difficult to get off until you are back on the ground. Perhaps the most important things we have learned are the need for a full understanding of the business and an evaluation of the customer.

We have also seen that even after the loan is on the books, we must continue to watch it closely, in order to take prompt action if problems develop.

Finally, it would be wise policy never to make a loan unless we know how we are going to collect it if everything turns sour.

13

Agricultural Credit

The principles underlying the extension of agricultural loans are similar to those in the granting of any other type of credit. Differences come in administration, owing to several unique features of agriculture. Generally, agriculture is an individual and a family enterprise, although corporate ownership is increasing. Control of all the assets is in the hands of a husband and wife, or perhaps a son or son-in-law is included in the operation. The organization can be a proprietorship, partnership, or corporation. Any of the organizations can be equally financed. Depending on the form, various statements of documentation are necessary. Tax purposes, estate planning, desire to limit liability, and other reasons determine the organizational form adopted by a certain enterprise. Agriculture is a capital-intensive industry: A tremendous amount of capital is required, including land and machinery, in relation to annual sales and net income. Costs of production in relation to gross income continue to increase. In 1980 it took $.90 in operating expense to produce $1 of income. In 1947 it took $.72; in 1927, $.65; and in 1907, $.44. Farming and ranching is no longer a matter of hard work but more a matter of smart business and managerial ability. Agricultural prices are very elastic. A slightly larger production will bring prices down drastically, and conversely a slightly smaller production will cause prices to skyrocket.

The supply/demand factor is very sensitive. Since most agricultural products are highly perishable, a quantity cannot be held from market for great periods of time to allow prices to adjust upward. Farm products generally require time to increase production in response to higher price levels. Grains and vegetables take a summer season from spring to fall. Animals, fruits, and nuts take more than one year due to their physiological makeup. A uniqueness of agricultural products and their value as collateral is the fact that there is always a ready market for them. Marketing of agricultural products has various forms—individually through cooperatives, direct sales, indirect sales, through terminal markets, and marketing go-betweens. Size of operations continues to increase, while the numbers involved in production are decreasing and stand at less than 3 million units. They continue to drop each year.

Agricultural credit is measured in terms of the maturity of the loan. There are three major categories of agricultural credit. Short-term loans are usually due and payable within 12 months and are used for the production expenses necessary to get the product ready for market. They are repaid from the sale of assets which the loan proceeds helped produce. Intermediate-term credit is generally 2 to 10 years in maturity repayable on an amortized basis, generally annually. Proceeds of these loans would be for the purchase of depreciable assets such as breeding stock, machinery, and equipment. These loans are repaid from the profits generated from the operation of the farm or ranch. Long-term credit is from 10 to 40 years repaid on an annual amortization basis and again from the profits generated from the operation.

Tools of Agricultural Loans

Again agricultural credit is not unique. The application for credit identifies the applicant and the type of business organization. It would include the purpose of the loan, when it will be repaid, and the primary as well as the secondary source of repayment. The loan officer should include his compelling factors and unfavorable factors as well in his loan analysis as they are determined during the interview and subsequent analysis.

PROPERTY STATEMENT

One of the more important credit documents is the property statement or balance sheet (Figure 1) of the credit applicant. The assets are listed in the order of their liquidity, from cash to land, which generally would not be sold unless the entity went out of business. The assets are further categorized into: (1) current assets—cash and near cash, that is, accounts receivable, grains, and livestock that are to be sold within 12 months and other assets that likewise will be converted to cash within one year; (2) intermediate assets—those that will not be sold or converted to cash within 12 months and are generally of a depreciable nature, that is, machinery, equipment, and breeding stock; (3) long-term assets—those assets used to produce products to be sold each year and have a useful life in excess of ten years or will not be converted to cash during the ordinary course of business or until after 10 years, that is, land and buildings.

The liability section of the balance sheet includes all of the indebtedness the entity is obligated to pay. Liabilities are listed in order of the maturity and order of payment in regard to due date. Current liabilities are those that are to be repaid within the next 12 months. Intermediate liabilities are those due within 13 months to ten years and generally are due to the purchase of intermediate term assets. Long-term liabilities are due after ten years and are generally against the land used in the agricultural operation.

Net worth is the resultant difference between the total assets and the total liabilities as listed. Thus, net worth, the amount the owner has in his operation, and liabilities, the amount his creditors have in his operation, will equal the financial assets he has at his disposal.

This balance sheet is to be prepared by the borrower on an annual basis. It should be prepared at the same time each year so a measurement of the financial progress of the operation can be determined by comparison with previously submitted statements. Generally, current assets are listed at market value, intermediate at the depreciated basis, and long-term at market less applicable sales expense and income tax considerations upon sale. If assets are carried at comparable figures year after year, a simple comparison of net worth will reflect financial progress or the lack thereof. Current market values make the comparison as a determinant of profit more difficult. However, in most agricultural operations, the profits are maintained in additional inventories, equipment, or land, not necessarily cash or cash equivalents.

Balance sheet analysis includes working capital, the difference between current assets and current liabilities. This is the amount of assets that provide a cushion for short-term creditors. An acceptable current ratio would be 1.5:1 or greater. Liabilities to net worth is considered another factor of balance sheet analysis. Here a ratio of 1.5:1 would be considered acceptable. Anything greater than that would cause concern for the lender as well as the borrower since the larger debt service would be a deterrent to the sound operation of the entity and ample retainage of income for continued operation.

CASH FLOW

A cash flow statement (Figure 2) merely presents on an expected or budgeted basis periodic income and expenses. The period usually is a month but may be a quarter. The statement shows total income and total expense per month, with the difference being the net cash flow. If it is positive, then debt can be repaid; if negative, new debt must be arranged. The cash flow presentation to the lender will determine the total amount of a line of credit that must be provided for the continuous operation of the entity. A negative cash flow for an operating season means that the operation may be unprofitable if inven-

Figure 1

THE OMAHA NATIONAL BANK   STOCKMAN
                                                                                                            OR
                                                                                                        FARMER

FROM _____ ADDRESS _____

TO _____

FOR THE PURPOSE OF OBTAINING LOANS AND DISCOUNTING PAPER WITH YOU, AND OTHERWISE PROCURING CREDIT FROM TIME TO TIME, I FURNISH YOU WITH THE
FOLLOWING STATEMENT AND INFORMATION, WHICH IS A TRUE AND CORRECT STATEMENT OF MY FINANCIAL CONDITION ON _____ 19 ____

I AGREE TO AND WILL NOTIFY YOU IMMEDIATELY IN WRITING OF ANY MATERIALLY UNFAVORABLE CHANGE IN MY FINANCIAL CONDITION, AND IN THE ABSENCE OF SUCH NOTICE, OR OF A NEW
AND FULL WRITTEN STATEMENT, THIS MAY BE CONSIDERED AS A CONTINUING STATEMENT AND SUBSTANTIALLY CORRECT; AND IT IS HEREBY EXPRESSLY AGREED THAT UPON APPLICATION FOR
FURTHER CREDIT, THIS STATEMENT SHALL HAVE THE SAME FORCE AND EFFECT AS IF DELIVERED AS AN ORIGINAL STATEMENT OF MY FINANCIAL CONDITION AT THE TIME SUCH FURTHER CREDIT
REQUESTED.

(FILL ALL BLANKS, WRITING "NO" OR "NONE" WHERE NECESSARY TO COMPLETE INFORMATION)

ASSETS				LIABILITIES	
CASH IN BANK			$	UNSECURED INDEBTEDNESS TO BANKS	$
SAVINGS OR C.D.					
GOVERNMENT BONDS				SECURED DEBTS ON LIVESTOCK TO BANK	
LISTED SECURITIES * (LIST ON BACK)					
CASH SURRENDER LIFE INSURANCE				DEBTS ON MACHINERY TO BANK (CURRENT PORTION)	
ACCOUNTS RECEIVABLE & GOVT PAYMENTS					
	AVG. WT.	PRICE PER HEAD		LIENS ON FARM IMPLEMENTS & AUTOMOTIVE EQUIPMENT	
COWS				TO DEALERS & OTHERS (CURRENT PORTION)	
HEIFERS 2 YRS. OLD BRED OPEN FD LOT					
HEIFERS 1 YR. OLD BRED OPEN FD LOT				OTHER LOANS	
HEIFERS - CALVES					
BULLS					
STEERS 2 YRS OLD RANGE FEED LOT				CCC LOANS	
STEERS 1 YR. OLD					
STEER CALVES				ENDORSEMENTS & GUARANTEES FOR OTHERS	
STEERS - FEED LOT					
BREEDING HOGS				LIFE INS. LOAN	
FAT HOGS & PIGS				ACCOUNTS PAYABLE	
RANGE SHEEP				INTEREST PAYABLE	
FEED LOT LAMBS				REAL ESTATE TAXES	
FEED AND GRAIN				REAL ESTATE PAYMENT (CURRENT PORTION)	
				PERSONAL TAXES	
HAY AND ROUGHAGE				INCOME TAXES	
				LEASE PAYMENTS	
OTHER FEED				ALL OTHER DEBTS	
FERTILIZER & CHEMICALS					
OTHER				TOTAL CURRENT LIABILITIES	
TOTAL CURRENT ASSETS					
GROWING CROPS ACRES OF			DO NOT INCLUDE ESTIMATED VALUE		
GROWING CROPS ACRES OF				TERM DEBT ON MACHINERY & EQUIPMENT	
OTHER INVESTMENTS (ITEMIZE ON BACK)					
FARM IMPLEMENTS					
AUTOMOTIVE EQUIPMENT * (LIST ON BACK)				TERM DEBT ON REAL ESTATE	
IMPROVEMENTS * (LIST ON BACK)					
HOMESTEAD (LEGAL DESCRIPTION) * (LIST ON BACK)					
OTHER REAL ESTATE				TOTAL LIABILITIES	
OTHER ASSETS OR INVESTMENTS				NET WORTH	
TOTAL ASSETS				TOTAL	

(FILL IN ALL BLANKS AND SIGN ON REVERSE SIDE)
(OVER)

C.C. 132

FARM IMPLEMENTS AND AUTOMOTIVE EQUIPMENT

MAKE AND TYPE	YEAR	MODEL	COST	PRESENT VALUE	LIEN:
			$	$	$
IF ADEQUATE SPACE NOT PROVIDED ABOVE, ATTACH SCHEDULE		TOTALS	$	$	$

REAL ESTATE SCHEDULE

ACRES	LEGAL DESCRIPTION (show county and state)	TITLE IN	VALUE	LIENS	NATURE OF IMPROVEMENTS
			$	$	$
IF ADEQUATE SPACE NOT PROVIDED ABOVE, ATTACH SCHEDULE		TOTALS	$	$	$

OTHER INVESTMENTS

STOCKS	VALUE	STOCKS		VALUE
	$			$
OTHER		OTHER		
	$			$
			TOTAL	$

TAXES PAID TO _____ 19 _____   MORTGAGE INTEREST PAID TO _____ 19 _____
(DATE)   (DATE)

I HAVE UNDER LEASE _____ ACRES OF LAND IN _____
(COUNTY AND STATE)

THE RENTAL PRICE BEING $ _____ PER ACRE WHICH HAS BEEN PAID TO _____ 19 _____

HAVE YOU ANY PARTNERS IN YOUR BUSINESS? _____ IF SO, STATE PARTICULARS _____

HAVE YOU EVER BEEN ADJUDGED A BANKRUPT? _____ IF SO, STATE PARTICULARS _____

JUDGMENTS OR SUITS PENDING AGAINST ME AT THIS TIME $ _____ STATE PARTICULARS _____

LIFE INSURANCE $ _____ PAYABLE TO _____ IS THE RIGHT TO CHANGE BENEFICIARY RESERVED? _____

INSURANCE ON: BUILDINGS $ _____ GRAIN $ _____ LIVE STOCK $ _____ MACHINERY AND AUTOMOTIVE EQUIPMENT $ _____

I HAVE RESIDED AT PRESENT LOCATION _____ YEARS _____ MONTHS. FORMERLY RESIDED _____

I HAVE READ THE ABOVE STATEMENT, BOTH WRITTEN AND PRINTED, BEFORE SIGNING, AND IT IS CORRECT. _____

DATED AT _____ THIS _____ DAY OF _____ 19 _____

BEFORE SIGNING, SEE THAT ALL QUESTIONS HAVE BEEN ANSWERED AND ALL BLANKS FILLED.

WITNESS:

_____   (SIGNED) _____

_____   AGE _____ YEARS. MARRIED OR SINGLE _____

SUBSCRIBED AND SWORN TO BEFORE ME THIS _____ DAY OF _____ 19 _____

_____

(NOTARY PUBLIC IN AND FOR _____.)

(SEAL)

WE HEREBY CERTIFY THAT THE FOREGOING IS A TRUE AND CORRECT COPY OF A SIGNED FINANCIAL STATEMENT OF THE ABOVE MENTIONED INDIVIDUAL, FIRM OR CORPORATION NOW ON FILE IN THIS BANK, AND THAT, TO THE BEST OF OUR KNOWLEDGE AND BELIEF, THIS STATEMENT REFLECTS THE TRUE CONDITION OF THE BORROWER.

(NAME OF BANK) _____

(OFFICIAL SIGNATURE) _____
(TITLE)

Figure 2

CASH FLOW PLANNING FORM

Date Completed _____

Do in pencil
Round to dollars

Name _____
Address _____

CASH FLOW IN	1.	Beginning Cash Balance					
		Operating Sales					
	2.	Crops					
	3.	Livestock & Livestock Products					
	4.						
	5.	Other (Custom Work, Govt. Pmts., etc.)					
		Capital Sales					
	6.	Breeding Livestock					
	7.	Machinery & Equipment					
	8.						
	9.	Other					
	10.	Non-farm Income					
	11.	**TOTAL CASH AVAILABLE (Add lines 1 thru 10)**					
CASH FLOW OUT		**Operating Expense**					
	12.	Labor Hired					
	13.	Repairs & Maintenance					
	14.	Rents & Leases					
	15.	Feed Purchased					
	16.	Seeds & Plants					
	17.	Fertilizer, Lime & Chemicals					
	18.	Machine Hire					
	19.	Supplies					
	20.	Livestock Expense (Breeding, Vet, etc.)					
	21.	Gas, Fuel, Oil					
	22.	Storage, Warehousing					
	23.	Taxes (Real Estate & Pers. Property)					
	24.	Insurance (Property, Liability, Hail)					
	25.	Utilities (Electricity, Telephone)					
	26.	Freight & Trucking					
	27.	Auto (if not included in other items)					
	28.						
	29.	Feeder Livestock (purchased for resale)					
	30.	Miscellaneous					
		Capital Expense					
	31.	Breeding Livestock					
	32.	Machinery					
	33.						
	34.	Other					
	35.	Family Living Expense					
	36.	Income Tax & Social Security					
	37.	Fixed Term Loan Payments Due — Principal					
	38.	— Interest					
	39.	**TOTAL CASH REQUIRED (Add lines 12 thru 38)**					
SUMMARY	40.	CASH AVAILABLE less CASH REQUIRED (11-39)					
	41.	Money to Be Borrowed (if line 40 is negative)					
	42.	Debt Payments (if line 40 is positive) — Principal					
		Interest					
	43.						
	44.	Ending Cash Balance					
	45.	**OPERATING LOAN BALANCE (at End of Period)**					

tory does not increase. Enterprise cash flow on each individual enterprise may help determine the losers that should then be dealt with in more detail. The cash flow helps the lender to establish a line of credit available to the borrower, helps him budget and arrange for lendable dollars to fund loans, and determine the repayment plan. Agriculture lends itself to cash flow lending quite well since funds are used for production of a product and repayments come when the product is ready for market and sold. The cash flow statement also lends itself to a comparison of actual income and expenses with the original projections—after the completion of the period, usually one year or a full season. Assumptions used in individual income items must be given so the lender may be able to judge the validity thereof. Depreciation and other noncash items are not included in the cash flow. Only those items are included that require expenditures of cash and which develop cash inflow.

PROFIT AND LOSS STATEMENT

The profit and loss statement is developed at the end of the operating cycle and is the measure of actual income and expenses. Increases or decreases in inventory by addition to beginning inventory and deduction of ending inventory plus noncash items, such as depreciation, are included in the profit and loss statement but are not included in the cash flow statement. Most farm operations keep their income and expense records on a cash flow basis, taking into consideration only the receipt or expenditure of cash. For Internal Revenue Service purposes, the cash method of accounting is acceptable, in most cases, for reporting Federal income taxes. The categories of income and expense should match the categories included in the cash flow so a comparative analysis can be made. Both positive and negative variations need to be explored to determine the reasons for them. Again enterprise accounting and a profit and loss statement for each enterprise would be helpful to both producer and lender to identify profit makers and losers.

COMPARATIVE ANALYSIS SPREAD

Most lenders will include in the credit file on agricultural borrowers a spread sheet of balance sheet and profit and loss statements. Individual items of these accounting reports are recorded in columns so a comparison is possible for any number of years. Trends in various items can be readily seen and analyzed. For example, are liabilities increasing faster than net worth, or are current liabilities increasing faster than current assets?

Trends in working capital, liabilities, and net worth are most important. These ratios determine the financial progress or the lack thereof. Negative trends should be discussed immediately with the borrower. He must know what makes him a better borrower and what causes him to be a poorer credit risk—for instance, purchasing intermediate or fixed assets from working capital or short-term borrowing can cause the short-term lender concern because his equity position has been eroded. A constant increase in the debt to worth ratio concerns lenders and should also concern borrowers. Additional debt growth over and above net worth growth creates additional debt service, both interest and principal, and therefore requires additional net income. If the cash flow does not materialize as expected, then debt service becomes difficult and can lead to loan delinquencies and negative credit ratings. It is far better for the borrower to discuss purchases or changes in the operation before the fact rather than later and then find his credit has been put into jeopardy because of his actions.

All of the previously described tools of loan analysis have been objective in nature. As with any credit decision, subjective material needs consideration. Most of the subjective information can only be gleaned from personal conversations with the applicant, a visit to his operation, and character and credit checks with trade suppliers and other creditors. Personal credit references can expose a great deal about character and habits. Previous dealings with creditors and trade suppliers likewise reveal credit handling in the past.

The Farm or Ranch Visit

Perhaps the single most important factor in loan analysis is an on-site visit by the lender. Information can be gleaned, such as the state of housekeeping of the farmstead, machinery and equipment, land and facilities, livestock, crops, and grains. The visiting official should be familiar with the assets as reported on the balance sheet. He can verify the quantity, quality, and values as placed by the borrower in the financial statement presented with his credit request. Knowledge by the official of the value of equipment, livestock, grain, and other feed stuffs is very important. Some knowledge of animal husbandry and agronomy is helpful to be able to judge the borrower's abilities in crop production and soil and livestock management. The signs of a poor operator are readily apparent. A poor manager is exposed in the financial analysis but also is exposed in the farm or ranch visit. There is such a thing as being a good operator but not a good manager. He can be an excellent producer but very poor in marketing or financing and can turn out to be unsuccessful in the long run.

Verification of assets which will be taken as collateral for the loan can be determined on the visit. The borrower is on his home ground rather than the lender's office and therefore much more at ease and able to express himself. In fact, he is proud to show off his operation to the visitor. There is also the opportunity to see him in the act of managing people and assets.

Negative items which would count against the applicant would be excessive death loss and poor performance in animal production, poor agronomy practices, including the improper use of chemicals, herbicides, insecticides, and fertilizers, and equipment and facilities in disrepair. Excessive evidence of these negative factors should lead to a turndown of the credit application. A poor operator manager generally turns out to be a less favorable borrower, with the risk factors being in excess of what the lender is willing to accept. The visit then is both objective (an audit function) as well as subjective in nature.

Upon the return to the lending institution, the official must start the process of loan analysis, weighing the financial data, the farm or ranch visit, and the apparent risks in the financing request. Risks are inherent in every phase of lending. However, in agriculture some additional risk must be identified, the degree determined, and to what degree the risk can be minimized or eliminated. Risks such as hail, drought, and destruction by natural causes in relation to crops and intermediate and fixed assets can be insured against by a third party. Good farming practices, ground preparation, cultivation and harvest, correct type of seed for the climate and conditions of the region, application of fertilizer, chemicals and irrigation, and proper storage management of the harvested crop can diminish to a great degree the risks that are passed on to the lender through the borrower. Marketing risks can be minimized using several techniques to be discussed later in this chapter.

When and where insurance is appropriate, it should be requested and assigned to the lender. If a claim is filed, the claim proceeds will flow to the lender. The Federal Crop Insurance Corporation writes coverage which can be assigned as collateral through the United States Department of Agriculture. Private insurance companies also write insurance on livestock, grain, equipment, and buildings. The more of these risks that can be laid off, the less risk that the borrower assumes and the safer the loan to the lender. The amount of risk that cannot be reduced by other means generally determines the amount of down payment, equity, or margin to be required of the borrower for the benefit of the lender to cover the exposure in regards to the uncovered risks. The margins can generally range from 10 percent on grain that has market risk and hazard risk eliminated to 40 percent on high-expense specialty crops and breeding livestock. Animals for meat production would normally require a 25 percent equity position. Intermediate- and long-term assets, machinery and equipment, land, and buildings would normally require a 10 to 30 percent equity.

Leasing of intermediate-term assets has grown substantially during the past ten years. Credit decisions to be made by the lessors are equal in all respects to the decision to lend the money on an installment loan or conditional sales contract. Differences in accounting by the lender, including the ability to keep investment tax credit and depreciation, make the net interest charge somewhat less to the lessee and important when the lessor can more readily use the tax advantage than can the lessee. Those in a higher tax bracket can use the advantages better than those in a lower bracket. Generally it would be up to the user of the equipment to determine the advantages and decide on leasing or financing. The credit decisions remain the same for the lessor and lender. Special care in determining residuals must be exercised so that at the expiration of the lease, the asset is worth that much or more so no loss is taken on the transaction. The property generally reverts back to the lessor or an option to purchase by the lessee can be offered.

Marketing of Farm Products

Effective marketing by producers can eliminate some of the risk of lenders. Most agriculture products are sold on the open market. Several methods can be employed, including: (1) forward contracting; (2) futures hedging; (3) direct selling; (4) terminal markets; and (5) auctions. The first two instances allow for pricing the product prior to having the product ready for market. The remaining methods necessitate the product being in a marketable condition.

Forward Contracting. The seller can price his produce in anticipation of delivery when it is ready for market. The buyer and seller will agree on a fixed price and fixed quantity to be delivered at a future date, and the financial strength of the forward contract purchaser to fulfill his obligation. An advantage is the fixing of the price.

Futures hedging is done on a formal basis with a recognized public futures trading exchange, for example, the Chicago Board of Trade or Chicago Mercantile Exchange. Here the seller can pick the time and price at which he will sell for future delivery, or at least the future price. A third party, a broker, is necessary to complete the transaction. Advantages include the fact that delivery is not necessary providing the contract is lifted or bought back before the delivery date specified. If the quantity and date of delivery cannot be met, then the position can be lifted and delivery is not necessary. Disadvantages include a good faith deposit that must be placed with the brokerage house. No deposit is required in the forward contracting method. Any changes in the market against one's position must be met with additional "margin calls" or additional deposits. Therefore, additional funds may need to be loaned to keep the borrower's position in place in order that his position not be involuntarily removed, creating a loss of all previously deposited funds.

Direct selling allows the buyer to bid on the product while it is still in the hands of the producer. A prime example would be a packer/buyer coming to the feedlot and negotiating the price. The seller has the right to reject the bid and it costs him nothing in the way of transportation or commissions for going to market and having to return the livestock to the feed yard.

Although *terminal market selling* has diminished in the past 20 years, it is still used by smaller operations. The product must be moved to market and it is sold for the best bid received by the commission man to whom the product has been consigned.

Auction markets continue to be a very viable marketing alternative. Any number of buyers bid against each other for the product and it goes to the highest bidder. Competitive bidding should bring the top price of the market at the time. Some negatives to this type of marketing include the fact that the product must be transported to the auction area and generally one must sell for the top bid, over which one has little control. The seller must take the price offered.

Legal Instruments

As with any other type of credit being extended by a lending institution, a promissory note must be executed by the borrower. No special note forms are necessary. Amount, due date, and stated interest rate in percentage form are necessary. If it is corporate or partnership indebtedness, then appropriate authorization instruments are necessary to document the authority of the signing parties to procure funds and execute debt instruments. Almost all jurisdictions are now covered under the Uniform Commercial Code in respect to taking collateral. A financing statement listing the collateral given for the loan, and signed by the borrower, and filed with the appropriate public official, according to each state's law, constitutes public notice. The execution of the security agreement outlines the specific collateral and rights given to the lender as a secured party. Farm products are generally treated differently than inventory for a commercial business. The lending officials should be cognizant of the procedure and methods in order to perfect the security interest so it will stand up against the defenses placed if legal action becomes necessary. These are the required collateral instruments for personal property, equipment and farm products, livestock, crops, and grain inventories.

Real estate mortgages and/or deeds of trust continue to be the proper instruments for real property. They likewise would be filed with the authorities, usually the register of deeds in the county where the property is located.

A search of government records for prior liens on property offered for collateral is essential. A lender should generally not be satisfied with anything less than a first lien position. Split line credit, financing with more than one short-term lender for crop or livestock production, should be avoided since neither lender has complete control over the total short-term credit extensions. Other lenders on an intermediate or term basis are acceptable since they will have collateral different from the short-term lender, who would be interested primarily in short-term or current assets.

C's of Agricultural Credit

Most lenders have their criteria for lending which include both subjectivity and objectivity. The application of the following six C's of credit, as they apply especially to agricultural credit, and a positive answer to each can help in making a better lending decision: (1) Character—probably the most important since the borrower is the one who is utilizing the funds and must return them at the time previously designated. (2) Capacity—this includes the capabilities of the agriculturalist. Does he have the ability to handle the size and kind of operation that he is proposing for financing or is he biting off more than he can chew. In some instances a successful operator and manager of a small operation will fail if he moves the size and scope of his operation up in order to achieve the efficiency of scale generally expected. (3) Capital is the amount of working assets the operator has under his control, owned or leased. Are these assets sufficient for an efficient operation and ample enough to provide an adequate net income to sustain his financial needs? (4) Conditions—the agriculturalist and the agricultural lender must be cognizant of conditions such as weather, markets, governmental influences, new technology, anything that has an influence on the production and product. Conditions create risks and likewise opportunities, and one must be flexible enough to capitalize on such changes. (5) Collateral—the loan should not be made strictly with the thought that the creditor must liquidate the security in order to pay the indebtedness it secures. Normally lenders are poorer liquidators than are borrowers or owners of the collateral. It is, however, important to take security even though repossession and sale are the last resort for payment. Collateral is important in the case of bankruptcy or other litigation against the borrower. (6) Communication—the two-way dialogue between borrower and lender. Prior knowledge by the lender will keep him from becoming nervous at any sign of something out of the ordinary. The borrower likewise is entitled to know of any change in previous plans.

Management Ability

During the past 25 years, technological progress has changed the degree of management expertise necessary on the part of the owner/operator. Purchased inputs including mechanization, hybrid seeds, herbicides, pesticides, commercial fertilizer, and marketing stretched out over the entire year have brought about the need of the operator/manager role. On operations grossing a half million dollars or more, most of the agriculturalist's time will be spent on management and supervising hired labor. More and more producers have a four-year degree from a state agricultural college. A number of them may also have a business degree from a state university. Farming and ranching is no longer just "a way of life." With fewer than 2.8 million farmers and ranchers, each one is producing for himself and 80 other people, plus exporting to the far corners of the earth.

Management is the important ingredient that combines physical assets, risks, and capital to cover these costs, plus profit for future expansion. Without proper management, assets and capital will dissipate in short order.

Because of this increase in management expertise on the part of the farmer and rancher, the lender must make sure he likewise grows in knowledge and ability. This requires continuing education on the part of the loan officer and the management of the lending institution to understand technological changes within the agricultural industry.

Sound administration of agricultural credit, both from the lender and the borrower's point of view, is important since much of the wealth of the country is derived from the soil. The independence of the individual operator/manager has been a fact since the beginning of America. Since this country is the breadbasket of the world, the sound financial administration of agricultural credit is of the utmost importance to the world, country, community and the lending institution. Agriculture is made up of three main facets, production, marketing, and financing. Without the correct blend, the operation is destined for failure.

14

Commodity Loans

There are two types of commodity loans, secured and unsecured. The purpose of this chapter is to discuss the secured loan, as the unsecured loan should be extended only to the largest and most creditworthy companies.

In this discussion the lending function is divided into the following phases:

1. Value of collateral
2. Proper margin
3. Proper control documents
4. Uniform Commercial Code
5. Governmental policies
6. Conclusion

Collateral Value

Most commodity firms are highly leveraged and have enough working capital to carry only minimum levels of inventory without the use of debt. A commodity loan, however, is essentially a self-liquidating transaction, and therefore the risk is not as great as it would seem. Since the loan cannot be repaid until the collateral is sold, it is vital to know the value of the collateral, which is usually in the form of either inventory or accounts receivable.

When considering inventory collateral, one must keep in mind the distinct difference between the value of inventory which is sold in the ordinary course of business and that which is sold by the lender to liquidate a loan. The concept of collateral values and required margin are closely intertwined, but collateral value must be reliably established before the correct amount of margin can be determined. The spot market is probably most used to value collateral, as it reflects the price for immediate delivery of the commodity.

The futures market can also be used to value collateral. However, when using the futures market to determine the value of a commodity, keep in mind that the futures contract is for a particular grade of the commodity delivered at a certain designated point at a specified time. Additionally, the seller has the option of delivering certain other grades at premiums or discounts based on market differences for such grades prevailing at designated spot markets. The demand and supply for the different grades at the various locations are influenced by many factors. Therefore, the relationship between the price for a particular grade at a particular location and the futures price is constantly changing. This difference is called the "basis," and simply stated is the difference between the spot price for the particular grade at the particular place and the current futures price. When using the futures market to value commodities, always keep in mind the "basis" and use it correctly.

A third method of valuing collateral is to use the sale by the borrower for future delivery of the physical or actual commodity. In this case, the borrower has determined an exact value for the collateral by finding a buyer willing to pay a specific price for the delivery of the commodity to a designated place at a specified time. In using this method the lender should remember to deduct carrying charges, such as transportation, storage, insurance, and interest costs to the delivery date, from the value of the collateral. This approach should be used only to value collateral which has been sold but not yet delivered.

Usually, inventory collateral is represented by negotiable warehouse receipts or some other type of title document. One of the things that must be considered when valuing collateral covered by warehouse receipts is accrued storage. In some instances, no storage charges are paid until the goods are shipped from the warehouse. Other warehouses require storage charges to be paid on a monthly or quarterly basis. If the collateral has been in storage for a long period of time, the warehouseman's charges could be considerable. A lender should determine what the accrued storage is and deduct it from the value assigned to the collateral, as the warehouseman has a lien on the goods stored which must be satisfied before he is obligated to release the goods. Where a negotiable warehouse receipt is involved, the warehouseman's lien for storage is limited only to the goods represented by that particular receipt. If those goods are released by the warehouseman without payment of those particular charges, the lien cannot attach to goods stored by the same party under other warehouse receipts. On the other hand, if nonnegotiable receipts are involved, the warehouseman's lien for storage of goods previously released may attach to any goods still remaining in the warehouse.

When considering the value of collateral in the form of accounts receivable, the lender should keep in mind that in many cases he no longer holds a title document as evidence of his collateral, but rather has a security interest in an account receivable which may be an unsecured obligation of the purchaser. It is therefore of the utmost importance that the lender satisfy himself as to the capacity of the purchaser to pay the obligation when it is due.

Proper Margin

In evaluating a loan, two basic concepts are usually employed. These are the "going concern" and the "liquidation" concepts. The more important aspects of the going concern concept are as follows:

1. Ability to pay loans as they come due
2. Ability to earn profits
3. Ability to borrow funds as needed

The liquidation concept is more concerned with how the loan will be repaid in the event of unexpected difficulty. Important aspects of this concept are:

1. Ability to convert assets or collateral into cash to pay debts if the borrower gets into trouble
2. Ability to cover liabilities with sufficient collateral after allowance for collateral shrinkage in the event a forced sale of assets is required

The commodity lender considers all of the above, but should pay particular attention to the liquidation concept. One of the most important aspects of commodity financing is the maintenance of adequate margins at all times.

After establishing a value for the collateral, the next step is to determine what amount of margin the lender should have. A good definition of margin is found in *Webster's New Collegiate Dictionary,* 7th Edition, which states that margin is "cash or collateral that is deposited . . . to secure . . . from loss on a contract or a customer's equity if his account is terminated at prevailing market prices." Most commodity lenders require that their margins be in the form of liquid assets, preferably cash, or sufficient equity in the commodity being financed to be able to retire the loan completely by selling the collateral at current prices. The two most important ingredients in determining how much margin should be maintained are price stability and the marketability of the goods held as collateral.

Price stability is certainly helped by hedging the commodity in the futures market should one exist for the commodity being financed.

Hedging has been described in many ways. Some simply say that hedging is insurance against price fluctuation. A booklet published by the Kansas City Board of Trade explains:

The term hedging as it applies to any commodity which has the benefit of futures trading means the taking of such action as will result in offsetting possible losses in transactions previously made or about to be entered into. Actually, when expressed in terms of action, it involves one of the following:

1. The sale of one or more futures contracts to eliminate the possible decline in value of ownership of an approximate equal amount of the actual or "short hedge."
2. The purchase of one or more futures contracts to eliminate or lessen loss from possible advance in the value of the actual commodity not yet owned and needed to fill commitments at set prices. This is called a "long hedge."

Space will not permit us to discuss completely futures markets, as they are a separate subject. However, they are essential to commodity merchants and should be understood by all commodity lenders.

The marketability of a commodity is very important in determining how much margin should be required. The longer it takes to liquidate an inventory, the more risk is incurred, and therefore the more margin required. An established market for the commodity is a real plus. The collateral can be sold much faster, and there is a much better insight as to its value, which usually reduces the selling expense in times of trouble.

The lending officer must be cognizant of the fact that the margin requirement cannot be satisfied when the loan is made and then forgotten, as the value of the collateral constantly changes. Probably the hardest decision which a lender has to make is deciding when there is insufficient margin and it becomes necessary to call the loan and liquidate the collateral. Once the decision is made, immediate action must be taken, as the whole concept of margin is to sell the commodity and pay the loan before the collateral value drops below the amount owed.

Proper Control Documents

The documents most commonly used in secured commodity lending are as follows:

1. Warehouse receipts
2. Bills of lading
3. Accounts receivable documentation
4. Trust receipts

Warehouse receipts are by far the most important documents used and can take many forms. Some of the most important characteristics which a lender should understand are:

1. Negotiability
2. Licensed and bonded
3. Information required by the Uniform Commercial Code to be listed on each warehouse receipt
4. Private or public warehouse
5. Field warehouse

Warehouse receipts are either negotiable or nonnegotiable. Under the Code, a warehouse receipt is negotiable if by its terms the goods are to be delivered to the order of a named person or bearer. Any other warehouse receipt is nonnegotiable. Negotiable receipts are transferred from one holder to another in much the same manner as any other negotiable instrument. Receipts drawn to "order" must be endorsed; however, this is not necessary if the receipt is made out to bearer. A lender accepting negotiable warehouse receipts as collateral should determine that they are valid, properly endorsed, and accurately describe the commodities represented.

Nonnegotiable warehouse receipts should be accepted as collateral only when the receipts are in favor of the bank. These receipts may be transferred by assignment and do not have to be surrendered to the warehouseman for delivery of the commodities.

Many times the phrase "licensed and bonded" is misunderstood as absolute protection. One must determine licensed by whom and bonded for how much. Public warehouses may be licensed by either the state or the Federal government. This system affords some measure of assurance to the bank and warehouse receipt holder that licensed warehouses meet certain standards; however, inspection procedures and enforcement of standards vary from state to state.

Bonds are obtained in amounts proportionate to the capacity of the warehouse licensed. They extend protection to the holder only up to their face amount. Though bond amounts are low in comparison to the value of the products, experience has been good and losses infrequent.

The Uniform Commercial Code does not specify a specific form which the warehouse receipt must take but it does state it must contain the following information:

1. Consecutive numbering of receipts
2. Location of warehouse
3. Date of issue
4. Storage rate
5. Description of goods or containers in which they are stored
6. Whether the goods are to be delivered to the bearer, to a specified person, or to the order of a specified person
7. Signature of the warehouseman or authorized agent
8. A statement by the warehouseman of any lien or security interest claimed by him
9. Whether the warehouseman solely or jointly owns any of the goods for which a receipt has been issued

In most cases, public warehouses have no ownership in the goods stored and provide their services for a fee. They act only as a "bailee for hire" and are engaged in the business of storing goods for a profit. In the event the warehouseman does own some of the goods stored, it must be plainly stated on any warehouse receipt covering those particular goods. This is not true with private warehouses, as they are under the direct or indirect control of the firm owning the stored goods. The primary business of the controlling company is not warehousing; it is the merchandising or processing of the commodity stored.

Banks accepting private warehouse receipts as collateral should use caution when there are close ties between the owner of the pledged goods and the warehouse that is storing them. Keep in mind that the receipt could be worthless, as control of the goods remains directly or indirectly in the hands of the borrower.

There are times when a commodity merchant needs to borrow funds from the bank, pledging as security commodities stored in or on his own facilities. As mentioned before, a bank should be hesitant to lend on this type of collateral without adequate controls. Field warehouse receipts provide this control. The fundamental difference between a public warehouse and a field warehouse is that a field warehouse is a custodian of the goods and routinely holds them in an area on the owner's premises. The area is normally leased from the owner of the goods and fenced off from the rest of the premises to prevent unauthorized entry. Even though the goods need not be moved from the owner's premises, they must be physically separated from the owner's other goods in order to execute a transfer of possession. Usually the field warehouse company hires an employee of the owner of the goods to take charge of the field warehouse and act as custodian of the goods.

In addition to exercising control over the goods for the warehouseman, the custodian frequently continues many of the day-to-day duties that he had as the employee of the owner of the goods. In some bankers' minds, this causes some problems, as employees of public warehouses are answerable only to the warehouse owner for their acts, whereas field warehouse custodians usually are "former" employees of the commodity owner and should there be a need to terminate the field warehouse arrangement, they would probably return to the payroll of the owner. Experience has proven the "former employee" concept satisfactory, as the field warehouse company is fully liable for all acts of the custodian. The field warehouseman likes this arrangement as the custodian is familiar with the owner's operation. In the final analysis, the relationship between the owner and the field warehouseman must be confined to that of lessor and lessee and bailor and bailee.

The second most important document used in commodity financing is the bill of lading. These documents are issued by the transportation company charged with moving commodities from one place to another, with each carrier having a form to fit his particular needs. However, lately there has been a trend to standardize the terms. Basically, bills of lading come in two forms; order bills of lading and straight bills of lading. Order bills of lading are preferred by bankers, as they are true title documents and must be surrendered to the carrier in order to take possession of the goods. Even when using order bills of lading, there are two essential phrases to look for: "on board" and "clean."

When goods are loaded aboard a ship, the bill of lading is stamped "on board," and if the goods are damaged or there are any irregularities, they must be so noted on the bill of lading. If no damages or irregularities exist, the bill of lading is marked with the word "clean." Also, export bills of lading are generally issued in a "set" which may consist of two to four negotiable copies. They should be treated as a "set," as only one copy is needed to obtain possession of the goods from the carrier.

The basic difference between an order bill of lading and a straight bill of lading is that the consignee can obtain the goods from the carrier when shipped on a straight bill of lading without a copy of the lading. All the consignee is required to do to obtain possession of the goods is to identify himself. Needless to say, this form of bill of lading should not be used when control of the collateral is vital.

As mentioned earlier, most commodity loans go through an accounts receivable financing stage before final payment.

A security interest in this collateral is perfected by the filing of a financing statement under the Uniform Commercial Code. Control is best exercised over this type of collateral by the lender notifying the account debtor of its interest and requiring that the payments be remitted directly to the lender. The lender should be aware of and protect himself against any rights of offset which may exist between the borrower and the account debtor.

Trust receipts are probably used more in commodity lending than in any other type of financing. Most bankers are not proud of this fact, as a trust receipt is not a true title document. However, many times this is the only instrument available to retain a security interest in the goods. Negotiable warehouse receipts must be returned to the warehouse before the goods can be shipped, and the borrower usually cannot repay the loan until the goods are shipped and payment received. Therefore, the lender is forced to release the warehouse receipt on trust receipt.

Any trust receipt accepted by a lender should contain at least the following:

1. Date documents are released
2. A complete description of the collateral released
3. An agreement by the customer to keep the goods as well as the proceeds received from their sale separate and distinct from other goods and funds

Owing to the legal status of trust receipts in each separate state, a lender should consult his attorney as to the form which should be used and its validity period.

Uniform Commercial Code

The first step that should be taken before attempting to perfect a security interest under the Code is to research the appropriate records to determine if there is already on file a financing statement covering the proposed collateral. The Code's general rule of priority, with a few exceptions, provides that the creditor with the earliest perfected security interest has priority over other creditors. After a determination has been made that there are no filings outstanding, a security agreement should be obtained and a financing statement filed.

A security interest in a negotiable document can be perfected in the following ways:

1. Taking actual possession of the document
2. Filing a financing statement
3. When new value is given pursuant to a written security agreement, it is temporarily perfected for 21 days.

There are also three ways in which a security interest can be perfected in collateral in the possession of the bailee who has issued a nonnegotiable document. These methods are:

1. By taking possession of an assigned nonnegotiable document issued in another name and notifying the warehouseman of your interest
2. By issuance of the document in the name of the lender
3. By filing a financing statement

Most commodity bankers file financing statements as well as maintain possession of the warehouse receipts.

A good working knowledge of the Code is essential to all commodity bankers. However, each particular transaction and procedure should be reviewed by the lender's attorneys.

Governmental Interference

It would be unfair to leave out the role played by the U.S. government in any discussion of commodity lending, as it has been a major factor in the financing of agricultural products for many years. Since 1929, the U.S. government has sought to create and maintain strong prices for agricultural commodities. Policies affecting commodities have included restrictions on production and marketing, loan and purchase programs, export subsidy payments, benefit payments, surplus commodity disposal programs, crop insurance, loans to foreign governments for the purchase of commodities, barter, lend-lease, and relief and rehabilitation transactions. Space will not permit us to discuss these various programs, but each and every one has had a direct bearing on the financing of the commodity involved.

The 1978 soybean embargo made clear that export controls were not in the best interest of our country. That embargo was brought about by short supply conditions. The 1980 embargo on grain to the U.S.S.R. was the result of different considerations, foreign policy and national security. Full consequences of this decision will take years to unfold. However, the embargo's immediate economic effects were downward pressure on grain prices, reduced farm income, chaotic markets both future and spot, disrupted grain flow, and a devastated grain export industry. The period of uncertainty was short but it did vividly reflect what government policy can do to a healthy market. Anyone financing grain on January 4, 1980, had some uneasy moments.

Management

One of the most important points in appraising any credit risk is the evaluation of the character and ability of management. Character is the most difficult of all elements to evaluate, and strong reliance must be placed on the management's reputation as a reflection of its character. Personal reputation should be considered, as well as business reputation. Business reputation is best measured by management's relations with its employees, customers, and the public in general. Personal reputation involves the personal habits of the members of the management group and includes such things as their willingness to pay personal obligations and participation in various community activities.

The ability of management is the one most important element in any successful commodity firm and is usually measured by the depth and breadth of its numbers, skills, and personal abilities. A very important consideration in measuring management is the ability and experience of the individual members of the management team to manage an organization as opposed to technical skills. Some of the things to be considered are the financial progress of the company and the willingness and ability to meet changing competitive conditions.

CONCLUSION

Commodity lending is a very specialized type of lending, but in terms of risk, properly handled, can provide a safe and liquid loan. The keys to successful lending are the loan officer's intimate knowledge of the customer and his operation and an understanding of the commodity industry which is being financed.

15

Commercial Bank Real Estate Lending

Real estate loans, that is, loans that are principally secured by liens on real property, are a part of almost every commercial bank loan portfolio. The amount of emphasis placed on this type of loan varies significantly from bank to bank, and these variations are not explainable by any single consideration. Bank managers may be influenced from time to time by the deposit-generating capabilities of certain types of residential lending, by the above average yield offered by construction lending, or by less tangible factors such as competitive or public interest concerns. Whatever the motivation, most bank managers consider it important to have some real estate lending capacity.

The types of real estate loans a bank may make can be categorized by the type of real estate against which they are made. Subject to legal and policy considerations, a number of which are discussed below, a bank may make loans for the acquisition or holding of *improved* (that is, developed) or *unimproved* real estate. Improved real estate may be further defined by the use or purpose to which the property is dedicated. Property improved by a single-family dwelling is generally known as *residential* real estate, as the use of such property is usually as a primary or secondary residence. If the real estate is improved with a structure which, through lease or sale, is to be used for the production of income, then it is known as *income-producing* real estate. Examples of income-producing properties are shopping centers, office buildings, apartments, hotels, and other commercial structures. While the great majority of commercial bank real estate loans that are secured by improved property are on residential or income-producing properties, there are *specialty* categories, such as those improved with churches and private clubs.

Real estate loans may be broadly defined by the use to which the loan proceeds are put and the method of repayment. A *construction loan* eventuates when the loan proceeds are for the acquisition of real estate and the erection of a residence or income-producing structure. These loans are short-term, usually being extended just for the period of the construction and then repaid from another resource. *Permanent loans* result from the extension of credit for the long-term holding of real estate, and these loans are usually payable on an amortized basis with principal and interest combined in a single, uniform monthly payment over a period of twenty to thirty years. Combined construction and permanent loans are also made with interest only payable on the principal until the completion of the construction.

Commercial banks participate in a nondirect way in real estate lending through credit facilities extended to other companies concerned with real estate finance such as *mortgage bankers.* The mortgage banker makes loans on residential or income-producing properties pending the sale of these loans to other institutions such as insurance companies or pension funds, which then become the *permanent lender.* Large inventories of these loans may be accumulated by the mortgage banker prior to the time the conveyance to the permanent lender can occur. During this inventory period commercial banks may finance these inventories by taking a secured position in the mortgage banker's loans. This type of financing is frequently referred to as *mortgage warehousing.*

A wide array of other real estate loans may be extended constrained only by law and policy. *Land and development loans* are made for the purpose of acquisition of unimproved land and the preliminary development work necessary to a specified further use. *Bridge loans* may be made on income-producing property pending the resetting of financing on a permanent basis. *Swing loans* are made principally to facilitate the acquisition of a residence pending the sale of another residence. Loans secured by *junior* or *secondary liens* may be made for short periods of time to allow some percentage of owner equity to be drawn from the property for use in another legitimate business purpose.

This list, which of course does not exhaust the possibilities, gives some definition to commercial bank real estate activity. Most banks restrict their lending to a few types of loans. The reasons why this is so becomes more apparent as the legal and business characteristics of these loans are explored with some particularity.

Legal and Governmental Policies

Legislative regulation of bank real estate loans is perhaps more comprehensive than of any other type of loan. Although some of the most restrictive legislation appears in the National Banking Act, state chartered institutions also have constraints imposed on them by statute and administrative fiat. Reference to legislative history does not seem to reveal the reason for this approach, but, at least for national banks, the commencement date of any capability in respect of real estate lending is clear. It occurred in 1916, when an amendment to the National Banking Act first authorized national banks to make such loans.

The concept of the regulatory approach can be seen from a summary review of the salient portions of the National Banking laws. In general these acts provide that a bank may make loans secured by unimproved or improved real estate in which the ownership interest of the borrower is a fee simple or, under certain circumstances, a leasehold. Loan amount to value of the property ratios are imposed, with lower ratios being prescribed for unimproved properties. For certain improved property loans involving higher loan-to-value ratios and for all residential loans, amortization of the entire principal is required within a period of not more than thirty years. The aggregate of all real estate loans may not exceed the capital and surplus of the bank or the amount of its time and savings deposits, whichever is greater, but numerous loans may be excluded from this aggregation process. For instance, many government guaranteed loans and loans which have conforming takeouts from another financially responsible lender need not be counted. Special provisions and ratios are established for construction loans and loans secured by junior liens.

Although the regulations are constraining, recent trends have been toward liberalization of controls and the creation of programs designed to promote real estate lending. One reason for this trend is that public policy has been increasingly directed toward the stimulation of the housing industry by creating a climate in which more mortgage funds are available. This action has had a powerfully stimulating effect on mortgage markets generally but, as will be seen, has had a much more moderate effect in respect to commercial bank real estate lending.

In 1934 a major step was taken with the creation of the Federal Housing Administration (FHA). FHA provides insurance to lenders on loans granted for homes and apartments provided those loans meet certain criteria as to the maximum amount, downpayment, maturity, and a number of other factors. The Veterans Administration (VA) offers a loan guaranty program which tends to have the same effect. Importantly, both FHA and VA loans have a stipulated maximum interest rate which can be charged, and this limits their desirability to many banks.

The government influences real estate lending in other ways. The Federal National Mortgage Association (FNMA) provides a secondary mortgage market where lenders can sell portions of their mortgage loan portfolios to maintain liquidity at desired levels. Originally this secondary market was available only for FHA or VA approved loans, but amendments to the law during the early seventies enabled FNMA to become a purchaser of conventional (that is, uninsured) loans as well.

Further order to the mortgage market is provided by the Government National Mortgage Association (GNMA). This organization guaranties individual securities which are backed by a pool of FHA and VA insured mortgage loans. These securities have achieved significant market acceptance and add a level of liquidity to real estate financing not previously known.

Bank Real Estate Lending Policies

In practice most banks restrain real estate lending less because of the impact of regulations than because bank managements voluntarily choose to do so. Several characteristics of real estate loans which contribute to a conservative portfolio policy are that they have long maturities and frequently are made at a fixed interest rate. The volatile financial markets of 1979–80 have poignantly demonstrated the earnings pressure that can be occasioned when banks are forced to gather funds at extremely high rates to fund portfolios of this sort.

Because of the above problem, a growing number of banks and other lending institutions such as savings and loan associations have attempted to devise indexed, or variable-rate, mortgages (VRM). Although the VRM takes many forms, the underlying concepts are the same. A cost of money index is chosen and on the basis of that index the loan rate changes from time to time. Usually there is a limitation placed on the amount of change that may be effected at any one time and on the aggregate amount of change which may occur over specified periods. The effect of these changes is realized either in monthly payments on the loan or the note maturity is changed with the monthly payment remaining the same. At present, bank managements have not embraced the VRM in any of its forms with great enthusiasm. Difficulties in selecting the appropriate cost of money index and in setting the amount of fluctuation to be permitted have resulted in VRMs which have not gone as far toward solving the problems as bankers had hoped. Further, the VRM is thought by some to introduce a pricing structure which cannot be readily understood by the frequently inexperienced real estate borrower. Despite this reluctant start it is clear that if unstable interest rates and inflation persist, as many think they will, then many new lending formats will be devised which may seem as foreign to today's practices as the long-term level amortization loan is to the three- to five-year interest-only loans of earlier times. In the meantime most bank mortgage portfolio managers will continue to contain the problems discussed here by constrictive and selective policies in respect of the type of real estate financing in which they engage.

Commercial banks are generally biased against permanent mortgages on income-producing property. The principal difficulty with this type of loan is that it is usually for quite large amounts and is of a very long maturity. Another problem is that these asset-oriented loans do not usually produce demand deposit balances proportionate to their size. However, there are exceptions, and banks will often consider income-producing property loans where the user of the facility is otherwise a customer of the bank. Nonetheless, the principal providers of funds for permanent loans on income-producing properties are life insurance companies.

Highly specialized properties such as churches and clubs are usually not considered appropriate security for bank permanent loans. These properties are single purpose and therefore if the bank would inure to ownership of the property through foreclosure, alternate uses are infrequently available. These loans are thought to be subject to a higher risk of default since there is no orthodox credit support to maintain debt service in that the borrowers are dependent upon voluntary or charitable contributions. Again, exceptions are made, and these usually turn upon the bank's overall relationship with the individuals comprising the borrower.

In contrast to permanent loans on income-producing properties, banks are very active in the business of providing construction loans. These loans have found increasing favor at commercial banks since the middle 1950s and often form the bulk of a bank's real estate portfolio. The enthusiasm with which they are regarded is in part because they allow the bank to avoid some of the problems noted above. First, they are ordinarily made at fluctuating rates relating to prime and are often several percentage points above the prime rate. In addition, loan service fees are generally charged which further increase the yield. They are generally extended for short periods of time (usually 12 to 24 months, although larger projects may require as much as four years) and, particularly when there is a takeout commitment, offer considerable liquidity. From a community or civic standpoint they offer tangible evidence that the bank is contributing to the social and economic development of their market areas. Relationships with developers (the appellation generally attributed to companies, whether proprietorships or corporations, who engage in the business of constructing and owning buildings as investments) have bank significance in that developers maintain demand deposits and require other bank services somewhat in line with other commercial enterprises. Finally, this type of loan is frequently shared with other banks through participations and therefore offers opportunities for improving bank relationships.

Despite the interest rate risk and liquidity problems created, the substantial majority of loans in bank mortgage portfolios are residential loans. Bank managements recognize that individuals will carry their checking and savings accounts at banks that provide mortgage financing to them. Beyond this there are less tangible benefits such as improving the image of the bank as a responsible member of the community which is interested in the growth of the area. Within this large loan category, however, banks continue to demonstrate selectivity. Despite their safety as to principal and interest, FHA or VA insured loans usually do not form a large proportion of a bank's residential lending portfolio because of the interest rate ceiling attendant to these loans. Banks favor conventional, noninsured loans, which do not have this feature. Further, in times of tight or expensive money, banks tend to limit their mortgage lending practices by pricing these loans so as to reduce their desirability to the customer. Nonetheless, this is such a major function at many banks, and the lending is so specialized, that separate real estate departments or divisions are formed for the origination and servicing of these loans.

The financing of mortgage bankers is an important function at many banks. Mortgage banking is a relatively new industry which came to prominence following the depression of the 1930s. With the real estate development boom that began at about that time, it was frequently necessary to go beyond local lending institutions to gather funds for these projects. Insurance companies and others had become thoroughly committed to real estate loans, but were more willing to make these loans if there was a local intermediary who could guide them through the maze of laws which governed them. This need was filled by the mortgage banker. In simplest terms, a mortgage banker originates and disburses mortgage loans and after an interim period of holding sells these loans to permanent lenders, which the mortgage banker often refers to as its investor. After the sale they service the loans, that is, they collect the principal and interest payments and remit them to the investor, maintain insurance and tax escrows collected from the borrowers, and generally keep the investor apprised of the status of his mortgage loans. Typically, mortgage bankers are thinly capitalized and to conduct their business require funds amounting to many times that which they can create through earnings. It has become popular for banks to lend funds to mortgage bankers, usually via secured lines of credit, to carry these mortgages pending the sale to investors. The security taken is of course the notes and mortgages evidencing the liens. For this extension of credit the mortgage banker pays a market interest rate which fluctuates and relates to the bank's prime rate and perhaps, more importantly, generates highly desirable demand deposit balances which arise from the collection of tax and insurance escrows from individual borrowers.

Construction Lending

Commercial banks' involvement in construction lending is significant, and some of the reasons for this have already been set forth. Although they are involved both in the business of financing the construction of residences and income-producing properties, the procedures dealt with here relate primarily to the latter.

This market opportunity arises for a commercial bank since, with some exceptions, life insurance companies, the principal holders of long-term real estate loans, do not wish to provide financing during the construction period. This period is associated with an amount of risk and uncertainty that they do not feel comfortable in attempting to manage. Most banks involved in this activity were powerfully reminded of the impact of these risks during the recession of 1974–75, when billions of dollars of construction loans fell into default and the banks were forced to foreclose, complete construction, and dispose of the finished structure. Even the most experienced banks encountered problems during this period. Some of these risks are apparent and others are quite subtle. For instance, contractors and subcontractors who commit to build the structure may, because of a lack of technical expertise or management capabilities, be unable to maintain quality standards and time control. Since these entities are usually in thin working capital positions, these problems can create financial pressures which may make contract compliance impossible. The contractors, architects, engineers, lawyers, and local building authorities associated with the project may have difficulties understanding or communicating with each other, and these situations may result in disputes, delays, or even total curtailment of the project. The developer, who is charged with the responsibility of bringing all these elements together, is therefore faced with constant delicate management decisions. Even if these matters are managed well, there are uncontrollables such as labor disputes, bad weather, and unanticipated cost increases that may contribute to delays and the need for additional funds which the moderately capitalized developer cannot provide. In the zeal to grow, the developer may have undertaken too many projects at once, which magnifies all of these problems for him and for the construction lending bank. Because of risks of this sort, construction lending is considered one of the most sophisticated and often most profitable forms of real estate lending.

Construction loans fall into two categories—those with takeout commitments and those which are open-ended. The construction loan with a takeout commitment is generally preferred by bankers since this structure insures, if the many conditions of the takeout commitment are satisfied, that there will be funds available to repay the construction loan at the completion of the project. A takeout commitment is a contract obligation issued by an institution, usually a life insurance company, to become the permanent lender in respect of the project when their conditions are satisfied. In the case of the open-ended construction loan, no takeout commitment exists and the bank depends upon the borrower to place a permanent loan on the facility at some later date from a source which is not identified at the outset of the construction loan.

Irrespective of whether there is a takeout or the loan is to be open-ended, the bank analysis of a construction loan opportunity begins with an analysis of the developer and proceeds to an analysis of the project which is the subject of the loan.

Analysis of a developer's statement will pose problems to a bank officer which are peculiar to the real estate industry. Since the form of business organization usually chosen by the developer is that of a proprietorship, partnership, or closely held corporation, the statements will often be internally prepared, and even if prepared by an outside accounting firm will usually not be set forth in accordance with generally accepted accounting principles. One effect this will have is that the real estate assets which typically comprise the bulk of the total assets shown will be valued at fair market value instead of at cost minus accumulated depreciation, as accounting principles (with some qualifications) require. The bank officer's job in the first instance is to determine how these fair market values were decided upon. This procedure entails a review of all projects shown. Often the developer will determine fair market values by capitalizing the income streams emanating from the projects. Verification requires a review of the leases or other contract instruments from which the projects derive income. In briefing these items consideration should be given to the creditworthiness of the lease obligors and to all terms affecting the obligation to pay including, of course, the number of years the obligation has to run. Having established the amount and quality of the income, the officer considers the project expenses such as utilities, maintenance and security, real estate taxes, insurance, debt service, and any other expense for which the developer may be contractually responsible under the leases. Finally, the officer reviews the capitalization factors applied to these cash flows in light of his knowledge of the equity markets for real estate assets of like kind.

The liability side of the balance sheet will also present concepts not encountered with ordinary commercial concerns. Most of the projects will be subject to permanent mortgage debt, and the very high debt-to-net worth ratios thereby created are indicative of the industry. The mortgage instruments evidencing this debt should be reviewed to verify debt service and to insure that the developer is not in default. His exact financial responsibility in respect of this debt should be determined. Since the early 1950s an increasing amount of mortgage debt has been on a non-recourse basis. This means that should the mortgage go into default and the permanent lender begin enforcement proceedings, the lender is limited to recovery of the real estate and no other asset, real or personal, of the developer can be obtained to satisfy the debt. Today almost all permanent debt on real estate is of this variety. This factor could lead to the conclusion by the officer that the developer's enterprise could withstand the failure of an individual project.

The officer analyzing the long-term debt of a developer must come to this process with a perspective about debt and its relationship to net worth which differs from the ordinary commercial credit analyst. It must be borne in mind that it is the ordinary course of business for the developer to create debt of this sort, and soundness is governed not so much by lesser amounts of debt, but rather by the quality and quantity of the income stream which covers the debt. Extending this perspective, it is short-term debt, or any debt that does not have an adequate income stream specifically pledged to cover it, that will most concern the officer. The latter type of debt may have been incurred to invest speculatively in unimproved property, to cover project costs that exceed other construction loans, or because of some other unplanned financial discription. Sometimes the developer will have no credible plan for retiring this debt. Finally, the officer must determine the amount and nature of the developer's contingent liabilities such as guaranties for completion of construction projects. Of course, the analysis will be completed by an investigation of all construction in progress, as well as the development of ordinary credit information supplied by other banks, contractors, credit bureaus, and other investors who have worked with or financed the developer.

The second stage of construction loan underwriting is an investigation of the proposed project. This begins with verification of the detailed breakdown of the costs of the project as prepared by the developer. This is a crucial stage of construction loan underwriting since the officer must be certain that the construction loan proceeds will be adequate to complete the construction in strict accordance with the development plan and in accordance with the provisions of any takeout commitment which may exist. One of the most disastrous lender mistakes leading up to the real estate debacle of 1974–75 was the failure to determine adequately the cost of projects before proceeding. When many loans failed and these projects were obtained in a partially completed state through foreclosure, banks were forced to the unhappy realization that, in some cases, millions of dollars in excess of the original estimates were necessary to complete the facilities.

The choice of a method of construction cost analysis is determined by the circumstances. In the simplest situations the officer is dealing with a form of construction with which, by his previous experience, he has become conversant. His duties here are limited to an analysis of the construction contract for completeness, a comparison to previous costs, and appropriate updating to reflect known increases in certain types of expenses such as construction loan interest. In a more complex project, or in one with which the officer is not familiar, he may choose to obtain the consulting services of an architectural or engineering firm which will prepare a comparative cost analysis. Some banks maintain the services of such professionals on staff.

At this stage the terms and conditions of the construction loan begin to take shape. If the construction loan which the bank is willing to make is not sufficient to cover all legitimate costs, then the developer will be required to provide the necessary assurances that these funds will be available. With financially strong entities these assurances may be in the nature of guaranties, but more often the officer will require that the difference between the loan amount and the estimated costs be invested in the project by the developer prior to the commencement of construction advances. Sometimes it will be agreed that if additional security is provided or other evidence of cash availability is given, the investment may be delayed until a later stage of the project.

During this initial structuring phase, the officer is devising the conditions, which he will later require by his commitment letter, before the bank will lend money for the project. The structure he chooses will be the one he considers most likely to add certainty and reliability to the development process. In his concern for maintaining the costs of the project in accordance with the agreed upon cost breakdown, he will therefore require that the building costs be evidenced by a fixed price contract with a financially responsible and experienced contractor. He can assume that in the arm's length negotiating process that will occur between the developer and the contractor, the most accurate cost figure will be obtained. Further, should for any reason the actual costs exceed this, it will be the contractor's obligation and the integrity of the loan should be preserved. This step represents the thought process the officer should follow in underwriting the construction loan in respect of each of the requirements he views as critical. In other words, he attempts to control the outcome of the development process at the critical points by a series of enforceable contracts. Building on this theory, he might next require that the contractor enter into an attornment agreement with the bank whereby the contractor agrees that if the bank should become the owner of the project (as through foreclosure), then the construction contract will remain valid and enforceable between the bank and contractor as if it had been originally between them. This will insure the ability to complete within the original cost framework. Last, a third contract, known as a performance bond and labor and material bond, might be required to support the contractor's ability to perform. This is a contract issued by a corporate surety which promises that the contractor will fulfill all terms of the construction contract and will pay all amounts due pursuant thereto.

The next major procedure in underwriting is to make a valuation of the project when completed according to the development plan. Returning to the experiences of 1974–75, mentioned above, a second area of lender imprudence appears. The nation was at that time in the throes of a building boom, and many lenders, banks and others, were competing aggressively to provide the financing. Often, particularly in cases where takeout commitments existed, lenders gave little if any consideration to the ultimate value of the project, with the result being that many projects obtained in foreclosure never attained the estimated value against which the loan was made.

The process of establishing value is known as an appraisal. Bank real estate officers and professional appraisers refer to three approaches to value, often called the cost approach, the income approach, and the market approach. The decision as to which approach to use is an esoteric one but the income approach is frequently employed. Irrespective of which approach is utilized, all appraisals consist of the gathering of a comprehensive amount of data about the project and the organization of that data so as to reveal all factors that have an effect on value. A few of these are the city of location, the neighborhood, the specific site, land sales in the vicinity, income produced by the property through leases, and type of facility and construction.

How to undertake the appraisal will be dictated by the circumstances. The value of a building to be tenanted by a single high-credit tenant at a specified rent may be a relatively easy question. Multiple occupancy or multiple use facilities are much more complex and may require the services of an experienced professional appraiser. Sometimes such appraisers exist on the bank staff but in other cases this work may be performed by independent professionals.

Since value is one of the two most important loan considerations (the other being cost), the officer will, as the appraisal is reviewed, begin to evolve the provisions of the loan structure which deal with the creation and maintenance of value. Once again the emphasis is on creating a network of contracts which affect various aspects of the value components. Examples of how this works are fairly obvious. If in the income analysis of a building, rent was estimated at $10 per square foot per annum, then this number is given validity by the existence of a commitment to lease at that rental. If this commitment is assigned to the bank, the legally enforceable contract support for the income stream spreads to the bank directly. If the commitment is to lease the whole facility, then the entire income and expense statement for the building can be reliably established and value upon completion can be confidently predicted. In certain types of construction, such as apartments, contractually obligated income and expenses cannot be obtained, so that pinpointing value at the preconstruction stage is more difficult. As value assumptions weaken risk increases, and the officer will make decisions about pricing and acceptability on this basis.

The officer completes the underwriting of the construction loan by examining the source of repayment. The preferred construction loan as to rate and risk will have a takeout commitment. The commitment in addition to providing a source of repayment provides some additional verification of value, although it should never be the sole index of value. The commitment issued by most permanent lenders is a relatively fragile agreement. The standard conditions make it apparent that in the event the developer and construction lender do not perform during the construction phase in certain very specific ways, the permanent lender's obligation to fund the commitment is abrogated. Some of the commonly occurring conditions are that the building must be built in accordance with plans and specifications approved by the permanent lender, the title to the property must be valid and insurable, the survey must be acceptable, the building must be completed by a specified date, an architect or other independent professional must certify the completion in accordance with plans and specifications, and a certificate of occupancy must be provided. Frequently the commitment will provide that the developer, construction lender, and permanent lender enter into a triparty agreement in which the developer agrees that he will accept no other permanent financing for the building, the construction lender agrees that he will accept repayment of the loan from no source other than the permanent lender, and the permanent lender acknowledges an assignment of the loan proceeds to the construction lender. Often it is required that this document be executed by a certain date.

In order to insure that the property achieves the appraisal value that the permanent loan was granted against, the permanent loan commitments will often provide rental achievement clauses. Introduction of such a provision results in a two-tiered commitment or a commitment which has a lower tier amount, which is known as the floor, and a higher tier amount that is advanced only upon satisfaction of the rental achievement clause, which is known as the ceiling. The difference between these two amounts is usually referred to as the "gap" and is frequently 15 to 20 percent of the ceiling amount. Construction lenders who are faced with a request for a construction loan equal to the ceiling amount will often require that the developer provide a commitment from another lender to provide financing equal to the gap amount or come forward with a bank letter of credit or additional security in this amount.

Sometimes, usually during periods of exceptionally high long-term interest rates or tight money periods, a construction lender will be asked to make a loan where the repayment source is a standby commitment. Unlike takeout commitments, standby commitments do not require the developer to deliver the loan on completion and the undertaking of the standby lender is not to make a permanent loan, but a short-term loan is made upon completion pending obtaining permanent financing. The terms of these loans, if made, are generally quite onerous and discourage funding. Since neither the developer nor standby lender wishes to fund these loans, banks view with considerable skepticism the value of these commitments.

The documentation of the construction loan is a complex process requiring the services of a real estate lawyer. Conveyancing and mechanics' lien laws vary substantially from state to state. Since the loan is advanced incrementally over the period of construction, other claimants, such as judgment creditors of the developer and contractors, labor and material men supplying goods and services to the project may develop complex and often conflicting rights in respect of the property. Sometimes these rights can affect the mortgage interest of the construction lender. For this reason extreme care must be exercised in the documentation and disbursement of the construction loan.

Typical basic loan documentation consists of a mortgage note, a mortgage, an assignment of leases and rentals, and financing statements, although special loan considerations may result in many more instruments. Local laws dictate the exact documentation and the place of filing. A key document, when there is a permanent commitment, is the triparty agreement. Beyond the purposes previously indicated for this document, the parties will usually use it to further clarify the contractual arrangement existing among them. From the construction lender's standpoint, he will endeavor to have the permanent lender acknowledge his approval of all of the conditions of his permanent commitment that can be satisfied at the preconstruction stage. In other words, the construction lender seeks to have the permanent lender agree that he has approved the plans and specifications, the current state of title to the property, the survey, and any other conditions that can be so dealt with.

Despite the increased reliability provided by a well-negotiated and drafted triparty agreement, the construction lender must always remember that during the pendency of the permanent loan commitment conditions will change, and some of these changes may affect the permanent lender's attitude toward the commitment. If, for instance, the monetary climate is much tighter at the date of funding or if financial markets have moved in such a way that the rate on a permanent loan is below market, the permanent lender may be encouraged to review his commitment with a high level of scrutiny. Conversely, if rates have moved downward, the developer will be inclined to look at the permanent commitment with an eye toward avoiding it. The wise construction lender reviews the permanent commitment in light of changing conditions throughout the development process and acts quickly to obtain satisfaction of any outstanding conditions precedent to funding.

The administration of a construction loan involves a multiple advance situation which is unlike any other type of lending and consumes a great deal of personnel time. The administration phase is merely an extension of the underwriting judgments and structure determinations previously made. The administrator must be aware of the effect that changing conditions have on the two chief underwriting principles of cost and value. In addition, he must be sensitive to the effect that these changes may have on the obligation of the permanent lender and the effect they may have on the priority of the construction lender's lien. Regrettably, 1974–75 problems again point up serious problems brought about by poor administration. With loan volumes and expectations running high, construction loans were frequently disbursed without regard to sound principles. The result was that all too often construction lenders found that their first mortgages had fallen junior to intervening lien holders, that funds had been advanced well beyond the stage of actual completion, and that funds which had been disbursed might never have reached the persons for whom they were intended. Upon foreclosure, construction lenders were in tenuous situations *vis à vis* the other parties to the development process and other creditors of the developer.

Sound administration requires that the administrator conduct a complete project review at the time of each advance. It is necessary to determine the stage of completion aggregately and since the time of the last advance, and to compare this progress with other chronologies such as maturity of the note and the expiration of the permanent commitment. An estimate must be made of the cost to complete and the availability of funds. For this the administrator will lean on the expertise of the inspecting architect (who may be staff or an outside consultant), who should inspect the project at the time of each advance. During his physical inspection of the job, the inspecting architect verifies that the dollar amount of the work requested by the loan advance has been accomplished and should further verify that all work to date has been completed in accordance with plans and specifications. If the triparty agreement so provides, he should issue his progressive certificate to the permanent lender. Depending upon the title laws of the jurisdiction, it may also be necessary to coordinate the advance with the title insurance company so that they may continue their search of the real property records to the date of the proposed advance and, if necessary, issue an endorsement to the title policy.

Periodically the construction lending officer or administrator should visit the project to familiarize himself with the conditions on the site. A disorderly site or the existence of a large number of unsupervised personnel indicates forthcoming problems. It is not unusual, and in fact likely, that because of costs or market conditions developers will make changes from time to time in the plans and specifications. The changes which increase the cost of the project must be approved by the permanent lender. A substantial amount of record keeping must be done by the administrator. An audit procedure must be established to spot check periodically to see that the loan proceeds are being disbursed in the proper amount and to the proper payees.

Construction lending is a highly profitable but risky form of real estate lending. Banks engaging in it successfully must, by and large, take the development process as they find it and refrain from treating it as they wish or hope it would be. Since it involves so many variables, in the final analysis it is the developer/customer who, having an appetite for risk and a desire for great reward, determines the success or failure of the process. If, through application of good underwriting practices, the bank officer locates the right developer, he will, through his efforts and integrity, make up for what the officer does not know and cannot control. It is, as one successful developer described his life's work, "a cacophony of activity in which zoning commissions cry for trees they never had, undercapitalized contractors rail for payment for work they will do tomorrow if they get paid for it today, and architects, engineers, accountants, lawyers, and bankers attack your plans with a dizzying array of conflicting (and only sometimes relevant) requirements, only to retreat until the time they can say, 'We knew that wouldn't work.' "

Residential Real Estate Lending

As noted previously, residential mortgage lending continues to be the most important, in terms of dollar volume, and type of loan in the commercial bank real estate portfolio.

There are basically two types of mortgage loans in the residential area which are made by commercial banks today. There are insured loans, in which FHA and VA government insurance or guaranties are involved, and conventional loans. As has been pointed out, the FHA insured or VA guaranteed loan offers some benefits since the bank is assured of its ability to recover principal and interest in the event of a default. The chief difficulty with these loans is the red tape involved in the origination and enforcement of them and, probably more importantly, the limitation on the interest rate imposed. For this reason the vast majority of commercial bank residential mortgage lending is in the form of conventional loans, where no interest ceiling (other than applicable state usury statutes) exists. The rising use of private mortgage insurance in recent years has given conventional loans some of the attributes of government insured loans.

Residential mortgage loan policies have undergone radical changes since commercial banks first became active in this business prior to the 1930s. In pre-depression years the concept of a long-term, level amortization mortgage loan was by and large unknown. At that time most mortgages were made with a term of a maximum of five years and generally were set on an interest-only basis. In some other countries, such as Canada, this is still the basic mortgage term. The mortgage insurance program of the FHA was primarily responsible for the advent of long-term mortgage loans. These increased maturities, while extending the possibility of ownership to many who would not otherwise qualify, have posed many interest rate and liquidity problems to banks. However, for reasons mentioned elsewhere, banks are a significant participant in this market.

Many of the principles of real estate finance observed in the discussion of construction loans are applicable to residential mortgage loans. The approach to the underwriting of the individual loan is dominated by a concern for the creditworthiness of the borrower and by the value of the property which is offered as security.

Of course, the applicant for a residential real estate loan is usually an individual who intends to occupy the property either as a primary or secondary residence. In determining the credit standing of the borrower, the beginning point is the amount and quality or stability of the borrower's income. Numerous ratios have been developed as standards to determine the appropriate amount of income to support a residential real estate loan. One rule is that the price of the residence being purchased should not exceed 2½ to 3 times the borrower's annual income. A more conservative approach is that the price should not exceed 2½ to 3 times the borrower's income after taxes. Other rules have been devised which focus on the ratio between monthly take-home income as it relates to debt service on the mortgage. Formulas are devised to deal with installment debt other than the mortgage, and bankers by policy adopt attitudes toward the recognition of second incomes. None of these rules is regarded as more reliable than others and none has been shown to be a more effective credit tool than others. Often these rules are relaxed in recognition of the fact that many factors are involved in determination of the creditworthiness of a borrower. Those persons who have had stable employment over a long period of time will be preferred to persons just recently entering the job market. Individuals who have had a history of successful home ownership will be favored over those who have a spotty previous record. In any event, whatever rules the banker uses and however they are applied in the individual situation, an analysis of the borrower's credit and financial stability is always the first step in underwriting the residential mortgage loan.

Since these loans are extended for long periods of time, a significant emphasis is placed on the value of the security. Over these long maturities substantial changes can occur in the condition of the borrower which will affect the repayment potential and require the bank to look to the security for payment.

The appraisal process in respect of residential property is fraught with uncertainty since many factors influence value, and determining factors are difficult to isolate. In income-producing real estate it is usually possible to develop and rely on the income stream in making the evaluation. Residential real estate values frequently turn on factors which are much less tangible. Many times considerations such as architecture or positioning on the site are important. In certain areas brick construction may be preferred over frame. In other locations the converse may be true. Despite these difficulties, it is essential to the bank that as comprehensive an evaluation as possible be made. There are some determinants considered more reliable than others. Many times a market approach will be taken by the appraiser, which means determining the value of the property from the values of other similar residences located in the immediate vicinity. Extensions of this approach will lead to investigation of population trends for the area and will emphasize the location of the residence in relation to schools, churches, and recreational facilities. It is also important to consider the availability of publicly sponsored services such as water and sewer connections and police and fire protection.

Whatever technique of appraisal is chosen, the results will have some limitations. The best protection for the bank in this regard is to have the appraisals prepared by persons having considerable training or experience in this field.

The terms of residential mortgage loans and the perfection of a security interest in the real estate collateral present the banker with different considerations and technicalities than are encountered in other types of bank loans. This is primarily because of the laws governing mortgages, which vary substantially from state to state. In documenting the residential real estate loan, the banker is concerned with the creation of a lien on the property which will enable the bank to obtain the property in satisfaction of the debt if in the future the borrower should default under the agreement. In order to obtain a lien on the property, it is, of course, first necessary that the borrower be the owner of a lienable interest. One of two methods is usually employed in obtaining satisfactory evidence that the borrower has legal and beneficial title to the property to be mortgaged. In many areas, and in almost all urban areas, the bank will insist that the borrower provide a policy of title insurance issued by a substantial title insurance company. In addition to establishing the ownership of the property, the bank will usually insist on a mortgagee's policy which establishes the priority and enforceability of the bank's mortgage instrument. If title insurance is not employed, as is sometimes the case in smaller communities, the determination of ownership usually is the responsibility of an attorney who, after examination of the land title records, issues his opinion to that effect. Whatever method is chosen, the bank will always insist that their lien be a first and prior lien. If the examinations of the title insurance company or the attorney should show the existence of any prior liens, then at the closing of the loan, these liens must be discharged by payment or by operation of law.

The lien on the property is created either by a mortgage or a deed of trust, depending on the law of the jurisdiction. While there are legal theory differences between a mortgage and deed of trust, they have essentially the same effect. It is in the mortgage that the borrower's principal obligations to the bank are expressed, and in this sense the document does not differ significantly from other bank loan agreements. The mortgage will provide for the payment of principal and interest at specified times (usually monthly) and in specified amounts. In addition, the mortgage will usually place significant obligations on the borrower in respect of the management of the property of which one of the most important is the requirement to pay all taxes or special assessments which may be levied against the property. In almost all cases the mortgage will require that the amounts necessary to pay these taxes be escrowed with the bank, usually at the time of the payment of principal and interest installments. The borrower will also be obligated to maintain insurance against hazards on the property in a form and amount satisfactory to the bank, and the insurance premiums may also have to be escrowed with the bank.

Foreclosure, which is the process whereby the bank obtains title to the property if there is a default under the mortgage, is strictly governed by laws, which vary from jurisdiction to jurisdiction. It is typically not an easy process, and substantial rights are given to the borrower to cure defaults before the impact of foreclosure is realized. These rights are generally referred to as rights of redemption. Because foreclosure is sometimes an awkward process and because the maintenance and subsequent disposition of residential real estate by a bank is often time-consuming and expensive, most banks are quite liberal in giving the borrower an opportunity to correct defaults under the mortgage.

Bankers are careful in determining the amount and term of the residential real estate loan. In determining the amount the chief consideration is the ratio of the loan amount to the value of the property. Banks tend to favor a low loan-to-value ratio although today the loan-to-value ratio is almost always in excess of 50 percent. Obviously, the lower this ratio is the more likely the loan will be collectible if the collateral has to be realized upon. Lower loan-to-value ratios tend to reduce the debt service and thereby increase the likelihood that the borrower will be able to maintain the principal and interest payments. A lower loan-to-value ratio also allows for changing conditions which may affect the value of the property and for mistakes which may have been made in the original appraisal analysis. Shorter maturities are also preferred by bankers since the risk of nonpayment is reduced by virtue of the fact that the borrower develops equity at a more rapid pace. Shorter maturities also lessen the interest risk period to the bank.

Despite bankers' desires for shorter terms and lower loan-to-value ratios, the trend in residential real estate lending has been in the other direction. Lower down payments and longer terms are governmentally supported by the

FHA and VA loan programs. To encourage banks to follow this trend, laws have been amended to allow banks to make loans of longer maturities and higher loan-to-value ratios. With some banks following these trends, a competitive pressure has been applied on others, and today loans of up to 90 percent loan-to-value, with up to a 30-year repayment term, are not uncommon. Frequently, however, the bank will require that the amount of the loan which exceeds a 75 percent loan-to-value be insured by a private mortgage insurance lender. This insurance is paid for by the borrower and the bank usually requires that it remain in existence for a period of time sufficient to reduce the loan-to-value ratio through equity build-up.

Interim Financing of Mortgage Bankers

As has been pointed out, the expansion the country experienced in both residential and income-producing properties after the depression of the 1930s and the broad acceptance of real estate mortgage loans as an investment for large national companies such as life insurance companies provided the impetus for the development of the mortgage banking industry to access this debt market. Today mortgage bankers have become an integral part of the real estate financing network. The mortgage banker is principally a service organization, and from a financial statement point of view has the characteristics of most companies within the service industry. Mortgage bankers are usually modestly capitalized when viewed in respect to the large dollar volume of mortgages they originate. While there are exceptions, such as the very large nationally oriented mortgage bankers which are sometimes owned by banks or other financial companies, they are quite often closely held and their fortunes tied to the skills of a few key managers. Some develop specialties in certain types of real estate finance while others offer a full range of real estate loans. No matter how wide-ranging their activities, however, they all have in common that they never act as the permanent source of funds for real estate. Their ordinary areas of activity can be summarized as follows:

1. They originate long-term loans on existing residential real estate. Mortgage bankers often refer to these loans as the spot market.

2. They offer land and development loans on tracts to be improved with single-family residences. Their principal reason for making these loans is to obtain the opportunity to provide the long-term financing on these residences when completed. In this regard they may also offer the developer construction financing for the residences erected on the developed property.

3. They originate commitments for long-term financing on income-producing projects.

The mortgage banker's income is principally made up of fees earned for the origination of the above loans and servicing income derived from charges they assess the permanent lender for administering the loan. Their servicing responsibilities include the collection and remittance of principal and interest on the loans and the collection of tax and insurance escrows from the property owners.

Mortgage bankers which do substantial spot financing or other single-family residential mortgage financing create large demands for bank-type credit. The origination of a loan in these cases involves the solicitation, documentation, disbursement, and temporary holding or inventorying of the loan prior to its sale to a permanent lender. These mortgage bankers do not have the working capital to finance internally a profitable volume of these loans. Conversely, mortgage bankers which operate principally in the income-producing loan area usually do not have bank financing needs. As to these loans, the mortgage banker negotiates a loan commitment with a permanent lender which funds directly when the conditions of the commitment have been satisfied, so that there is no inventory period.

The types of credit devices sought by mortgage bankers are in the nature of lines of credit (ordinarily referred to as mortgage warehousing) to provide money to carry loans which are (1) closed and held in inventory pending sale in accordance with existing commitments from permanent lenders; (2) loans which are closed but have not yet been committed; and (3) unsecured loans to enable them to finance tract developer construction loan activities. Many banks are unwilling to provide the latter type of financing given the financial structure of the mortgage banker and the fact that the loans are of a high-risk nature. Many banks are also unenthusiastic about financing mortgage banker inventories which are not committed for sale. These loans are subject to an interest rate risk which will cause them to depreciate (or be discounted) in value if mortgage rates rise before the sale occurs. The extremely volatile mortgage rates of 1979–80 have pointed up these dangers. Sometimes from the date of origination until a sale commitment can be arranged, the market may have shifted by two or three percentage points, and if this happens a 15- or 20-point drop in the value of the mortgages will occur.

The financial structure of a mortgage banker almost always dictates that they be financed on a secured basis, and the officer's analysis of these companies begins, naturally, with their financial statements. The balance sheet will almost always reveal a high debt-to-net worth ratio. Many times the only debt shown will be for mortgage warehousing, and an argument can be made that the officer might curtail his request for security since all debt would be of the same priority in bankruptcy. However, even with the strongest mortgage bankers this is usually not looked upon favorably. The rationale is that the efficient origination, documentation, and sale of the mortgages is the only method by which the bank can be paid, and since the business is primarily being operated with borrowed funds, the bank should have a position which enables it to examine and to some extent control this process. In reviewing the balance sheet most bankers are willing to augment the mortgage banker's net worth by some valuation of the servicing portfolio which is undisclosed by the statements. These servicing portfolios have a somewhat liquid value, particularly to other mortgage bankers who may have an underutilized or expandable servicing capability. The bank officer will be concerned with the size and age of the mortgage inventory and with what percentage thereof is committed for sale. This concern will become particularly acute during periods when rates are, or are predicted to become, unstable. During these conditions the mortgage banker may be caught with a volume of loans which are uncommitted and are depreciating in value. Unless these can be warehoused economically, a large loss on disposition may occur. The income statement should be relatively straightforward, comprised principally of servicing income, origination fees, and interest earned on the loans during the time they are in inventory. In assessing the quality of the income and future projections, the officer should consider the effect of the short-term financial markets. Because the mortgage banker finances the inventory at rates relating to prime and because, based on recent experience, prime may be for sustained periods in excess of permanent mortgage rates, a negative carrying cost may result in a loss which cannot be offset by origination fees and servicing income.

The documentation and administration of lines of credit to mortgage bankers involve some techniques not common in other types of commercial bank lending. Some form of master note in the total amount of the credit facility is usually entered into, and provision is made for the notation of repayments and reborrowings thereunder on the face of the note. Advances under the note occur as mortgage loans are disbursed by the mortgage banker, and repayments occur when a block of mortgage loans is delivered to a permanent lender. The bank note will recite that it is secured by mortgages from time to time in existence.

The method of perfecting a security interest in each of the individual mortgage loans is a matter of some debate and is determined primarily by the law of the jurisdiction in which the mortgaged property lies. Although it was stated previously that the distinction between a mortgage and a deed of trust is not conceptually important, there are technical differences which affect mortgage warehousing. It is usually agreed that a security interest in a mortgage is obtained only when an assignment of the mortgage is recorded in the land title records where the mortgage itself was recorded. No recording is necessary in the case of a deed of trust. The recording of a mortgage assignment is a rather cumbersome procedure, particularly in light of the short assignment period, and should usually be dispensed with where the borrower is of significant financial strength or there are no other major creditors who might have priority claims in bankruptcy. Fraudulent dealing with the mortgage loan is by and large eliminated by requiring that the original mortgage note be endorsed to the bank and delivered into its possession.

At the time an advance is made against a mortgage loan, the bank should receive evidence that the loan was properly made and is enforceable. In addition to the original mortgage note, it should receive a certified copy of the mortgage, which will be in the process of recordation, a copy of the commitment for title insurance insuring that the lien created is a first and prior lien on the subject property, a certificate of hazard or fire insurance, a survey, and a copy of the truth in lending disclosure statement. In addition to this, certain types of lending such as FHA or VA loans may require other documents to comply with regulations and, to the extent that any of these documents can affect the enforceability of the insurance or guaranty, evidence that they were properly obtained should be given.

The bank should establish a periodic review procedure to determine the existence of the necessary commitments, in accordance with the warehouse agreement. This is especially true during a period of rising mortgage rates or scarce money, when these commitments are difficult to obtain and when breaches of these commitments occur with some regularity. The bank should be particularly attentive to the creditworthiness and reputation of the institutions from which the mortgage banker is obtaining these commitments. Regular review procedures, which should occur not less than once a year, should also be established to evaluate the collateral held by the bank as against the records of the mortgage banker.

16

Consumer Credit

It is inconceivable to imagine our modern economy without consumer credit. The majority of Americans have been participating in a buy-now, pay-later credit explosion, with the ability, if they wish, to do anything and everything on credit. Babies are born on credit, young people attend college on deferred time payments, and even funerals are paid on credit.

Because of the rapid growth in consumer credit (Table 1) and the inflationary spiral of the United States economy, credit controls not invoked since World War II were reestablished in March, 1980. The Credit Control Act required that banks within certain size criteria place additional reserves with the Federal Reserve Bank on any increases in unsecured and secured nonpurchase money loans outstanding. The purpose of the act was to moderate inflationary pressures and return our country to stable economic growth.

Total outstanding consumer installment credit dropped in April, 1980, for

Table 1 Consumer Credit Oustanding
(Millions of Dollars)

	1919	1929	1939	1949	1959	1969	1979
Total	2,642	7,116	7,222	17,334	51,544	111,146	382,022
Installment	800	3,524	4,503	11,590	39,247	97,105	311,122
Non-installment	1,842	3,592	2,719	5,744	12,297	24,041	70,000

Source: Economic Research Division, Federal Reserve Bank of Kansas City.

the first time in five years, and the restrictive measures of the Act were cut in half in May as the recession reached unexpected depths. Controls were virtually eliminated in early July, 1980.

Consumer installment debt continued to drop as the last vestiges of the credit tightening measures still made some consumers wary of incurring debt.

Early Development of Consumer Credit

Despite its record growth in recent years, consumer credit is not a modern development. Several types of consumer credit institutions developed in the period from 1800 to the Civil War. The merchant, the physician, and the pawnbroker all extended consumer credit during this period. Furniture stores may represent the first major industry to have entered the credit field. As early as 1807, the Cowperthwait and Sons New York Furniture House used an installment system to finance the purchase of home furnishings.

Pawnbrokers were among the first to make cash loans to the consumer in this country. By 1800 they were operating in New York City, Philadelphia, and Boston on an extensive scale. However, pawnbrokers are not technically consumer credit agencies because their transactions involve no explicit promise to pay. Their claim is against the property which is pledged in exchange for the cash loan, which technically is a conditional purchase of the borrower's personal property.

Dramatic economic changes took place in our country after 1860 as large numbers of people were drawn from farms to the large cities, manufacturing industries grew rapidly, and many department stores and chain retail institutions were founded.

Credit policies in effect prior to 1860 were liberalized as widespread extension of consumer credit developed along with the growth of several important consumer credit institutions and associations. Household Finance Corporation was established in 1878, and along with other contemporary personal loan companies, spread rapidly to the principal cities of the East and Middle West. However, in many other states there were few lawful lenders because the limitations imposed by existing usury statutes (specifying the maximum rate of interest which could be charged) tended to exclude lawful enterprises from the small-loan field.

Effective principles for making cash credit available on fair terms to the consumer borrower were not developed on a national basis until the twentieth century. In 1908 the Russell Sage Foundation, a philanthropic research agency, created a division of remedial loans to study the problems involved in making small loans, with particular emphasis on the possibility of government regulation. In 1911 Massachusetts pioneered the first comprehensive and workable system of small-loan regulation. New Jersey followed suit in 1914, New York, Ohio, and Pennsylvania did the same in 1915. The best solution to the problem came with the drafting of the Uniform Small Loan Law in 1916 after eight years of study of the small-loan business by the Russell Sage Foundation. Today, after many revisions and improvements, the statutes of most states generally follow the pattern of the Uniform Small Loan Law.

Passage of the Massachusetts Credit Union Law in 1909 opened the way to formal credit union development in the United States.

During this period, the "industrial bank" also came into existence. This is a financial institution which invests its funds chiefly in personal loans and which obtains or is authorized to obtain its funds from individual savers, either through the acceptance of deposits or the sale of investment certificates. The first industrial bank was organized in Norfolk, Virginia, in 1910 by Arthur J. Morris. Industrial banks expanded rapidly thereafter, using the "Morris Plan" approach.

This approach, used to eliminate the problem of the usury laws, provided that repayments would be credited to a non-interest bearing deposit or investment certificate account rather than to the loan. When the proceeds of the deposit or certificate equaled the loan amount plus interest, the balance was transferred to pay off the loan. This approach returned a rate of interest to the bank almost double the rate apparently charged, and often almost double the lawful usury rate.

During this same period, automobile manufacturers found their production and sales restricted because lack of cash prevented customers from purchasing their products. For this reason the General Motors Acceptance Corporation was formed in 1919, and Universal Credit Corporation (by Ford Motor Company) in 1929. These corporations financed the retail contracts resulting from the sale of automobiles to consumers and assisted dealers with inventory financing, also called floor plan financing.

Thus consumer credit developed as a vehicle to facilitate mass production and mass consumption.

Consumer Credit in Commercial Banks

There are no reliable statistics available to determine how many banks were making consumer installment loans during the pioneer days in consumer credit, but it is probable that there were very few.

In 1928 the National City Bank of New York announced the opening of a department to supply credit for consumer needs. This was the first large bank to enter the business in a formal way. In 1929 Bank of America, in San Francisco, with branches serving the entire state of California, entered the consumer installment loan business. These experiments were observed by bankers nationwide, but few were willing to accept this type of lending activity as a viable bank service. Historically, bankers have tended to be rather conservative and slow to accept radical changes until those changes have been tested and proven. Bankers during this period of time were used to looking at the net worth on a financial statement and the tangible collateral offered in passing judgment on the soundness of the credit quality. It was something new to evaluate loans strictly on the basis of character, personal and vocational stability, and the future income potential to repay the debt.

In the opinion of many bankers, the Federal Housing Administration was the major factor influencing banks to enter the field of consumer installment credit. On August 10, 1934, the Federal Housing Administration announced that it would furnish a liberal guarantee to all authorized lenders who would grant credit for home repairs and modernization.

The experience of lenders with FHA Title 1 loans furnished convincing proof that installment credit could be extended to qualified individuals on a safe and profitable basis. Within two years after the beginning of the FHA program, sufficient interest had developed on the part of many bankers to investigate other phases of installment credit. By 1938 almost 4,000 banks were engaged in some form of the business.

Recognizing that consumer credit was an essential part of the economy and the banking system, the American Bankers Association formalized a Consumer Credit Department within the organization in the early 1940s. The department continues today, assisting banks in improving their methods and procedures through publication of installment credit statistics (and other information) and by organizing conferences enabling installment bankers to discuss common problems and interests.

Today, banks are firmly entrenched in this important retail function and bank customers can obtain credit on installment terms for almost any worthwhile purpose.

Despite its humble beginning, the expansion of consumer credit was rapid and dramatic in the 1960s and 1970s because the individual consumer and the businessman became increasingly dependent upon the consumer's ability to use credit to fulfill varied wants, desires, and needs.

Installment transactions (loans repayable in two or more installments) are the major component of the broad consumer credit category. Commercial banks have attained a dominant position, as indicated by their 48 percent share of all installment credit outstanding at year-end 1979 (Table 2).

Acquiring Installment Business

There are two basic methods available to a bank for acquiring installment business; the direct loan and the indirect (dealer) approach. Many banks use a combination of both methods.

Direct loans involve only two parties, the bank and the borrower. The interviewer is able to insure that sufficient and complete information is obtained on the credit application and develop any further information necessary

Table 2   Consumer Installment Credit by Major Holder
(Millions of Dollars)

	1919	1929	1939	1949	1959	1969	1979
Commercial banks	19	201	1,079	4,439	15,227	42,421	149,604
Sales finance companies	73	1,074	1,197	2,944	9,880	‡	‡
Finance Companies						27,846	68,318
Credit union	4	22	132	438	3,280	12,028	48,186
Consumer finance companies	†	†	†	†	3,337	‡	‡
Others*	68	448	657	1,436	1,407	1,694	17,108
Retail outlets	636	1,779	1,438	2,333	6,116	13,116	27,916
Total	800	3,524	4,503	11,590	39,247	97,105	311,122

* Includes savings and loans associations and mutual savings banks.

† Consumer finance companies are included in other financal institutions until 1950.

‡ Finance companies consist of those companies formerly classified as sales finance companies and consumer finance companies.

Source: Economic Research Division, Federal Reserve Bank of Kansas City.

to explain what may be obvious weaknesses or inadequate or incomplete statements on the application which may hinder the credit investigation and the timeliness of a proper credit decision on the bank's part. Direct loans are often used for purchase of consumer durable goods, but a large portion is to meet such unusual expenses as medical and dental expenses and college fees and in some cases to consolidate credit obligations where a change in economic status may have affected the borrower's ability to meet obligations on a current basis.

Indirect loans, on the other hand, are three-party transactions where the seller of goods or services obtains the credit application and completes necessary documentation at the seller's place of business. The majority of bank installment credit outstanding is generated through retail sales contracts, or indirect financing. Although almost any goods or services may be financed on an indirect basis, most commercial banks are active in purchasing contracts on larger-ticket items which develop a better profit margin.

Establishing Consumer Installment Credit Policies

There are four major reasons a bank participates in an installment lending operation:

1. To serve the financial needs of the community
2. To meet competition
3. To generate additional profit
4. To attract customers for other bank services

The scope of an installment loan operation varies from bank to bank and depends on many factors. The successful operation is guided by a written loan policy which is developed through input from senior lending officers and senior management and is reviewed and approved or ratified by the bank's board of directors.

Establishing loan policy is not an easy task, and once it is established it must be continuously reviewed and updated to reflect changes in local and national economic conditions, customers' demands, the knowledge and ability of the bank's officers and staff, and any other internal and external restraints which could have an effect on the bank's liquidity position.

The first consideration is the expertise of the bank's officers and staff to whom the responsibility for the installment lending function is assigned. With a staff that is knowledgeable and experienced in all phases of installment lending, the bank is able to derive the maximum benefits from an installment credit operation.

Consumer compliance policy is a major concern. The board of directors of every bank should, as a part of the bank's policy and procedures or in a separate resolution, issue a nondiscriminatory practices statement and state the bank's intent to comply with all consumer laws and regulations. The absence of policies and procedures and/or a compliance resolution will make it extremely difficult to eliminate violations of consumer regulations.

Banking has long been one of the most highly regulated industries in the United States, but until recently regulation centered on safety, soundness, and solvency. In the last decade, however, an additional emphasis has evolved. Since the passage of the Consumer Credit Protection Act in 1968, the banking industry has been virtually deluged with a flood of consumer protection legislation. It is a rare bank that can hope to comply with this varied legislation without an individual charged with the responsibility of overseeing consumer compliance responsibility. This varies from a part-time individual in smaller banks to consumer compliance departments with in-house legal expertise. Whether the bank is big or small, the job of the individual (or individuals) charged with consumer compliance cannot be overemphasized. As with the overall operation of the bank, the board of directors is legally charged with the responsibility to provide the impetus for the bank's compliance efforts. It is realized that the board cannot actually supervise all facets of line activity. Consequently, the responsibility is generally delegated to senior management officials whose activities are closer to those of line management. It is appropriate for the board formally to appoint a "compliance officer," who is delegated not only the responsibility for compliance but also the authority to insure it.

The compliance officer must insure development, administration, and maintenance of internal controls sufficient to insure compliance with all consumer laws and regulations. The officer must be thoroughly or at least fundamentally familiar with all Federal and state consumer laws and regulations and be aware of related interpretations. He should be charged with responsibility for reviewing the bank's policies and procedures regarding consumer laws and regulations; development of written policies (for senior management and board approval); various facets of consumer regulation; development of an efficient method to keep personnel aware of legal changes; and the constant review of procedures, forms, and legal documents. He should assist with training new personnel and be responsible for the ongoing training of other personnel. In conjunction with the auditor, he should also periodically review all applicable facets of the bank's operation for consumer compliance.

In many banks the consumer compliance officer is named in a board resolution which further defines the duties and responsibilities of the job and his relationship with other bank departments and divisions to insure complete cooperation. This resolution is usually disseminated throughout the bank to all departments and division heads. This serves not only to develop the importance of consumer compliance but also to assist in developing the compliance effort which will minimize or eliminate the possibility of civil liability for violation of consumer laws and regulations.

MARKET POTENTIAL

The market potential must be carefully weighed. When policy for installment credit is established, it is imperative that the policymakers be aware of the types of customers they may expect as well as the types of merchants in the community who will generate installment paper.

COMPETITION

Competition is another major factor influencing policy decisions of a bank. This will determine the type of endorsement a bank may hope to receive on dealer paper as well as influence rates and terms which may be used competitively. Generally, bank rates tend to be somewhat lower than nonbank competitors. As a result, banks cannot afford to accept as high a risk. Therefore, it is not uncommon to find that bank policies often are more conservative than those of nonbank competitors.

ALLOCATION OF FUNDS

The amount of funds available for allocation to the consumer installment loan function is an important consideration. If funds are limited it may be necessary to confine operations to direct lending on a highly selective basis. A bank will rarely eliminate the consumer installment credit function, because good long-time customers depend on it. State usury rates may have some effect on the allocation of funds. If state consumer usury rates are at so low a level (as occurred in late 1979 and early 1980) as to eliminate the profitable operations of a consumer loan program, funds may be significantly curtailed except to the most creditworthy bank customers. Consumer loan availability is presently adversely affected by low usury loan rate ceilings in many states. Some states are revising their rates in order to hold this business within their states.

An additional constraint that has limited bank consumer lending recently has been the sharp increase in the incidence of personal bankruptcies facilitated by the Bankruptcy Act of 1978.

TRADE TERRITORY

The trade territory in which a bank is willing to extend consumer installment credit should be a part of the bank's loan policy. This has been somewhat simplified by the Community Reinvestment Act Notice, which is written, reviewed, and approved by a bank's board of directors on an annual basis. The local community is clearly delineated and the loans which the bank is willing to make are clearly stated along with a statement explaining what the bank is doing to meet the credit needs of the local community. When any change in the bank's lending policy or CRA is anticipated, both the policy and the CRA statement should be examined for compatibility.

TYPES OF LOANS

The types of loans a bank is willing to make are also a part of the CRA statement. When determining the types of consumer installment loans to be offered, the profit potential must be considered. And in a period of high money costs, only a naive banker concentrates much time and effort in the acquisition of small loans.

RATES AND TERMS

Rates and terms are another very important consideration. It is always important to be aware of rate competition and to remain competitive but profitable. To most customers and dealers, when a bank is involved in indirect credit, service is almost as important as rates, and many banks are paid a slightly higher rate for excellent service rendered. But it should always be remembered that being competitive but not profitable does not warrant involvement in installment lending. As terms become longer and longer due to inflation, we must consistently stay in touch with down payment requirements. On most consumer durable goods the smaller down payment should have a correspondingly shorter term to shorten the time the bank is in a negative equity position.

LENDING AUTHORITY

The authority to approve loans depends a great deal on the ability and experience of the officers and staff. Inexperienced lending personnel should have lower, more restrictive loan authority, requiring them to obtain advice from more experienced officers. This advice and counsel should enable them rapidly to gain the experience and judgment necessary to warrant higher lending limits. The lending authority should also state whether the limits apply to secured or unsecured loans and the types and sizes of loans which must be approved by the loan committee. Lending authority is an important policy consideration, and in determining it the bank must consider the customer who wants and expects a prompt decision from the bank.

The policy should also set out application requirements, the definition of a formal application, and loan review procedures to assist strict adherence to consumer compliance legislation.

Once a policy and procedures guide is established, it must be continuously reviewed and updated. Our local and national economy changes continuously, as does the deposit mix of a bank's customers. Policy and procedures must be constantly reviewed to provide the liquidity, solvency, and safety requirements for a particular bank. An up-to-date, well-written policy is an excellent tool to develop sound, profitable installment loans for the bank and to develop knowledgeable, skilled installment loan personnel.

Other Considerations

PHYSICAL FACILITIES

Equal success has been obtained in banks with open platform arrangements and banks with private interview rooms or offices. The most important consideration is to provide the applicant with warm, friendly, pleasant surroundings in which he feels comfortable in transacting his business with the bank.

More and more banks are housing their installment loan operations in areas away from the main bank lobby to provide access to customers both before and after regular banking hours. This may be a consideration in a community where market potential is primarily employees whose job schedules may conflict with traditional banking hours.

PERSONNEL

In many banks the installment loan operation is handled in the retail banking department or division. This is an indication of the type of service offered. Installment lending is a retail business, and as with other retail operations it requires knowledgeable, tactful, courteous, and friendly personnel who can deal with large numbers of borrowers from every socioeconomic stratum. Many banks have expanded the services offered by installment loan officers into a retail banking concept where the personnel are well trained in all phases of retail banking. This requires better educated and well-trained personnel but offers a dividend by giving the customer the convenience he demands and by giving the bank a better opportunity to recognize and exploit sales opportunities.

DOCUMENTS AND FORMS

With the advent of consumerism and the resulting consumer laws and regulations, it is almost impossible to use legal documents and forms for a long period of time without some modification to meet changing legal requirements. Although there are a number of excellent professional forms companies and correspondent banks willing to share their expertise, only an unwise banker adopts forms and documents blindly without consulting legal counsel. Systematic review procedures must be established to assure that all legal documents and forms are periodically reviewed by in-house counsel, the consumer compliance officer, and/or legal counsel to insure that they comply fully with all existing consumer laws and regulations.

SOURCE OF ADDITIONAL INCOME

When legally permissible, the collection of service charges and fees helps defray the cost of making and collecting installment credit transactions. Some states permit lenders to charge an acquisition fee or at least to retain a minimum fee on any account that is paid in full a short time after the transaction was put on the books. The cost of filing or recording legal documents may often be passed on to the customer. The additional expense of collecting delinquent accounts may be partially recovered through late charges.

Many banks offer creditors group life insurance, accident and health insurance, or other forms of liability insurance in connection with installment transactions. These forms of insurance and the rates charged are closely regulated in most states, and many states now require full licensing of a bank agent. Commissions on these types of insurance can make a good contribution to installment loan department profit. Banks are urged to examine closely all laws dealing with offering creditor's insurance and to leave the purchase optional as required in Regulation Z. Banks writing insurance in excess of 80 percent of their loans will be closely examined by regulatory authorities.

BUSINESS DEVELOPMENT METHODS

Since there are a number of banks and nonbanking organizations competing for the installment lending business, any bank desiring a substantial volume of business must be aggressive in the marketplace.

Direct loan business is most successfully generated through extensive promotional efforts. This includes newspaper, radio, television, billboards, statement enclosures, lobby displays, and direct mail. Many banks use a combination of these methods or perhaps all of them when economic conditions provide available funds and rates which are profitable to the bank. Many banks have been successful in soliciting additional or future business from present loan customers by using direct mail at a predetermined point in the life of the customer's current loan. These borrowers are usually very loyal to the bank and will return so long as they are treated fairly and receive prompt, personal consideration. They are also an excellent source of new business for other areas of the bank.

Indirect business, on the other hand, is generally developed through public relations efforts with the various dealers who can provide profitable business to the bank. The dealer must be shown that he can receive prompt, efficient services by knowledgeable, skilled bank officers to enable him to use the bank's credit services as a sales tool.

It is equally important in business development that a bank maintain up-to-date procedures and ideas. One way is to visit other banks to analyze their methods and procedures. Bankers should attend installment conferences and subscribe to the best books and magazines available through the various banking publishing houses. This does not mean that others' systems or methods should be copied but rather that new systems and new methods which will improve the bank's installment loan operation should be compared and investigated.

Qualifications of A Good Installment Credit Risk

The ability and willingness of a prospective borrower to repay generally insures a good credit risk.

For years bankers have used such old standbys of credit—character, capacity, collateral, capital, and conditions. However, in recent years, bankers have begun to recognize that these tests do not form an exclusive classification system and that it is not always possible to separate the facts that bear on character from those of capacity and those bearing on capacity from those bearing on capital. Most bankers find it desirable to list and discuss all personal credit qualifications which appear essential and valuable to the applicant. Discussion of the qualifications of a good installment credit risk takes into consideration other qualities pertinent to the credit decision.

Willingness to repay is a reflection of the applicant's character. Is the applicant a good moral risk? If the investigation reveals deliberate misstatements by the applicant, conviction for criminal offense, embezzlement, moral turpitude, or other indications of poor character, the application is usually rejected without further consideration. A good risk, on the other hand, will furnish a relatively accurate statement and the investigation will develop that the record of meeting past credit obligations has been satisfactory.

The ability of the applicant to repay is reflected by his vocational stability and financial capacity. Does the applicant have sufficient income to repay the loan? It is almost impossible to analyze each applicant's budget in detail, but it is necessary to appraise the ability to repay by evaluating the factors of dependency, shelter payments, fixed expenses, various insurance programs, and other items listed in the credit application. The applicant must have a margin of income above his fixed obligations and other necessary expenses to qualify as a good credit risk.

The continuation of income is very important in evaluating the ability and capacity of the applicant. The applicant who changes jobs frequently is less likely to be a good credit risk than one who has established seniority on the job in a well-established organization. The stability of the employer and the size of his business are also important factors to consider. While it is unfair to single out any particular type of employment as an undesirable credit factor, it is a known fact that the state of the economy will have more effect on some industries than others. It is important that bankers be aware of the local and national condition of the various industries in our communities to enable us to evaluate the future income potential of applicants from these particular types of businesses or industries.

Too often bankers lull themselves into a sense of false security by assuming that adequate collateral exists to secure a loan in the event that unforeseen circumstances adversely influence a borrower's capacity to repay. The purpose of the loan should be as much a part of the credit evaluation as other credit factors. Is the applicant making a necessary purchase or purchasing impulsively, being lured into the purchase not because of good quality or reasonable price but because the payment terms are easy? Is the applicant making a purchase now because of an attractive sale or special, because of the likelihood that a necessary item will have a substantially higher price in the near future, or solely as a morale booster or perhaps to raise the current standard of living above what he or she can afford on present income? Is the applicant borrowing because of a genuine emergency or is he actually overusing his credit and as a result failing to maintain an adequate cash reserve? Bankers have not only an obligation to preserve the funds of depositors but also a moral obligation to the community to assist with the proper use of credit and avoidance of future financial problems.

Capital is another measure of the creditworthiness of an applicant. What does the borrower own which provides a margin of safety in the event of adverse circumstances resulting in inability to meet installment obligations? Ownership of tangible collateral sometimes enables a bank to be more liberal than normal in term or advance criteria when evaluating an applicant.

Conditions must always be considered in determining the aggressiveness or conservativeness of a particular bank's installment loan operation. Inflation cuts into the disposable income of the consumer and the excess of income over expenditures available for repayment. Recession results in a downturn in industrial output with resultant layoffs or elimination of jobs. Both the local and national economy must be considered by banks in all phases of lending.

Investigation and Credit Decision

The purpose of the credit investigation and analysis is to secure, classify, and grade facts. To make a proper decision for both the bank and the applicant, it is necessary that the information given by the applicant be verified, his manner and habits in making payments established, and any other information necessary to enable a prompt and proper decision be developed.

There are four basic sources from which a bank may obtain credit information. Perhaps the most important, from a bank's standpoint, is the bank's own records. Has the applicant had previous credit experience with the bank, and, if so, was the credit handled in a satisfactory manner? A previous account resulting in a charge-off or extensive collection work may preclude an applicant from further consideration.

Another source of credit information is directly to check the references given on the credit application and to obtain a detailed reference. This reference will include the date the account opened, the opening amount, present balance, amount and number of monthly payments, collateral used if any, and the manner in which the borrower is making his payment.

CREDIT BUREAU

An alternative or supplement to direct credit information used by most banks is the credit bureau. The bureau is a membership organization that may be a cooperative, a nonprofit organization, or a profitmaking organization.

Credit bureau procedures are fairly standard. Normally a merchant or other businessman pays a yearly membership fee. When he wants to make an inquiry, he telephones the credit bureau, identifies himself by a prearranged code number, and gives the applicant's name and address, social security number, name of employer, previous address, credit references, and as much information as he can give in order to avoid mistakes or mistaken identity.

The report will normally give the customer's employer, when employment was verified, and credit references from various firms used, indicating opening balances, current balance as of the date of the last check, and whether payments have been satisfactory. Any history of bankruptcy or civil or criminal litigation, including suits filed and collection accounts, will generally appear if within the time limits established by the Fair Credit Reporting Act.

A local credit bureau provides the cheapest and fastest information a creditor can obtain. It generally has a high degree of reliability and completeness, although not always completely accurate.

If a report is outdated, most credit bureaus will update the file by calling all of the previous references and open accounts to obtain current information, but will generally make an additional charge. Many banks supply information on all new consumer loans to their credit bureau to help assure the completeness of information in the file. In addition, most banks conscientiously report repossessions, charge-offs, and troublesome accounts to assist the bureau in giving the most complete, accurate file possible.

If no problems are reported to the bureau, it will simply state that everything is satisfactory as far as known. The best news it will state is that there is no bad news.

A source of verification of employment is the applicant's employer. Generally, given the various privacy regulations, the employer will only verify employment and give little additional information.

Credit checking is necessary and important, but we must realize that it will not guarantee that we will not have losses. Even if we learn everything possible about a potential customer from all available sources, about his present circumstances and his past record, the future will remain uncertain. People and circumstances both change. A good past record provides an indication of future behavior but extension of credit still involves risk. Marital difficulty, unexpected medical expenses, or other financial difficulties beyond the customer's control may adversely affect ability to repay.

After verifying the facts given on the credit application, obtaining such other information as is available concerning the applicant, and determining the market value of the collateral offered, an appraisal of the risk must be made.

Credit Evaluation

Time-tested guidelines of consumer credit have determined that regularity of income, reliability and stability of the source, and a clear credit record are the necessary attributes of a good credit risk. If these factors have been determined, and there is sufficient net income to pay monthly fixed obligations and other related expenses with adequate additional margin, the application will normally be approved.

The traditional method of evaluating credit applicants is called the judgmental credit evaluation process. A credit analyst examines the applicant's characteristics, evaluates the applicant's creditworthiness, and decides to approve or decline the applicant. This process is based on the experience and human judgment of the individual analyst. Most banks use the judgmental evaluation process, but others employ an empirical credit evaluation known as credit scoring. This system uses a numerical formula to predict the credit risk of an applicant by assigning points to specific applicant characteristics such as income, current debt level relative to income, and years at current job. By law, certain variables such as sex or marital status may not be included in a credit scoring system. The total of the points indicates the credit risk of the applicant (low points imply high risk) and is compared to a cutoff score. If the applicant's score equals or exceeds the cutoff, the applicant is accepted; if it does not, the applicant is declined. Through this quantitative analysis, the credit granting function becomes less dependent upon subjective factors.

The ability and efficiency of the bank are reflected in its responsiveness to applicants and customers. Regardless of the action taken, it is imperative that a prompt decision be made and relayed to the applicant. Many applicants, including those who have excellent credit and will receive ultimate approval, are somewhat apprehensive about applying for credit. The bank will improve its image, build good will, and perhaps generate additional customers for other bank services by taking quick action on a loan request. If conditional approval is granted for an amount other than that applied for or on different types of collateral, the applicant should be notified as quickly as possible and given the reason for the action.

Rejected applications should receive the same courtesy. From a public relations standpoint, many applicants rejected or granted conditional approval may have future potential as excellent bank customers. They may be applying for credit which is not currently within their means or is not properly secured. This could change in the future, and it is impractical to preclude them from ever doing business with the bank by discourtesy and improper handling of the present application.

For other than approved applications it is necessary to establish a system to assure that proper notification, as required under the Fair Credit Reporting Act and the Equal Credit Opportunity Act, is made and that file copies are maintained for the required time.

Direct Lending

Direct lending as previously defined is a two-party transaction between the applicant and the bank. Many banks quite appropriately participate only in direct lending due to the absence of qualified dealers to generate profitable business in sufficient quantity, competitive situations in which the bank does not care to compete, or due to inexperienced installment loan personnel not yet ready to cope with the faster-moving dealer situation.

In a direct lending environment, various elements of the loan portfolio can be controlled to a greater extent. Perhaps the bank wishes to remain somewhat conservative in volume and outstandings or wishes to maintain better control over quality and the size of loans or participate in only certain types for which funds can be allocated on a more conservative basis. Generally in this type of environment it is much easier to train and develop bank personnel into executives because the pace is somewhat slower than a dealer operation. With bank personnel conducting the interview and granting the credit, the experience is more beneficial than in a dealer operation, which involves no personal contact with the applicant. Loan authority for trainees in a direct loan operation is generally restricted to enable more experienced loan officers to assist with credit approval and documentation, which provides training and development.

With closer control over quality, and therefore over delinquencies and losses, a direct lending operation is often more profitable than an indirect operation. But at this point we should remember that direct loan volume is acquired through more extensive advertising and promotion than an indirect operation requires.

THE LOAN INTERVIEW

It is important for the interviewer to remember why an applicant comes to a particular bank:

1. The applicant was invited to do so by solicitation through advertising
2. The applicant is a depositor or a customer of another department
3. The bank was recommended to the applicant
4. Or, the applicant needs financial assistance and selected a special bank.

As a result, the applicant is entitled to cordial and pleasant treatment and should receive the utmost consideration from the bank.

The purpose of the interview is to produce adequate reliable information to establish definite identification of the applicant, to permit prompt and easy checking of his credit through credit bureaus and other sources, and to facilitate quick verification of other features of the loan request. This enables the credit officer to make a proper decision for the applicant and the bank, as well as aid in the collection of the account if it becomes delinquent.

The interviewer must have a sound knowledge of the bank's lending policies and the ability to apply them, as well as an understanding of the bank's internal installment credit operation including a knowledge of the collection procedures and the legal means available. The interviewer must exhibit mature judgment and ingenuity to build a good loan clientele for the bank in a highly competitive market, and develop discretion and understanding in encouraging worthy applicants, as well as a sincere desire to understand problems of borrowers. He should show skill in converting as many applicants as possible into good loan customers.

During this initial phase of the interview, the interviewer must relieve tension resulting from the applicant's apprehension in applying for credit, gain the applicant's confidence and encourage him to talk willingly and freely. The interviewer should actually guide and control the course of the interview toward the facts and details so important in establishing the character and capacity of the applicant which enable the credit officer to make proper and prompt decisions.

During the course of the interview, the interviewer may develop information often referred to as "danger signals," which may not preclude the applicant from further consideration but may require development of additional information and more detailed credit investigation. The interviewer should always be alert for these potential danger signals and ask sufficient questions to ascertain that they will not cause additional risk should the bank approve the applicant's loan request. The following is a list of potential danger signals which should alert the interviewer to proceed with care:

1. Definite identification is not available.
2. The applicant applies at a bank far removed from his home or work.
3. The applicant's mail is directed in care of a friend or to a post office box.
4. An applicant is in a tremendous hurry to obtain the loan and attempts to do some fast talking regarding his desirability as a credit risk.
5. The information furnished on the application is contradictory, or weaknesses are disclosed which raise a question as to the honesty and integrity of the applicant.
6. The applicant is employed intermittently, is a job shifter, or has just started another job.
7. The applicant does not have an established place of business and only rents desk space or has a telephone answering service.
8. The nature of the applicant's business or occupation cannot be satisfactorily explained and may be illegitimate.
9. There is difficulty obtaining prior credit history or background.
10. An applicant's income is at a mere subsistence level.
11. An applicant is overextended in debt.
12. There is evidence of frequent renewals for increased amounts.

The interview which results in accurate and complete credit information facilitates prompt and easy verification of the applicant's credit standing and desirability as a good credit risk.

THE CREDIT APPLICATION

There is a wide variance of opinion regarding the most effective method of taking credit applications. Some banks require that the applicant complete the application process while in the bank, with the interviewer asking the questions and filling out the application. Other banks have the applicant complete it on his own and review questions with the interviewer, while yet others encourage the applicant to take the application to complete. It is suggested that somewhere between the application and loan completion process, an interviewer or loan officer take the time to review the application with the applicant to ascertain completeness and assess the maturity of the applicant.

Indirect or Dealer Financing

As previously defined, indirect financing is a three-party transaction with the seller obtaining the credit application, relaying it to the bank for consideration, and drawing up the necessary notes and documents to complete the loan.

There are advantages to participating in this type of financing. Indirect or dealer financing is a quicker volume builder than a direct loan operation; it requires only a modest advertising effort (primarily public relations) and is an excellent source of new customers who might not otherwise be doing business with the bank. However, the indirect or dealer business is not without risk. While elimination of the interview time and the time necessary to prepare loan documents provides economy, it also creates certain problems. The attitude of the customer about his obligation to pay is not as good as a direct loan transaction, with the borrower dealing directly with the bank. If the customer becomes dissatisfied with the merchandise or service, he may associate the bank with the seller and collection problems may arise.

Other problems may arise from the lack of contact between the applicant and the bank. The dealer's employee in effect represents the bank and often may be more interested in selling the merchandise than taking care of the credit aspects. Consequently, application information may be more limited and less accurate than that obtained during an interview, and the dealer's pressure for speedy credit decisions does not always permit a thorough investigation, possibly resulting in a careless credit decision. Any bank entering the indirect, or dealer credit, field must be equipped for fast-moving situations, and be willing to accept a higher level of collection effort and expense than is considered desirable in direct lending. To participate in the dealer field, a bank must develop special accounting procedures and auditing systems to protect itself against possible fraud situations such as fictitious paper, double financing, down payment misrepresentation, and undelivered merchandise.

A bank may also have to provide other types of credit to a dealer to attract any volume of retail paper. The typical credit provided is floor planning, or financing of dealer inventory available for resale. There is a high degree of risk and a below normal return for this type of financing. There is always a possibility that a dealer may sell the bank's collateral without making the required payment to the bank, resulting in a situation known as "sold out of trust." Many banks, balancing this risk against the lower than normal return, may decide to restrict their installment credit to the direct lending field and whatever dealer paper they can acquire without furnishing credit directly to the dealer.

There are various other types of credit which may be necessary for the dealer, such as short-term working capital requirements to cover seasonal fluctuations of business, tax payments, advances against manufacturers' holdbacks and term loan credit for expansion of the business. Credit may be needed also to purchase equipment, to purchase the interest of other principals or owners, to provide working capital to an otherwise undercapitalized venture, and for real estate, a somewhat risky credit due to the generally single-purpose nature of the buildings and improvements.

All of these factors must be taken into consideration when selecting and soliciting a dealer for indirect business. The financial qualifications of the dealer must be thoroughly investigated, and even though a bank may be participating in indirect credit with a dealer whom they are not otherwise financing, periodic financial statements must be required to determine that the dealer is in sound financial condition and is operating at a profit.

The background of the dealer is equally important. Character and reputation must be checked to determine the dealer's knowledge, experience, and performance in both the territory he serves and the product he sells. This verification can not be lessened because most transactions are secured. On the contrary, the potential for fraud is great both in purchasing paper and in floor planning the inventory. Dealer selling policies are important to the bank because the public associates the dealer with the bank carrying the paper. Unethical practices and high-pressure methods not only adversely affect the quality of the paper but also damage the reputation of the bank.

The trading area served by the dealer should generally conform to the trade area served by the bank. Any business obtained from areas outside of the bank's normal trade territory is more difficult and dangerous to handle. Credit checks are harder to make and more expensive, collections are more costly and less effective, fraud becomes harder to detect, and customers outside the normal banking area are unlikely to generate other forms of business for the bank.

DEALER PROTECTIVE AGREEMENTS

There is a wide variety of dealer agreements available in connection with the purchase of installment paper from dealers.

1. *Full recourse.* Under this plan the dealer unconditionally guarantees all paper sold to the bank. This plan is generally used when a fully responsible dealer in excellent financial condition desires to obtain the minimum discount rate and is willing to take the risks. To assure that the dealer remains financially solvent and the bank does not accept undue risks, all applicants should be required to submit a full credit application and the bank should check and approve all credit.

2. *Limited liability.* There are many types of limited liability, such as the dealer retaining full recourse until a certain number of payments have been made on the contract, or on the basis that the dealer's liability is limited to the sum on deposit in a special loss reserve. Any losses that subsequently occur are charged to the reserve account. Should the account be depleted, the bank has no further recourse to the dealer.

3. *Repurchase plan.* Generally this type of plan provides that when an account is in default, the dealer will repurchase the merchandise involved if

tendered to him at his place of business within a prespecified period of time after original default. The obligation of locating and repossessing collateral is vested in the bank. Generally this type of plan will have an agreement to extend the repurchase period in the event of litigation or insolvency or bankruptcy proceedings.

4. *Nonrecourse.* Paper purchased from dealers under this plan bears only the warranties from the dealer that the transaction is genuine, that proper title and security interest is transferred, and that the terms of the sale are as stated in the instrument. Once a dealer endorses the note to the bank, he is relieved of liability for nonpayment except that resulting from breach of warranty on the dealer's part as established under the Federal Trade Commission's rules and regulations and the Uniform Consumer Credit Code in many states. The nonrecourse endorsement usually returns a higher rate to the bank than the recourse arrangement. If a bank's particular market bears some type of endorsement, a bank should use extreme caution before establishing a "without recourse" purchase plan and purchasing lower-grade paper. Under this plan a bank must obviously select the paper carefully, using as its prime consideration the credit qualifications of the purchaser.

There are many variations of the protective agreements previously described, but for the purpose of this chapter the descriptions are confined to those most generally in use.

DEALER RESERVES

Merchants often derive substantial income from the sale of contracts to financial institutions. This income is derived from charging a particular rate to the purchaser and discounting the paper with the financial institution at a lower rate with the difference being credited to what is referred to as a dealer reserve account. If a protective agreement between the bank and the dealer imposes some liability on the dealer for losses, the bank will likely hold some portion, if not all, of the reserve account, with this account serving as a margin of safety to both the dealer and the bank in the event the dealer cannot comply with the terms of his agreement. In other cases, such as without recourse endorsement, the bank will establish a level at which it wishes to keep the balances to cover rebates of precomputed loans and generally pay the excess to the dealer at the end of certain intervals of time. For recourse or repurchase contracts a reserve account building to 3 to 5 percent of outstandings is fairly customary within the industry.

Collection Procedures

The ultimate goal of any collection system is to recover the amount owed. To establish creditability a bank must develop well-defined collection policies and procedures. This means that past due notices must be prepared and mailed on a timely basis, that those accounts not responding to notices be assigned to a collector or collection department for personalized letter or personal contact on a predetermined basis, and that those borrowers failing to keep payment promises be contacted immediately after the promise date. It also means that delinquent loans should be consistently reviewed, and, when it becomes apparent that the borrower has neither the ability nor the intention to pay, that the necessary action be taken to repossess collateral or bring legal action to enforce payment. Chronic delinquencies take advantage of haphazard, nonprofessional collection procedures, resulting in excessive delinquencies and higher losses.

A common sense approach must be used with regard to the notice or reminder policy. Sending out a past due notice on the day following the due date of an unpaid installment is an unnecessary expense, as over 90 percent of all payments are received within five days of due date. Many banks give a customer a grace period of five to seven days before sending a reminder, while others wait as long as ten days, or the period required by state law, to permit addition of any late fee allowable. Some banks send only one notice prior to personal contact, while others send two. The number of notices is unimportant. Either may work for a particular bank. What is important is that there be a consistent procedure. If payments are not received after notice, the next step is assignment of the account to a collector after a predetermined number of days. In many banks the collection efforts are conducted by officers who made the loans, in others a specialized collector or collection department may be assigned the account to avoid the personal relationship that has developed between the borrower and a particular loan officer. Regardless of the method used, the best results are obtained by a close follow-up. It is important that contact be made and that the reason for the delinquency be determined to assist the customer in solving his delinquency problem. A persistent, well-organized collection effort will hold delinquencies and losses to a minimum, and strong collection measures are seldom necessary.

If it is determined that the customer is uncooperative and unwilling to pay the debt, stronger effort in the form of repossession or legal action may be necessary.

The primary purpose of any collection effort is to bring an account up to date, receive future payments as contracted (to avoid further collection expense), and retain the customer's good will. Few customers go past due on purpose. For many of them it is merely a temporary setback such as unforeseen medical expense, a temporary job cutback, illness of the primary wage earner, or other unexpected expenses. If close contact is maintained with the customer, the delinquency status of the account should work itself out, and the bank should retain a potential good customer for the future.

Charged-off loans should never be overlooked in the collection function. There is often a tendency to work only those accounts which are currently on the books and which show up in various departmental reports as part of the delinquency. However, persistently working charged-off accounts will result in recoveries and a lower loss ratio. Charged-off loans should also be studied and reviewed with the bank's lending officers to determine why particular loans resulted in losses. By reviewing such loans, a bank is often able to determine that a particular problem with policies or procedures exists.

Operational Procedures

After the necessary documents are completed, the loan proceeds are paid to the borrower by check or deposit to an account—in a dealer situation, to the merchant in exchange for assignment of the retail contract to the bank. Dealer contracts are checked for completeness and accuracy before disbursement of the funds.

The loan documents should then go to a loan processing area to complete any required perfection of security interest and to process any insurance written in connection with the loan.

After the transaction has been checked, the total amount of the loan will be charged to consumer loans and will be offset by necessary entries to the officer's checks or the consumer's checking account, unearned discount, dealer reserve or holdback, insurance premiums, or other accounts.

Computer input is prepared either on hard copy or directly if on-line capabilities exist. If a manual operation is used, ledger cards are prepared. This section is also responsible for preparation or ordering of a coupon book, establishment of a casualty insurance follow-up card to insure receipt of a policy, typing of index cards, and any other records necessary for servicing an account. With an automated installment loan system, many of these records are produced by the computer.

Some banks purchase insurance to protect their interest rather than establish an insurance follow-up system. Others with a high-volume operation may establish a self-insurance system.

Regardless of the system used and the extent of follow-up desired, one officer should be designated to oversee the procedures and development of reports to management.

Income Accrual

Accrual methods vary from bank to bank and by size of loan portfolio. A cash-basis bank takes discount and interest charges into income immediately, while others accrue income as frequently as daily. These banks must determine what basis of accrual will be used: sum of the digits, level or straight line, or average interest. Determining the method and mechanics can be a difficult task due to various rates and terms. A manual operation using sum of the digits accrual may establish focal points with all loans maturing on the same date grouped for ease in computation. Those using a level or straight line accrual generally divide the discount or interest by the number of months in the contract and accrue on a monthly basis. Using this approach, prepaid loans on the "rule of 78's" rebate system create plus adjustments to the bank's income.

Fortunately most banks have access to computers, either through purchase or acquiring the service from a correspondent bank, which simplifies the computations.

The best method used is the one which will accurately or very closely approximate the actual earning on the installment loan portfolio.

Rebate of Installment Loan Charges

Many banks are changing to the "simple interest" method of writing loans, accruing interest on the principal balance and applying payments received first to interest and then the balance to principal. However, some banks still write what are known as precomputed loans; the contract is written to include in the face amount the finance charge for the entire period of the loan. When such an obligation is paid in full prior to maturity, the unearned finance charge and any applicable insurance written in connection with the loan are refunded to the borrower. Most states govern rebates by statute.

The most common rebate method used on precomputed loans is the sum of the digits, or "78's," method. This method derives its name from the application to a 12-month loan; the sum of the digits 1 to 12 is 78. The charge is split into 78 units. The first month, 12 of these units are considered earned (66 units left unearned); second month, 11 months earned (55 units left unearned); and so on. Accurate manual computation of unearned interest on each loan is impossible in a large bank. Most computer software on the market has "rule of 78's" capacity for consumer application.

However, it is still necessary for the loan officer to have an understanding of the system and how it works. A simple formula for computing the rule of 78's rebate is:

$$\frac{S\,(S+1)}{N\,(N+1)} \times \text{Total finance charge} = \text{Customer rebate}$$

where S = number of payment periods that are anticipated (remaining) in accordance with time elapsed, not payments made

N = number of payment periods in the original contract

Although this system was developed as a substitute for simple interest, it is difficult for the typical consumer to understand. It is probably best explained by noting that interest earned is larger on the higher outstanding principal balance and declines on lower balances (as is the case for amortized loans).

On longer-term loans (for example, purchase of mobile homes), the rule of 78's is recognized by consumer advocates as a penalty for prepaying loans in the early stages. Consequently, legislation is being considered which would abolish or limit the use of the rule of 78's to precomputed contracts of shorter terms.

Charge-offs

Although charge-offs are the last resort in collection procedures, a bank should establish and define procedures for repossession and legal action necessary to remove questionable assets from the balance sheet. Banking regulatory agencies have defined what they will classify as loss accounts. The bank should establish a charge-off policy which parallels these definitions on a systematic basis.

Managing Profitability

Many factors must be considered by a bank in establishing the rates to be charged for installment credit services. Needless to say the cost of funds, collection costs, and administrative and overhead expenses are important factors, but consideration must also be given to the cost of advertising, interviewing, credit investigations, accounting and other operations incidental to acquiring and servicing an installment credit transaction.

A well-managed and profitable installment loan operation is based on a sound knowledge of costs. Generally the total expenses allocated to an installment loan department can be determined without too much effort. However, determining the amount of allocation to acquisition or maintenance of loans will require more detailed analysis of the jobs and other activities of the department.

The cost analysis of the Anytown Bank (Table 3) illustrates the procedure in allocating funds to acquisition or maintenance and develops an acquisition cost of $30.42 per loan and a maintenance cost for processing each monthly payment of $1.03.

Many banks will expand on this procedure and add a cost of funds factor and loss factor to develop a break even chart (Table 4). A table of this type can be very helpful not only in managing a profitable installment loan portfolio but also in establishing policy and developing new programs that generate adequate size loans for a proper return. The figures compiled by the American Bankers Association (Table 5) show a great variance in gross expense per installment loan both by geographic region and by bank size. These figures are available annually from the American Bankers Association and would be of valuable assistance in estimating costs for those banks not performing a more detailed analysis. Regardless of the method used to determine or estimate cost, it is important that all banks recognize all inherent costs associated with the

Table 3   Cost Analysis Installment Loan Department
Anytown Bank

Expense Item	Total	Acquisition	Maintenance
Salaries and benefits	$114,269	75,417	38,852
Occupancy cost	15,240	11,430	3,810
Advertising	357	357	
Stationery and supplies	2,154	1,077	1,077
Legal	2,456		2,456
Postage	978	245	733
Service contracts	128	64	64
Telephone	8,698	3,479	5,219
Travel	1,515	758	757
Entertainment	1,435	1,435	
Schools and seminars	960	960	
Dues and subscriptions	365	365	
Repossession expense	5,212		5,212
Credit bureau	2,651	2,651	
Xerox	323	323	
FHA #1 insurance	4,115	4,115	
EDP expense	4,480		4,480
Miscellaneous	2,534	1,267	1,267
Coupon books	3,500	3,500	
TOTAL	$171,370	$107,443	$63,927

Acquistion Cost Per Loan

3532 Loans Made
$107,443 divided by 3,532 = $30.42

Maintenance Cost Per Loan Payment

5157 Average number of Loans Outstanding
Total number of Payments Processed
61,884
$63,927 divided by 61,884 = $1.03

Table 4   Installment Loan Department Anytown Bank
Size of loan required to break even at various annual
percentage rates*
(Rounded to the nearest dollar)

	12%	13%	14%	15%	16%	17%	18%
12 months	$2487	$2087	$1639	$1345	$1141	$990	$875
18 months	2176	1584	1246	1026	871	757	668
24 months	1636	1310	1033	851	724	629	555
30 months	1545	1138	898	741	631	549	485
36 months	1372	1015	805	665	566	493	435

* Cost includes cost of funds at 9% and a loss factor of .5%.

lending function and make some provisions for periodic review to assure an adequate return on the funds allocated to the installment loan function.

Special Forms of Consumer Installment Credit

Installment credit is a subject so comprehensive that only the surface can be scratched within the space of this chapter. Books have been written on single phases of this credit. It is a business within a business, and its administration requires considerable ability.

Only the basic concepts of consumer direct and indirect lending were discussed. No mention was made of installment loans to small businesses, lease financing, commercial and industrial equipment financing, insurance premium financing, student loans and financing of a wide variety of services, all of which are facets of a successful installment loan operation. However, there are some special forms of consumer installment credit that have attracted considerable interest in recent years and which merit brief discussion.

CREDIT CARDS

The bank credit card combines the features of a regular retail credit account, installment loans for various types of durable goods or services, and personal loans. A customer who receives a credit card has, in effect, a line of

Table 5   Average Total Gross Expense Per Installment
Loan, 1979
(To Acquire, Service, Collect Loan)

By size of deposits and census region

Census Region	Deposit Size Categories (in Million Dollars)				
	Under 25.0	25.0— 49.9	50.0— 99.9	100.0— 499.9	500.0 and over
New England	–	–	–	$55	$73
Middle Atlantic	–	$40	$44	55	84
South Atlantic	$45	47	55	75	87
East North Central	–	40	65	61	89
East South Central	40	–	43	63	73
West North Central	46	48	41	65	77
West South Central	35	45	49	76	93
Mountain	40	44	46	87	99
Pacific	–	–	–	–	–

Number of Banks Reporting: 131

Source: 1980 Retail Bank Credit Report, American Bankers Association

credit with the issuing bank which can be used to purchase goods or services from participating merchants or which can be used to obtain a cash advance from a participating bank. Originally, banks did not charge the customer a fee for the card and no charge was made if payment was made within some predetermined number of days after the billing date. However, with the high 1980 interest rates, many issuing banks began to use an annual card fee of $15 to $20 and considered the abolition of any free interest periods. Generally, rates range from 15 to 22 percent on the unpaid balance for customers desiring to pay their account on an installment basis.

Merchants who accept the cards agree to pay the bank of deposit a fixed percentage of credit sales. This generally ranges from 2 to 5 percent based on volume and ticket size. A major advantage to many merchants who accept credit cards is that they need not spend the time and effort required (or make the investment) that an in-house credit operation would require. The fee paid to the bank is often less than the cost of managing an in-house operation, and, in addition, the potential customer base is substantially greater than that which the merchant could hope to draw with his own credit plan operation.

The benefits to the individual also increase because the card holder has access to a much broader range of goods and services than he would if he opened an account with each merchant. He can consolidate all of his credit purchases on one account. This makes it easier and more convenient for him to manage his expenditures. And he may often still take a predetermined number of days after billing statement date to pay his purchase in full without being assessed an interest charge.

Many banks entered the credit card field in the 1950s, but due to significant losses and difficulty in establishing a sufficient merchant base and customer base, the number of card issuers has dwindled to a few, with Visa and MasterCard the two most widely held cards.

The Visa card originated with Bank of America in the mid-sixties in California. In order to operate within the law in most states (which prohibited out-of-state banks from operating within their borders), Bank of America began to license banks across the country to issue and service Bank Americard accounts. An interchange arrangement was made between banks in various areas to facilitate credit purchases in states other than the card holders'. As the number of participating banks increased, a private corporation (National Bank Americard Corporation) was formed, which was owned by all participating banks, to control licensing and exchange and to facilitate cooperative national advertising. Foreign banks joined the National Bank Americard Corporation, and Bank Americard became a card used throughout the world.

Competing banks joined to set up a separate credit card organization called Interbank Card, using MasterCard credit cards. Today most banks belong to either Visa, successor to the Bank Americard, or MasterCard, issued by the Interbank system.

Both cards can be used throughout the United States and in many parts of the world. The use of bank credit cards has grown rapidly and is expected to continue.

A major advantage to the card-issuing bank is the availability of an efficient way to handle small personal loans and installment loans for durable goods. Once a card is issued, assuming the customer maintains his account in a satisfactory manner, the bank can offer overdraft protection and cash advances for small purchases. This eliminates the need for interviewing the customer, checking his credit, and other time and expense associated with acquiring and servicing the loan. In addition to being less expensive for the financial institution, it also provides a prompt, efficient method of advancing funds, which is so much demanded by customers.

Another objective is the acquisition of new customers and establishment of a banking relationship with merchants who are qualified to become customers for the service. Theoretically, the bank can become the merchant's credit department (and operate it more economically than the merchant).

There are various options available to a bank as to the extent of involvement in a bank card operation. They may become an agent of one or more of the national cards and become a card-issuing bank. This involves a substantial investment in staff, advertising, promotion, specialized equipment, forms, and imprinters. This may be impractical for many banks. Another alternative is to become an associate with a larger, card-issuing bank and participate in the profit by obtaining merchant depositors and card holder accounts issued due to the bank's solicitation and salesmanship.

CHECK CREDIT AND OVERDRAFT PLANS

Check credit and overdraft plans are forms of installment credit connected with a bank checking account. They were developed independently of bank credit cards. These plans have appeared in a variety of forms, but the primary feature is establishment of a specific line of credit or reserve to which the customer has immediate access through a checking account.

The plan is simple in operation. The customer fills out an application form, in some banks applying for a specific amount of credit, or in others the amount being based on income or the amount of payment desired by the customer.

Some banks allow a credit line of one to two times the applicant's monthly income, while others allow 12 to 20 times the monthly payment desired by the customer. Repayment requirements range from $\frac{1}{12}$ to $\frac{1}{20}$ of the balance owed on the statement date.

When the customer's credit is approved, a "check credit" or "overdraft" agreement is signed, and on certain plans the customer is furnished special checks which may be used to activate the revolving line of credit. Other banks use the customer's regular checking account to activate the line of credit when overdrafts occur, or at the request of the customer, transfer funds from the line of credit directly to a regular checking account. This unique form of installment credit was introduced by the First National Bank of Boston in 1955 and developed in a number of banks as a less costly alternative to bank credit cards.

The customer applies for credit only once, and, if it is handled in a satisfactory manner, the line remains available for use. As payments are made the unused portion increases and is available to the customer. The customer is not restricted to particular merchants who accept various credit cards and no cost other than routine checking account cost is involved until service is used. Overdrafts can be paid on authorized reserve accounts even though there may be insufficient funds in the checking account, thus saving the embarrassment of unintentional overdrafts.

The bank receives the benefit of lower cost because once the loan is approved and placed on the books, there is no further acquisition cost for processing advances against the line of credit. The line may revolve for a number of years with only routine maintenance. This plan also improves customer retention and enhances the bank's image and prestige.

Certain disadvantages should be recognized. The customer may tend to stay in debt longer at a somewhat higher rate than with a closed-end loan because of the ease with which funds may be obtained. Also a customer may pay interest on funds not actually needed because many banks use minimum increments of up to $100 to cover any resulting overdraft even though it is a very small amount.

A considerable policing effort is required to minimize problems. Most banks review lines at least annually in an effort to minimize losses. Most losses occur at or near the top of the unsecured line. This results in a loss ratio unacceptable on closed-end credit.

Energy-related Loans

With shortages and accelerating petroleum prices, many banks have developed special loan programs to promote energy-saving home improvements. These programs usually involve insulation and storm windows and doors, but may also include more sophisticated solar heating devices. The loans are usually written at rates lower than those prevailing for other types of borrowings.

The benefits to the customer and bank are obvious. The customer saves money through lower utility bills and at the same time conserves energy resources. The bank offers a valuable community service and enhances its image by contributing toward conservation.

Legal Consideration

The installment credit manager must develop an understanding of all state and Federal laws and regulations to comply efficiently.

Complying with consumer legislation is not easy, and the consumer credit manager must work with the compliance officer, read the various laws and regulations, purchase the best compliance material available, and seek help in obtaining and interpreting state laws through a state bankers' association or the bank's legal counsel when necessary. The results are worth the effort in establishing an efficient, effective, and profitable installment credit operation.

SUGGESTED READINGS

Consumer and Commercial Credit Management, by Robert H. Cole, Richard D. Irwin, Inc., 1980.

Installment Credit, a series of twelve installment credit reference manuals, American Bankers Association, Washington, D.C., 1979.

Comptroller's Handbook for Consumer Examinations, Office of the Comptroller of the Currency, Washington, D.C., 1977.

Handbook for Credit Training, American Bankers Association, Washington, D.C., 1978.

Loan Interviewing Training Program, American Bankers Association, Washington, D.C., 1978.

A Planning Guide for Consumer Compliance, American Bankers Association, Washington, D.C., 1979.

Consumer Compliance: A Source Book of Materials and References, American Bankers Association, Washington, D.C., 1979.

Retail Bank Credit Report, American Bankers Association, Washington, D.C., published annually.

Periodicals

Banking, Journal of the American Bankers Association (monthly), 90 Park Avenue, New York.

Bulletin of the Robert Morris Associates (monthly), issued by Robert Morris Associates, Philadelphia.

The Burroughs Clearing House (monthly), published by Burroughs Adding Machine Company, Detroit.

Federal Reserve Bulletin (monthly), published by the Board of Governors of the Federal Reserve System, Washington, D.C.

17

Payment Commitments—Banker's Acceptances and Letters of Credit

This survey of the banker's acceptance and letter of credit as a means of enabling a bank's customer to obtain goods, services, or money is addressed primarily to lending officers. It does not deal with the niceties of law or the details of operation, but is intended to focus attention on the problem of accommodating customers without detriment to the bank. For coverage of the omissions from this discussion, the reader is urged to refer to the materials cited at the end of the chapter. These include relevant portions of the Uniform Commercial Code, the Uniform Customs and Practice for Documentary Credits, and texts that record comprehensively governing law, operating procedures, and accounting requirements.

In general terms, a bank responds to the financial requirements of its customers by permitting them to use its assets; in other words, by making loans. The assets thus deployed may be the proceeds of the bank's own borrowing in the form of deposits or capital obligations, the proceeds of equity contributions, or that intangible but real asset, the bank's credit. As a matter of convention and convenience, the term "loan" is applied to advances to a customer of the "cash" proceeds of the bank's own borrowings or equity contributions. The price of such accommodation necessarily includes the cost to the bank of the "cash" advanced. In a wide range of circumstances, however, the customer's need is not for "cash" but rather for a satisfactory assurance to a third party that "cash" will be payable at a future date. In such case a loan of the bank's credit, that is, the bank's commitment to disburse "cash" for account of the customer at a future date, is indicated, and will ordinarily be provided in the form of a letter of credit. In other circumstances, when the customer has a present need for "cash," it may more readily and cheaply be satisfied by selling to third parties a bank obligation in the form of a banker's acceptance than by an advance from the bank, which depletes the bank's store of "cash," or by offering to third parties the customer's own obligation in the form of a promissory note (commercial paper).

Loans of bank credit in the form of banker's acceptances and letters of credit is the subject of this chapter.

The Banker's Inventory

The instruments by which a banker extends credit to his customer have in common an engagement by the banker to make payment to a third party. The form of the instrument reflects both the customer's desires as to the terms and conditions on which such payment will be made and the extent to which the banker is prepared to accommodate those desires. Form is therefore of vital importance, not for conceptual reasons, but in order to define the expectations of the parties concerned.

Familiarity with the many specific credit instruments is essential to successful use of the device. In the context of this view from the lending officer's desk, however, it will be presumed that such familiarity exists or can be derived from more comprehensive texts listed at the end of this chapter. The following description of types of instruments is, therefore, confined to the general categories, an understanding of which is basic to application of credit judgment to particular transactions.

Acceptances

An acceptance is the instrument best suited to conveyance of an unconditional promise to make a payment at a future date. Although commonly regarded as such, an acceptance is not in fact a discrete instrument. It is, rather, the means by which the drawee of a draft or bill of exchange undertakes, in legally enforceable form, the obligation to carry out the order of the drawer or maker. That order is ordinarily a direction by the drawer to the drawee to pay a specified sum at a specified future time. If the direction is to pay to a specified person, the instrument lacks an essential element of negotiability; if, as is most often the case, the direction is to pay to a specified person or upon the order of that person, the draft or bill is a negotiable instrument. In its initial form, it confers on the payee or subsequent holders no rights against the drawee. When, however, the drawee signifies his obedience to the drawer's order, the drawee becomes the primary obligor and is unconditionally liable to the holder to make payment at the time and place and in the amount specified.

That assumption of liability is ordinarily signified by the drawee's placement on the face of the instrument of the word "Accepted," followed by the date of acceptance and his signature. In effect the drawee has become the maker of a promissory note, and the obligation of the drawer is secondary. If the acceptor is a bank or banker, the instrument is a "banker's acceptance"; in other cases, regardless of the vocation of the acceptor, the instrument is a "trade acceptance."

In normal practice, the future payment promised by the accepted draft or bill is immediately converted to a present receipt of funds by negotiation of the instrument. The draft or bill may provide for interest to maturity, but more frequently is for a principal amount only, in which case it is sold for less than the principal amount, or discounted. Ordinarily, the banker/acceptor effects the original discount, that is to say, buys back its obligation by paying the discounted cash value of the instrument. The bank then has the option of holding the instrument to maturity or of recouping its outlay by reselling or rediscounting the instrument. In either case, the price of the instrument will be determined by reference to the rate for bankers' acceptances, which is normally more favorable to the borrower-vendor than the rate for paper that does not embody a banker's primary obligation.

Letters of Credit

Like an acceptance, a letter of credit is (1) an undertaking to make a payment at a future date; (2) a direct and primary obligation of the issuer or acceptor, as the case may be; and (3) it is an engagement by the obligor to the beneficiary or holder, made at the request and for the account of a third party who may or may not be named in the instrument. Unlike an acceptance, however, a letter of credit conveys a conditional promise and is not a negotiable instrument,* nor does it create or convey any liability of the party for whose account it is issued. Use of a letter of credit is indicated where it is desired to assure performance of the payment term in an independent contract or other arrangement.

Letter of Credit Distinguished from Acceptance. Apart from the differences in legal structure and effect, a letter of credit differs functionally from an acceptance. A letter of credit promises payment upon performance of certain conditions. An acceptance, in practical effect, is payment. The point is so basic as to need no elaboration, but an illustration can do no harm.

S. Simon, Ltd., makes a contract with A. Pieman, Inc., for the purchase of a pie for a penny, payment to be made 30 days after delivery. Because of previous unfortunate experience with Simon, Pieman insists on an assurance

---

*It is possible to create a letter of credit that is a negotiable instrument, just as it is possible to create a nonnegotiable acceptance. There is little point in such an exercise, other than to trap a hapless student on a law school examination.

of payment. Simon proposes that at the time of delivery he will hand over his check on the Baker's Bank, certified by that institution. Pieman, however, is unwilling to commence preparation of the pie until he has his assurance of payment.

Simon then offers to cause Baker's Bank to issue a letter of credit in favor of Pieman, the bank thereby undertaking to pay Pieman upon delivery to it of Simon's receipt for one pie. That payment would, in the usual course, be made by delivery of Baker's Bank's cashier's check to Pieman.

Now Simon expresses dissatisfaction. Payment is not due until 30 days after delivery, yet if, at the time of delivery, Simon's check is certified, or if the bank delivers its cashier's check, Simon's account will be charged or he will be obliged to reimburse the bank for its payment under the credit. Accordingly, the letter of credit is rewritten to provide that, upon presentation of Simon's receipt for the pie, the bank will accept Pieman's draft on it at 30 days sight, that is, the bank will undertake a direct and primary obligation to pay Pieman on order 30 days later.

It will be noted, as of course it should, (1) that the condition qualifying the promise to pay is delivery to the bank of Simon's receipt, rather than actual delivery of the pie to Simon; and (2) that the instrument by which the bank purports to effect payment, whether it be a cashier's check or an acceptance, is a negotiable instrument and thus conveys an unconditional promise to pay.

Letter of Credit Distinguished from Guaranty. Letters of credit and guaranties are alike in that each is used to reinforce a contract or arrangement to which the issuer or guarantor is not a party. The essential difference is that the obligation of the issuer of a letter of credit is independent of any other contract or arrangement to which it is ancillary, whereas the obligation of a guarantor is measured by actual performance or nonperformance of such other contract or arrangement.

As in the mythical cases of the nonnegotiable acceptance and the negotiable letter of credit, an idle and mischievous mind can conceive of a letter of credit so inartistically drawn as to require the issuer to make a factual determination as to a state of affairs or as to the performance or nonperformance of an independent contract; and a guaranty may be so cunningly conditioned that the guarantor's obligation is confined to that customarily undertaken by the issuer of a letter of credit. Whether the product of design or ineptitude, however, such instruments are aberrational and interfere with sound practice by putting form and function at odds with one another.

In the course of dealing between S. Simon, Ltd., and A. Pieman, Inc., the contract now provides for 52,000 mince pies at ten pence each, C.I.F. Simon's Tavern; shipment to be in equal weekly instalments; terms cash on delivery; secured by prime banker's letter of credit; seller warrants pies to be first quality, containing only pure ingredients, in all respects wholesome and suitable for human consumption. For account of S. Simon, Ltd., Baker's Bank issues a letter of credit in favor of A. Pieman, Inc., valid for 14 months, undertaking to pay Pieman's sight drafts on Baker's Bank up to the aggregate amount of 520,000 pence upon presentation at the bank of each such draft for the full invoice value of 1,000 pies, accompanied by: invoice for 1,000 A. Pieman Mince Pies, at ten pence per pie, C.I.F. Simon's Tavern; truck bill of lading consigned to Simon's Tavern marked freight prepaid, and insurance certificate.

Simon—simple but no patsy when it comes to pastry—demands and obtains from Consumers and Morticians Indemnity Co. a surety bond whereunder the indemnity company guarantees that A. Pieman, Inc., will duly perform the mince pie contract entered into February 30, 1980, between it and S. Simon, Ltd., and will indemnify Simon against loss consequent on breach by Pieman, not exceeding 520,000 pence.

Upon presentation of the documents described in the letter of credit, the bank is required to pay Pieman, even though it breached its contract with Simon. Upon demand by Simon for payment under the guaranty, the indemnity company is required to pay only if there is an actual breach by Pieman of its contract with Simon.

Liabilities Created by Letters of Credit. Inasmuch as a letter of credit is a legally enforceable promise to make a payment upon the terms and conditions stated in the instrument, the issuer's liability is such as he may assume. It consequently varies widely from case to case. A detailed classification of credits in general use, such as is contained in some of the works cited at the end of the chapter, is beyond the scope of this chapter. For present purposes, it is sufficient to examine the nature of liabilities undertaken by issuance of the major categories of letters of credit. This analysis requires only two inquiries:

1. *What is the character of the commitment?* The engagement undertaken in a letter of credit is enforceable according to its terms without requirement of consideration moving to the issuer. Those terms, however, are strictly—in proper case literally—construed. Thus, the initial inquiry with respect to every credit relates to the nature of the commitment.

In the first instance, the question relates to duration. The commitment embodied in a revocable letter of credit or in most types of authorities to purchase or pay may be terminated, without notice to the beneficiary, at any time prior to actual performance by him of the conditions stipulated in the instrument. The commitment embodied in an irrevocable letter of credit, on the other hand, may not be terminated, nor may its terms be altered, prior to the expiration date stated in (or derived from the terms of) the instrument.

The nature of the commitment also serves to distinguish a letter of credit (whether revocable or irrevocable) from an advice of credit. More often than not, the fact that a credit has been established and the terms and conditions on which it is available are conveyed to a beneficiary by one other than the issuer. That notification, commonly called an advice, constitutes no commitment on the part of the one giving it, and, as a matter of precaution, the advice will ordinarily so state. A bank that advises a credit issued by another, or which notifies a beneficiary that it is authorized to pay or purchase drafts or demands drawn or made on another, is liable for the accuracy of its advice, but it has no liability in the event that the issuer fails to honor its commitment.

Frequently the advising bank is requested to add its confirmation, and when it does so in appropriate form, the result is a confirmed credit. The effect of confirmation is that the confirming bank "becomes directly obligated on the credit to the extent of its confirmation as though it were its issuer and acquires the rights of an issuer" [Section 5107(2) of the *Uniform Commercial Code;* see also Article 3b of *Uniform Customs and Practice for Documentary Credits,* ICC Publication No. 290].

2. *Who may enforce the commitment?* Unlike the commitment contained in a negotiable instrument, the obligation of the issuer of a letter of credit may be enforced only by one who is explicitly invited to rely on it. In the case of a negotiable instrument, including the conventional banker's acceptance, the promise of the primary obligor, to pay a sum certain on a day certain at a certain place, is open-ended as regards the identity of the obligee.

In the case of a letter of credit, only a person identified by the issuer may enforce the instrument. As the nature of the commitment is ascertained by reference to the particular instrument, so is the identity of the person or persons who may enforce it.

Considered from that point of view, namely, identification of the obligee, the relevant major categories of letters of credit are "straight" or "negotiation," and each of these may be divided into classes known as "transferable" or "nontransferable."

A straight credit is one whereunder the duty undertaken by the issuer creates enforceable rights only in the named beneficiary. The beneficiary cannot create any rights in a third party that alter the precise duty undertaken by the issuer. That duty is to make payment to the named beneficiary upon performance by the named beneficiary of the terms and conditions of the credit.

When, however, the issuer of a straight credit expressly denominates it as transferable, the named beneficiary (frequently referred to as the "prime beneficiary") may nominate a substitute to perform some or all of the terms and conditions of the credit and to demand and receive some or all of the payment promised by the issuer. Transferability of a credit (whether straight or negotiation) involves observance of a series of rules that are at once complex and confusing. (See *Uniform Customs and Practice for Documentary Credits,* Article 46 and 47; *Uniform Commercial Code,* Section 5-116; and Harfield, *Letters of Credit,* pp. 95–103.) For purposes of this discussion, it is sufficient to note that a credit, whether straight or negotiable, is not transferable unless expressly stated to be so, and that the effect of transfer, when authorized, is not to enlarge the duties of the issuer, but only to entitle a named transferee to enforce them; subject always to the terms and conditions of the credit.

A *negotiation credit* is one whereunder the issuer's duty of payment, upon compliance with the terms and conditions of the credit, is enforceable by a bona fide holder of a draft or demand for payment that conforms to the terms and conditions of the credit. The distinction from a straight credit is signaled by inclusion in the letter of credit instrument of a statement that the issuer engages with drawers, endorsers, and bona fide holders of drafts (or other demands), as well as with the beneficiary, that such drafts or demands will be honored (that is, paid or accepted) if drawn under and in compliance with the terms of the credit.

It is essential to observe that the fact that the invitation in a credit to negotiate drafts or demands does not imply that the credit itself is a negotiable instrument, nor that its terms and conditions are performable by one other than a named beneficiary. Thus an engagement with holders of demands may not be equated with an authorization to transfer. Accordingly, an issuer's duty of payment may not be enforced, even by a bona fide holder in due course of a draft or demand purporting to be drawn under a credit, unless (1) the draft or demand is drawn by the named beneficiary or an authorized transferee and (2) the terms and conditions of the credit are met.

To sum up, a holder of a draft or demand under a straight credit acquires no right to enforce the issuer's promise, notwithstanding the fact that the credit may be transferable. A holder of a draft or demand under a negotiation credit may enforce the issuer's promise to pay or accept, provided that the terms and conditions of the credit are met by the named beneficiary or an authorized transferee, but the act of negotiation (purchase) does not constitute the negotiator an acceptable substitute for the named beneficiary or authorized transferee in performing the terms and conditions of the credit.

Structure of Financing

As a matter of law, acceptances and letters of credit are free-standing instruments, independent of any other contracts, arrangements, or relationships out of which they may arise, or to which they are ancillary. From a banker's point of view, however, there is an essential linkage of the acceptance or letter of credit to the relationship between the banker and the customer for whose account the credit facility is created. Creation of an acceptance or establishment of an irrevocable credit renders the banker liable, as a principal, to make a payment and enables a third party (the holder of the acceptance or the beneficiary of the credit) to enforce that liability. Acceptance or letter of credit financing, therefore, eliminates one of the safeguards ordinarily included in a credit agreement between a banker and a customer. The point deserves detailed attention.

All forms of credit accommodation have in common that whatever value the bank places at the disposal of its customer must be returned, together with compensation for use of the value. As a matter of sound banking practice, that understanding is evidenced in one form or another.

The simplest arrangement is a cash advance to the customer, the obligation to repay being evidenced by the customer's promissory note, payable on demand together with interest from the date of the note to the date of repayment.

When the arrangement between bank and customer/borrower contemplates that the loan shall be outstanding for a fixed period, or that advances shall be made from time to time so that the bank cannot terminate the arrangement at will, it is customary to enter into a written agreement that spells out conditions for borrowing and circumstances justifying acceleration of the maturity of fixed-term obligations. The purpose and hoped-for effect of such provisions is to provide an opportunity to apply credit judgment contemporaneously as well as prospectively, and to curtail the lender's risk by recalling or withholding the value advanced or promised to the borrower.

Acceptance of a draft or establishment of an irrevocable credit puts the value (the bank's commitment) in the hands of the holder or beneficiary, as the case may be, rather than in the hands or at the disposition of the borrower. Because the engagement made in the acceptance or credit is independent of the arrangement between the bank and its customer/borrower, an alteration in the circumstances of the customer/borrower that might justify the bank's refusal to make contemplated advances or to exact repayment of advances made does not excuse the bank/lender from honoring its commitment embodied in the acceptance or credit.

It is axiomatic that a prudent banker will create acceptances or establish letters of credit for a customer only pursuant to a written agreement by the customer to put the bank in funds to meet maturing acceptances or to reimburse the bank for payments under the credits and to pay the bank's related charges. The Comptroller of the Currency has declared (I.R.7.7016) that as a matter of sound banking practice, "the bank's customer should have an unqualified obligation to reimburse the bank for payments made under the credit," and a similar commitment is a logical prerequisite for creation of a banker's acceptance. It should be noted, however, that these are minimum requirements to conform to sound banking practice; prudence mandates more.

Precisely because agreements between bank and customer cannot reduce the bank's liability under its acceptances or letters of credit, such agreements can and should contain whatever covenants are deemed useful to secure the customer's obligation to the bank. As in the case of loan agreements, the application and agreement, pursuant to which acceptance or letter of credit financing is provided, should include provisions, if appropriate, for collateral, mandatory prepayment, or acceleration of the customer's obligation, and the like. The primary purpose of such provisions is protection of the bank against the risk of deterioration of the bank's asset (the customer's obligation) when the bank cannot reduce its liability (the obligation on the acceptance or irrevocable credit); and one can envisage other uses.

Preliminary Appraisal

Creation of an acceptance or issuance of an irrevocable credit is the functional equivalent of a loan of money. Indeed, in modern practice, what is commonly called a loan of money involves no "money" in the narrow sense of that word but is an exchange of credit. Nevertheless, the legal and regulatory consequences of an extension of credit vary considerably, depending upon the way in which the accommodation is structured. For the sake of convenience, in the following summary the word "loan" is used in the narrow sense of a present advance, and no attempt is made to cover the laws of individual states, nor to describe a pattern that fits banks that are not members of the Federal Reserve System and which are not insured by the Federal Deposit Insurance Corporation.

Loans. Generally speaking, banks may not lend to one customer more than a stated percentage of the bank's capital funds (the per-customer lending limit). There are other restrictions and exceptions, such as the purpose of the loan, the status of the borrower, and the nature of security.

Letters of Credit. Prior to 1973, letters of credit were not included in per-customer lending limits. In the event that the bank did not obtain immediate reimbursement for its outlays under the credit, that forbearance was treated as a loan; the bank's commitment under the letter of credit, although actually a loan of the bank's credit, was not treated as a loan for lending limit purposes. In 1974 the Federal bank supervisory authorities decreed that a defined class of irrevocable credits, used as financial guaranties rather than as commercial payment devices, must be included, at the time of establishment, in per-customer lending limits.*

It is important to recognize that the variant treatment by bank supervisors of so-called "standby" or financial credits and of so-called "commercial" or goods-related credits is not indicative of legal or functional differences in the types of credit. The bank's liability, created by the letter of credit, is not affected by the purpose for which the credit is used. The character of the bank's asset—the value of the customer's obligation under the banker/customer agreement pursuant to which the credit is issued—is, on the other hand, directly affected.

When the purpose of a credit is to effect payment for goods, there is a prospect—but by no means a certainty—that sale or employment of the goods will generate funds to reimburse the bank for its outlays. The transaction is described (sometimes overoptimistically) as "self-liquidating." No such prospect exists when the trigger for payment under the credit is a failure by the

*12 C.F.R. § 7.1160; 12 C.F.R. § 208.8(d); 12 C.F.R. § 337.2.

bank's customer to discharge an obligation. In effect, in the latter case upon issuance of the credit the banker has undertaken a commitment to make an advance to his customer at a time in the future when the customer's cash flow may be inadequate.

The foregoing in no way suggests that the establishment of financial, as distinct from goods-oriented, credits is unsound banking. It is evident, nevertheless, that the evaluation of the risk factors in accommodating a customer's financial requirements requires consideration of elements that differ from those involved in a trade financing. Illustrative of these variant considerations is the fact that if security is desired, it will ordinarily have to be provided from sources extraneous to the transaction facilitated by the credit.

Acceptances. There is virtually no conceptual difference between a customer's receipt of funds through encashment of a banker's acceptance and his receipt of funds through encashment of a cashier's check. There are, nevertheless, real differences both in the pricing and the availability of the accommodation which require careful attention at the time the financing is structured. As a matter of law and regulation, these differences turn on the distinction between eligible and ineligible acceptances.

Eligible and Ineligible Acceptances. Viewed from the point of view of liability management, an acceptance is an acceptance whether it is characterized as eligible or ineligible, just as a letter of credit is a letter of credit whether it is characterized as commercial or standby. The distinction between eligible and ineligible acceptances is arbitrary and artifical.

An eligible acceptance is a banker's acceptance which has the tenor and grows out of one of the transactions described in Section 13 of the Federal Reserve Act (12 U.S.C. Section 372) and it, therefore, is eligible for discount by the Federal Reserve Banks. As a matter of interpretation, discount of an acceptance by a Federal Reserve Bank is not equated with purchase of an acceptance by a Federal Reserve Bank at a discount. There is undoubtedly some economic or legal reason for the distinction, but it is extremely difficult, if not impossible, to determine what it is.

However obscure the rationale, the consequences are clear. Unless the acceptance precisely meets the statutory description of the Federal Reserve Board requirements for discount, it is not an "eligible acceptance," and any banker's acceptance that is not an eligible acceptance is an ineligible acceptance. The significant consequential differences are the following.

Per-Customer Limitations. Eligible acceptances may be created for a customer notwithstanding the fact that the customer has fully utilized the accommodation available to him under the bank's lending limits. The restrictions imposed by 12 U.S.C. Section 84 have no application to credit extended through the creation of eligible acceptances. Creation of eligible acceptances, however, is quantitatively limited by 12 U.S.C. Section 372. That limitation, broadly stated, is that a bank may not have outstanding acceptances created for the account of any one customer in excess of 10 percent of the bank's capital funds unless the excess is secured by actual security growing out of the same transaction as has generated the acceptance. On the assumption that a bank has $1,000,000 of capital funds, customer X may borrow $100,000 and in addition thereto may be obligated to the bank in respect of an additional $100,000 of eligible acceptances created for his account, and in further addition thereto may be obligated to the bank for an unlimited amount of eligible acceptances if the excess obligations are secured by actual security growing out of the respective acceptance transactions.

The accommodation is available only for eligible acceptances. If the acceptance is ineligible—either because the form and tenor of the instrument or the transaction out of which it grows does not meet the requirements for eligibility—the customer's obligation in respect of it must be included in the bank's lending limit.

Aggregate Limitations. In addition to the limitations imposed upon the accommodation that may be accorded any one customer, 12 U.S.C. Section 372 imposes limitations on the aggregate amount of eligible acceptances that a bank may have outstanding at any one time. As in the case of the bank's lending limits and its per-customer acceptance limits, the aggregate limitation is determined by reference to the bank's capital funds.

The interplay of quantitative limitations is fairly clear. The aggregate limitation imposed by 12 U.S.C. Section 372 is 50 percent of the bank's capital funds or if the approval of the Federal Reserve Board has been obtained, 100 percent of the bank's capital funds. A bank enjoying such approval and with capital funds of $1,000,000 may, therefore, accept eligible drafts for a customer up to the amount of $100,000, provided that eligible drafts accepted by it for other customers and outstanding do not exceed in the aggregate $900,000. So far as the per-customer limitations are concerned, that bank may accept drafts aggregating $10,000,000 if it holds actual security for such acceptances in excess of $100,000, but in practice the volume of acceptances, however secured, cannot exceed $1,000,000. There are some exceptions which provide possibilities for enlarging the accommodation.

The aggregate limitation is construed to apply only to acceptances outstanding. Thus, if a bank discounts an acceptance and holds the discounted acceptance in portfolio, the amount of that acceptance need not be included in the bank's aggregate limitations. The Board has also ruled that if an acceptance (or, accurately, the customer's obligation on the acceptance) is secured by cash collateral, the acceptance need not be included in the bank's aggregate limit, whether held in portfolio or outstanding.

As in the case of the exclusion from lending limits and the per-customer limitation on acceptances, the aggregate limitation applies only to eligible acceptances. Thus, a bank which has reached its limit in the creation of eligible acceptances may, nevertheless, undertake acceptance financing for a customer if the acceptance created is ineligible and the amount thereof when combined with other nonexempt extensions does not exceed one per-customer limit.

Pricing. In addition to the quantitative limitations on the creation of acceptances, Federal regulations impose cost differentials that are reflected in the price of the accommodation. Regulation D of the Federal Reserve Board requires maintenance of marginal reserves against deposits. Prior to 1973 a bank's liability on acceptances outstanding was not treated as a deposit. In 1973 the Board recognized, by formal ruling, that a bank's legal power to create acceptances derived from the bank's charter and not from the provisions of 12 U.S.C. Section 372. Thus, state member banks which had charter power to create acceptances in any category of transaction or national banks, which the Comptroller has ruled are not restricted by the character of the transaction, were recognized as capable of creating eligible as well as ineligible acceptances. The Board's ruling, further, was that the quantitative limitations of Section 372 applied only to eligible and not to ineligible acceptances.

An economic consequence of the discovery of these legal facts of life was that banks could use acceptances created in purely financial transactions as funding mechanisms in like manner as certificates of deposit. The Board observed the possibility of a serious erosion of the containment dike it had erected to implement monetary policy by controlling the flow of funds through the banking system. Certificates of deposit (no more than the evidence of a particular banker-depositor relationship) were and always had been "deposits" and thus attracted reserves under Regulation D. The funds obtained by a bank upon rediscount of an acceptance were not and never had been regarded as deposits. The Board was understandably concerned that ineligible acceptances would be used instead of certificates of deposit in order to fund bank loans for purely financial (and possibly speculative) purposes, and in so doing the imposition of reserve requirements would be avoided.

Accordingly, the Board amended Regulation D so as to include in the definition of deposits a bank's liability on acceptances used by it to obtain funds for its banking business. The amendment, to that extent, meant that if a bank made an advance to its customer by way of discount of the bank's own acceptance and thereafter recouped that advance by selling the acceptance, the proceeds of the resale would be treated as a deposit for reserve purposes. The Board recognized, however, that such action would increase the cost of acceptance financing of the movements of goods, a result that was neither intended nor desired. In an attempt to maintain monetary control without unduly burdening trade financing, the Board excepted from the definitions of deposits a bank's liabilities on acceptances of the kind described in Section 13 of the Federal Reserve Act and eligible for discount by the Federal Reserve banks; that is to say, eligible acceptances.

As a consequence of the foregoing, the ability of banks to provide acceptance credit free of what some might regard as the archaic limitations on the creation of eligible acceptances carries an offsetting penalty of increased cost, because the reserve requirements preclude a bank from recouping the same amount of the usable funds as it has disbursed by way of original discount.

Acceptance Letters of Credit. For convenience letters of credit are often divided into categories of "sight" or "acceptance." The distinction rests entirely on the performance stipulated in the letter of credit. A sight letter of credit is one in which the bank engages that it will pay the beneficiary's drafts drawn at sight. An acceptance letter of credit is one in which the bank engages that it will accept the beneficiary's draft drawn for payment at a specified time after sight.

The Federal Reserve Board has ruled that the quantitative limitations on the creation of eligible acceptances do not restrict the establishment of letters of credit that contemplate acceptance of a beneficiary's drafts, whether such drafts when accepted are eligible or ineligible. An irrevocable letter of credit that contemplates the creation of an ineligible acceptance, however, will, in accordance with the regulations of the Comptroller of the Currency, the Federal Reserve Board, and the Federal Deposit Insurance Corporation, be treated from the time of its establishment as an extension of credit subject to the bank's lending limits.

In view of the fact, as noted above, that the ineligible acceptance thus contemplated will become a liability subject to deposit reserves when the bank sells it after effecting the original discount, it is evident that in structuring such a transaction, the banker must take into account, and should provide for in the customer's agreement, two factors that affect the cost of the accommodation. The first of these is the economic effect of the marginal reserves. The second is that the banker's commitment under the letter of credit deprives him, *pro tanto,* of the benefits of other forms of accommodation that are subject to the lending limit. The point may be illustrated as follows.

Bank X has a lending limit of $1,000,000. Its best, or prime rate, is 12 percent per annum. It charges a commission of 1 percent for the establishment of letters of credit. The discount rate for eligible acceptances is 10 percent. Midas & Co., a valued customer of the bank, borrows $500,000 for a term of one year at 12 percent per annum. Midas thereupon obtains from the bank a standby letter of credit valid for one year, contemplating acceptance of a 30-day time draft. Upon establishment of that credit, for which the bank charges at the rate of 1 percent, the bank is precluded from making any further loans to the customer at the rate of 12 percent. Moreover, if there is a drawing under the credit and the bank discounts its own acceptance at 10, it will be obliged, upon rediscount of the acceptance, to set aside, for example, 5 percent, of the proceeds as a deposit reserve. The adverse economic consequences to the bank are apparent.

What is less apparent but certainly should be taken into account by the banker is that the amount recouped by the bank on disposition of the ineligible acceptance cannot now be lent to Midas & Co. because the bank has lent them its limit and, therefore, there is pressure on the banker to lend at a higher rate to one who is likely to be less creditworthy.

Collateral Risk Factors

Creation of an acceptance or issuance of an irrevocable credit is reflected on a bank's books by recording a liability to the holder or beneficiary and an asset consisting of the customer's obligation to put the bank in funds or to reimburse it, as the case may be. Whether or not the liabilities are actual or contingent, and whether accounting conventions do or do not require that they be shown on the balance sheet, their existence is manifest. Less evident is a second tier of contingencies which, for want of a better phrase, may be characterized as collateral risk factors. These create a potential for loss when a transaction is not carried out in accordance with the expectations of the parties. The following stories illustrate some but by no means all of the possibilities.

1. At the request of Beaver Construction Corporation, a valued customer, Security and Prudent Bank (SAP) issues its negotiation credit in favor of Mole Mfg. Co., funds to be available against draft, invoice for 10,000 Supermole shovels, and clean on-board bill of lading. Heartlands Bank negotiates a draft under the credit, presents it, with attached documents, to SAP, and is paid. When SAP tenders the documents to Beaver, they are rejected and reimbursement is refused. Beaver points out that the bill of lading recites shipment on deck of the schooner *Marie Celeste,* and is thus a nonconforming document under Articles 19a iii and 22a of the Uniform Customs and Practice for Documentary Credits.

SAP thereupon demands repayment from Heartlands, the negotiating bank. Heartlands responds that, as a negotiating bank, it has made no warranties as to the conformity of documents to the credit, citing Section 5-111(2) of the Uniform Commercial Code and prior decisional law.

SAP then writes to Mole, the beneficiary of the credit, referring to Section 5-111(1) of the Code, whereunder the beneficiary is believed to have warranted to all interested parties that "the necessary conditions of the credit have been complied with." A lawyer replies, stating (1) that he has doubt *(a)* as to the applicability of that section in a case where there is no claim that the documents were in any way false or fraudulent, and *(b)* as to the validity of a statutory sentence that ends with a preposition; and (2) that Mole Mfg. is bankrupt and its principal shareholders have gone underground.

In the light of this advice, SAP proposes to cut its losses by selling the 10,000 shovels it has inadvertently bought. It therefore presents the bills of lading to the agents of the *Marie Celeste,* only to learn that the vessel, and whatever cargo it carried, has been lost at sea. Inasmuch as neither SAP nor Beaver (which, in the event, could not care less) had thought to require that a policy of insurance accompany the invoice and bill of lading, and in view of the fact that the lending officer who structured the financing is a nephew of the chairman, SAP's only recourse is to fire the document clerk who failed to observe the deficiencies in the bill of lading.

2. Beaver Construction Corporation has won a contract to build a pleasure dome for Kublai Khan. The contract provides, *inter alia,* that materials are to be paid for at the time of shipment and that Beaver is to pay an agreed amount as liquidated damages in the event that the dome fails, within two years of delivery, to keep water out of the interior of the structure. The Royal Bank of Xanadu establishes its irrevocable credit, in favor of Beaver and/or transferees, and containing an engagement to drawers, endorsers, and bona fide holders of drafts drawn thereunder that payment will be made against documents as specified therein. At the instance of Beaver, and upon its undertaking to pay related charges, Xanadu asks SAP to confirm the credit.

At the same time, and in lieu of depositing cash to cover liquidated damages, Beaver causes SAP to issue a credit in favor of Khan, funds to be available by Khan's sight draft accompanied by his statement that water has accumulated within the area of the pleasure dome.

Beaver transfers to True Grit Mines the right to draw under the confirmed credit for the invoice price of 100 tons of cement, drafts to be accompanied by on-board order bills of lading. Beaver draws under the same credit for the invoice price of one prefabricated dome, accompanying its draft with appropriate shipping documents, and is paid by SAP. Heartlands Bank presents to SAP True Grit's draft, invoice for 100 tons of cement, and appropriate shipping documents. Prior to payment of that drawing, however, SAP is advised that the Court of First and Final Instance in Xanadu has issued an injunction restraining payment by the Royal Bank of Xanadu and by SAP of True Grit's draft on the ground (which appears to be correct) that the invoice was false and fraudulent in that the shipment consisted, not of cement, but of a rather poor grade of sand.

Upon SAP's failure to pay, Heartlands Bank institutes suit at SAP's domicile in the United States and is granted summary judgment on the grounds *(a)* that as a bona fide holder of drafts and documents which on their face conformed to the terms of the credit, it is entitled to payment notwithstanding latent defects, in accordance with Section 5-114(2)(a) of the Uniform Commercial Code, and *(b)* that the injunction of the Xanadu Court has no extraterritorial effect. This causes SAP some anguish because a suit in Xanadu would be met by a defense, certainly valid there, that the local court's order was controlling, at least insofar as Royal Bank's liability is concerned; and Royal Bank has no assets in the United States out of which SAP could satisfy a judgment even if it were able to obtain jurisdiction. Beaver, of course, contributes nothing but sympathy, as it did no more than effect a substitution, *pro tanto,* of True Grit for itself under Royal Bank's confirmed, transferable credit.

But there is more to come. The cement was intended for the foundations of the pleasure dome. Sand will not suffice. The pleasure dome remains a hole in the ground, beside which the prefabricated dome lies in its original wrappings. It rains—for forty days and forty nights. The excavation fills, and on the forty-first day, Khan draws under SAP's "standby" credit. Without waiting for an attempt by Beaver to intervene in the courts, SAP refuses to pay. Khan sues. The court grants judgment in favor of Khan. His statement was as required by the credit; it was literally correct; the credit was an engagement by SAP wholly independent of the contract or arrangement between Beaver and Khan. Although the judgment may seem incredible, read the opinion of the Supreme Court of Connecticut in *New York Life Insurance Co. v. Hartford National Bank & Trust Co.* (22 UCC Rep. Serv. 761). These things happen.

Fortunately, Beaver was not in bankruptcy. However, the amount it owed SAP under the credit had not been taken into its cash flow calculations, with the consequence that SAP was a creditor for money borrowed and not only for credit used.

The purist will note that SAP's losses are not liabilities in the usual and narrow sense of the word. Nevertheless, they represent exposure to loss that is inherent in any letter of credit transaction, and that a banker ignores at the peril of his bank.

The risks are a function of the independence of the agreements creating the bank's matching asset and liability. In the case of acceptance financing, the special risks are largely of failure to conform in some respect with complex regulatory patterns; the bank's liability as acceptor is unconditional, and the offsetting asset, the customer's obligation to put the bank in funds to meet the acceptance, is or should be equally unconditional.

In the case of a letter of credit transaction, however, both the agreement creating the liability (the letter of credit) and the agreement creating the asset (the customer's undertaking to reimburse) contain conditions. Thus, although the agreements are independent as a matter of law, the bank's ability to enforce the customer's obligation is dependent upon its ability to show that it correctly performed the obligations undertaken by it in the letter of credit. It should therefore be evident that in structuring a letter of credit accommodation, a prudent banker must take into account the transaction financed as well as the customer's financial condition.

In like manner, the prudent banker will recognize that a letter of credit is not necessarily a self-securing extension of credit. That fact is evident in the case of a standby credit, used in lieu of a guaranty or performance bond. The beneficiary's statement, against which the bank pays, is ordinarily nothing that can be converted into cash.

The situation is conceptually different in the case of a goods-related credit, when the bank's payment is made against, for example, documents conveying or securing title to merchandise. Even in such cases, however, it must be remembered that in letter of credit transactions the parties deal in documents and not in goods. To the extent, therefore, that the banker looks to the subject matter of the credit as a means of securing his customer's obligation to reimburse, the banker should make the same sort of investigation as to and evaluation of collateral as in the case of any secured loan.

CONCLUSION

The safe and sound use of banker's acceptances and letters of credit requires conformity to an undeniably complex set of regulations, and familiarity with an increasingly large body of decisional and statutory law. From the banker's point of view, however, these bases must be covered in addition to, and not as substitutes for, fundamental principles that inform credit judgment.

Accommodation in the form of acceptances or letters of credit is, in essence, a loan the proceeds of which are disbursed to one other than the borrower, who is legally entitled to enforce the bank's commitment to disburse, free of any defenses the bank may have against the borrower and notwithstanding material adverse changes in the financial condition of the borrower.

Administration of such extensions of credit is facilitated by a body of law and practice that minimizes the risk of mechanical failure. There is, however, no present, nor probable future, law or regulation that can dictate when to grant or decline accommodation to a specific customer at a specific time and in specific circumstances.

BIBLIOGRAPHY

a. Article 5 of the Uniform Commercial Code.
b. Uniform Customs and Practice for Documentary Credits, ICC Publication No. 290.
c. Henry Harfield, *Bank Credits and Acceptances,* 5th Edition, John Wiley & Sons, Inc. (formerly Ronald Press, Inc.), 1974.
d. H.C. Gutteridge and Maurice Megrah, *The Law of Bankers' Commercial Credits,* 6th Edition, Europa Publications, Ltd., 1979.
e. Boris Kozolchyk, *Letters of Credit in the Americas,* Part I, Matthew Bender & Company, 1966.
f. Henry Harfield, *Letters of Credit,* ALI-ABA, Philadelphia, Pa., 1979.

18

Term Loans

Term lending to business has become a major commercial banking activity in recent decades. Such lending now represents an important, steady source of profitable business for banks, while at the same time providing a readily available and flexible source of financing for creditworthy bank customers.

The basic definition of a term loan describes it as a loan repayable by its terms more than one year from the date it was made or committed to the borrower. In general, a bank term loan has the following characteristics that distinguish it from a current loan: (1) the term runs for a period of at least one year up to about ten years; (2) repayment is expected to be provided from future earnings or cash flow rather than the short-term liquidation of assets; and (3) the provisions of the loan arrangement are detailed in and governed by a signed agreement between the borrower and lender.

The banking industry in the United States did not make term loans as such before the early 1930s. The making of loans in excess of a year was frowned upon by bank management, as well as by both regulators and bank examiners, all of whom viewed such loans as undesirable risks and as running counter to the principles of maintaining a sound and liquid loan portfolio. Although banks certainly had loans on their books for continuous periods in excess of one year, they were generally carried on the current ledger and renewed on a regular basis. A more realistic analysis of the nature of bank loans, emphasizing soundness rather than current liquidity, allowed for changes in policy by the various authorities, and banks began to make such loans on a modest basis.

Since that time, term lending has grown to become a major commercial bank activity. For the larger banks and many of the medium-sized banks, the term loan portfolio now constitutes over half of all loans to corporate and commercial customers. For these banks, term loans have provided a major and steady source of profitable lending. If approached on a sound basis, the risks have been demonstrated to be reasonable, and the loss experience over the years has been very satisfactory. Such lending has permitted the banks to fill an important niche in their customers' needs at the same time that they have been losing some of their historical lending opportunities to competing sources of lendable funds (such as the commercial paper market, through which major companies obtain substantial amounts of the current, working capital financing that used to be provided by the banks).

From the perspective of the bank's customers, term loans have provided a needed source of funds under very flexible arrangements. Small to moderate-sized companies that do not have ready access to the public markets have been able to expand their operations at a faster pace with an assured source of funds. Larger corporations have been able to use bank term facilities for greater flexibility of term and under more liberal financing provisions than other sources might allow. Bank term lending has also provided needed flexibility for project-related financing that might otherwise be unavailable.

It is interesting to note that the substantial growth of term loans came during several decades of great prosperity, moderate recessions, and relatively low inflation. It has been a period during which continued growth became expected, and in which financial projections of companies with proven track records could be generally relied upon to be met or exceeded.

The risk to a bank in making a term loan should be a normal banking risk. It is not intended that such loans be higher-risk assets. The analysis, however, is quite different than that for a current loan, and needs to be done in considerably greater depth. Although the expected source of repayment is also different, the confidence in the ability to meet the scheduled repayment should be equally great in either case. A term loan is not a solution to a problem credit.

Types of Term Loans

One of the important advantages of a term loan is flexibility in adapting it to the special requirements of the borrower. Initially, term loans were in most cases obligations payable serially over the life of the loan. As the needs of borrowers changed, new types of term credit evolved, such as revolving credits and standby credits, most of which contain an additional feature permitting the borrower to convert the commitment into a term loan under certain conditions.

SERIAL TERM LOAN

Under this type of term credit, funds are made available to the borrower immediately, and the obligation is repayable serially over the life of the loan on a monthly, quarterly, semiannual, or annual basis. The serial term loan has been used where prompt availability of the proceeds is necessary, such as for financing the purchase of a plant, machinery, and equipment; re-funding existing long-term debt; funding existing current debt; or acquiring another company.

REVOLVING CREDIT

This bank credit permits the borrower to avail itself of funds from time to time up to the maximum amount of the commitment, with the right to repay and reborrow during the life of the credit. It is actually a line of credit for a period extending beyond one year (usually up to three or four years), for which the borrower is willing to pay a commitment fee based on the daily average unused portion of the credit. Generally, the borrower has the right to terminate the credit at any time by giving the prescribed notice, or to reduce the credit whenever it is determined that the full amount is no longer necessary. Revolving credits are, as a rule, used to provide seasonal working capital needs, but may also be used for interim construction financing when there is a pronounced seasonal factor in the flow of cash from operations and flexibility is desired. In more recent years major companies have been establishing revolving credit agreements for such purposes as assuring a source of funds during a tight money period, supplying a backup to commercial paper sales, and providing for general and unspecified corporate purposes.

STANDBY CREDIT

Under this arrangement the borrower is granted a commitment by a bank for a period which permits it to borrow from time to time, up to the maximum amount available, to the expiration date. This differs from the revolving credit in that there exists no privilege to repay outstanding notes and to reborrow. Notes usually mature at the expiration of the standby period, and a commitment fee is charged for the unused portion on the basis of the unused daily balance. The borrower generally has the right to reduce the credit upon furnishing proper notice. This type of loan is commonly used for interim financing for construction purposes. The borrower either sells equity or places long-term notes with institutional investors for permanent financing when construction is completed. In some instances it may be desirable for a bank to have a "take-out" letter (that is, a commitment for long-term financing) from an institutional investor as an inducement to provide the interim standby credit.

REVOLVING OR STANDBY CREDIT CONVERTIBLE INTO A SERIAL TERM LOAN

Often a revolving or standby credit grants the borrower the option to convert any outstanding notes and any unused portion of the credit, on or before the expiration of the revolving or standby period, into a serial term loan repayable over a period of years. This gives the borrower the opportunity to use such funds as may be needed during the interim period, terminate or reduce the credit in accordance with its needs, and convert into a term loan only the amount required. Such credits may be used for working capital purposes over a longer period of time or for construction purposes. If money conditions are not favorable during the revolving or standby period, the borrower has the flexibility to convert into a term loan. In the case of a construction standby serial term loan, earnings generated by the new facilities should be expected to service, at least in part, the term obligation.

MULTIPLE-BANK TERM LOAN

A number of banks may be asked to participate in a term loan if the amount of the credit is large and exceeds the legal limit of one or more of the borrower's banks of account. This is generally the case with large national companies. Also, a borrower of larger size may have accounts with several banks and may want to have some or all of them participate in a term financing. The principal bank usually negotiates the terms and conditions of the loan agreement with the borrower and then offers to the other participants the amounts suggested by the borrower, subject to the approval of a satisfactory loan agreement and required documentation. The principal bank may also be designated as agent for the processing of all borrowings and payments under the agreement on behalf of all participating banks. The agent bank generally receives no fee unless the work involved is excessive or the loan is extremely complex. Sometimes there is no agent bank, and the borrower deals directly with each participant on all matters pertaining to the credit.

COMBINATION BANK–INSURANCE COMPANY TERM LOAN

It is not uncommon for banks and insurance companies to provide term financing on a joint basis. Banks often encourage insurance company participation when the loan period required is longer than that permitted by the lending policy of the bank. These loans are substantially confined to serial term loans and standby serial term loans. The bank or banks may take the first five to seven years of maturities, and the insurance company the later maturities up to perhaps 15 or 20 years. Insurance companies often welcome such an arrangement, especially when the relationship with the borrower is new to them. In some instances both the insurance company and the bank execute the same loan agreement. Generally, however, each insurance company has a separate agreement covering its loan, with financial covenants essentially the same as those in the agreements of other participants in the aggregate credit. In accordance with usual practice, the insurance company portion of such loans is almost always at a fixed rate of interest.

Factors Affecting the Credit Risk

The factors involved in the extension of short-term bank credit are considered in other chapters of this book. While most of these are also important when considering the extension of longer-term financing, many additional factors must also be studied. A major difference between short- and long-term financing is the expected source of repayment for the loan. For example, when extending short-term credit to a cannery to pack a corn crop, a banker will be interested in whether the borrower will be able to market the product profitably within a number of months and thus retire the obligation out of the proceeds of the sale of the canned goods. If, however, the borrower obtains longer-term credit to expand plant and equipment, with the loan running for a period of five or seven years, and with monthly or quarterly payments of principal, the banker will be vitally interested in the earnings and cash flow generated by the company over that period of time as the primary source of repayment.

A banker obviously needs all the help he can get in determining whether future earnings and cash flow will be adequate to repay a loan being considered. First, he should carefully study the past record of the prospective borrower, noting especially such things as size and trend of earnings, ability to withstand downturns in the economy, and other uses of cash flow generated (dividends, fixed asset expenditures, increased working capital, and other debt repayment, for example). The borrower's industry should also be carefully reviewed to understand the company's strength and position relative to its competition and developing trends that will affect its general outlook. The company's labor situation, its relationship with the government, and its relationship with other creditors are other areas of consideration that should not be ignored.

Once he has a general feel of the past and present so far as the borrower's financial and competitive positions are concerned, the banker needs to develop an idea of what he feels the future will bring. This is usually done with considerable help from the borrower. Financial projections prepared on a realistic basis, including income statements, source and application of funds statements, and balance sheets, are generally prepared for the next several years, preferably for the length of the loan. In some cases it is also helpful to have prepared a schedule of cash receipts and disbursements, especially for the near-term outlook. Such projections should be prepared on a monthly or quarterly basis for the first year and annually thereafter. It is important for the banker to understand the assumptions that were used to prepare the projections and to determine if he is satisfied with them or feels some adjustments should be made. He should also keep well in mind that projections become progressively less reliable the further out they get from the present time. This does not diminish their value, however, if they have been thoughtfully constructed. In addition to determining company management's best estimates of what it expects to accomplish in the future, projections also reflect management's thinking on such things as dividend policy, fixed asset requirements, and the use of leverage. Furthermore, how well the projections are constructed gives strong indications of how well management understands and controls its own business. The banker needs to have an awareness of all these matters, as well as the financial outlook, if he is contemplating entering into a long-term financing arrangement with the company.

In studying the projections for ability to repay, merely comparing the future expected earnings with required debt repayment is not enough. It is necessary to study all components of the cash flow to be generated by operations and to compare the totals with the expected uses of that cash flow. The stability and quality of the cash flow must also be considered.

As indicated above, it is very important to develop a confidence in the ability of management. In the long run capable management running a sound business will generate and retain the funds necessary for the repayment of term financing.

A prospective borrower's corporate structure is another matter worth some consideration prior to making a loan, especially if that structure is complex. In situations where most of the assets are in a subsidiary company or where a large percentage of the company's earnings are generated in a foreign subsidiary, a bank lender could find himself in a junior position in relation to other creditors unless he is careful about the manner in which he structures the loan. In the first example above, for instance, he may be better off lending directly to the subsidiary with the guaranty of the parent company. In the second example, perhaps a portion of the loan should be made directly to the foreign subsidiary. Bank counsel can be most helpful in studying such situations.

In most cases term loans are made only to substantial companies of demonstrated earning power. The soundness of a term loan, therefore, is generally measured by the financial strength of the company and the expected adequacy of future earnings and cash flow to retire the loan. As a result, most term loans are made on an unsecured basis. It is sometimes prudent, however, to require adequate collateral as security for the loan, especially when the earnings record is not well established or the balance sheet is not as strong as would be desirable. Various types of assets are pledged as security for term loans, with the most common being plant, machinery, equipment, or other fixed assets. The pledging of collateral is more common for term loans in specific industries, where such collateral may consist of railroad equipment, ships, or the proceeds from the production of oil and gas.

The Term Loan Agreement

One of the characteristics of a term loan is that a written agreement between the borrower and the lender is usually signed at the time the loan is consummated. The agreement is one of the conditions of the loan and is designed to fit the requirements of the particular term loan being considered. It should serve as a mutual understanding between the borrower and the bank as to the terms and conditions under which the loan is made. Although there is a common format, and there are language and provisions that are found in almost all agreements, the agreement itself should be tailor-made for the particular borrower and transaction involved.

Legal counsel should be familiar with this type of lending, so that the language in the agreement will accurately state the mutual understanding reached between the parties, particularly in regard to the financial covenants. While some banks have house counsel who handle the legal details, most banks have outside counsel, whose fees are generally paid by the borrower. While experienced counsel can be invaluable in drafting and designing a sound loan agreement, it is the banking officer involved, and not the counsel, who determines what the language is to reflect. In order to give the counsel adequate information with which to draft an agreement, many banks require the banking officer to prepare for him a detailed outline of what should and should not be included in the agreement.

The term agreement consists of five principal sections: (1) description of the credit, (2) representations and warranties, (3) closing requirements, (4) financial covenants, and (5) default provisions.

DESCRIPTION OF THE CREDIT

This section should set forth the amount of the credit, the participants, if any, and their proportionate shares, and the period of availability if it is a standby or revolving credit. It should state the maturity of the notes, rate of interest, commitment fee if any, collateral security if any, voluntary prepayment provisions, and reduction or termination privileges.

Both fixed and fluctuating interest rates are used in connection with term credits. Fluctuating rates are usually stated as being at the prime rate, a fraction over prime, or a multiple of prime, with the rate changing as the prime rate changes. Many borrowers prefer a fixed rate since that establishes the known cost over the life of the loan. Banks, in turn, generally prefer a fluctuating rate because they normally fund such loans with shorter-term funds. Some agreements will call for a fixed rate for the first few years of the loan, converting to a floating rate to maturity. Because of the longer-term risk, banks generally charge a slightly higher rate or spread over prime than they charge the same customer for a current loan. (A notable exception to this, however, occurs in the earlier years of a revolving credit, where the rate is often the same as for a current loan.) On many term loans, the rate will increase during the life of the loan, or at the time of conversion from a revolving or standby credit to a term loan. As with current loans, compensating balances are often a factor in the overall pricing of a term loan, although the understanding on balances is only rarely written into the agreement itself.

REPRESENTATIONS AND WARRANTIES

In considering the application for the loan, the lender has relied on certain information furnished by the borrower. The borrower, therefore, is required to represent and to warrant that such information is true and correct as of the date the loan agreement is executed. Among the principal items covered are:

1. Annual audit for the latest fiscal year, certified by independent accountants
2. Latest interim financial statements, certified by a responsible officer of the company
3. That the borrower is duly organized and is authorized to execute the agreement and the notes
4. Outstanding liens on assets
5. Funded debt outstanding
6. Investment in subsidiaries and other entities
7. Guaranties of obligations of others
8. Pending litigation
9. Latest year for which Federal income tax returns have been audited and cleared by the Internal Revenue Service.

CLOSING REQUIREMENTS

There are always certain basic documents that are to be provided by the borrower in connection with the finalization of a term loan agreement. It is essential that the documentation be acceptable to counsel for both the bank and the borrower. In addition to a fully executed loan agreement and a signed note or notes, documents normally reviewed and provided include a borrowing resolution relating to the specific transaction, the written opinion of the borrower's counsel that the agreement and notes are validly authorized and executed and are binding obligations of the borrower, and copies of the borrower's articles of incorporation and by-laws. Where appropriate, such items as full collateral documentation, guaranty agreements, subordination agreements, evidence of insurance, governmental approvals, and borrowing certificates may also be required and should be obtained at the time of signing the agreement.

FINANCIAL COVENANTS

A key section of any term loan agreement is that which spells out the financial covenants the borrower agrees to comply with during the life of the agreement. The primary reason for the bank to desire a sound and realistic set of covenants is to protect its position in case of adversity, especially in relation to the other creditors of the company. Whether the covenants are few and basic or many and detailed will depend on the quality of the credit. Even more so than in most other sections of the term loan agreement, the covenants need to be designed to fit the particular circumstances of the borrower, the industry, and the outlook for the future. They should be no more restrictive than the policies that any prudent management would follow to maintain and build a good credit rating, but should be designed to give an early warning of any material deterioration in the financial condition of the borrower.

If there should be a violation of one of the covenant provisions, an event of default (discussed later in this chapter) shall have occurred, and, under the terms of the agreement, the bank should be in a position to accelerate the maturity of the loan if it is in its best interests to do so. Generally during the term of an agreement, owing to changing circumstances or changing events, the borrower will, for valid reasons, need and request a modification of a covenant, a waiver of a restriction, or a consent to an action taken. If matters are going relatively well, the bank is generally willing either to agree immediately or to resolve the matter easily after some negotiation. It is important, however, to protect both its negotiating position with the borrower and its position in relation to other creditors, that the bank retain the right to accelerate the maturity of its notes should it deem it necessary.

Among the more important covenants generally included are the following:

1. Purpose for which proceeds of the loan are to be used
2. Proper maintenance of property owned by the company
3. Furnishing of financial statements annually, quarterly, and occasionally monthly
4. Maintenance of minimum working capital and, in some cases, minimum current ratio

5. Maintenance of a minimum net worth level
6. Restriction on pledge of assets to others
7. Restriction on creation of other indebtedness
8. Restriction on payment of cash dividends and repurchase of shares of own capital stock
9. Restriction on investment in, loans and advances to, and guaranties of debts of others
10. Restriction against merger with or consolidation into any other entity
11. Restriction against sale of principal assets other than in the ordinary course of business
12. Restriction on amount that may be expended for acquisition of fixed assets
13. Restriction against sale and lease-back transactions and lease rentals
14. Restriction against sale of notes or accounts receivable
15. Restriction against voluntary prepayment of other outstanding term debt

As indicated above, not all of these covenants will be included in every agreement. Other covenants that are appropriate for a particular company or industry may, in turn, be included. What is included and the manner in which it is drafted will depend on the credit strength of the borrower and those events and actions for which the bank feels it needs adequate protection in the particular situation.

There is an obvious interrelationship between many of the above covenants. Such actions as borrowing long-term indebtedness, paying dividends, and spending for fixed assets, for example, all can have a major effect on the level of working capital. These interrelationships must be kept in mind when designing sets of covenants, so that individual covenants are not in conflict with each other. Also, in cases where less restrictive covenants are acceptable, a maintenance of working capital covenant may give satisfactory protection without requiring covenants relating to all of the other activities included in the list. It should be noted that many of the items in the list use the word "restriction" rather than "prohibition"; the intent in each case is generally to design, with the borrower, limitations and guidelines which give the bank protection but permit the management of the borrower the flexibility to continue to operate its own business in a productive manner. A bank definitely does not want to be in a position of, in effect, managing its borrower's business.

As a final word on covenants, it should be pointed out that, important as they may be for helping the bank to protect its interests, they merely reflect what has already happened (maintenance covenants) or set limits on future actions (restrictive covenants). They are not a substitute for either good credit analysis or a well-managed and successful business, and do not represent a source of repayment.

DEFAULT PROVISIONS

Upon breach of certain provisions in the agreement, the borrower may be granted a period of time after notice by the lender to remedy the breach, and if this is not done, an event of default occurs. In some situations an event of default may be automatic, requiring no action by the lender to accelerate maturity, while in other instances it may be required that the lender notify the borrower that the lender has declared the obligation due and payable. Following are common default provisions:

1. Any representation or warranty by the borrower in connection with the agreement proves to be materially false
2. Nonpayment of principal when due
3. Nonpayment of interest within a specified time after it becomes due (usually up to ten days)
4. Breach of any negative covenants
5. Default upon or failure to pay any other obligation when due
6. Bankruptcy of the borrower
7. Failure of the borrower to deny and have vacated within a specified time any bankruptcy or reorganization proceedings instituted against it (frequently 30 days)
8. Appointment of a trustee or receiver for a substantial part of the borrower's property in any involuntary proceeding and not vacated within a specific time (frequently 30 days)
9. Consent by the borrower to appointment of a trustee or receiver for a substantial part of its property
10. Assignment by the borrower for the benefit of creditors or admission by him in writing of inability to pay debts as they become due
11. Failure of the borrower to discharge any judgment against it within a specified time (frequently 30 days)
12. Breach of any other provision (including an affirmative covenant) of the agreement which is not remedied within a specified period after written notice from the lender (frequently 15 to 30 days)

Servicing the Term Loan

The signing of the term loan agreement and the first advance of funds mark only the beginning of a close working relationship between the banker and his customer. It is important for the banker to stay well informed about the company's activities throughout the life of the loan. If the results of operations are as good as or better than plan, then the banker has no reason to be concerned; in fact, good results are most likely to result in an increased need for loans or other banking services.

It is essential, however, to be aware as soon as possible if a customer is having difficulties and if there are problems developing in its ability to repay the loan as scheduled. In many cases the banker's awareness of such a situation will come through an on-going good communication with the customer. A continuing thorough review of the financial statements also will be likely to identify problems, reflected either in poorer operating results or decreased liquidity in the balance sheet.

In connection with a term loan, however, additional early warning signals are usually received through the close monitoring of the customer's compliance with the financial covenants in the loan agreement. Most of the information required to determine compliance can be found in the financial statements. Frequently, the agreement calls for the company's independent accountants to furnish a certificate, at the time of preparing the annual audit, stating whether any violations of the loan agreement were observed in the conduct of the audit. The chief financial officer of the company may also be required to furnish a similar certificate when delivering interim financial statements, together with his certification that, to the best of his knowledge, no default exists under the terms of the agreement.

Even with this outside help, however, it is important for the bank to establish regular procedures that call for competent personnel to review the financial statements and determine if the borrower is in compliance with the financial covenants in the agreement. The handling of this task varies among banks, with the responsibility sometimes resting with the lending officer or assistant and sometimes with the credit department.

Most violations of covenant provisions do not end up with the bank declaring a default and accelerating the maturities of the loan. As indicated earlier, it is rare that a loan agreement runs to its maturity without the requirement for an amendment or waiver, or often even a refinancing. The banker's flexibility and willingness to keep informed and to be involved in periodic negotiation and occasional refinancing of the term loan agreement are important reasons why bank term financing is so attractive to customers of the bank.

19

Equipment Leasing

The leasing industry since the mid-1950s has grown into a very important and acceptable method of acquiring the use of assets. It is estimated that over $150 billion in equipment is now being leased worldwide. Leased equipment ranges from ocean-going supertankers to office copiers. There are certain types of equipment for which leasing is the preferred method of acquiring an asset. The obvious example is computers.

Why do bankers need to understand the leasing industry? Primarily, for two reasons. Their customers, from the large corporations to the individual consumers, are more and more seriously considering leasing their equipment whether it be an automobile, a computer, or aircraft. Because of their reliance on the banker's experience and knowledge in understanding their funding requirements, the banker may be called upon to give them direction in their evaluation of alternative methods of funding their equipment needs. This chapter may be of some help should a bank wish to establish some form of leasing activity. The second reason a banker may need to understand the leasing industry is that the bank may be called upon to make a direct loan to a leasing company.

During the 1960s the Federal government encouraged capital asset investment because of its large spending in such areas as the space program, the interstate highway system, and the Vietnam War. During this period many companies who were undercapitalized needed to acquire more equipment. The majority of the companies were far too small to enter into the debt and equities markets to obtain the needed capital to finance their growth. Their bankers would not extend credit to them beyond their working capital requirements, and these companies could not pay cash from internally generated funds. The equipment lessor who was an "expert" at understanding the cash flow needed to fund the assets and the resale value and remarketability of the collateral matched the yield with the risk being taken to make a viable lease transaction. The lessor then provided the five- to seven-year amortization needed to match the lessee's projected revenues from the newly acquired equipment to the lease rentals. The general equipment lessors' rates of return were high but so was their risk.

When the bank-related lessor entered the general equipment leasing market, its method of doing business differed greatly from the independent lessor and the captive lessor. The independent lessors were primarily made up of innovative entrepreneurs who were risk-oriented. The captive lessor and the independent lessor were collateral-oriented first, and the financial strength of the user-lessee was a secondary consideration. The bank-related lessor's cost and availability of funds were usually more favorable than the nonbank-related lessor, who usually is more credit-oriented than collateral-oriented. The difference in the investment philosophies of the bank-related lessor and a captive lessor can be substantial. A vice president of a captive leasing company stated that "Given enough advance rentals, we would lease our equipment to anyone"; while a vice president of a money-center bank stated that "We would lease rubber bands to General Motors."

The bank-related lessor was willing to include "soft dollars" in its yield analysis, that is, depreciation, investment tax credit, and the timing of these benefits. This enabled the bank to provide lease rates that were competitive with bank financing and, in many cases, they were able to build their lease receivables with better-quality credits.

Although there are various types of leasing entities within the leasing industry and their businesses vary greatly, they have all helped to build the leasing industry into today's giant that it is. They all had one thing in common —they attracted highly motivated young people who had tremendous persistence and who were eager and hungry to close deals.

General equipment lessors group themselves into three marketing categories: the large lessor who writes leveraged leases and single investor leases in excess of $500,000; the middle-market lessor whose marketing strategy is to write leases in the $50,000 to $500,000 range; and the small-ticket lessor whose leases are $50,000 or less.

There are numerous types of leasing companies, and their motives for entering into the leasing industry vary with each company. A captive leasing company usually finances only its parent's equipment, although some captive finance companies have provided additional cash flow and benefits to the parent organization. Investment bankers and brokers usually do not have a continuing interest in the lease transaction, that is, they only match the investor with the lessee. For their services they receive a fee, and upon completion of the lease they exit the transaction. Independent lessors may specialize in one type of equipment such as IBM computers or they may lease to one specific industry such as transportation or agriculture.

The type of marketing strategy employed by each lessor will greatly depend upon its capital structure and the quality of its people. This chapter will be devoted to an understanding of the bank-related equipment lessor.

Basics of Leasing

What is a lease? A lease is a contractural obligation to rent specific property for a specific term at a predetermined rental rate.

Almost any type of property is being leased. Leased property can be either personal or real but, in almost all cases, the property has a useful life of more than one year, can be depreciated for tax reporting, and usually has some resale value after the base lease term.

HOW DOES A BANK-RELATED LEASE WORK?

Most leasing transactions develop in the following manner. The user-lessee has a need for a certain type of equipment. The need develops either because of a replacement of an existing piece of equipment or because of expansion. After the user-lessee decides on a specific manufacturer's make, model, modifications of equipment, and attachments, it negotiates the purchase price, delivery date, and service work that is to be performed during the warranty period and the terms of any maintenance contract.

After the user-lessee finishes the negotiations with the vendor, the search starts for the most attractive method of funding the equipment. The user-lessee usually requests a written lease proposal which includes a brief description of the equipment, cost of the equipment, lease term, amount of each rental, type of lease, and who is to benefit from the investment tax credit and depreciation. Other considerations are whether the lease is cancelable or noncancelable and whether the rentals are fixed or vary with the use of the equipment. Additional important items included in the first proposal are responsibility for the insurance (and in what amounts), maintenance and taxes, shipping costs and installation charges, and, in the case of computer leasing, whether or not the leasing company will include programming costs in the amount to be leased. It is necessary also to determine the purchase and renewal options and when the lease can be terminated.

After the lessee accepts the lessor's proposal, the proper financial statements are reviewed and a credit decision is made. The lessor's lease proposal will usually be quoted for equipment which will be delivered within a specific time, such as 30 days.

TYPES OF LEASES

A *true lease* is the most common type of lease. The lessor is the true owner and holds title to the property. Since the lessor is the owner of the property and assumes the risks of ownership, the lessor is eligible for the tax benefits such as investment tax credit and depreciation. The Internal Revenue Service allows the owner-lessor either to retain the allowable investment tax credit or to pass it through to the user-lessee. For tax reporting, the lessee may deduct the rentals paid as an operating expense but is not eligible for the depreciation associated with the property being leased. During the lease term, the lessee is not building any equity in the leased property but, generally, after the base lease term, the lessee is given three options: to return the property to the lessor, to renew the lease, or to purchase the property at its then fair market value.

A *leverage lease* is the most complex of all leasing transactions. The dollar amounts of a leverage lease can be substantial, and usually an institution or investor is not willing to provide all the money necessary to fund the lease transaction. United Airlines, Inc., leased twelve Boeing 727-222 and four McDonnell Douglas DC 10-10 aircraft at a total lease amount of $320,453,314.

This type of lease involves a minimum of three participants, the owner-lessor, the user-lessee, and the lender. Also included in the leasing group are the manufacturer, the vendor, and the trustee. The lessor's initial investment usually ranges from 20 to 40 percent of the cost of the leased property. The balance is provided by the lender on a nonrecourse basis. Although the lender's loan is secured by a first lien on the property, the lender cannot look to the lessor for the lease rentals. Each party in a leverage lease gives up some economic benefit and receives another benefit in its place. Figure 1, below, should make the leverage lease easy to understand. The lessee selects the property to be leased, pays the rentals to the trust, and then obtains the use of the property during the lease term.

The manufacturer receives the cash purchase price of the property and passes title to the trustee.

Figure 1

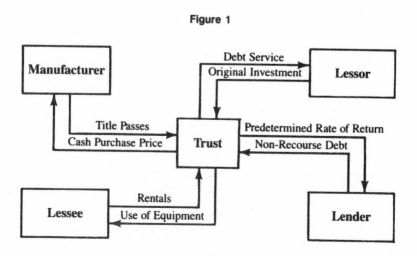

The lessor or investor provides the equity money, which is usually 20 to 40 percent of the purchase price of the property being leased. The lessor is eligible for the following benefits: the full amount of tax benefits usually associated with ownership; the excess rentals after the lender and trustee have received their interest and fees; interest expense on the nonrecourse debt; and any residual or resale value of the property at the end of the base lease term.

The lender, who has a lien on the property being leased and provides the remaining 60 to 80 percent of the funds to finance the lease transaction, expects only to receive a predetermined fixed rate of return on its investment.

The trustee holds title or maintains a security interest in the leased property. It receives the lease rentals from the lessee and disburses the funds to the lender and any other creditor. Any "free cash" is paid to the owner-lessor.

The above explanation of a leverage lease is somewhat oversimplified and not meant to be an in-depth analysis.

The *conditional sales lease* is a "lease" where title is retained by the lessor until the lease obligation is paid in full. This form of a full-payout lease usually has a stated or bargain purchase price at which the lessee can purchase the property after the base lease term. For tax reporting, the lessor is not the true owner of the property being leased, and it is not eligible for the tax benefits of ownership.

The term *full-payout lease* can have several meanings. Some lessors use this to mean that, after the original lease term, title can pass to the lessee for an amount sometimes as low as a dollar. The more accepted meaning is that the owner-lessor, during the lease term, recovers the original purchase price of the property plus the cost of funding the property, and a rate of return associated with the lease term and risk of the lease transaction. In the case of a true lease, ownership still remains with the lessor after the original lease term.

A *master lease* establishes a lease line of credit for the lessee, and there are two basic reasons a lessee would desire this type of funding. First, the lessee is contemplating an expansion and would like to establish a lease line of credit so that it knows how much equipment it can acquire through leasing. In many cases the lessor will write a letter to the vendor stating that, once the equipment has been delivered to and accepted by the lessee, the lessor will pay the agreed upon price. Second, a lessee has multiple locations and would like to keep all purchases controlled through a central purchasing department. A prime example would be the automobile manufacturer with several plant locations who would like to replace its lift trucks at a predetermined point, say every 60 months, in order to reduce down production time and to control maintenance costs.

Why Lease?

There are numerous reasons why companies and individuals lease. To understand leasing, it is important to understand that not all decisions to lease are based on the economics of the lease transaction. If a lessee has excessive cash or cannot obtain a high rate of return on its dollars employed, and can use the tax benefits associated with ownership, then the lessee would be better off to purchase rather than lease. Some of the most common reasons leasing has become an acceptable method of acquiring equipment are:

Cost. One reason, but certainly not the most important reason for a company or individual to lease, is that it may be the least expensive method of funding or acquiring the use of a specific asset. If the lessee cannot utilize the investment tax credit or accelerated depreciation, it could be better off leasing because most lessors will lower the lease rentals if the tax benefits are being retained by the lessor. Another cash savings for lessees is that during the lease term leasing companies usually do not require fees or balances, which are usually required by conventional bank financing.

Cash Flow. One of the biggest advantages to leasing equipment is that 100 percent of the cost of the equipment (and, in some cases, shipping costs and installation charges) is advanced by the lessor. Leasing allows the user-lessee to match the cost of the equipment being leased with the cash flow which is being generated by the equipment over an extended period of time. Lessors do not require any cleaning up of a lease for a 30- or 60-day term such as bank financing, and leases are set up to match the cash flow of the lessee. An example of this would be annual payments for farmers and skip rentals for ready-mix operators, or step-up rentals, that is, rentals which are lower in the first year and then step up in dollar amount during the remaining years.

Convenience. Next to cash flow, the second most important reason leasing has become an acceptable method of acquiring assets is convenience. Many leasing companies that work through vendors generate business because they were there at the time of the sale. U. S. Leasing, a leader in establishing national vendor programs, and captive leasing companies such as John Deere, Clark, and Allis Chalmers are successful not because they have low lease rates but because they are recommended or introduced to the lessee by the vendor or dealer. Most non-leveraged leases are also written on standard lease documentation, and no legal fees which are associated with a bank line of credit are required to be paid by the lessee.

Lease Term. The term of the lease is another important reason why lessees lease. Leases are usually structured to match the useful life of the equipment. It is not uncommon for a leasing company to provide a lease term of seven to ten years for equipment such as flat-bed trailers. The longer lease term will allow much more equipment to be acquired with the same monthly cash flowing out of a company. A bank loan at 12 percent for 25 flat-bed trailers costing $12,000 each would be about $7,900 per month for 48 months. A tax-oriented lease for eight years with a lease rate of 5 percent and monthly rentals of approximately $3,800, however, would allow the same trucking company to acquire double the trailers that could be purchased through a bank loan.

Additional Line of Credit. During periods of tight credit and high interest rates, many companies will turn to alternative sources for the funding of their equipment. They want to save their bank lines of credit to fund their accounts receivable and inventory, or to take advantage of cash discounts which may increase in times of tight credit.

Some banks will recommend leasing to their customers if the bank's loan-to-deposit ratio is high, or if the customer is starting to reach the legal lending limit of the bank or the credit limits established for that customer.

Loan Restrictions. This is not so important as some of the other reasons why a company or individual would lease, but it is worth relating. Lessors usually do not require that a lessee maintain any minimum financial ratios such as net working capital requirements or a certain debt-to-equity ratio. There may be some cases where a company may be worried about public disclosure of information specifically associated with industrial revenue bonds or other debt instruments. These public disclosures may not be required under a lease contract.

Off-balance-sheet Financing. If a lease qualifies as an operating lease, the lease transaction does not have to be recorded as a liability for financial reporting to shareholders. There are certain assets such as aircraft which management usually prefers to keep "off balance sheet."

An operating lease may have an important impact on such financial ratios as net working capital, debt to equity, and several of the liquidity ratios. It is highly advisable when reviewing the financial statements of companies and individuals that you include all noncancelable leases with a one-year or longer term in the financial ratios as debt.

Hedge Against Inflation. In periods of high inflation, the lessee is repaying the leasing company with cheap or inflated dollars. The lessee should determine the present value of the stream of minimum lease rentals in order to determine what the true cost of funding the asset will be during the lease term.

Budget Limitations. The majority of computers being leased are leased because of budget restrictions. Most data processing managers are given limited amounts of money with which to run their data processing centers. The budget amount in no way allows for the cash purchase of a large central processor or the peripheral equipment it takes to operate a complicated computer center. Almost all data processing managers are keenly aware of the latest computer technology and are always measuring the price-to-performance ratio of each generation of computer systems. In many cases leasing provides the most attractive method for staying within the budget while, at the same time, providing the output required.

Regulation Y

The Federal Reserve System through the Bank Holding Company Act of 1956 controls the activities of bank holding companies and their subsidiaries. Regulation Y applies to *de novo* and nonbanking activities. For a bank holding company to engage in a nonbanking activity such as leasing, it must make an application on Form F.R.Y.-4. The application must demonstrate that the activity is closely related to banking, that the activity will produce a benefit to the public, that it will not create any unfair competition, that there are no conflicts of interest, and that this activity is not an unsound banking practice. After it has been shown that the proposed activity does not violate any existing laws or other regulations, the Fed will publish in the Federal Register a notice of such application. This notice will allow interested persons an opportunity to express their views. Unless the bank holding company receives notification to the contrary, it may engage in leasing activities 45 days after the application has been approved.

Section 225.4 of Regulation Y permits the leasing of both personal and real property. Section 225.4(6)(a) addresses itself to the primary problems of the type of lease, term of the lease, and purpose of the lease pursuant to personal property.

The lease must be a full-payout lease in which the owner-lessor recovers its full investment during the lease term plus the cost of financing the lease. To calculate the yield, the owner-lessor may include the stream of rentals received during the lease term. Also, the lessor may include the tax benefits to be realized from the lease transaction such as the investment tax credit and depreciation. The lessor may include the expected resale value or residual to be gained after the base lease term. However, the residual value to be used in calculating the yield cannot exceed 20 percent of the original cost of the leased property.

Leases which are governed by Regulation Y must be "net" leases, that is ones in which the user-lessee absorbs such costs as taxes which may be assessed against the leased property and maintenance such as service or repair work. The user-lessee must provide other costs such as insurance and license fees.

The regulation does allow for some exceptions such as the leasing to Federal, state, and local governmental entities and for "bridge" lease financing of personal property. Many governmental entities may not enter into a lease agreement exceeding their fiscal funding authority, which is usually one or two years. When leasing to governmental entities, the owner-lessor must reasonably anticipate that the lease will be renewed until the owner-lessor is fully compensated for its investment.

The full-payout provision of Regulation Y prohibits short-term, cancelable leases. This part of the regulation makes it difficult for most bank-related lessors to compete against leasing companies, who may lease property based upon usage or who may lease property such as automobiles for a term as short as one day. Since Regulation Y restricts bank-related leasing companies from providing service work or providing a backup unit in case of a breakdown such as in truck leasing, growth in these specialized markets has been restricted.

Many independent or captive leasing companies, because of their expert knowledge of the leased property, can build in a residual far in excess of the 20 percent residual limit imposed by Regulation Y. The bank-related owner-lessor may not speculate on future property values and must purchase the leased property for a bona fide leasing transaction.

There have been cases where specialized leasing companies have placed an order for equipment months in advance of the anticipated delivery date. Just before the equipment is to be delivered, they try to find a lessee who can use the equipment at the time of delivery. An example of this is some independent leasing companies who placed orders for IBM computers and have been rewarded handsomely for speculating on computer equipment values. Since they lock the price in months in advance of the anticipated delivery dates, secondary profits have been achieved because of availability or because the computer companies have had one or more price increases during this period. It is not recommended that bank-related lessors be allowed to speculate in this manner, but some of the limitations imposed by Regulation Y should be noted.

FAS #13

The statement by the Financial Accounting Standards Board defines a lease as an agreement conveying the right to use property, plant, or equipment usually for a stated period of time.

Prior to FAS #13, there were great inconsistencies in accounting for leases both by lessors and lessees. One of the purposes of FAS #13 was to eliminate these inconsistencies and to establish standards of accounting by lessors and lessees. The symmetry in accounting for leases required by the FASB provides the groundwork but much work is still needed.

FAS #13 not only identifies what a lease is but also standardizes various leasing terms and concepts. Although there are still many gray areas, this statement has been successful in setting standards for what a lease term is, who the related parties in the leasing transaction are, and the inception of the lease.

FAS #13 also classifies leases and sets the criteria to be used when determining the type of lease and how to account for the transaction. FAS #13 classifies a lease as either an operating lease or a capitalized lease. The criteria for classifying leases are shown in Figure 2 below.

Figure 2

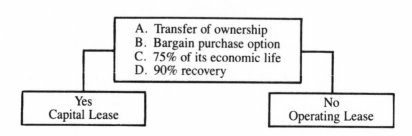

A. Transfer of ownership
B. Bargain purchase option
C. 75% of its economic life
D. 90% recovery

Yes
Capital Lease

No
Operating Lease

If a lease transaction meets at least one of the criteria, then it is to be recorded as a capital lease.

a. Transfer of Ownership. If, after the base lease term, title transfers to the lessee, then this must be recorded as a capitalized lease.

b. Bargain Purchase Option. If, after the base lease term, the lessee has a provision to purchase the property at a price lower than its fair market value, then the lease must be capitalized.

c. 75% of Its Economic Life. If the lease term is equal to or exceeds 75% of its economic life, then the transaction must be capitalized. To illustrate, if a computer has a useful life of 10 years and the lease term is 7½ years or longer, then the lease would have to be recorded as a capital lease.

d. 90% Recovery Test. If the present value of the minimum lease rentals to be paid by the lessee during the lease term equals or exceeds 90% of the fair market value of the leased property, then it is a capital lease.

When determining the minimum lease rentals, executory costs such as insurance, maintenance, and taxes that are paid by the lessor are excluded. The lessee shall use his incremental borrowing rate when computing the present value of the minimum lease rentals. The lessor shall use the interest rate implicit in the lease minus any investment tax credit being retained, also any other payments that the lessee may be required to make because he fails to renew or extend the lease or is to pay a penalty.

The reason many companies would want the lease transaction to be an operating lease is that the lease is recorded as "off balance sheet" debt. The asset being leased is not recorded as an asset or a liability by the lessee but only the lease rentals being paid are recorded as an expense. The operating lease can have the effect of lowering the lessee's debt-to-equity ratio, and it could have an adverse effect when negotiating a loan agreement if it were to be recorded as a capital lease. In many cases, most lessees would prefer the lease transaction to be recorded as an operating lease, but the 90 percent test is the hardest requirement to meet.

Tax Benefits

Who is to receive the tax benefits associated with ownership of leased property is important to the lease transaction. It is important to understand how valuable the investment tax credit and depreciation are to the transaction. There is an important difference between investment tax credit and depreciation. The credit is a direct reduction of a tax liability and depreciation is a deferral of a tax obligation.

INVESTMENT TAX CREDIT

In November, 1978, President Carter signed the Revenue Act of 1978. Some of the most important provisions of this act were to reduce the corporate income tax on earnings in excess of $100,000 from a maximum of 48 to 46 percent. The 10 percent investment tax credit was made permanent and is to increase from a maximum of a 50 percent reduction of a tax liability to 90 percent. The increase is to take place gradually over the next four years. Property which qualifies for the tax credit was expanded and the $50,000 limitation on used property was increased to $100,000. (There are many other important provisions of this act, but their effect on the leasing industry is minimal.)

For property to qualify for the tax credit, it must be used primarily in the United States, be an integral part of manufacturing or production, have a useful life of greater than three years, and be eligible for depreciation.

The maximum amount of allowable investment tax credit is 10 percent of the fair market value of the asset. For an asset to qualify for the maximum 10 percent, it must have a useful life of seven years or longer. If the useful life of the asset is greater than three years but less than five years, only one-third of the credit may be used to reduce the taxpayer's liability. The maximum allowable amounts are as follows:

Equipment Cost	Estimated Useful Life	Percent of Credit	Dollar Amount of Credit
$100,000	Under 3 years	0	$ 0
$100,000	3 to 5 years	3.33	$ 333
$100,000	5 to 7 years	6.66	$ 666
$100,000	7 years or more	10	$ 1,000

The owner-lessor may elect to pass the investment tax credit to the lessee if it is qualified new property. A lessor cannot pass the credit to a lessee for used property. If, at the inception of the lease, the credit is passed to the lessee, then, after the base lease term, the lessee purchases the property, the lessee is not entitled to an additional tax credit.

The owner-lessor is not eligible for the tax credit when leasing to a governmental entity or to a tax-exempt organization unless the property is used to produce unrelated business taxable income.

Loans to a Leasing Company

When structuring a loan to a leasing company, there are some basic points which should be considered. Some of the more important elements of the loan should be:

The credit should state what type of loan will be extended by the bank. It should include the principal dollar amount of the loan and its maturity date. Other areas should be the minimum amount of takedown and minimum amount of principal reductions.

The manner of borrowing should include the number of days' advance notice the bank needs before takedown can occur and the method of notification to the bank, how and when the proceeds are to be forwarded to the leasing company, confirmation, and when the bank's liability ends.

The *pricing* should include commitment fees and method of calculation, the specific date when the fees are to be paid, compensating balance requirements, and the interest rate to be charged, along with the method of calculation.

Prepayments. Will the leasing company be allowed to prepay the note, will there be any premium for early termination, and what will the specific penalty amounts be to terminate?

Place of Payments. Where and in what manner should payments of principal, interest, and fees be made, and by what dates should payments be made along with any penalties for late payments?

Liens, Indebtedness, Acquisitions, Mergers, and Sales. Before any of the above mentioned can occur, express written consent from the bank should be given in order not to jeopardize the bank's position.

Financial reporting to the bank should include the quarterly and annual balance sheet and income statement along with a sources and application of funds statement, lease delinquency report, quarterly write-offs, and new policies approved by the board of directors. The bank should also have the corporate by-laws and a list of the directors and the major officers along with their titles. Once a year the bank may wish to get a breakdown of types of equipment being leased, to what industries the equipment is being leased, and in what geographical area the equipment is located. These statements should be signed by the chief executive officer or the chief financial officer.

The leasing company should verify that the following are being performed or that they are true statements:

1. That the leasing company is authorized to carry on its business and is licensed in all jurisdictions where it conducts its business
2. That the loan agreement does not violate any existing agreements or its charter or by-laws
3. That there is no litigation or governmental proceeding pending or any adversities which would materially or adversely affect the financial condition of the company
4. That all taxes are current and that the Internal Revenue Department has examined and approved as filed past returns

The general covenants should state that the leasing company will preserve and keep in force all licenses and permits necessary to conduct its business, and that all taxes will be paid unless they are being contested in good faith and by appropriate proceedings. The leasing company will maintain a system of accounting in accordance with sound accounting practices.

The bank may impose an insurance requirement which will state that the leasing company will insure or cause to be insured public liability, product liability, and property damage by a responsible insurance company.

Other restrictions which the bank's credit committee may wish to impose are minimum net worth requirements and maximum debt-to-equity ratios. Still other information may include the maximum contract or dollar amounts to any one customer or industry, the maximum term of a lease contract, and the minimum amount of loss reserve that must be maintained at all times. If the leasing company is a division or subsidiary of another company, the bank may wish to impose some restrictions on dividends, management fees, and contracts with affiliates which may have an effect on the health and welfare of the leasing entity.

There are still other considerations when making a loan to a leasing company that cannot be qualified. Are the owners or investors serious about the leasing industry or are they fly-by-night promoters or super salesmen who use a hard sell to get someone to sign a lease agreement and then disappear after a few years? Does management understand the collateral being leased or is it trying to be everything to everyone?

The leasing industry will continue to grow and many changes will occur over the next few years. The progressive banker should continue to follow such changes.

20

Loan Portfolio Management in a Community Bank

The loan portfolio in the normal community bank comprises about 65 percent or more of the bank's total assets. High-performance managers aim to maximize income and minimize risks in loan portfolio management. The suggestions made in this chapter are aimed at those two objectives.

Liquidity

It is essential that liquidity needs be determined and provided for. Such a determination will accommodate the blend of complexities of hard-core deposits, seasonal fluctuations in loan demand and deposits, and the needs of the community. The regulatory agencies have formulas designed to determine if a bank has adequate liquidity. Every community bank manager should be familiar with the requirements of the agency to whom the bank reports. In addition, however, it is imperative that the peculiarities of the local community and the bank itself be accounted for.

Fund allocations and liquidity provision might be diagrammed and allocated as in Figure 1. Scientific management determines the liquidity requirements for each class of liability and provides for it. A simple form for regular calculations of liquidity is illustrated in Figure 2. This exercise done in some manner on a regular basis can be a most fruitful one for the bank.

The purpose of this chapter is not to discuss liquidity or describe how to

Figure 1

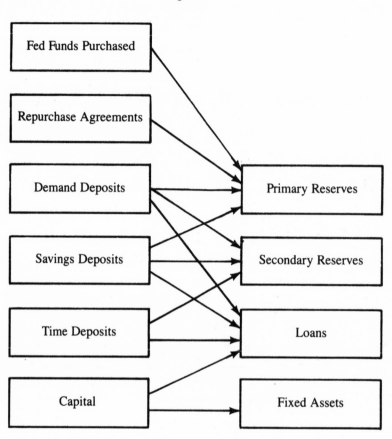

Figure 2

Date

Liquidity Analysis Schedule

1. TOTAL LIABILITIES (Exclude valuation reserve & capital)   _____
            (Includes _____$ Fed Funds Purchased)
   a. Less Deductions (C Ds over one year and Treasury Tax and
            Loan)   _____
2. NET LIABILITIES   _____
3. Cash and due from banks (Accounts 130-000; 132-000 & 133-000)   _____
4. Unpledged U.S. Governments (market value)   _____
5. Other unpledged securities—one year maturities or less   _____
6. Federal funds sold ($_____) (112-600); U.S. and other
   securities purchased under agreements to resell in which the
   term of the agreement does not exceed 30 days.   _____
7. Commercial Paper and Bankers Acceptances and Negotiable
   C Ds   _____
8. GROSS LIQUID ASSETS (sum of lines, 3, 4, 5, 6 & 7)   _____
9. Less Deductions (Required Reserve)   _____
10. NET LIQUID ASSETS (line 8 minus line 9)   _____
11. PERCENT: Net liquid assets to net liabilities (line 10 as a percent
            of line 2)   _____
            Liquidity percent considered
            desirable_____%

Memoranda

1. Other unpledged securities with maturities over one year   _____
2. Profit (or Loss) in U.S. Governments shown in item #4 above   _____
3. Profit (or Loss) in all other unpledged securities—one year
   maturities or less   _____
4. Firm Loan Commitments to be funded within 90 days:
            Commercial/Agricultural (customer loans)   _____
            Real Estate Loans   _____
            Other Loans (Including $_____ large C Ds (negotiable)   _____
            TOTAL   _____
5. Letters of Credit Outstanding   _____
6. Firm Payments anticipated within 90 days:
            Commercial/Agricultural   _____
            Real Estate Loans   _____
            Other Loans   _____
            TOTAL   _____
7. Total Loans_____Total Tax Exempts_____Total Deposits   _____

Recommendations (Asset changes to effect optimum liquidity and
profitability)_____

| Jan. | Feb. | Mar. | Apr. | May | Jun. | Jul. | Aug. | Sept. | Oct. | Nov. | Dec. |

fill out forms. It is however, an integral part of loan portfolio management in the community bank. Careful estimating of the future cash flows is also important. This estimate can be developed simply on a form as shown in Figure 3.

In order to avoid the hazards of "lending long and borrowing short," many community banks today use the gap ratio determination. The gap ratio can apply variable rate loans for the period (one month, three months, six months, or one year) against variable rate deposits for the same period (see Figure 3). The bottom part of this form identifies a simple method of laying out this risk. The ability to cover liability rate changes with income is a survival matter in the current volatile economic society.

Asset Allocation

Many matters determine the allocation of loan funds.
Some of these are:

- Community needs and characteristics
- Staff capability and availability
- Desirability for diversification of the portfolio
- Yield opportunities on various types of loans
- Risk analysis and loss potential on various loan types
- Growth opportunities for the bank

As a part of the planning process, identify an appropriate allocation of funds on an annual or more frequent basis. Cash flows from repayments, new funds, or reallocations may be assigned as available to various loan departments.

Appropriate loan departments or categories might be:

- Commercial loans
- Agricultural loans
- Consumer loans
- Real estate loans, commercial and residential

Most community banks sub-ledger their loans in conformity with current supervised call report requirements.

Loan Policies

Policies in many community banks are more informal than their metropolitan counterparts. Management should insure that policies are in writing, workable, and complied with. They should reflect the objectives of the bank and the needs of the community. Under the Community Reinvestment Act, all community banks need to have a Community Reinvestment Act policy (Figure 4).

Figure 3

Name of Bank _____

ESTIMATE OF FUTURE CASH POSITION FOR MONTH OF _____

(4-day average figures)

Deposits:	Last Month	This Month	+ or −	3 Months Hence	+ or −	6 Months Hence	+ or −
Checking Account							
Public Funds							
Other							
Total Demand							
Savings & Works							
C Ds							
Total Time							
Treasury Tax and Loan Notes Account and Repossessions							
Total Deposits and Treasury Tax and Loan							
Loans: (Fed Funds not included.)							
Real Estate Mortgages							
Customers							
Outside Paper							
Installment							
Total Loans							
Net Liquidity Change							
Fed Funds Sold (Purchased)							
Other Borrowed Funds							
Other Salable Loans Held							
Rate Sensitive Assets*							
Rate Sensitive Liabilities†							

} Ratio − _____

* Total all assets maturing or changing in rate within six months, including real estate amortization, customer loans, outside paper, money market instruments, bonds and Fed Funds sold.

† Total all liabilities maturing within six months, including C Ds, Treasury Tax and Loan, and Fed Funds purchased. Add in your estimate of savings net outflow for six months.

Jan	Feb	Mar	Apr	May	Jun	Jul	Aug	Sept	Oct	Nov	Dec

Figure 4

COMMUNITY REINVESTMENT ACT POLICY
ANY BANK
ANYWHERE, U.S.A.

I. The CRA statement (effective February 4, 1979):

A. Community Reinvestment Act Notice:

The Federal Community Reinvestment Act (CRA) requires the FDIC to evaluate our performance in helping to meet the credit needs of this community, and to take this evaluation into account when the FDIC decides on certain applications submitted by us. Your involvement is encouraged.

YOU SHOULD KNOW THAT:

You may obtain our current CRA statements for this community in this office. (Current CRA statements for other communities served by us are available at our head office, located at 102 South Center, Anywhere, U.S.A.)

You may send signed, written comments about our CRA statements or our performance in helping to meet community credit needs to Thomas R. Smith, President, Any Bank, Anywhere, U.S.A., and to Federal Deposit Insurance Corporation, 1700 Farnam Street, Omaha, Nebraska 68102.

Your letter, together with any responses by us, may be made public. You may look at a file of all signed, written comments received by us within the past two years, any responses we have made to the comments, and all CRA statements in effect during the past two years at our office located at 102 South Center Street, Anywhere, U.S.A. (You may also look at the file about this community at Meadow Lane Office, 1904 South Center Street, Anywhere, U.S.A.)

You may ask to look at any comments received by Federal Deposit Insurance Corporation, 1700 Farnam Street, Omaha, Nebraska 68102. You may also request from the Federal Deposit Insurance Corporation, 550 17th Street N.W., Washington, D.C. 20429, an announcement of applications covered by the CRA filed with the FDIC. We are a subsidiary of Any Banks, Inc., a bank holding company. You may request from the Federal Reserve Bank of Chicago, 230 S. LaSalle St.,Chicago, Illinois 60690, an announcement of applications covered by the CRA filed by bank holding companies

II. Any Bank Statement of Objective:

It is the intent of the bank to meet the responsible credit needs of our community. We seek to assist our customers to achieve their desired life styles and career paths. We particularly seek to make loans that will upgrade the potential, opportunities and capabilities of our customers and the community. Our programs are designed to assist customers in improving their positions and not just to perpetuate debt.

We intend to make loans in the geographic area hereinafter described. From time to time as we purchase loan participations from other banks, we will attempt to lay off similar dollar amounts to other banks in return in order to maintain a constant flow of available loan dollars.

Loan policies and practices will be designed to provide responsible loan and payment programs within the abilities of the customer to repay, the safety of depositors' funds and responsible profitability, safety and liquidity of the bank.

III. The bank's market area is located in the surrounding four counties.

IV. The specific types of farm loan services which we offer in order to meet the responsible credit needs of our community are:
   A. Seasonal loans for crop production
   B. Seasonal loans for livestock production
   C. Term loans for purchase of farm equipment
   D. Term loans for farm expansion
   E. Loans to young farmers to help them start farming

V. The specific types of other loan services we offer in order to meet the responsible credit needs of our community described as the effective lending area for "other types of loans."
   A. Consumer loans for purchase or ownership of new or used cars, appliances, recreational vehicles, college education or for other purposes as may comply with objectives as described in Paragraph II.
   B. Commercial loans for carrying inventory and accounts receivable on a seasonal basis. We also make term loans for purchase of equipment or expansion. We make loans through the Small Business Administration.
   C. We purchase General Obligation and Revenue Municipal Bonds and Industrial Development Revenue Bonds in the area defined as the effective lending area for "other types of loans" as well as nationally, subject to the bank requirements and the credibility of the offerings.

VI. Real estate loans will be made available only in the county in which the bank is located.

VII. The credibility of our effort to meet community responsibility in the past is demonstrated by a few statistics:
   A. In the last 18 months we have made single-family dwellings loans to 36 moderate-income families through the Iowa Housing Finance Authority for a total of $1,470,000 at an average loan of $40,833.
   B. We have 282 student loans outstanding totaling $297,868.
   C. We have 14 Small Business Administration loans outstanding for a total of $1,250,313.
   D. Loan officers assisted in processing 113 disaster loans in 1977–78.
   E. Forty-one young farmers under the age of 30 use our loan services presently.
   F. All officers are requested to commit one day per month of bank time to worthwhile community activities.

An agricultural loan policy for a community bank (Figure 5) works, is enforceable, and is easily interpreted by personnel.

Policies should provide for geographic distribution of loans, economic distribution of risk, government loan program participations, placement of overlines, and community development loans.

Figure 5

AGRICULTURAL LOAN POLICY
ANY BANK
ANYWHERE, U.S.A.

Our objective is to provide sound credit and related banking services to all creditworthy farm customers and agri-business customers in the outlined market area of our Community Reinvestment Act Policy.

Our intention is to provide forward planning of farm program needs on an annual basis. This process will insure the proper credit management of their short, intermediate and long term financing. We should obtain a new financial statement during the period December through March. At that time, we will have an annual review with both spouses and recap the line of credit, future plans, estate planning and land changes.

UNSECURED LINE

Farmers and agri-businesses with a net worth in excess of $100,000 and no current debt may be eligible for a line of unsecured credit based on their repayment capacity, current ratio and debt to worth ratio. Spouses should generally sign unsecured credits in excess of 15% of net worth. Cross guarantees could be used to fulfill this requirement.

SECURED LINES

A Uniform Commercial Code I filing with the Secretary of State containing the general farm clause should be used on all secured credit. This statement is good for a five-year period which should be reviewed annually to make sure that we maintain a current filing. Also, land changes (either owned or rented) should prompt a new filing.

Farmers with a full line of credit should present a marketing program, profit and loss statement or tax forms and cash flow statements at the time the new statement is presented. Those should be workng documents used for periodic review.

An Ag Reserve line of credit for operating expenses should be considered for all active farm lines. This should be a master note with sufficient collateral listed to justify the credit. It should also include a current crops clause and supporting legal descriptions of owned and rented land.

Large machinery purchases, feeder cattle and feeder pigs should be on a customer note. Breeding livestock and machinery should be programmed on a term repayment basis using a variable rate clause unless there is an extremely current liquid position available for repayment.

    a. Large machinery purchases should list specific serial numbers on the security agreement. A Uniform Commercial Code I filing is optional depending on the credit. We should encourage term loan repayment for the capital purchases, such as machinery and breeding stock, with terms running up to maximum of five years. Supporting documentation on term loans should include economic feasibility and debt service determinations. If loan extension is made then purchase price Uniform Commercial Code I should be extended also.

    b. A loan may be made for the full purchase price of feeder cattle and feeder pigs providing the farmer is carrying feed on hand in inventory or will have it available from crops. Debt load on current crop inventory should be taken into account. This will also be subject to adequate experience and a satisfactory current position. There are times when it might be necessary to require forward contracting or hedging to protect the profit on the purchase. If it is necessary for the farmer to purchase the feed we should never loan over 80% of the total cost of the cattle and the feed.

Farm inspection calls should be made on all customers with full lines of credit at least once a year. On large lines over $35,000, young farmers, or closely margined lines, additional calls may be necessary.

LEVERED LINES

On large lines an inventory report will be secured quarterly. Farm calls are an excellent opportunity to verify inventory. Also bank profitability analysis should be performed to strengthen relationships and determine pricing equities

Lines of credit that require close supervision should be placed on a base security agreement listing specific collateral including equipment, livestock, increase, grain and crops. Future advances on security agreements should be tied back to the original security agreement. Both spouses should sign or have cross guarantees.

Farm real estate loans are to be reviewed on an individual case basis with primary referral to Federal Land Bank or to insurance companies for long-term money. On contract purchases or farm down-payment on cash purchases we should insist on long-term take-outs or program the repayment through a term loan on the machinery or breeding stock, unless there is very strong liquidity in the current position that can repay the down-payment within one year. A cash flow statement should be prepared by the farmer and lender to determine feasibility of the purchase.

NEW OR YOUNG FARMER LINES

New lines of credit require an on-the-farm visit, credit check and a history of progress, also, we need to know the future plans of this particular farm operation. New lines of credit above $25,000 will be approved by the loan committee.

We will make an effort to encourage and develop young farmers. In some cases it will be necessary to make loans to young farmers with low net worths and highly levered positions. These need to be handled on an individual case basis. We require good management ability and progress. We should encourage young farmers to complete cash flow statements and to participate in a recordkeeping program. FHA direct or an FHA guarantied program should be considered in every case.

SPLIT CREDIT ON NONPROFITABLE LINES

Split lines of credit as a general rule are not acceptable. Such loans may be made to gain entry to new business and direction set for a complete Fidelity Brenton Bank customer. Loans should also be discouraged with marginal operators who are not making good progress or who have extremely low equity position. We also discourage making loans to farmers that have poor repayment habits and who do not carry adequate balances and accounts with our banks.

CLOSING

Heavy advances to customers with full lines of credit, watch loans or work-out loans should be cleared with the Executive Vice President or with the loan committee, which will meet every Friday morning at 7:45 a.m.

(continued)

Machinery, Equipment & Facilities

	Margin	Term
New	80%	5 years maximum
Used	50%	2–4 years

Livestock

	Margin	Margin	Term
	Feed Owned	Feed Purchased	
Cows	100%	80%	Maximum 4 years
Cattle	100%	75%	1 year
Sows	100%	80%	Maximum 2 years
Pigs	100%	75%	150 days

Loan Approval Process

Community banks generally have an informal loan approval process. Loan limits may be assigned to individual officers. Loan applications in excess of the assigned dollar limits or with more than normal risk are referred to a loan committee, which may or may not include members of the board of directors. Loan officers should be aware of the policy documentation requirements. Incomplete applications cause delays, negative decisions, or bad answers. Progressive community bankers know that proper counseling with the borrowers is a significant part of the loan service. Turning down a loan because "It's too big," or because "We don't make those kinds of loans," or "I think your application is reasonable but the committee turned it down" are not acceptable answers to customers in today's market place. Prompt decisions with effective counseling are a trademark of the effective community bank loan officer. In any event, loan approval responsibility should be designed to make loan officers accountable.

Commitments

Rate volatility and limited funds availability have led to more careful consideration by bankers issuing commitments. Bank customers, on the other hand, have come to want some assurance that their credit lines will be available to them. When written commitments are issued, it is important that the documents be carefully worded. The following items might be included:

1. Amount of the loan
2. Purpose of the loan
3. Collateral
4. Conditions
5. Rate
6. Expiration date

7. Maturity
8. Repayment requirements
9. Acceleration clause in event of violation
10. Other conditions:
    a. Fixed asset investment limitations
    b. Other borrowings and banking relationships
    c. Insurance requirements
    d. Financial reporting to bank
    e. Salary limitations to principals
    f. Dividend limitations

A written commitment on a residential real estate loan is shown as an example (Figure 6). Care should be taken to insure that the bank is not at risk with commitment liabilities. A control must be maintained to alert management of this exposure.

Figure 6

Real Estate Mortgage Loan Commitment

To:_____   _____, 19_____

The undersigned have made application for a mortgage loan in the amount of $_____at an annual rate of_____% for a term of_____years. This loan is made for the purpose of_____property located at_____

Special considerations of this commitment are
_____
_____
_____
_____

The undersigned agree that they will, within thirty (30) days from the date hereof, do any and all things necessary to formalize said loan, including the execution of all loan papers and documents requested by the creditor and the furnishing of evidence of a credit rating satisfactory to the creditor.

_____

                                                             Applicant

By:_____

                                                             Title

By:_____

                                                             Title

Subject to furnishing abstract showing merchantable title, an appraisal, a survey, appropriate approval by insuring agency or Guarantee Insurance Carrier, or assignee, and the conditions set forth herein, the Creditor agrees to make the above requested loan, hereby

(continued)

consummating the transaction. This commitment shall remain in force for_____days from the date set forth below at which time it shall expire.

Dated _____

                                                 _____

                                                                  Creditor

By: _____

                                                 _____

                                                                   Title

Pricing

Community banks routinely identify the cost of funds and price loans at an appropriate spread to achieve budgeted profits. A form that might be used to calculate the net interest margin is illustrated in Figure 7. Regular monitoring is required to insure that targeted rates and yields are being achieved in each loan area.

Figure 7

INTEREST MARGIN REPORT
(In Thousands)

Bank _____ Date _____ Prepared by _____

	Monthly Avg. Balance (A)	Yield or Cost (B)	Annualized Income (C)
1. Real Estate Loans			
2. Customer Loans			
3. Outside Loans			
4. Finance Loans			
5. Total Loans			
6. Fed Funds Sold			
7. Securities Purch. U/A to Resell			
8. C Ds Purchased			
9. Other			
10. Total Liquidity Loans			
11. Governments and Agencies			
12. Municipals and Tax Exempt Loans Tax Equiv.			
13. Other Investments			
14. Total Investments/Tax Equiv.			
15. Total Earning Assets/Tax Equiv.			
16. Savings			
17. Regular C D			
18. 6-month C D			
19. 30-month C D			

20. Large C D	————	————	————
21. Total Interest Cost Deposits	————	————	————
22. Fed Funds Purchased	————	————	————
23. Securities Sold U/A to Repurchase	————	————	————
24. Other Borrowed	————	————	————
25. Capital Notes	————	————	————
26. Total Borrowed Funds	————	————	————
27. Total Interest Cost Liabilities	————	————	————
28. Net Interest Income/Tax Equiv. (Col. C Line 15 Minus Col. C Line 27)	————		
29. Net Interest Margin (Col. C Line 28 divided by Col. A Line 15)	————		

**Historical–Margins
(Previous 12 Months)**

	Jan.	Feb.	Mar.	Apr.	May	Jun.	Jul.	Aug.	Sep.	Oct.	Nov.	Dec.
Year	——	——	——	——	——	——	——	——	——	——	——	——
Margin	——	——	——	——	——	——	——	——	——	——	——	——

The geographic barriers are continually breaking down so competitive pressures certainly are a part of the pricing mechanism. Shopping competitors for price comparison is a part of the marketing function in the community bank. It too is a part of the pricing process.

In periods of rapidly escalating interest rates, banks have found it appropriate to use the so-called "hurdle rate" method of pricing. New loans are priced at the desired margin over the highest cost of the most recently acquired liabilities (see Figure 8). This system is particularly necessary to preserve the margin in periods of rapidly escalating interest rates.

In order that all personnel can properly explain services to customers and prospects, a price sheet, updated regularly, can be made available to all departments and loan officers. Most community bank loan portfolio managers have moved to variable rate pricing or relatively short-term renewable loans to remove the rate risk from the portfolio.

Account Profitability Analysis

In order to price individual loans profitably, an analysis of the total account relationship must be made. The profitability of individual account relationships can be determined. This might be done as indicated in Figure 9. Sampling techniques in the community bank may give sufficient indications for appropriate pricing. The superior bank manager's design is to have all accounts profitable.

Figure 8

Hurdle Rate

DATE_____

Assumptions
1. A return on average assets of 1.1%
2. There is no long-term debt in the bank.
3. The capital to asset ratio is 7.
4. The bank's effective tax rate is 46%.
5. The estimated operating expenses associated with the lending function are 70% of the loan.
6. The estimated provision for loan losses is .55% of the loan.
7. The expected cost of incremental funds is 13%.

Loan Pricing for Profits

		Calculation	Value	Your Bank
I.	Develop a target margin			
1.	Define your bank's return on assets goal: e.g., 1.1%			
2.	Convert return to a pretax margin: return on assets ÷ (1 − tax rate)	$\dfrac{1.10}{1.00 - 0.46}$		2.04
3.	Add noninterest lending expenses: estimated annual expenses ÷ estimated average loan outstanding			.40
4.	Add provision for loan loss			.55
5.	Subtract value of equity capital			
	a) Determine capital to asset ratio: e.g., 7%			
	b) Forecast value of funds rate: e.g., 15.25%			
	c) Calculate capital credit	7% X 15.25		1.66
	Required Margin (Hurdle Rate) To Meet Profit Goal			1.93

II. Communicate the current target margin and interest rate forecast to the lending officers.
III. Determine the maximum rate achievable for the individual customer.
IV. Structure the credit in terms of rates, balances and fees to achieve the maximum rate in light of the customer's financial situation.

Figure 9

LOAN PROFITABILITY ANALYSIS

NAME _____

FUNDS STATEMENT
    Average Loans Outstanding $ _____
    Investible Funds Supplied $ _____
    (Collected Balances X .93) $ _____

    Net Funds Used $ _____
         $ _____

PROFIT STATEMENT
    Interest Income_____ $ _____

Less: Cost of Funds_____ $ _____

Less: Loan Handling Cost_____ $ _____

Net Spread $ _____

                                     $ _____

Net Spread
Net Funds Used $ _____

Rate of Return $ _____

                                     $ _____

Comments:

Documentation

It is imperative that all advances meet the necessary documentation requirements:

1. Proper projections
2. Appropriate appraisal values
3. Loan to value margins
4. Identifiable security
5. Meet all commitment requirements
6. Authorized signatures on all documents
7. Perfected security interest
8. Insurance coverage and bank interest identified

Experienced loan officers realize that in doing 99 things right and one wrong, it will be the one wrong thing that will haunt you in the collection process.

Laws and regulations change frequently. Legal counsel should advise lenders on appropriate documentation.

Loan Review

Community banks generally do not have separate loan review sections. The function can be accomplished in a variety of ways.

1. Senior officer review of loans
2. File review to identify any shortfall in documentation or creditability
3. Loan review committee
4. Separate loan review section

A simple way to identify loan portfolio risks is to use a loan rating system. Such a system is described in Figure 10.

The community bank may from time to time choose to make a loan with more than normal risk. Typical of such loans are those to young farmers, businessmen, or professional persons. Such loans might be classified on a watch

Figure 10

Loan Ratings

ONE   Loans with the least risk. Loans considered prime on the basis of financial strength and/or readily marketable collateral, and consistently good performance of the borrower. Unquestioned repayment ability. Generally not a term loan.

TWO   Safe loans with no problems anticipated. Loans considered sub-prime, but requiring only a normal degree of watchfulness. Well collateralized loans, or unsecured loans to a borrower with financial strength and one who performs as expected. Good repayment ability.

THREE   Safe loans with the need for trends and fluctuations to be followed by the lender on a continuing basis. These loans, considered standard, are an acceptable risk. Their initiation and continuation is warranted because of the potential they represent. No repayment problems anticipated.

FOUR   Substandard loans that are an unacceptable risk under present circumstances. They are still considered collectible, but, if not paid in full, must have corrections to reduce the risk and to result in a payment program.

FIVE   Doubtful loans that are not collectible in a reasonable period of time, and are a potential charge-off. Intensive collection efforts, including control of collateral, legal action, and/or refinancing elsewhere should be initiated immediately.

list to insure that they receive more than normal administrative attention from senior loan officers.

In order to facilitate the loan review function, a documentation check list is helpful. Such check lists are shown in Figure 11.

Collection Procedures

Loan portfolio quality discipline is a never-ending task because of a wide variety of economic, environmental, governmental, and personal factors impacting individual loans. Good loans can become problem loans. Continued review will strengthen or move out weak loans to the benefit of the borrower and the bank. Community bankers identify these as "work-out" loans. Some of the symptoms of problem loans are:

1. *Inability to pay a note at maturity.* We should always find out what happened to the funds that were supposed to pay the note when it was advanced, and determine why the program did not come off as planned.

2. *Excessive expenses over budget.* When advances are substantially over budget, we should determine from the borrower what has happened to the funds.

3. *Breakdown of communications with the borrower.* If the borrower becomes evasive, stays away from the bank, or does not answer questions directly—in other words, if the borrower stops communicating—we should investigate to see what is happening.

4. *Inability of borrower to margin loans properly.* This indicates a loss of working capital, which may mean a loss situation in the business or a leak of assets of some kind.

5. *Bank account problems.* If there are continued overdrafts, return items, or the customer is calling the bank daily for balances and covering requirements at the last minute, we should become suspicious.

6. *Delinquent Notes.* If a customer lets notes run past due, it may mean a weakening of his responsibility and creditworthiness.

In the event the above and any other signs surface that indicate problems on the loan, the following procedures are recommended:

1. Make an on-site visit and discuss the situation fairly and firmly with the borrower.

2. Get all the answers from the borrower so that we know precisely what has happened and what the program of action will be.

3. Attempt to get interim numbers. We cannot always get operating figures or a new statement but we can perhaps get receivables outstanding or inventory balances at least and determine what has happened.

4. Make only a temporary extension if any extension is made at all. Do not make a one-year extension. Make an extension until such time as more information can be developed and the situation clarified. Tell the borrower you want to review the loan with the loan committee so that all concerned can get properly oriented and make a reasonable judgment on the credit.

Collection policies should define timing and responsibility for the effort. Slovenly procedures leave the bank with weakened assets and a low-yielding portfolio. Overstaying with a problem loan can be time-consuming and costly. High-performance community banks have consistently lower portfolio losses than average banks.

Reporting Procedures

Some community bank boards of directors review all loans. Others identify loans of a given size or type. Management can report these in summary fashion. Smaller loans may be reported by name only. Complete candor in loan reporting and analysis is a must.

Management should have access to loss and delinquency ratios for various loan categories and each loan officer. Policy should direct acceptable parameters. National figures are available from the trade associations in order to help define such parameters. Many community banks today find loan officer objectives a useful device for determining volume per loan officer along with loss ratios.

Figure 11

Installment Loan Review Check Sheet

	Car Dealer	Car Direct	Personal	Mobile Home	Home Improvement	Second Real Estate Mortgage	Camper Boat	Other
Application								
Current date	X	X	X	X	X	X	X	X
Complete		X	over $1M	X	X	X	X	X
Date of birth	X	X	X	X	X	X	X	X
Social security number	X	X	X	X	X	X	X	X
Phone number	X	X	X	X	X	X	X	X
Loan value	X	X	X	X	X	X	X	X
Employer	X	X	X	X	X	X	X	X
Nearest relative	X	X	X	X	X	X	X	X
Note—Security Agreement								
Form acceptable	X	X	X	X	X	X	X	X
Security description	X	X		X	X	X	X	X
Cost shown	X	X	X	X	X	X	X	X
Credit life insurance	X	X	X	X	X	X	X	X
Accident and health insurance	X	X	X	X	X	X	X	X
Interest rate to two decimals	X	X	X	X	X	X	X	X
Signed by owners	X	X		X	X	X	X	X
Purchase price money clause checked or wife signs	X	X		X		X	X	X

Other

				over $10M		
Other						
Appraisal					X	X
Two pictures					X	X
Disclosure					X	X
Right of recission					X	X
Insurance					X	X
Title						
Name recognizable	X		X	X		XC
Lien recorded	X		X	X		X
Uniform Commercial Code I						
Name recognizable		X				XB
Equipment adequately described		X				X
Date of filing noted		X				X

Portfolio Risks

Cyclical disintermediation as well as cash outflows out of rural and suburban communities can create a shortage of lendable funds for community banks. Often it is desirable to book loans of more than normal risk for community developmental purposes. Community banks have historically been supported in these efforts by various governmental loan guaranties and participations.

Use of Small Business Administration and Farm Credit Bank services can expand funds availability with the agricultural and the commercial loan areas. Funds from the Federal National Mortgage Association can expand the bank's capabilities in meeting community needs in housing.

Participations with correspondent banks, other area banks, and competitive lending institutions like Production Credit Associations are all ways to expand the bank's funds.

SUMMARY

High-performance community banks generally tend to have higher-yielding loan portfolios and lower loan losses than average banks. They also tend to have slightly less of their total assets allocated to loans.

Aggressive community bankers feel that meeting loan needs of the area is a desirable way to help the bank grow.

The breakdown of geographic competitive barriers along with disintermediation have compounded the community banker's problems in meeting the needs of his community. Loan demand and fund availability appear to be on a collision course in community banks. It is imperative therefore that systems be designed to insure a portfolio of sound, productive, profitable loans.

It behooves the community bank loan portfolio manager to be totally aware of all options.

21

Loan Participation Problems of Smaller Banks

There are over 14,000 independent banks in the United States, and the majority of them do an outstanding job in serving their respective communities. This situation is unique in the world. In other countries banking is concentrated in a few large banks which operate branches—hundreds of them in some instances—to serve their banking customers.

One reason our system may be so successful is the existence of correspondent banking relationships. Simply stated, in correspondent banking relationships two banks work with each other to deliver maximum service to their customers. In most cases the relationship is between a smaller bank and a larger one, with the larger bank providing its smaller correspondent with the availability of certain services it could not otherwise provide its customers because of its limited size. Compensation for the larger bank usually comes through a non-interest-bearing deposit account maintained with it by the smaller bank.

In a correspondent relationship the smaller bank is generally referred to as a "country bank," while the larger bank is referred to as a "city bank." In some instances, a bank of medium size may be considered a city bank to its smaller country bank correspondent while, at the same time, it may be considered a country bank to the large city banks with which it may carry on a correspondent relationship.

One of the most important services a city bank can provide its country correspondent banks is the purchase of loan participations. When a city bank buys a loan participation, the bank agrees to the purchase of a portion of a loan that has been originated by the country bank. In most cases the country bank needs to sell the portion because, for example, the total loan would be in excess of its prescribed legal lending limit; or it does not want to assume a risk as large as the total loan; or, sometimes, a country bank just does not have the funds available to make such a large loan.

This discussion will deal primarily with actual experiences in selling loan participations "upstream" to a city correspondent bank—the type of participation with which the majority of bankers become involved. Even though a bank has $500 million in resources, it may be considered a country bank when compared to banks such as Citibank, Chase, First Chicago, and Bank of America. Consideration will be given chiefly to *problems* that may be encountered. Without any problems, it can be assumed the transactions work smoothly for both the city bank and country bank, as they do in the great majority of loans.

The term "city correspondent bank" refers to a bank (not necessarily a large city bank) at which the principal deposit account of a country bank is maintained. In exchange for the use of these deposit funds, the bank expects its city correspondent bank to make available certain services among which are some it is unable to offer its customers because of its size—particularly involving loans in excess of its legal lending limit, necessitating the sale of overline participations.

When country banks sell overline participations they generally retain their legal limit to show their good faith in the credit. It is important to the purchasing bank to see that "You put your maximum money where your mouth is." In other words, if the country bank does not wish to bet on its "horse" (loan customer) to the maximum, the city bank probably will not wish to bet its money either.

There are not always problems when a country bank tries to sell a participation to a city correspondent. If the country bank has a AAA-1 credit, a ten-year completely documented credit file, a loan for 30 days or less, a rate in excess of prime, and average collected balances with the city bank four or five times the amount of the participation request, the country bank may encounter no problems at all! In fact, the city correspondent may even appear to be happy to have been called.

Before some readers conclude this may be unwarranted criticism of the handling of loan participations by some city correspondent banks, it should be said that most city correspondent banks are helpful to country correspondent banks in many ways. However, this discussion deals with *problems* in loan participations with city correspondent banks, and not routine transactions.

Perhaps it would be helpful to relate typical experiences in selling loan participations. This will illustrate some problems a country bank may experience.

Credit Information

The city bank will usually have a more sophisticated credit department than the country bank from which it buys its participations. In many small banks most of the credit information on a customer may be filed inside the cashier's head.

The country banker should give the city banker all the credit information he has—whether good or bad—and not hold back when he feels the information is confidential or "just between him and his customer." There is nothing so confidential that it should be withheld from the city bankers who are buying the participation. For example, if a relative of the banker has a financial interest in the borrower, then the correspondent banker should be told about it.

To the best of its ability, the country bank should provide the city bank with full information on the borrower to enable it to make its credit decision. As long as the participation is outstanding, it has a continuing obligation to provide both good and bad information about the borrower as it becomes available concerning—but not limited to—management, financial condition, change in corporate structure, sale or acquisition of fixed assets, known contingent liabilities, or anything it believes could affect the city bank's desire to continue as a participant. There is an obligation to keep participants fully informed about the borrower. Adequate and complete disclosure of facts is essential.

The risk of incomplete disclosure includes being sued, losing a correspondent relationship, or having to repurchase a share of the loan—which could violate the country bank's legal lending limit.

Medium-size banks may have a reasonable amount of credit information in adequate form. The city bank's credit information request should consider the size of the bank and the amount of the loan requested. Asking a small-town customer to fill out a Robert Morris Associates five-year cash flow projection may be just the thing to convince the customer he really does not need a loan from the bank.

Audited statements are necessary for proper credit analysis, and all loans over a certain amount must be supported by an audited statement. What about the customer who needs the money now and did not know it last year when his statements were prepared without an audit?

Small banks are inclined to make loans to people rather than to balance sheets and profit and loss statements. Requests for credit information should be in line with the ability and size of the bank and customer who are to provide it.

However, the correspondent banker may have had more experience in this particular field than the country banker, who may wish therefore to consider carefully the correspondent banker's comments about the quality of the credit.

There may be some pitfalls in the type of credit under discussion that have not occurred to the country banker in his credit analysis.

Company Visitation by Correspondent Bankers

Most country banks recognize that city bankers are generally highly capable individuals who make a good impression on their customers. If a customer gets to know the city banker well, the customer may establish a direct relationship with the city correspondent bank—this is especially true if the city correspondent is a regional bank instead of a large metropolitan bank. The country bank believes the city banker has the right to a tour of the customer's plant and an introduction to the management, but it does not like to see one visiting the customer *alone* on a regular basis—or even telephoning on a regular basis—until the customer moves a part or all of its account to the city bank. The city bank should respect the country bank's ability to appraise and monitor management.

A look at the country bank's charge-off record of loan losses over several years may provide some idea of its ability to appraise management. The correspondent bank may wish to compare the country bank's charge-off record with that of its own bank. There must be mutual respect and understanding if loan participations are to work satisfactorily.

Dual Relationships in the Same Town

The experience of one country bank may be instructive. After five years of solicitation a bank secured an important customer who required an overline participation. Everything about the credit was good, so the bank was sure it would encounter no problem in placing the overline.

The banker went to the city in which its correspondent was located. The discussion was going well until the city bank asked what bank was losing the account. Upon hearing the name, they promptly said they had a problem. They had recently obtained a correspondent deposit account from that bank, the country bank's major competitor, and it was their policy not to participate in loans that would help one correspondent take business from another in the same city. The country bank therefore made other arrangements. However, *not all city correspondents follow this policy.*

Country banks generally believe the city banker should decide which bank it wishes to do business with in each community. There is danger in trying to serve two masters, particularly in buying loan participations from competitor banks.

Need for Prompt Action

Some city bankers have officers who are essentially information gatherers and cannot make commitments until they take the information back to their credit department and their superiors.

One country bank needed to sell a participation in a floor plan loan for an auto dealer. Most bankers are familiar with the letters that have to be given the automobile manufacturer, agreeing to pay drafts for shipments. These commitments are usually good for a certain number of days and can result in a substantial exposure if the factory continues to ship and the dealer does not sell. This bank had a situation like that, in which the floor plan was near its legal limit and the factory was shipping. In short, it had an excess of cars— a great many cars floor-planned.

The country bank asked its correspondent bank for an overline, and was told their representative would be in the country bank the following morning. He was there, and the country banker was quite relieved. However, at the end of the day the representative said that he would take the information back to his superior and the credit department. The country bank would then hear from them. That was not satisfactory, because the next day's drafts would put the country bank over its legal lending limit. It was suggested that the representative call his superior on the telephone and explain the situation. He did. The city bank bought a participation, and the country bank's problem was solved.

There are times when decisions must be made in the field, and it is important to have someone there who can make decisions if the situation warrants. Whether the answer is yes or no, the country banker deserves a prompt reply.

If a bank is well established as a correspondent, has kept an account profitable for the city bank, has a good loan charge-off record, and has sold participations before, there is every reason to expect an attentive ear, a sympathetic approach, and prompt service.

Loan Participations and Deposit Accounts

A country bank agreed to open a major account relationship with a large city bank, as it felt the city bank could help in check collections. Before opening the account, it was suggested that the city bank might wish to look at some of the bank's overline participations. If they were to receive a major account, the country bank would wish them to handle some of their credit overlines.

The city bank reviewed the overlines and said, frankly, that they could take everything but the auto floor plans and leasing company loans. It was their policy not to make such loans. The country banker understood the city bank could not buy these kinds of participations if they did not have them in their own portfolio. The deposit account was therefore not opened. The city banker should be aware that buying all types of loan participations ordinarily goes along with holding country bank deposit accounts.

Participations and Tight Money

A period of tight money—a situation that exists from time to time—is when many country banks need help with participations.

Contrary to previous comments in this discussion, the country bank may wish to retain less than its legal limit in an effort to improve its liquidity position. This is a satisfactory arrangement if the correspondent is told why the country bank is retaining less than its legal limit.

If a country bank gets a turndown on the basis of a tight money period, it may be a bit of a shock if the city bank has used the country bank's deposits for a number of years in the past. Some city banks will offer to buy an overline if the country bank will buy from them a like amount of their loans. This is known as a downstream loan participation. Many country banks do not believe they should have to carry deposit balances for a number of years to work out this kind of relationship with a city bank. If the city bank expects the country bank to carry balances at all times and to maintain a profitable account, it should be in a position to take care of the country bank during a tight money situation that may be of short duration.

In some instances, however, the country bank may wish to buy downstream loan participations to expand its loan portfolio if local demand is not sufficient. Many city banks provide this service to their country correspondents. If a country bank purchases a downstream loan participation, it is on a no-recourse basis and requires the same credit analysis as if the bank made the loan itself. The city bank does not expect to buy the loan back in the event of default.

Soliciting Business in Correspondent's Territory

Sometimes a city correspondent is so anxious to service the country bank's customer that it will call on the customer even before it is offered the loan participation. The country bank hopes that the city bank will not seek to solicit its customers. It feels that the city bank is entitled either to the country bank's balances or to those of the customer on a direct basis—but not both. The country bank does not wish to maintain deposit balances with its competitors. It believes the city correspondent must respect the country bank's relationship with its borrower. However, the country bank's balances should usually be more than nominal or token accounts.

Interest Rates

When buying a participation, some city correspondents may encourage the country bank to increase the interest rate to yield a better return. Prime customers to the country bank may not be prime rate customers to city banks. If the country bank account relationship is worth anything at all, it should take care of any differential in rates charged by the country bank versus that desired by the city bank.

Delay in Crediting Accounts

Generally, the country bank arranges to have copies of all the necessary loan participation documents mailed to the city bank so they arrive on the day on which the loan is to be closed. Sometimes, when a participation is sold, the city bank simply telephones to say the documents have arrived, a participation certificate is being mailed, and the country bank's account is being credited.

However, occasionally, the telephone call comes into the country bank too late to transfer the money out of its account at the correspondent bank. So the country bank gets no benefit from the participation credited to its account until the following day, even though the city correspondent is earning interest on the funds.

Last In, First Out Participations

Generally speaking, there is nothing wrong with a last in, first out participation. However, there can be some problems if there is deterioration in the loan while the participation is outstanding. Here is an experience related by a country banker. This bank had made a no-liability feeder-cattle loan to a farm corporation—in which case the bank looks only to the security for repayment of the loan. While the loan was outstanding, the price of feeder cattle dropped substantially. When the cattle were ready to be sold, their value was not sufficient to cover the principal and interest of the loan, even though the farmer had paid for some of the feed.

Since the cattle were sold in different lots at different times, the first monies went to pay the city correspondent bank in full. The country banker said the city bank got paid in full from the first lots of cattle sold—on a last-in basis. After all the cattle were finally sold and the balance of the proceeds had been applied to the country bank's loan, there was still a loan balance due, which the bank examiner made the country bank charge off as a loss. The country banker's question was, "Why should we have had a loss and the city bank not have had one?" This is an example of poor communication between the two banks. The country banker should have explained the entire situation in detail to the city banker. If the possibility of a loss was recognized before the collateral was sold, the city correspondent might well have offered to share pro rata in the loss.

Even if the loss would not have been recognized before the cattle were sold, it would still have been better to talk with the city banker. City bankers understand this type of problem and would not intentionally avoid their pro rata share of a loss at the expense of a country bank. They understand that loan participations are purchased on a no-recourse basis, and the selling bank is not required to bail them out in the event of loan deterioration.

Many of these types of problems can be avoided through a proper understanding before the participation is sold. All participants should understand the degree of risk involved and should be sure it is acceptable to them. Many times it is advisable to reduce to writing the responsibilities of both banks as to expenses, losses, policing of collateral, and all items which make it possible to avoid misunderstandings that might occur at a future date. They should be incorporated into the participation certificate. It is always a good idea to have an attorney review the loan participation certificate.

A loan participation certificate can be an important part of the transaction —not if the loan is paid as agreed, but especially if problems are encountered during collection of the loan. Many city correspondents will accept the certificate if it contains the standard provisions, and the bank should use its own counsel-approved certificate whenever possible.

These are some of the major problems in the loan participation area. However, it is recognized that city correspondent banks can be extremely useful and provide valuable services. It should not be expected that the services will be free. Generally speaking, the correspondent banker's service will bear a direct relationship to the collected balances the country bank maintains.

Loan participations are helpful both to the city bank and the country bank and its customers.

22

Asset-Based Financing

Accounts receivable, inventory, and equipment financing have long been the tools of the commercial finance industry in providing working capital or acquisition financing to American business. However, it was not until the 1970s that the banking industry developed significant interest in this financing technique. One reason for this was the inability of the small to medium-size firm to generate adequate inflation-adjusted profits to fund its growth. In the years 1965–1974, real after-tax profits dropped 58 percent and, during the same period, the effective tax rate paid on inflationary profits increased in real terms from 44 to 75 percent. This trend continued throughout the 1970s and appears likely to continue at least through the early eighties.

The result of this "profits depression" was an increase in the need for external financing. Thus, the ratio of debt to equity rose and it became increasingly difficult for banks to lend in the "traditional" manner. Faced with the choice of making riskier unsecured loans, prudent lenders looked for collateral to back those loans.

For the purpose of this discussion, all loans secured by accounts receivable, inventory, or equipment are not asset-based loans. There are many loans that are basically cash flow or balance sheet loans, with collateral taken as an abundance of caution. Asset-based loans should be classified as those loans where, given the inability of the borrower to achieve projected operating results, repayment will have to be predicated on the value of the collateral securing that loan. The discussion that follows shows some of the considerations required of a lender who considers asset-based financing.

The most important question an asset-based lender must ask himself is, "What is my exposure in this loan if the company fails?" The question does not imply that an asset-based lender gets involved in numerous insolvency proceedings, but it does put the nature of an asset-based loan in the proper perspective. The asset-based lender must anticipate problems inherent in a liquidation before the fact so that, as far as it is possible, the exposure can be quantified. A determination that the liquidating value of the collateral will support the loans the company requires is an absolute essential, irrespective of the company's prospects and projections as to future viability. Thus, while many banks have secured loan departments, many of them approach credit differently than the true asset-based lender. Because the asset-based lender relies primarily on the liquidating value of collateral, the techniques involved in handling this collateral may be significantly different than many banks' accounts receivable lending operations.

There are three distinct aspects of asset-based lending—legal structuring, credit structuring, and credit administration.

Legal Structuring

There are two indispensable sources of guidance in determining the legal ramifications and complexities of structuring an asset-based loan. They are the Uniform Commercial Code and the Federal Bankruptcy Law. The importance of working with legal counsel intimately familiar with the workings of the Code and the Bankruptcy Law cannot be overemphasized. Proper legal guidance is crucial in structuring loans involving parent-subsidiary relationships, or the financing of stock or asset acquisitions.

Credit Structuring

Credit structuring refers to the collateral taken as security and the appropriate rates of advance against the collateral. In determining the appropriate rate of advance against accounts receivable, the quality, as well as the quantity, of the accounts receivable must be determined. Since the liquidating value of the collateral is of primary importance, anything that affects this value must be considered before the loan is made.

ACCOUNTS RECEIVABLE

Accounts Receivable Aging. The percentage of accounts receivable more than 30, 60, and 90 days from invoice date tells something of the paying habits of the account debtors and the attention the borrower devotes to collections. Those amounts of accounts receivable over 90 days from invoice date are normally excluded from the borrowing base because it may indicate an inability of the account debtors to pay their obligations or that the accounts receivable are in dispute.

Invoice Date or Due Date Aging. Is the aging from invoice date or due date? If from due date, is the borrower selling on dating terms, that is, are account debtors permitted to pay in three, six, or nine months or longer from invoice date? Datings are quite common in seasonal businesses such as agriculture or the ski trade. It is not unusual for an asset-based lender to accept accounts receivable subject to dating terms. However, datings in excess of nine to twelve months are usually made ineligible, and those due in less than that time are made ineligible once they are 30 days past due date.

When financing datings the lender must be aware of redating practices. Redating occurs when the borrower rolls over the dating at due date for another extended dating term. It may be argued that datings are, in essence, guaranteed sales. If the dating period comes and goes and the merchandise has not been sold by the borrower's customer, the lender may receive the inventory in lieu of payment of the account when the lender attempts to collect.

Concentrations. Concentrations in account debtors are an important factor, that is, we need to know which, if any, of the borrower's accounts make up large percentages of the total accounts receivable.

There are three issues involved in concentrations. The first is the creditworthiness of an account debtor that makes up more than 5 to 10 percent of the total accounts receivable. If a concentration customer were unable to pay it would seriously jeopardize the collateral base. The second problem is that, not withstanding creditworthiness of the account debtor, if there are disputes due to the quality of the goods sold, large offsets or returns could be charged against the accounts receivable. The third concern relates less to impairment of collateral than it does to jeopardizing the viability of the borrower. What happens to the borrower if it loses a major customer? Obviously, this could have a negative impact on the borrower.

Conversely, there is a problem with too many account debtors. That problem is the enormous collection expense incurred in liquidating thousands of small accounts.

Consignment or Guaranteed Sales. Consignments and guaranteed sales make up another area of concern. Consignments are not truly sales until the consignee has consummated the resale of the product. Therefore, consignment invoices are not bona fide accounts receivable and should not be considered part of those accounts receivable that make up the eligible collateral. The same is true of guaranteed sales. In this case the account debtor may return the merchandise if it does not sell.

Contra Accounts. Contra accounts should be discovered by comparing an aging of accounts receivable to an aging of accounts payable. Contras occur from the buying and selling of merchandise to and from the same party. If the lender attempted to collect the outstanding accounts receivable, the account debtor would offset against the accounts owed him. Accounts receivable with offsets against them should not be accepted as eligible collateral, but if they are, then only to the extent that the accounts receivable exceed the accounts payable. Obviously, this balance could fluctuate and create exposure.

Late Delivery. Purchase orders must be reviewed to determine that shipments are not being sent out after the expected delivery date; for example, merchandise that is to be delivered for the Christmas selling season is of little use in January and is subject to return.

Affiliates and Employees. Sales made to affiliates should be excluded from the collateral base. There is too much temptation for creation of accounts receivable to generate additional loan availability if an affiliate's accounts receivable were accepted as eligible collateral. Similarly, employee accounts receivable can easily be created and, even if bona fide, can be offset because of wages due the employee.

Billings in Excess of Orders. Purchase orders must be analyzed to determine that more merchandise is not being shipped out than has been ordered. It is highly likely that this merchandise will be returned, creating offsets to the accounts receivable.

Warranty. The asset-based lender could find it difficult to collect accounts receivable that are subject to warranty in the event the borrower were to go out of business. The borrower's customers are likely to refuse or withhold payment in anticipation of warranty problems that can no longer be honored by the borrower. For example, a borrower selling a sophisticated electronics device of its own design and manufacturer offers a one-year warranty for parts, labor, and service. The borrower goes out of business and the lender attempts to collect the accounts receivable. It is highly probable that the account debtors would point to the warranty and ask for it to be honored. Since the lender is in no position to honor the warranty, they will not pay, or will reserve for anticipated problems. The asset-based lender must carefully evaluate the risk involved in financing accounts receivable subject to warranty provisions.

Progress Billings. This problem is very prevalent with construction or contractor accounts receivable. These accounts receivable arise from the partial completion and invoicing of work done pursuant to a contract for a total project. The difficulty is that the collectibility of the progress billing is subject to future performance by the borrower. Should the borrower not fulfill his contract, there could be damages arising to his customer for nonperformance and breach of contract. This could create significant offsets to the accounts receivable due to damages suffered and seriously dilute the value of accounts receivable financed. Progress billings should be excluded from the eligible collateral base.

Partial Shipments. Like progress billings, partial shipments provide only a percentage of what the customer has ordered. While there may not be a written agreement between the borrower and his customer, damages could arise from not receiving all the goods relied on by the customer. Such claims may be offset against existing accounts receivable.

Bill and Hold. A bill and hold accounts receivable is created when merchandise is sold but not shipped to the customer. Until the merchandise is shipped and bona fide accounts receivable created, bill and hold accounts receivable should not be accepted as eligible collateral.

Prebilling. Prebilling differs from bill and hold in that the merchandise is not even ready to be shipped. It is invoicing for merchandise expected to be shipped in the near future. It should be excluded from the eligible collateral.

Right of Stoppage in Transit. Occasionally the borrower has merchandise shipped directly from his supplier to the borrower's customer (known as a drop shipment). Terms of this sale may be such that unless the supplier is paid in a very short period of time the supplier has the right to recall the merchandise before it arrives at its final destination. In this situation there is no transfer of title of the merchandise to the borrower unless he pays within the agreed time. Should the borrower invoice and the lender advance against this accounts receivable and subsequently have the merchandise recalled, no payment will be coming from the borrower's customer.

Overbilling and Rebates. The selling practice of the borrower must be reviewed to determine if the borrower overbills, knowing full well there will be subsequent returns, or offers selling terms that provide for quantity, pricing, or advertising rebates. To the extent these practices dilute the quality of the accounts receivable, they must be reserved for.

Export. The primary problems with foreign accounts receivable are in determining creditworthiness of the customer and ultimately the difficulty in collecting an accounts receivable in a foreign country.

Retail. Retail accounts receivable are normally excluded from the eligible accounts receivable due to their quality and small size (collection expense).

Returns and Allowances. A thorough review of all returns and allowances is required. This analysis should discover all past patterns of credits to the accounts receivable. Among those to be watched for are price and volume discounts, advertising allowances, and product quality problems.

Ten Percent Rule. One other eligibility test used by some asset-based lenders is called the "ten percent rule." The rule is designed as an incentive to the client to maintain or help induce an intensification of his collection activities. The rule requires that whenever one of the client's account debtors allows his indebtedness to age to a point where 10 percent or more of the accounts receivable from that customer is more than 90 days old, *all* of the indebtedness from that account is declared ineligible. Therefore, if an account debtor of the borrower owes $10,000 and $1,000 or more age over 90 days from invoice date, the entire $10,000 becomes ineligible.

As can be seen, a thorough review must be made to determine the quality of the accounts receivable. To take comfort in lending substantial amounts of money against accounts receivable, the asset-based lender must be absolutely sure that the accounts receivable are collectible. Each accounts receivable must be examined—in detail—especially in regard to the areas of concern outlined above. This is exactly what experienced asset-based lenders do. The lender must send a specially trained examiner to review and analyze all potential borrower's accounts receivable. With the completion by the examiner of the analysis of accounts receivable and the determination of eligible collateral, a decision can be made as to the appropriate advance rate. Assuming a good clean accounts receivable base with a minimal amount of returns and allowances, an 80 percent advance against eligible accounts receivable is typical. The 20 percent reserve is needed to help provide the lender with adequate protection against accounts receivable deterioration and costs of liquidation. However, this does not imply that all receivables will collect out for 80 cents on the dollar. The value of the accounts receivable is very much determined by the viability of the business. While in business the accounts receivable are worth close to their face value, in liquidation they may bring less than 50 cents on the dollar.

It is one of the skills of the true asset-based lender to be able to gauge asset values as they relate to business viability. The asset-based lender must reduce his advance rates, that is, "work down" his loan in the event of borrower deterioration, so that if the accounts receivable must be collected under distressed circumstances the lender will not take a loss.

INVENTORY

Just as a thorough analysis of the accounts receivable is necessary to determine the value of that collateral, a similar analysis must be done of inventory.

Again, the question that must be asked is, "If the lender comes into possession of the inventory, what will be the forced sales value?" Therefore, guesses as to this value will not do.

First, the inventory must be reviewed in its overall components. Those are raw material, work in process, and finished goods. In viewing these components of inventory, common sense will dictate a first approximation as to the inventories salability. It is fair to say that the raw and finished goods components will usually have more value than work in process. In fact, except for scrap values, work-in-process inventory is usually valueless and, therefore, deemed ineligible collateral.

The more the raw material and finished goods approach commodity items, for example, goods with a wide degree of standardization and commercial usage, the greater the potential value. Items such as primary coil steel of standard gauge and width could have relatively high liquidation value, possibly approaching cost. Obviously then, as the marketability of products decreases, so does the advance rate. There will be many inventories that will have little or no value.

When reviewing the components of inventory and attempting to determine the eligible inventory and the appropriate advance rate, four important variables must be considered. They are quantity, mix, age, and technological or fashion obsolescence.

One method of determining the quantity of inventory is to rely on periodic reports by the client. Unfortunately, if there is a problem, reporting lags, inventory goes out without notice, and the lender is left with less inventory than counted on. One technique used to prevent this is to revolve the inventory loan, that is, to reduce the inventory loan daily by applying a portion of the advance that is being made against the newly created accounts receivable reflecting the sale of the goods coming out of the inventory collateral pool. For example, if the advance rate against inventory were 50 percent and the cost of goods sold was 80 percent of selling price, then when inventory is converted to accounts receivable, 40 percent of the gross value of accounts receivable, or one-half of the advance that would otherwise be made thereon, should be applied in reduction of the inventory loan rather than advanced directly to the client.

Concurrently, the inventory loan is only increased when the lender is assured of the new value of inventory delivered to the borrower's premises or has evidence of completion of newly manufactured goods being added to the inventory pool.

Particular attention must be paid to extremely fast-turning inventories such as food wholesale or meat-packers. In these cases institution of bonded field warehouse control may be necessary.

Mix refers to the movement of inventories from raw material to work in process and then to finished goods. The problem for the lender is in controlling this mix. Take, for example, the metal fabricator who starts with 48-inch-wide coils, slits them into 4-inch coils, and then stamps them into specific components. As the inventory progresses from raw to work in process to finished goods, it loses its liquidating value even though it gains in book value.

Age of inventory can only be controlled by physical inspections. An analyst must review each major inventory item to determine its historical usage and the number of days' or months' inventory of that item in stock. Typically, inventory that does not turn within one year should be excluded from the eligible inventory base.

The potential for fashion or technological obsolescence must be considered by the lender. High-fashion items that are in vogue this year may be worthless next year. Electronic products such as calculators, watches, and games are subject to significant price reductions or even obsolescence by technical innovation. The lender must never forget that ultimate repayment of his loan is predicated on the value of the collateral. Product subject to fashion or technological obsolescence can experience significant reductions in collateral value.

Quantity, mix, age, and technological or fashion obsolescence are all part of determining value. However, the ability accurately to determine value is dependent on the skills of an experienced inventory analyst. The asset-based lender must have inventory auditors who can inspect both the physical condition of the inventory and the inventory controls. These auditors must be able to review thoroughly the quantity, mix, age, and obsolescence factors; and determine eligible and ineligible inventory and the appropriate advance rate.

MACHINERY AND EQUIPMENT

Just as the lender attempts to determine the liquidating value of accounts receivable and inventory, he must also determine the liquidating value of machinery and equipment.

Book, fair market, or replacement value usually have little, if any relationship to liquidation or forced sale value. Therefore, an appraisal must be obtained that tells the lender what the equipment is worth "under the hammer," that is, at a public auction under forced sale conditions.

Most lenders use appraisers who conduct public auctions because of their intimate and inside knowledge of distress sale equipment values. In deciding upon whom to use, the inexperienced lender should inquire of other experienced lenders as to their choice of appraisers. A highly competent and qualified appraiser is indispensable.

Once the appraisal is complete, a reserve must be set up against this value to cover the appraiser's commission and expenses.

Consideration must be given to the amount of time the equipment may sit idle in the event of bankruptcy. During this time interest will accrue and the equipment can depreciate. In assessing the liquidating value, the lender must be aware of economic fluctuations. The market can move radically and drop 20 percent or more within a year. Also, the lender could incur expenses in preserving and protecting the equipment while awaiting auction. Once the liquidation value is determined, the lender must set up an amortization program consistent with both cash flow and depreciation.

Typically, asset-based lenders will lend up to 80 percent of forced sale value with amortization terms not to exceed five years.

Credit Administration

Successful asset-based lending requires two abilities: the first, discussed above, is being able to determine accurately the liquidating value of collateral; the second is credit administration or being able to control the daily changes in the collateral and keeping the loan in ratio.

Credit administration is probably the area that most distinguishes the true asset-based lender. Credit administration is the vehicle by which asset-based lenders mitigate the so-called high risk of the loans they make. The incremental rate charged by asset-based lenders is not a risk premium. It is the cost of administration required properly to monitor the collateral and, therefore, to prevent losses from occurring.

Daily control means the lender must examine the collateral every day: he must know every day what new collateral was created, and what collateral is ineligible for whatever reason. It is the control that is exercised over the accounts receivable and inventory—the daily control—that spells the major differences in approach by the true asset-based lender.

The most important aspect of control is the daily monitoring. The reason for this is the revolving nature of the loan; if on the day of payout of the loan there is $1 million of eligible accounts receivable and an 80 percent advance rate is appropriate, $800,000 would be advanced; but what happens on the next day? For one thing, some of the accounts receivable on which loans were made will be collected. The checks for those accounts receivable will arrive in the mail. In addition, new accounts receivable will be generated as new sales are made.

It can be seen that the accounts receivable as well as the inventory that created those accounts receivable change every day. The lender must account for those changes daily. He must use the collections to repay the loan and make new advances on the newly created accounts receivable. In effect, there will be a new and different loan outstanding at the close of business tomorrow than there is at the inception of the loan today.

The lender must be sure that if the loan is structured so that there is an 80 percent advance against eligible accounts receivable and a 35 percent advance against eligible inventory, the loan is in the prescribed ratio each day after accounting for the daily fluctuations in the collateral base.

It is fair to say that if the lender knows the liquidating value of collateral and keeps the loan in ratio, he will (except for fraud) rarely lose money. The fact is that well run asset-based lending companies lose less than one-half of one percent of funds employed.

Verification of accounts receivable is one very important aspect of credit administration. While the borrower states what its accounts receivable are, only the borrower's customers can truly confirm the amounts owed.

Verification can provide extremely useful insights into the nature of the accounts receivable. The lender can through verification find out the following:

1. Misunderstanding of selling terms
2. Dissatisfaction with product performance
3. Misrepresentations
4. Contra accounts
5. Unissued credit memos
6. Special terms, consignments, bill and hold, progress billings
7. Fictitious invoicing
8. Billing errors

Only through verification can the lender be reasonably sure that the accounts are as represented and under control.

Verification is typically done by telephone prior to payout of the loan and must continue throughout the term of the loan. A statistically significant sample of customers will be taken on a monthly basis and these customers will be called and their balances verified to the last dollar. All discrepancies must be reconciled so that there is a 100 percent resolution of the outstanding balance. Any accounts receivable that cannot be properly verified must be treated as ineligible.

While this extensive verification is costly and time-consuming, it is critical in controlling the accounts receivable. It not only keeps borrowers diligent in their reporting but also provides them with useful information the lender may have uncovered when in contact with the borrower's customers.

As discussed earlier, day-to-day processing is required owing to the revolving nature of the collateral. Since the lender is relying on ultimate liquidation values, he must know what the status of the collateral and loan is everyday.

The lender must provide same-day processing service to the borrower, that is, when the borrower sends in copies of invoices and inventory additions, they must be processed the same day. A competent processor must analyze each and every item, not only rechecking tapes and totals, but scrutinizing every individual invoice for evidence of ineligibility from delinquency, concentrations, or consignments. In addition, the processor must check the collections on accounts receivable the same day.

Each day the new loan availability must be computed. For example, let us assume that at the beginning of a new day there was $1 million of eligible accounts receivable and the lender was advancing 80 percent and the loan was $800,000. The daily work comes in and there is $100,000 of new accounts receivable and $50,000 of collections. Assuming there is $10,000 of ineligible accounts receivable included in the $100,000 of new accounts receivable and no inventory loan, what would be the new loan availability? The computation would be as follows:

Eligible collateral at beginning of day	$1,000,000
Less invoices paid	(50,000)
	950,000
Plus eligible collateral assigned today	90,000
Eligible collateral	1,040,000
Maximum loan available at 80%	832,000
Actual loan beginning of day	800,000
Less collections	(50,000)
Current loan balance	750,000
Additional loan available	82,000
(Maximum loan available minus Current loan balance)	

This type of calculation must be done every day by the processing people. These people must be highly competent and know how to look for dollars rather than just keeping track of pieces of paper.

A good processor will review large invoices to determine whether or not they exceed credit limits set on that account debtor. Other invoices may require immediate verification. The processor should also review shipping evidence that accompanies the accounts receivable. This review can uncover prebilling and bill and hold situations.

The borrower must send in an aged trial balance every month. This is reconciled with the previous month's trial balance to help determine the accuracy of the aging. Each month the new ineligibles are determined from the aging. Also, in the monthly reconciliation review the borrower's control is reconciled to the lender's. Large discrepancies can give clues to problems such as diversion of cash or unreported credit memos.

Quarterly or as needed, the lender must examine the borrower's books and records to determine the accuracy of the aging. The borrower's balance is checked against the general ledger, and additional spot checks are made to reconcile the lender's collateral figures with the client's.

The lender's field examination must also pick up any adverse trends in accounts payable, operations cash flow, and delinquent taxes as well to determine the overall quality of recordkeeping and the accuracy of financial information being supplied to the lender.

Of utmost importance is the technique used to handle the borrower's collections on accounts receivable. The lender must never allow the borrower to deposit collections into the borrower's operating account. The lender must insist on getting these collections either through a lock box or directly from the borrower. The lender must use these proceeds to reduce his loan. If you give up the proceeds of collections, you give up control. Remember, these collections must be viewed as the primary source of loan repayment.

As mentioned in the opening paragraphs, banks have traditionally been unsecured lenders, but in recent years many have entered the sphere of asset-based lending. A bank is faced with the choice of setting up its own asset-based lending operation, passing up the business entirely, or serving its customers' needs by involving a skilled asset-based lender as managing partner of the loan. If the first option is selected, a bank, in order to minimize its risk of loss, should staff a separate department to perform all the credit, administrative, verification, and examination functions that are required of the true asset-based lender. This is a complex organizational task because the work is highly specialized and competent people with asset-based lending experience are required. A more routine or less intensive approach to collateral administration, on the other hand, will quite often lead to significant bad debt exposure.

The second alternative—passing up the business—is not acceptable to most marketing-oriented banks since it would place them in a vulnerable position in respect to competition. The most practical option, then, for some money center banks, most regional banks, and virtually all local banks is to obtain professional management through "participations." The arrangement permits the bank to maintain an aggressive marketing posture, but at the same time minimizes their risk of incurring bad debts.

Through a participation arrangement, the professional asset-based lender structures and administers the loans while the bank participates in the financing package. The bank has the benefit of an account relationship, a satisfactory yield, and a minimal operating expense in relation to its investment. In addition, the bank can take the commercial finance company out of the loan whenever the financial condition of the company justifies traditional bank credit. The borrower is the beneficiary of a blended rate reflecting the relative percentage of the bank's and the asset-based lender's investments.

23

The Legal Aspects of Bank Loans

___

In today's rapidly changing business environment, the laws and regulations which apply to credit extended by banks are becoming more complicated. However, certain fundamental legal principles continue to apply no matter how complex or innovative is the lending transaction. To avoid needless litigation and to insure that each loan is a legally enforceable claim against the borrower, a banker should understand these basic principles. In addition to understanding the basic legal principles, the loan officer should be familiar with various state and Federal regulations governing the manner of extending as well as the method of granting credit.

Fundamental Principles

The following basic legal principles are applicable to all transactions to insure that the bank has an enforceable claim against the borrower.

The extension of credit should be evidenced by a writing setting forth the terms and conditions of the loan. Nothing prohibits a bank from lending money on the strength of the borrower's oral promise to repay. If the borrower elects not to repay in accordance with the bank's understanding of the terms of the oral loan, the bank is subject to all defenses the borrower asserts. The result would depend upon who the trier of fact believes. Even though the bank requires the borrower to sign a note or other written agreement, the borrower is bound by the terms of the writing. Unless the borrower is able to show fraud at the time of the execution of the writing or an ambiguity in the writing, the borrower cannot introduce oral testimony in an attempt to establish different terms. The law presumes that the borrower knows the contents of the writing.

Prior to having the loan document signed, the loan officer must determine who is the prospective borrower and that person's legal authority to borrow the money.

INDIVIDUALS

An individual must be of legal age and competent to contract. A person not of legal age may be emancipated under the laws of the state where the bank is located, and therefore has the capacity to contract. A bank should review with its counsel the applicable state law as to when a minor is emancipated, especially if it purchases installment paper from sellers of various consumer goods, such as automobiles, appliances, and furniture.

If an individual authorizes an agent or attorney-in-fact to execute the note or agreement, the bank should examine the underlying agreement under which the agent seeks to act to determine the extent of the agent's authority and whether it is in full force and effect. As banks develop various types of loan agreements which permit an individual to initiate a loan by writing a check or using an electronic device, the bank should provide that any party who may draw a check on or initiate an electronic transfer from such an account is authorized to act even though that individual does not sign the agreement. The agency created thereby may be terminated only after notice has been given to the bank.

When two or more individuals sign the writing, the document should state whether they are jointly and severally liable. If the document is a negotiable instrument, the Uniform Commercial Code, which has been adopted in all fifty states, provides in Sec. 3-118(c) that two or more persons who sign are jointly and severally liable. The majority of notes in use today are negotiable instruments, but the various other credit agreements are not negotiable instruments.

CORPORATIONS

Corporations have the power to borrow money for the purpose of carrying on their business. Though this power is implied since a corporation may act only through its authorized representative, a bank should require a general resolution of the corporation's board of directors giving certain parties, normally officers, power up to whatever limit the board decides. The resolution should set forth whether this is continuing or limited authority.

Though a general resolution is satisfactory for the short-term borrowings of a corporation, in the case of term loans, loans secured by security interests in the corporation's personal property, or mortgages on various pieces of real estate, a specific resolution of the corporation's board of directors should be obtained prior to making the loan authorizing the specific transaction. Further, since various corporation laws restrict the mortgaging or pledging of substantially all of the corporation's assets without prior approval of the shareholders of the corporation, a bank should discuss with counsel such a transaction to determine if shareholder consent is required. A common method of dealing with this situation is to obtain an opinion from the borrower's attorney that acts of the corporation are properly authorized and not in conflict with the corporation's certificate of authority, by-laws, or applicable state laws. These precautions should protect the bank from being subordinated to claims of other creditors under the terms of some indenture or preferred stock provision.

The execution of the writing evidencing the loan should show on its face that the corporation is the borrower. The corporate name should appear and then the name of the appropriate officer with the title. For example:

Rotbed Corp.
By:_____
Its President

If the writing is a negotiable instrument, Sec. 3-403(2) of the UCC states the general rule that if the agency does not appear on the instrument, the party signing is personally liable. To enforce payment against a corporation, the note or other writing should show on its face that the borrower is a corporation.

OTHER BORROWERS

In addition to individuals and corporations, the borrower may be a partnership, joint venture, lodge, church, union, governmental body, or not-for-profit corporation. No matter what type of entity the borrower is, the bank must ascertain the authority of that entity to borrow and who may exercise that authority. Usually this requires a review of the agreement, charter, or by-laws establishing and governing the operation of the entity. However, it may be necessary to review the law under which the entity is established to determine whether the entity may borrow. Having satisfied that the entity may borrow, the bank should require a resolution of the governing body authorizing certain parties to borrow money. The form of this resolution will vary depending upon the nature of the borrower. A loan made without first obtaining the appropriate authority may not be enforceable against the entity.

Basic Legal Requirements of Loan Documents

The basic legal requirements of every loan document are the amount loaned, the time and place of repayment, the interest to be paid, and the events of default. The demands for new and innovative types of loan documents other than the traditional promissory note require the loan officers to have a firm understanding of these. By analyzing various kinds of loan documents, a loan officer may better observe these in practice. Consider first a single-payment unsecured note similar to the one shown in Figure 1.

Figure 1

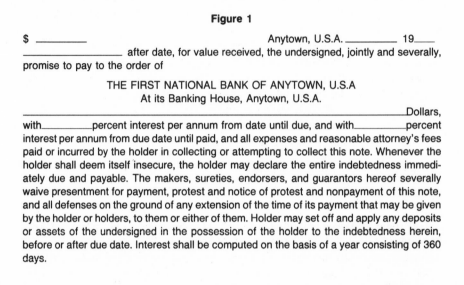

Since many of these notes are payable six months or more from date, a clause allowing the bank to accelerate the due date of the loan if it deems itself insecure is included. Section 1-208 of the UCC specifically authorizes such a clause provided that the action of accelerating the due date is taken in good faith. Such a clause may be included in any loan document whether or not it is a negotiable document. Without such a clause, the bank is unable to seek enforcement of the note prior to maturity, even though the financial situation of the borrower has dramatically changed.

If the bank uses 360 days instead of 365 days for a year in computing interest, it should so state on the face of the note, as shown in Figure 1. Otherwise the majority of courts have held that "per annum" means 365 days, notwithstanding the long-standing custom and practice in the banking industry of using 360 days for a year when computing interest.

Another widely used note form provides for payment in regular installments and is secured by personal property similar to the one shown in Figure 2.

The interest calculation on this note is different in that the total interest charged for the loan is what would have been charged if the loan was not prepaid in regular installments.

Figure 2

PROMISSORY NOTE

$ _____   Anytown, U.S.A. _____ , 19____

For value received, the undersigned promise to pay
to the order of
THE FIRST NATIONAL BANK OF ANYTOWN
At Its Banking House in Anytown, U.S.A.

the sum of_____Dollars in monthly installaments of $_____on
the_____day of_____, 19____ and $_____on the_____day of
each_____thereafter with final balance of $_____on
the_____day of_____, 19____, with interest at a rate of_____%
per annum upon all unpaid installments after the due date thereof.

If any payment of this note is not paid when due, or if the holder deems itself insecure, the holder may declare the entire amount remaining unpaid immediately due and payable.

The undersigned agree to pay a charge not to exceed $5.00 or 5% of any installment set forth in (b) more than ten days in arrears to cover extra expense caused by such default. The undersigned further agree to pay reasonable attorney's fees and costs incurred by the holder herein enforcing collection if the indebtedness is not paid when due.

Holder may set off and apply any deposits of the undersigned and assets of the undersigned in the possession of the holder to the indebtedness herein before as well as after maturity.

The makers, sureties, endorsers, and guarantors hereof severally waive presentment for payment, protest and notice of protest and nonpayment of this note, and all defenses on the ground of any extension of the time of its payment that may be given by the holder or holders, to them or either of them.

This note is secured by a security interest in the following described collateral: a new car.

A second variation from the single-payment note is that the amount of the note includes both principal and interest not principal alone. The default provision in this note is broadened to include the failure of the borrower to make any installment payment when due.

Finally, since this is a collateral note, the bank has a security interest in the personal property described in the note. The language of this note is legally sufficient for the borrower to grant a security interest to the bank; however, a prudent lender would require the borrower to sign a separate security agreement or incorporate additional language in the note which would cover various issues such as after-acquired property, future advances, care of the collateral, and remedies on default.

With the adoption of the UCC in all 50 states, the legal requirements for a bank to take collateral as security for the repayment of a loan have been substantially simplified and standardized. The UCC applies to any consensual transaction regardless of form where the collateral is personal property or fixtures and those transactions which involve the sale of accounts or chattel paper. This broad spectrum of collateral is divided into seven categories: two general categories, tangible personal property or goods and intangible personal property—general intangibles; and five specific categories, money, instruments, documents, chattel paper, and accounts. The UCC does not apply to an interest in or a lien on real estate.

For a bank to have an enforceable security interest, it must have either physical possession of the collateral or, if the collateral is in the possession of the debtor, a written security agreement signed by the borrower granting a security interest in certain described collateral. The note shown in Figure 2 satisfies this minimal requirement.

The bank's reason for taking a security interest in the collateral is to have something more than the borrower's promise as a source of payment for the loan if the borrower defaults. At the time of default, a borrower usually has a number of creditors seeking satisfaction out of the same collateral. The UCC establishes a procedure which, if the bank follows it, provides that the bank has the first right to the collateral that is subject to the security interest. This procedure is to "perfect" a security interest. The bank, except for certain categories of collateral, may perfect either by retaining physical possession of the collateral or filing with the appropriate governmental officer a notice of its security interest. The place of filing will vary from state to state. A bank must perfect its security interest in money and instruments—stocks and bonds—by having physical possession of the collateral. After a bank has perfected its security interest, Article Nine of the UCC establishes various priorities over other possible creditors.

The adoption of Article Nine of the UCC has resulted in a substantial increase in the number of secured loans made by a bank. The loan officer should have a basic understanding of the legal requirements of Article Nine.

Unfortunately, the traditional promissory notes are not satisfactory to use in many of the lending situations banks engage in today or will engage in in the future. Banks have developed and will continue to develop different loan documents to meet each situation. The four fundamental legal requirements —amount borrowed, time and place of repayment, interest charged, and events of default—should appear in each document.

A business loan agreement is a commitment on behalf of the bank to loan a given sum over a period of time. The amount may be taken down at one time or disbursed as requested by the borrower. Such an agreement is often used when the bank grants a borrower a line of credit.

If each disbursement is not evidenced by a promissory note, the method of disbursement should be stated to insure enforceability against the borrower. For example, when advances are paid directly to a party selling goods to the borrower upon receipt by the bank of certain specified documents, the bank should notify the borrower on a regular basis of said advances in order that the borrower does not deny receiving the money advanced.

Traditionally, the interest rate has been fixed for the term of the loan but this is rapidly changing. If the interest rate is to fluctuate to reflect market conditions, the loan agreement should state how and when the rate is to be adjusted. Wherever possible, a bank should base its change of rate upon a published standard—for example, the prime rate of another bank or some government index. Otherwise, the use of the phrase such as "our prime rate" is subject to dispute and in the event of litigation, subject to oral testimony to establish what was meant by the bank and understood by the borrower. If the bank is unable to use a readily ascertainable standard, the bank's formula should be set forth in detail in the agreement to reduce the area for misunderstanding.

Since loan agreements are simply contracts reciting the understanding between the bank and the borrower, a banker should consider including one or more of the following provisions: method of repayment, prepayment privileges, financial covenants, negative covenants, affirmative covenants, warranties, and default provisions. When a loan officer reviews a loan agreement, he should be able to state that the understanding of the parties is adequately reflected by the language.

With the development of electronic transfers and the wide acceptance of credit cards, banks have developed specialized consumer loan agreement forms. An example of such a revolving credit agreement form appears in Figure 3.

This loan agreement varies substantially from the traditional promissory note or business loan agreement; however, it incorporates four basic requirements necessary to establish an enforceable obligation against the borrower.

The agreement provides that upon the acceptance of the application, the bank shall establish and notify the borrower of the maximum amount of credit which the borrower may have outstanding at one time.

The borrower may obtain all or part of this line of credit by issuing a check or by accessing the credit via a debit card or some other electronic means. The bank must provide the borrower with a periodic statement showing when and how each advance was made and the total amount outstanding.

The interest rate is calculated monthly on the balance outstanding during the month. The formula should be explained in terms readily understood by a consumer.

The agreement establishes a regular repayment provision based upon the total amount outstanding. The default provision should provide for termination of the line of credit in the event the borrower defaults its obligations. This loan agreement is the sole writing containing the borrower's promise to pay the loan and the interest charged.

The variable rate note is increasing in popularity, especially for business loans and real estate mortgage loans. A key legal element to be considered when using a variable rate in a promissory note is to insure that the method by which the interest is calculated can be determined from the note or by reference to a readily ascertainable standard. Otherwise, the note may not be negotiable and, therefore, not salable to a third party in the event the bank needs liquidity. In addition, when the rate may be increased or decreased should appear in the note.

Figure 3

We request you, meaning The First National Bank of Anytown, U.S.A., to maintain a Reserve Cash Line of Credit under which you will make loans to us, subject to the following procedures and conditions.

LINE OF CREDIT

You will make one or more loans to us up to an unpaid balance of_____
___Dollars ($_____), herein called Line of Credit. You will advise us of our current approved Maximum Line of Credit as shown on our periodic statement.

ADVANCES

You will make advances under our Reserve Cash Line of Credit by any of the following methods:

1. Upon receipt of any check from any of us which overdraws our checking account in excess of $3.00, you will, without further notice or request, make a Reserve Cash advance hereunder in multiples of $100.00 or the unused portion of the line of credit, whichever is smaller, by depositing the proceeds to the credit of our checking account.

2. Upon presentation of any Card at any electronic terminal which accepts the Card and provides for cash withdrawals.

3. By depositing with you a signed and properly completed advance request on a form provided to us which will show the amount of the requested advance and the instructions for the disbursement thereof.

4. By instructing us by telephone or in person to make an advance by depositing the same to our designated account which action you will confirm to us in writing.

It is agreed that you need not pay any check or honor any request for a cash advance that will create Reserve Cash Line of Credit balance in excess of the approved maximum.

If more than one borrower signs this application, each of them may draw checks, obtain cash advances by use of the Card, sign advance requests or obtain advances on oral request without the countersignature or approval of any other borrower, and the obligation to make payments therefore shall be the joint and several obligations of all of us.

FINANCE CHARGE

We promise to pay all sums borrowed hereunder, together with a monthly Finance Charge of one and one-half percent (1½%) [being an Annual Percentage Rate of eighteen percent (18%) per annum] on the Average Daily Outstanding Balance during each monthly billing period. The average daily outstanding balance is determined by adding the outstanding principal balance in Reserve Cash Line of Credit on each day of the billing cycle, after having first deducted Payments and Credits received that day from each such balance and dividing the total by the number of days in the Billing Cycle. The Finance Charge is subject to change by written notice addressed and mailed by you to us not less than fifteen (15) days prior to when the new Finance Charges become effective for outstanding Reserve Cash Line of Credit balances. The finance charge does not include optional credit life premiums.

PAYMENT

Each month, we promise to pay you the minimum monthly payment according to the following schedule or such lesser amounts as shall pay the outstanding indebtedness in full.

Average Daily Outstanding Balance (Reserve Cash Line of Credit in Use) at Statement Date	Minimum Monthly Payment
$300 or less	$15
301 to $500	25
501 to 1000	50
1001 to 1500	75
1501 to 2000	100
For every $500 interval over $2000	add 25

All payments received shall be applied first to interest and insurance premiums, with the balance, if any, to be applied to principal.

The undersigned hereby authorize you to receive payment of any monthly installment of principal, interest, or any other charges by automatically deducting the amount thereof from our designated account on or after the date specified on the statement for payment to be paid. If the balance in our designated account on payment date is insufficient to make the minimum monthly payment due, but during the statement period there have been deposits (other than advances made pursuant to this application) the total of which exceeds the amount of said minimum monthly payment due, then further advances on the same terms will be made to us in an amount of $100.00 or the balance of our Maximum Line of Credit, whichever is the lesser, provided that the proceeds of this further advance, together with the balance in the account, are sufficient to make the payments then due. Any payment in excess of minimum payment will reduce the outstanding balance, but will not eliminate the amount of the monthly payment due, unless we make a separate payment equal to or greater than the scheduled payment between the date of the last statement and the next scheduled date of the payment. We may prepay all advances at any time.

PERIODIC STATEMENT

You are to render a periodic statement to us reflecting all loans made hereunder during the statement period, all finance charges made, all charges for credit life, all payments received, the beginning and ending balances owing hereunder, the annual percentage rate and the method by which the annual percentage rate is computed, which statement shall be considered correct and accepted by us unless we notify your audit department of errors within sixty (60) days of your statement date.

CREDIT LIFE

If we desire, one of us may elect to be covered by a group life insurance policy or policies accepted by you, subject to the terms and conditions of said policy, including the provision that such insurance shall not cover any loan outstanding after the undersigned's 66th birthday. An additional charge of 10¢ per month per $100.00 of indebtedness during the time any loan is outstanding is made for credit life insurance. Credit Life is subject to change as to future transactions by written notice addressed and mailed by you to the insured not less than fifteen (15) days prior to when the new Credit Life becomes effective for reserve Cash Line of Credit Balances.

(continued)

NOTICES

You will provide us with separate statements notifying us of our rights to dispute billing errors and other matters. IF WE HAVE ANY QUESTIONS, WE SHALL CALL YOU AT 010-1000.

DEFAULT

If we fail to make punctual payment of any amount when due hereunder or fail to perform any other obligations to you or if any one of us files for bankruptcy, makes a wage earner's assignment, dies or suffers an adverse change in our financial position, or if you should for any reason deem yourself insecure, you need not make any further Reserve Cash Line of Credit loans hereunder, and all sums owing by us shall become immediately due and payable without demand or notice and we promise immediately to pay the full amount then owing to you.

TERMINATION

Either you or any of us may terminate this agreement as to future advances, by written notice to the other, but no termination shall affect any check properly drawn and issued hereunder prior to your receipt of such notice. Neither shall any termination change the obligations of us to punctually pay all sums owing hereunder, together with finance charges and credit life charges, when due or the observance of any of the other terms hereof.

MISCELLANEOUS

If this application is accepted by you, your commitment for advances hereunder runs solely to us, and we will not attempt to assign any rights hereunder to any other party. In the event we shall designate or authorize any other party to draw checks upon or make cash withdrawals from this account, we agree and promise to be liable for all advances which may result from said authorization even though said party has not signed this agreement. Parties so designated shall not be liable for any loans created hereby.

The conditions of this agreement may be changed adversely to us by you, provided not less than 15 days' notice of the adverse change is mailed by you to us at the last address which you have for us.

The terms "we, our or us" whenever used shall refer jointly to the borrowers signing this agreement and to each of them severally. If this application is accepted, all signers agree that they are jointly and severally bound by all of the terms and provisions of this agreement.

We acknowledge that this agreement does not alter or affect the usual terms governing our deposit accounts with you or the usual terms governing the Card.

Loan Guaranties

Since banks often require the borrower to obtain a third party to guaranty a loan, bankers should understand the legal principles governing guaranties. Contracts of guaranty are divided into two categories—limited and continuing. A limited guaranty is of a specific note or for a fixed period of time. The continuing guaranty is in effect for future transactions between the bank and the borrower or until revoked by the guarantor.

The usual form of a limited guaranty is as follows:

For value received, the undersigned jointly and severally hereby guarantee payment of the within note and interest and all expenses and attorney's fees paid or incurred by the holder in collecting or attempting to collect his note, waive presentment, demand, notice, protest and diligence in collecting. Holder may set off and apply any deposits or assets of the undersigned in the possession of the Holder to the indebtedness herein, before or after due date.

This language is printed or stamped on the back of the note at the time the loan is made. Sec. 3-416 of the UCC states that the words "payment guaranteed" or their equivalent means that the bank may seek payment from the guarantor without first seeking payment from the maker or any other party to the note. However, when the words "collection guarantied" or their equivalent are used, the bank must take action first against the borrower before proceeding against the guarantor. Therefore, a loan officer should also use the magic words "payment guaranteed" on all limited guaranty forms, or otherwise the usefulness of the guaranty is substantially reduced.

The continuing guaranty form in contrast to the limited guaranty is invariably embraced in a separate instrument. This instrument contains a phrase guarantying the prompt payment when due of any and all obligations of the borrower to the bank, whether direct or contingent, now in existence or hereinafter arising by whatsoever means. The guaranty should either be up to a fixed sum or for an unlimited amount which is stated in the guaranty.

Because contracts of guaranty (other than surety company contracts) are frequently entered into solely as an accommodation for the borrower and without the guarantor participating in the benefits of the loan, the courts tend to construe contracts of guaranty strictly against the party claiming under the contract. It is widely accepted that "widows and sureties are favorites of the law." However, the rule of strict construction of contracts will not be so extended to invalidate a guaranty that is clear and unambiguous in its terms. Nor is the principle that the undertaking of the guarantor is to be strictly construed intended to nullify the plain language of the instrument of guaranty.

Unless the guaranty is given prior to or at the time the initial loan is made to the borrower, the guaranty may not be enforceable because there is no consideration—that is, the making of the loan in reliance upon the guaranty —for the guaranty. Caution dictates that a loan officer should not disburse any funds on a loan until the executed guaranty agreement is in the bank's possession.

A continuing loan guaranty agreement should contain waivers by the guarantor of various acts by the bank which otherwise would be a defense to the enforcement of the guaranty. For example, the guaranty should waive any defense arising out of the bank's release of collateral for the underlying loans without first obtaining the consent of the guarantor. This waiver should be broad enough to cover all acts the bank would take in the prudent management of the loans. If the guaranty is not so drafted, the bank should notify the guarantor of each action it takes which varies from the initial terms and conditions established at the time the loan was negotiated. Since any well-drafted guaranty agreement may not cover all the contingencies which may occur over the life of the loan, prudence requires the bank to advise the guarantor on a regular basis of the progress of the borrower. This is especially important when the guarantor is not familiar with the day-to-day activities of the borrower. If the guarantor is the major shareholder of the borrower, then such communication between bank and the guarantor may not be required. However, even then the bank should be able to show, if required, that the guarantor was aware of the status of the loan. An example, a continuing guaranty agreement which covers many of the predicable contingencies, appears in Figure 4.

If the proposed guarantor is some form of entity such as a partnership, joint venture, or corporation, the loan officer must determine whether such entity has legal authority to enter into the guaranty agreement. The general rule is that a corporation does not have the authority to guaranty the obligations of another person unless it is a surety company.

A general exception to this rule is when the corporation guarantees the debt of a third party in furtherance of a corporate purpose; for example, when an officer of the corporation purchases some real estate on behalf of the corporation. If the purpose of the loan to an individual or somebody other than a corporation is not in furtherance of a corporate purpose, then a careful examination of the appropriate statutes authorizing the corporation to do business should be made. Some corporation Acts specifically permit the corporation to guaranty borrowings of its officers, directors, or shareholders, whether or not those borrowings are in furtherance of a corporate purpose. Whenever there is any question about the corporation's authority to guaranty the proposed loan, counsel should be consulted and a special corporate resolution should be passed by the corporate board of directors specifically authorizing the execution of the guaranty.

Hypothecation Agreements

Quite often the loan officer is offered in lieu of a guaranty of the proposed borrowing a pledge by a third party of collateral belonging to that party. If personal property is involved, unless the bank takes physical possession of the collateral that is pledged, such as stock certificates or certificates of deposit, there must be a written pledge agreement, or hypothecation agreement. This is an agreement whereby the owner of the property grants a security interest in the collateral described therein to the bank to secure the indebtedness of a third party. Section 9-105(d) of the UCC defines the word "debtor" to include any third party who pledges its collateral for somebody else's debt. Consequently, Article Nine applies to hypothecation agreements.

Under Article Nine of the UCC, the bank must have physical possession of the stock and other negotiable instruments in order to perfect the bank's security interest. Banks often, therefore, just take possession of the stock certificates, plus stock powers endorsed in blank, in lieu of a hypothecation

Figure 4

LOAN GUARANTY AGREEMENT

FOR VALUE RECEIVED, and to enable_____of
_____hereinafter designated as "Debtor," to obtain credit, from
time to time, of The First National Bank of Anytown, U.S.A., the undersigned hereby request
said Bank to extend to said Debtor such credit as said Bank may deem proper, and the
undersigned hereby, jointly and severally, guaranty the full and prompt payment to said Bank
at maturity, and at all times thereafter, and also at the time hereinafter provided, of any and
all indebtedness, liabilities and obligations of every nature and kind of said Debtor to said
Bank, and every balance and part thereof, whether now owing or due, or which may hereafter, from time to time, be owing or due, and howsoever heretofore or hereafter created or
arising or evidenced, to the extent of _____ Dollars, and the undersigned,
jointly and severally, also agree to pay in addition thereto, all costs, expenses and reasonable
attorney's fees at any time paid or incurred in endeavoring to collect said indebtedness,
liabilities and obligations, and in and about enforcing this instrument.

   This guaranty shall be a continuing, absolute and unconditional guaranty and shall
remain in full force and effect until written notice of its discontinuance shall be actually
received by said Bank, and also until any and all of said indebtedness, obligations and
liabilities existing before receipt of such notice shall be fully paid. The death or dissolution
of the undersigned shall not terminate this guaranty until notice of any such death or dissolution shall have been actually received by said Bank, nor until all of said indebtedness,
obligations and liabilities existing before receipt of such notice shall be fully paid.

   The liability hereunder shall in no wise be affected by, and said Bank is hereby
expressly authorized to make from time to time, without notice to anyone, any sale, pledge,
surrender, compromise, settlement, release, renewal, extension, indulgence, alteration, substitution, exchange, change in, modification or other disposition of any of said indebtedness,
obligations and liabilities, either express or implied, or of any contract or contracts evidencing
any thereof, or of any security or collateral therefor. The liability hereunder shall in no wise
be affected or impaired by any acceptance by said Bank of any security for, or other
guarantors upon, any said indebtednesses, obligations, or liabilities, or by any failure, neglect
or omission on the part of said Bank to realize upon or protect any of said indebtedness,
obligations or liabilities, or any collateral or security thereof, or to exercise any lien upon or
right of appropriate of any moneys, credits or property of said Debtor, possessed by said
Bank, toward the liquidation of said indebtedness, obligations or liabilities, or by any application of payments or credits thereon. Said Bank shall have the exclusive right to determine
how, when and what application of payments or credits, if any, shall be made on said
indebtedness, obligations and liabilities or any part of them. In order to hold the undersigned
liable hereunder, there shall be no obligation on the part of said Bank, at any time, to resort
for payment to said Debtor, or other persons or corporations, their properties or estates, or
resort to any collateral, security, property, liens or other rights or remedies whatsoever.

   All diligence in collection, and all presentment for payment, demand, protest, notice
of protest, and notice of nonpayment, dishonor and default, and of the acceptance of this
guaranty, and of any and all extensions of credit hereunder, are hereby expressly waived.

   The granting of credit, from to time, by said Bank to the Debtor in excess of the amount
of this guaranty and without notice to the undersigned, is hereby authorized and shall in no
way affect or impair this guaranty.

   Authority and consent are hereby expressly given said Bank, from time to time, and
without any notice to the undersigned, to give and make such extensions, renewals, indul-

(continued)

gences, settlements and compromises as it may deem proper with respect to any of the indebtedness, liabilities and obligations covered by this guaranty, including the taking or releasing of security and of any one or more of the guarantors hereunder, and surrendering of documents.

In case of death, dissolution, liquidation, failure, insolvency or bankruptcy of said Debtor, filing by the Debtor of any petition for an arrangement or reorganization proceedings or the filing of any petition for an arrangement or reorganization of the Debtor or an assignment by the Debtor for benefit of creditors or of said liabilities, all of said indebtedness, liabilities and obligations, to the extent of the amount of this guaranty, shall, at the option of said Bank, become immediately due from, and be forthwith paid by the undersigned to said Bank, the same as though said debts, liabilities and obligations had matured by lapse of time.

This guaranty shall be construed according to the laws of the State of Illinois, in which state it shall be perfomed by the undersigned.

This guanty as to each signer shall be supplemental and additional to any other guaranty or guaranties, and security or securities heretofore or hereafter received by the Bank in connection with the indebtedness guaranteed, and the liability of the undersigned hereunder shall not be affected or impaired by reason of the taking or releasing of such other guaranty or guaranties, security or securities, other signer or signers, without notice to the undersigned.

This guaranty shall be binding upon the undersigned, jointly and severally, and upon the heirs, legal representatives and assigns of the undersigned, and each of them, respectively, and shall inure to the benefit of said Bank, its successors, legal representatives and assigns.

Signed and Sealed by the undersigned at_____, this_____day of_____, 19___.

_____ (SEAL)

agreement. Caution dictates that the bank always take a hypothecation agreement, which sets forth the bank's rights in the event of default and duty to care for the collateral.

Since a hypothecation agreement is similar to a guaranty agreement, the same general rules apply. The agreement must be delivered at the time the loan is made, the party hypothecating stock or other collateral must have the authority to pledge the stock, and finally in the event of default or change in terms of the initial loan, the bank should notify the party pledging the collateral of any change of terms or extension of the indebtedness secured. The bank should not accept as collateral stocks or other items which are listed in the borrower's name under the Uniform Gifts to Minors Act. The parents often will offer such security; however, this security may not be pledged nor may the bank enforce its security interest against such collateral since it is legally the property of the minor.

Subordination Agreement

A bank officer who is extending credit to a closely held corporation may wish to have the shareholders of that corporation subordinate any indebtedness of the corporation to the shareholders to the bank's loan. This is accomplished with the execution of a subordination agreement by the shareholders. In drafting such an agreement, the bank should insure that the officers are subordinating their indebtedness only to the loan to the bank, and not to that of other creditors.

A similar situation arises when a bank is asked to extend credit to the lessee of a tract of ground who is intending to construct a building on that ground. It is necessary for the owner of the ground to consent to the mortgage to the bank, and it may be necessary for the mortgage lender to the lessor also to consent. This is a variation of a subordination agreement and is required in order to insure that the security interest or lien of the bank has a priority over other lien creditors, as well as the owner of the property.

State and Federal Acts and Regulations

The legal principles which apply to bank credit discussed so far have not taken into consideration various regulatory acts which apply to the granting of credit by a bank. The foregoing principles determine whether or not the bank has an enforceable claim against the borrower. In addition to these basic principles surrounding the lending of money, the loan officer must be familiar with the various state and Federal acts and regulations which regulate the bank's authority to make a loan.

The fundamental regulation governing bank credit which has been in existence for a number of years and applies to banks chartered under both the National Banking Act and the various state banking acts is a limitation on the amount of credit that may be extended to any one borrower. This limitation is traditionally stated on the basis of a certain percentage of the capital accounts of the bank. For example, a national bank may not extend credit to a single borrower in an amount in excess of 10 percent of its capital, surplus, undivided profits, and certain other reserve accounts. However, a bank chartered in the state of Illinois is limited in extending credit to 15 percent of its capital and surplus accounts. Each state has varying restrictions as to how much money may be lent to any one borrower. The underlying principle behind these restrictions is that there should not be an undue concentration of assets in any one borrower. This concept applies even though the extension of credit to a related group of borrowers is permissible under either the National Banking Act or state banking laws. A common example is when a corporation borrows the maximum from the bank and the bank also lends the same amount of money to a shareholder of that corporation. Depending upon the appropriate chartering act, that loan may be considered one loan or may be considered two separate loans. However, the loan also may be criticized not for a violation of the specific banking act but for an undue concentration of assets.

Because of the restriction on the amount of credit which a bank may grant to any one borrower, there has developed the practice of a bank selling or participating part of its loan to another bank in order that they may satisfy the credit needs of the borrower who needs to borrow more than the limit. This is called a "participation." There are a number of ways a participation may occur. The customary method is that the borrower signs a note at the lead bank. The bank then sells an interest in that note pursuant to the terms of a participation agreement to one or more banks. Such a transaction should be evidenced by a participation agreement which spells out in detail the understanding between the lead bank and the participating bank. The participation agreement establishes who is paid first, what happens in the event of default, what happens to any setoffs which either bank receives, how the various expenses are divided, and who is responsible to collect the note in the event of a default. At the time a lead bank sells an interest in the loan, it must fully disclose all the information it knows about the borrower to the participating bank. If it does not, it will be liable to the participating bank for any loss which the participating bank may suffer in the event the borrower defaults.

A participation agreement may also occur when the borrower executes notes directly to the participating bank. Then, the participating bank's name should appear on any security document, such as security agreements, real estate mortgages, and hypothecation agreements, so that there is no question about its claim to the collateral. More and more participations are required in order that the lead bank or the bank in the area where the business or the individual is located be able to service its customer. Consequently, it is important that the bank officer study some of the other complex questions which arise in loan participations.

NONDISCRIMINATION IN THE GRANTING OF CREDIT

Prior to the adoption of the Equal Credit Opportunity Act in 1974 and its subsequent amendment in 1976, a loan officer could refuse credit for any reason that the officer determined. This refusal did not have to be based upon the credit information that was submitted to the bank, but on any sociological or other reason which the bank officer or bank chose to deny the applicant credit. The Equal Credit Opportunity Act applies to all extensions of credit whether for business or consumer purposes and specifically prohibits any creditor from discriminating against an applicant for credit on the basis of race, color, religion, natural origin, sex, marital status, or age (provided the applicant has the capacity to contract), or because all or part of the applicant's income derives from any public assistance program, or because the applicant has exercised in good faith a right granted under the various Consumer Credit Protection acts. Consequently, a banker may not turn down loans to married women who have sufficient assets and ability to repay the loan solely because they might become pregnant. A bank can no longer refuse to make a business loan to a farmer or a small businessman acting as a sole proprietor because the wife refuses to sign the note. There are many other examples of discrimination in credit which have existed over the years and been accepted by banks which are now prohibited.

This prohibition on discrimination in credit does not mean that the bank must extend credit to everyone who applies for it. Instead, the bank must judge each credit application upon the prospective borrower's assets and ability to repay. The bank may refuse the credit if it does not satisfy the banker's standards; however, the banker must tell the debtor why the credit is refused. This act does not prevent a bank from refusing to make a certain type of loan. For example, a bank may have a policy of not making any loans secured by first mortgages on real estate to purchase residences. As long as a bank can establish that this is its policy which is never deviated from, the bank may refuse all such applications.

The provisions of the Equal Credit Opportunity Act have been implemented through Regulation B issued by the Federal Reserve Board. The act, in addition to providing the appropriate supervisory agencies with authority to enforce the provisions of the act, also provides the borrower with various civil remedies directly against the bank. The effect of this legislation has been to change a number of the traditional practices of banks involving the granting of credit, and requiring the bank to consider each credit application on the basis of the borrower's assets and ability to repay and not on the basis of any other information or dislikes.

COMMUNITY REINVESTMENT ACT

In 1977 the Congress adopted the Community Reinvestment Act, which became effective November, 1978. The purpose of this act is to insure that banks meet the credit needs of the local communities in which they are chartered, consistent with the safe and sound operation of such institutions. Pursuant to the act, a bank which gathers deposits from its market area and makes all of its loans out of the market area will be subject to criticism by the appropriate regulatory body. In order to carry out the purposes of this act, the bank must make a formal designation of its market area and prepare and review on an annual basis a CRA statement stating its intention to serve the credit needs of the community. Each time a bank seeks permission from a regulatory authority to change some aspect of its business, open a branch, close an office, or change its location, the regulatory agency must review the bank's compliance with CRA. If a community group complains, or if the regulator believes that the bank is not complying with the Community Reinvestment Act, the application may be denied. The effect of the Community Reinvestment Act is to complement the Equal Credit Opportunity Act to insure that banks are extending credits to all segments of the community, both business and consumer, on the basis of the financial ability of the borrowers to service their debt.

Another area of regulation is whether or not the proposed borrower may qualify as a borrower from the bank. For a number of years there have been restrictions on the amount and kind of loans a bank could make to its executive officers. An executive officer has been defined traditionally as an officer who makes management decisions for the bank. The Financial Institutions Regulatory and Interest Rate Control Act of 1978 imposed additional restrictions on who may borrow money from the bank. When and how loans may be made to a director, an executive officer, or any person who directly or indirectly has control of the member bank have been carefully set forth and restricted. No longer may such people receive favorable interest rates, and their loans in excess of $25,000 must be approved in advance by the full board of directors. Further, this act places restrictions on loans to executive officers, directors, or persons who control more than 10 percent of another bank who seek to borrow from a correspondent bank and use the deposit of their bank as a basis for negotiating a favorable interest rate.

CONSUMER REGULATION

In 1969 Congress adopted the first of a series of titles to the Consumer Credit Protection Act. The primary title is the Truth-in-Lending Act, also known as Consumer Credit Cost Disclosure. The stated purpose of the Truth-in-Lending Act was to provide the borrower with an explanation of the terms of a loan so that the borrower could compare those terms with those offered by other creditors. No matter how salutary the purpose of the Truth-in-Lending Act was and still is, the act and the regulations implementing it have caused substantial confusion and litigation. So much so that Congress has now adopted amendments to the original Truth-in-Lending Act known as the Truth-in-Lending Simplification and Reform Act, which become effective March, 1982. The fundamental requirements of Truth-in-Lending are to disclose to a borrower obtaining a loan for personal, family, or household uses the annual percentage rate; that is, the rate of interest the borrower is being charged, and the total amount of interest the borrower will have to pay if the loan is not paid prior to maturity. In addition to disclosing these two primary facts, the bank is required to disclose any charges that are made in the event of default, any prepayment penalties, any security interests which are taken to secure the indebtedness, and whether or not various forms of credit insurance are required. If the loan is for other than acquiring a residence and is to be secured by an interest in real estate, a notice of right of recision must be given to the borrower three days prior to the disbursement of the funds. The implementation of the provisions of the Truth-in-Lending Act was delegated to the Federal Reserve Board, which issued Regulation Z. Unfortunately, although the Board has attempted to interpret the act in keeping with customary practices of the credit industry, the courts have been technical in their interpretation of the possible violations of the act.

In addition, the Truth-in-Lending Act governs the issuance of credit cards, the correction of errors in billings on credit card and revolving credit accounts, the use of credit reports, credit advertisement, and consumer leases. All of these regulations apply to credit extended to persons for personal, family, or household purposes. In order to comply with the various and numerous regulations, the majority of banks today have designated a person as a compliance officer and are constantly reviewing their forms and procedures to make sure that they are in compliance.

USURY RATES

For many years both the National Banking Act and state legislatures have imposed restrictions upon the amount of interest which a lender may receive as consideration for making a loan. The purpose of these acts, known as usury statutes, has been to protect the unsophisticated borrower from overreaching by the lender. However, as banking has changed, and the cost to the bank of obtaining deposits or monies to lend has substantially increased, a number of exemptions to the usury rates have been established. The primary exemption is that interest rates for loans for business or investment purposes are either not regulated or have a higher limit than loans for personal purposes. The Depository Institutions Deregulation and Monetary Control Act of 1980 removed all restrictions on the interest rate which a financial institution may charge on a loan secured by a first lien on residential property or similar property. This Federal preemption of the state usury laws will continue to be effective unless a state within the next three years specifically establishes different limits. Even though there is no limit on the rate which may be charged on first mortgage residential real estate loans, there are regulations limiting the variations which may be made in the rate after the loan is initially made. These regulations apply to variable rate mortgages and to renegotiated rate mortgages. The Act further preempted state laws as to the interest charged on certain agricultural and business loans.

The foregoing discussion of various regulations which further govern bank credit does not take into consideration the various state regulations. Some states require all consumer credit forms to be in simplified language. Others prohibit the practice of redlining. States have adopted the Uniform Consumer Credit Code, which regulates various types of consumer credit.

BANKRUPTCY CODE

The Bankruptcy Code of 1978 is a substantial clarification of the Bankruptcy Act, which had not been revised for over 40 years, and directly affects bank credit in the event the debtor defaults. If the bank has not perfected its security interest as required by the provisions of Article Nine of the UCC, nor has the bank properly recorded its mortgage or real estate lien as required by the provisions of the appropriate state law, then the trustee in bankruptcy may declare the security agreement or real estate mortgage void and proceed to liquidate the assets which were pledged as collateral to the bank and distribute them equally among all the creditors. This is in keeping with the underlying principle behind bankruptcy of equitable distribution to all the creditors. Obviously, it is important that a bank follow the appropriate steps to perfect its security interest or its interest in real estate in order that it retain the priority in certain collateral which it bargained for. If a bank does not take the appropriate steps at the time the loan is made, but does take the appropriate steps within 90 days of the bankruptcy, there is a presumption that this is a transfer for an antecedent debt; therefore, the trustee may void the security interest or lien as a preference.

The Bankruptcy Code further affects the bank's rights as a secured lender by providing in certain situations that the court may force the secured lender to leave its property with the debtor, while the debtor attempts to work out some type of payment program. This may be done provided the security is not diminished in value.

Without considering all of the other major or minor changes which have been made under the Bankruptcy Code, a bank should be aware of some other facts. For example, the Bankruptcy Code specifically recognizes the bank's right to set off any deposits of the borrower against any notes or claims which it may have against the borrower. However, the amount that may be set off is subject to review by the trustee in bankruptcy to determine whether or not the bank received more than it should have received. Without discussing the detailed formula, during the 90-day period immediately prior to bankruptcy the trustee has a right to review the amount that was on deposit on any given day against what was actually set off to determine if the bank received an advantage.

Another area to consider is the broadening of Chapter 13. Arrangements which used to apply only to wage earners now apply also to small businesses, providing their total secured debt does not exceed $350,000 and their unsecured debt does not exceed $100,000. The court has broad powers under a Chapter 13 arrangement to require the bank to leave its security with the debtor attempting to pay off the indebtedness.

SUMMARY

Throughout this chapter the discussion has been directed to alerting a bank officer to certain basic principles which apply to all extensions of credit to insure that the bank has an enforceable claim, and to certain regulations which apply to some specialized types of credit. No attempt has been made to detail the given requirements of any single transaction. However, if a bank officer will keep the basic principles in mind on every loan and not become lost in the technical details of the forms or documents, the bank should in the majority of cases have a valid and enforceable loan which will withstand attacks by the debtor or other creditors of the debtor and the regulatory agencies.

24

The Use of Financial Futures in Bank Loans

Inflation in the 1970s tore the lid off bank borrowing costs and forced the Federal Reserve to release its already tenuous grip on short-term interest rates. As a result there will be a great deal more volatility in the cost of funds affecting a bank's income statement in the years ahead compared to the seventies.

Without the use of futures contracts, banks have only two ways to respond to this environment of increased interest rate risk. One is through "floating" loan rates (usually changed on a day-to-day basis at the bank's discretion), the second through greater spreads between bank borrowing and lending rates. Neither action is likely to engender an enthusiastic response from bank customers.

The 90-day Treasury bill futures contract, traded on the International Monetary Market, a division of the Chicago Mercantile Exchange, allows banks to protect themselves from the ebbs and flows of interest rate tides without transferring the resultant risk to their customers. Furthermore, with the use of futures, banks may be able to increase substantially their share of the market for corporate funds without significantly increasing their risk exposure.

Banks today generally lend at a rate that changes automatically when the bank alters its prime rate. But this means the customer bears the risk of unexpected increases in borrowing costs. Many creditworthy bank customers have responded to this increased risk by rejecting bank loans as their principal means of financing, turning instead to the primary market for funds by issuing their own commercial paper. Fortunately, banks have not lost all revenues these customers had provided because commercial paper is generally backed by a line of credit with a bank, provided for a fee. Thus, the bank guarantees its corporate customer recourse to a bank line of credit in times of trouble. However, in exchanging loans for credit lines, banks have adversely affected the credit risk of their own loan portfolios.

The upshot of these recent trends—floating rate loans and the concomitant shift of borrowers to the commercial paper market—is that banks have lost some of their best customers and replaced them with less desirable customers who do not have access to the primary market for funds. (This absence of access is usually for the reason that the customer in question is not sufficiently creditworthy.) The floating rate loan also adds its own element of risk in that a rapid rise in the floating rate may itself result in insolvency for the customer.

In this volatile environment interest rate futures can reduce risk both for banks and for their customers, thereby permitting banks to seek loan business more aggressively. Used in this manner, futures contracts could revolutionize the banking industry by providing an attractive alternative to the commercial paper market. The 90-day U.S. Treasury bill futures contract presently is the most useful vehicle for hedging short-term liabilities of banks. This chapter will discuss the elements of that futures contract and strategies for its use by banking institutions.

The Treasury Bill Futures Market

The only liquid futures market in a short-term instrument is the 90-day Treasury bill contract, traded on the International Monetary Market. Two separate studies conducted by the Commodity Futures Trading Commission, the Federal agency which regulates futures markets, indicate that commercial banks do not yet make major use of the Treasury bill futures contract except in their trust and dealer operations. Currently the principal users of this market are commodity pools and funds, private individuals, and government securities dealers.

But the most logical users of Treasury bill futures contracts are organizations such as commercial banks which have a significant proportion of assets or liabilities in the form of short-term, interest rate-sensitive instruments. Treasury bill futures contracts should be useful to banks as a substitute for the temporary purchase or sale of Treasury bills, or the purchase or sale of other short-term money market instruments whose yields are closely correlated to Treasury bill yields.

For a bank the most important benefit of futures contracts is that they provide a means of bridging the gap between the average maturity of the bank's assets and the average maturity of its liabilities. In other words, through the use of Treasury bill futures, the bank can run a "matched book" without actually matching the maturities of liabilities to the maturities of assets.

This particular futures contract calls for delivery of Treasury bills having a face value of $1 million at maturity, 91 days after delivery date. The "price" of the futures contract is quoted in terms of the IMM Index. This Index is constructed by subtracting from 100 the bill's discount yield on a 360-day basis. For example, a T-bill priced to yield 5.5 percent on a bank discount basis would be quoted on the IMM at 94.5. The reason for the use of the IMM Index is this: When the Index declines, the contract loses value; when the Index rises, the contract gains in value, as is the case with other commodity futures contracts. The opposite would be true if the yield instead of the Index were traded. Newspapers carrying quotes on Treasury bill futures usually carry both the IMM Index and the implied interest yield. However, orders must be given to floor brokers in terms of the Index itself.

The minimum price fluctuation in Treasury bill futures, as in the cash market for Treasury bills, is .01 of an Index point, or 1 basis point. The value of a one-basis-point change in the Index is $25. The Exchange at present trades futures contracts for delivery in the so-called December (December, March, June, and September) and January (January, April, July, and October) cycles. The actual delivery date(s) for each of those months and the instrument(s) that can be delivered under the contract are specified in the Exchange rules.

In constructing a cross hedge between a futures contract in 90-day Treasury bills and a certificate of deposit or Eurodollar time deposit (bank *add-on* instruments with a principal amount that is a multiple of $1 million, paying principal plus interest at maturity), the user must bear in mind that the futures contract is for delivery of a *discount* instrument; that is, the Treasury bill pays $1 million at maturity with the yield determining the current cash value of the bill. For example a $1 million 90-day Treasury bill priced to yield 10 percent on a bank discount basis is currently worth $975,000 and is worth $1 million at maturity. A newly issued $1 million 90-day CD, on the other hand, has a cash value of $1 million, but is worth $1,025,000 at maturity.

Use of Futures by Banks

The three primary areas of bank operations that can benefit from the use of Treasury bill futures are (1) dealer operations, (2) liability management and loan policy, and (3) Euro-operations.

In dealer operations the primary risk is one of capital loss in the dealer's cash position in CDs. If this risk can be reduced, dealers could expand inventories—thus more readily servicing their customers during periods of rising interest rates. This risk is much more relevant in the CD market than in the market for Treasury bills, where shorting in the cash market is possible.

Treasury bill futures can, therefore, provide dealers with the ability to reduce the risk of carrying a CD inventory.

From the point of view of the liability manager, the most important use of Treasury bill futures is the ability to price borrowings in advance of the actual purchase of funds. If the liability manager anticipates that rates will be higher than those reflected in the futures market, he can lock in the cost of money before the rise, while doing the actual borrowing at the time the funds are needed. This ability to lock in yields in anticipation of the receipt of bank funds also provides the liability manager with the option of adjusting the average effective maturity of his liabilities up to a maximum of two years.

In Euro-operations, Treasury bill futures can help to solve problems in the Euromarket created by credit restrictions. Futures contracts can be bought and sold as a substitute for a comparable purchase or sale of cash deposits without regard for the credit risk on the other side of the transaction, since the Exchange steps between traders and is a seller to every buyer and vice versa. Since the Eurodollar market is primarily a time deposit market, the middlemen of that market—Eurodollar brokers—do not assume a position in bank liabilities. Hence, Eurobankers must take upon themselves many of the risk transfer services assumed domestically by brokers. Futures can be helpful to them in this endeavor.

DEALER OPERATIONS—HEDGING CD POSITIONS

A bank's corporate customers prefer to hold short-term CDs, since their CD investments are usually residual funds being stored in anticipation of tax or dividend dates, and such dates are usually less than three months in the future. Banks, on the other hand, would like to match the maturity of their liabilities to the maturity of their assets. Without using Treasury bill futures, it is difficult to satisfy the needs of the bank and the corporate customer simultaneously. One way this is done at present is through a CD dealer. The bank can, for example, issue six-month CDs, placing them with a CD dealer. The dealer might then sell the bank's corporate customer a three-month term repurchase agreement with the CD as collateral. This affords the bank reduced exposure to upward movement in short-term rates, and the reduced reserve requirements it desires, while providing the corporation with the shorter-term liquid asset portfolio it prefers.

Thus, the interest rate risk a corporation would face by purchasing a CD with a longer term to maturity than its desired holding period is absorbed by the CD dealer. The CD dealer also absorbs the interest rate risk the bank would face if it were forced to issue CDs with shorter maturities than its desired six-month holding period. The dealer, on the other hand, is left with the risk that CD rates will rise before the maturity of the term repurchase agreement, resulting in a capital loss when the CD is redelivered to the dealer.

Table 1

**Hedge Performance of 90-Day T-Bill
Futures Contracts Against
Three-Month Certificate of Deposit
March 1976–May 30, 1980***

Time Period	Hedge Ratio	Percentage Reduction in Risk
Daily	.240 (12.03)†	.119
Weekly	.834 (14.62)	.491
Monthly	1.166 (13.89)	.793

*See Appendix (p. 000) for methodology.
†T-Bill statistics in parentheses.

Since dealers cannot short CDs, there is no way to eliminate this risk, but it can be somewhat reduced by shorting the Treasury bill futures contract. However, in using Treasury bill futures to cover exposure in CDs, the dealer should bear in mind that CD rates frequently rise more rapidly than Treasury bill rates. This tendency can in part be offset by hedging with a larger futures position than the cash CD position. Tables 1 and 2 show that for holding periods longer than a month, this strategy would reduce the bank's risk exposure.

Treasury bill futures provide banks, corporate customers, and the middlemen, CD dealers, with a means of matching cash portfolio maturities to futures maturities, thereby reducing their risk at low cost.

Any one of the three participants in the CD market transaction described above could have attained his desired holding period without increasing the interest rate risk of the other two participants. For example, the bank could have sold three-month CDs directly to its corporate customer and shorted a Treasury bill futures contract for delivery three months hence. This would have reduced the bank's exposure to a change in the cost of funds over the following six-month period, as would the sale of a six-month CD, but without involving the CD dealer or forcing the corporation to purchase funds of a longer maturity than its preferred three-month maturity.

Alternatively, the dealer could remain the intermediary between the bank and the corporation as before, shorting the Treasury bill futures contract for delivery three months hence to reduce the risk of a decline in the value of the CD to be repurchased in three months.

HEDGING BY BANK LIABILITY MANAGERS

The most important concern for a bank intending to use futures contracts to balance the maturities of assets and liabilities is that changes in yield on the assets and liabilities being protected by the futures contract may not match yield changes on the futures contract itself. Fortunately, there are some straightforward procedures for determining this risk. Table 1 describes historical experience regarding such risk, along with the appropriate ratio of futures hedges to cash items being hedged. Spreads between Treasury bill futures and certificate of deposit or Eurodollar yields can change substantially over short periods of time for two basic reasons. The first is that when money market yields rise, investors often believe that the credit risk of a bank certificate of deposit exceeds the risk of holding a Treasury bill by a greater amount than at lower rates. The rationale for this shift in risk evaluation is that higher yields may lead to credit problems for the liability manager. The second is that when CD rates rise, dealers increase their bid-ask spread in order to cover the rising cost of carrying CD inventories.

The tables that follow display the ratio of futures contracts to cash CDs being hedged that has the least risk (known as the hedge ratio), and the percentage risk reduction that could have been achieved between May, 1976, and May, 1980 (Table 1), and between January, 1978, and May, 1980 (Table 2).

Tables 1 and 2 describe the relationship between yield changes in three-month secondary CDs and 90-day Treasury bill futures using ordinary least squares regressions. The results are typical of those obtained with most cross-hedges of private short-term debt against 90-day Treasury bill futures. As one

TABLE 2

**Hedge Performance of 90-Day T-Bill
Futures Contracts Against
Three-Month Certificates of Deposit
June, 1978–May 30, 1980**

Time Period	Hedge Ratio	Percentage Reduction in Risk
Daily	.240 (8.30)	.121
Weekly	.976 (11.77)	.570
Monthly	1.233 (11.05)	.840

increases the length of time the 90-day Treasury bill hedge is maintained, there is a concomitant increase in percentage reduction of the cash market risk exposure. The hedge ratio also rises; for hedges of three-month instruments maintained for periods of one week or longer, hedge ratios are in the neighborhood of one. That is, about $1 million of hedge is needed for each $1 million cash item being hedged.

The remainder of this section describes three possible hedging uses of the 90-day T-bill futures contract for banks, each more sophisticated than the one before. The first hedge could be managed by the chief of the funding department of the bank, acting independently of loan policies determined elsewhere. The second hedge uses futures to provide more flexibility to loan policy and hence would require the direction of top management. The third hedge actually changes the procedure for pricing CDs and hence represents a change in the technology of bank borrowing.

Hedge of a Floating Rate Loan Financed by Overnight Repurchase Agreements. Although banks presently do a great deal of what might appropriately be called hedging in the cash market without using futures, there remains some residual interest rate exposure even under current bank practices. A good example is the case of a bank whose loans are floating on a day-to-day basis but are tied to the prime and whose liabilities are to some extent overnight repurchase agreements with corporations. This example is developed primarily because a hedge of an overnight rollover is the most complex cross-hedge; so this example, once understood, should ease the development of other examples that would be useful to bankers.

Although banks have the latitude to protect themselves completely against movements in short-term interest rates by adjusting the prime on a day-to-day basis as their cost of funds changes, they are quite reluctant to do this, since day-to-day adjustment of the prime would tend to antagonize customers and cause a loss of business for the bank. To show how futures could be used by a bank to reduce the frequency of prime rate changes under these present-day circumstances, an example is constructed of a floating rate loan whose yield remains unchanged for one month, financed by overnight rollovers of repurchase agreements.

The interest rate exposure of a prime rate loan, fixed over a one-month period and funded by debt rolled over more frequently, is basically the risk that overnight rates will rise substantially during a one-month period in which the prime remains unchanged. This interest rate risk can be reduced using a Treasury bill futures hedge, although other sorts of risk remain. The remaining exposure includes the risk that repurchase agreement rates will rise more rapidly than Treasury bill futures, and any credit risk resulting from the repurchase agreement.

This hedge example shows what actually would have happened in December, 1979, with a hedge of a $90 million loan at the prime, maturing in one month, assuming the loan is being financed by overnight repurchase agreements. A rule of thumb for determining the size of the short hedge on a day-to-day basis was used:

$$S = \frac{L \text{ (days to maturity of loan)}}{90}$$

where $S =$ size of the hedge
$L =$ size of the loan
$90 =$ number of days from issue date to maturity date of Treasury bills deliverable on the futures contract

In this example a bank grants a \$90 million one-month fixed rate loan. The risk faced by the bank is the risk that the cost of money in the repo* market will rise above the interest charged on the prime rate loan. By entering the futures market and shorting 90-day T-bill contracts, the bank reduces its exposure to risk resulting from rising repo-market interest rates.

Table 3 describes the mechanics of the hedge. As column 1 indicates, the total position initiated at the start of the one-month hedge period is obtained from the hedge formula, where size of the loan $L = 90$ and days of maturity $= 31$:

$$S = \frac{90}{90} \times 31 = 31$$

Alternately, and more accurately, this hedge may be thought of as several hedges, one for each of the cash rollovers. This approach, known as the deferral accounting method, aligns the hedge with the cash purchase being

TABLE 3

T-Bill Futures Hedge
December 3–14, 1979

Date	Hedge Position	T-Bill Settlement Price	Margin Receipts Payments
3	31	11.42	Entry
4	30	11.42	—
5	29	11.47	$3,750
6	28	11.42	($3,625)
7	27	12.16	$51,800
10	24	11.86	($20,250)
11	23	12.08	$13,200
12	22	12.15	$ 4,025
13	21	12.41	$14,300
14	20	12.22	($ 9,975)

*An agreement to sell a security at a fixed price at a later date.

hedged and hence produces a daily record of hedge performance that is more closely related to the daily borrowing cost being hedged. For example, the bank's purchase of three futures contracts on December 8, reducing the net short position from 27 contracts to 24 contracts, may be viewed as the lifting of a hedge of a three-day $90 million loan. Hence, in the formula, $L = \$90$ million, days to maturity $= 3$, and $S = \$3$ million.

Accounting for futures margins in this manner is advocated by Arthur Anderson & Co. in their brochure *Interest Rate Futures Contracts, Accounting and Control Techniques for Banks* (September 1, 1978). This accounting method is preferred because the resulting income statement provides a clearer picture of the extent of the risk reduction the bank experiences using the hedge. The second column of Table 4 shows the effective reduction in interest cost resulting from the hedge. Table 4 compares repo rates and hedge performance during the two-week period. In this example, had the bank not entered the futures market, it would have had a net interest cost of 12.85 percent. With the use of futures, however, the corporation reduced interest rate risk, and average interest cost of funding the loan fell by 44 basis points to 12.41 percent.

On a short-term basis the degree of association between yield changes in overnight repurchase agreements and 90-day T-bill settlement prices is not high. In many instances yields on repos rise while those for T-bills fall, and the reverse. Consequently, hedging the interest rate risk associated with granting a fixed rate loan funded by overnight repurchase agreements via T-bill futures will not reduce exposure by a substantial amount on a day-to-day basis. However, as the length of time the hedge is maintained increases, the effective risk reduction also increases. Over the one-month period in question, the risk reduction is substantial.

TABLE 4

Finance Cost of Hedged Overnight Repos
Used to Finance a Fixed Rate Loan
December 3–14, 1979

Date	Repo Rate	Hedge Effect	Net Interest Cost
3	12.50	Entry	12.50
4	12.50	—	12.50
5	11.88	−.05	11.83
6	12.75	—	12.75
7	13.00	−.74	12.26
10	13.13	−.44	12.69
11	13.25	−.66	12.59
12	13.00	−.73	12.27
13	14.00	−.99	13.01
14	12.50	−.80	11.70
Average	12.85	−.44	12.41

Hedge of Fixed Rate Loan Over a One-Year Period Using T-Bill Futures.
In this second example bank loan policy is involved, so that top management
must ultimately be part of the development of this strategy. The use of futures
contracts allows banks to vary loan terms in order to make those terms more
attractive to potential customers. The 90-day Treasury bill futures contract
provides banks with a vehicle for protecting themselves against interest rate
exposure on such loans. This use of the contract highlights the most important
function provided by the futures market—risk protection at low transaction
costs.

The 90-day bill futures contract allows a fixed rate loan to be funded using
short-term certificates of deposit or other short-term purchased funds and
futures hedges. Table 5 describes how such a hedge would have worked in
September, 1978. This table illustrates the making of a one-year fixed rate $20
million loan, funded through the issue of a series of 90-day CDs and hedged
through a strip of short sales of Treasury bill futures, all entered simultaneously. The profitability of this loan is compared to the profitability of the same
loan funded with rollovers of 90-day CDs without hedging in the futures
market, during a period, September, 1978, to September, 1979, when short-
term rates moved upward, making fixed rate loans that were not hedged
unprofitable. Table 5 demonstrates that this hedge would have substantially
reduced the interest rate risk of such a loan in 1978.

In the case of our first hedge example, deferral accounting was used for
illustrative purposes but was not important for the purpose of informing the
bank's shareholders as the hedge period was too short to affect the quarterly
income statement. But in the case of a loan over a term as long as one year,
the use of accounting techniques other than deferral accounting could substantially mislead shareholders.

Table 6 shows the futures market yields that determined the ultimate cost
of funding the fixed rate loan in this example. The table was constructed using
actual futures yields on the appropriate 90-day Treasury bill contracts at
mid-month beginning in September, 1978. Table 7 shows futures gains and
losses by quarter and by futures contract.

The quarterly gains and losses on all hedges are calculated by summing

TABLE 5

Performance of Fixed Rate Loan
September, 1978–September, 1979

	Revenue and Cost	Yields
Revenue from loan	$1,850,000	9.25%
Cost of funding loan *without* CD hedge	$1,902,000	9.50%
Cost of funding loan *with* CD hedge	$1,718,000	8.59%
Net gain from using futures hedges	$ 183,500	.92%

TABLE 6

Treasury Bill Futures Yields at Quarterly Statement Dates

Futures Contract Months

Beginning of Quarter	September	December	March	June
Q1		7.94	8.05	8.14
Q2		9.34	9.39	9.50
Q3			9.54	9.50
Q4				8.92

TABLE 7

Futures Gains and Losses by Quarter for Each Futures Contract

Futures Contract Months

Quarter Ending	December	March	June	Total Quarterly Futures Gains
Q1	$70,000	$67,000	$68,000	$205,000
Q2	——	7,500	——	7,500
Q3	——	——	−29,000	−29,000
Total gains for each futures contract	$70,000	$74,500	$39,000	——
Total futures gains and losses				$183,500

the entries in Table 7 horizontally. For example, the futures gain during the first quarterly accounting period (Q1) is the cumulative gain in the December, 1978, March, 1979, and June, 1979, futures contracts (first entry in the column on the far right). With deferral or hedge accounting the futures position is entered on the balance sheet at the time the hedge is closed by lifting the futures hedge and issuing the CD. That is, the sum of the columns in Table 7, which represent accumulated gains and losses for a given futures contract, are entered in the income statement at the time the cash CD is issued and the futures position is liquidated. For example, the accumulated gains on the June, 1979, futures contract are entered in June, when a three-month CD is issued to refund the loan. The futures gains and losses due to the cash item being hedged and the cost of the cash item itself are entered on the bank income statement simultaneously. The result is displayed in Table 8 (page 333).

The Synthetic Fixed Rate Certificate of Deposit: Covering the Risk of Rising Interest Costs. Stabilizing the costs of funding inventories and capital expenditures will be one of the key problems bank corporate customers will

TABLE 8

Balance Sheet with Hedge Accounting

Quarter	Interest Income	(−)	Interest Cost	(+)	Futures Gains and Losses	(=)	Net Income
Q1	$ 462,500		$ 397,500		$ ——		$ 65,000
Q2	462,500		508,000		70,000		24,500
Q3	462,500		498,500		74,500		39,000
Q4	462,500		498,500		39,000		3,000
		(−)		(+)		(=)	
Total	$1,850,000		$1,902,000		$183,500		$131,500

face during the 1980s. The ideal solution is to turn the volatile costs of borrowing into fixed costs—a goal that can be reached with fixed rate loans. By and large, the corporate treasurer cannot now look to his banker for low-cost fixed rate loans. After all, the banker himself is exposed to the risk that volatile interest rates create, and before the advent of interest rate futures, he was forced to pass much of this risk along to corporate treasurers through the floating rate loan. For the most part, the cost of floating rate loans may vary on a day-to-day basis and is tied to the prime rate, which in turn is tied to the banker's cost of funds. In this treacherous environment there is demand by corporations for the reduced interest rate risk that fixed rate loans can provide. One of the tools that banks have not yet fully exploited in attempting to meet corporate needs is the interest rate futures market. Using this market, banks may grant fixed rate loans while simultaneously reducing their own interest rate risk.

The use of futures to cover the risk created by floating rate loans should also provide the astute banker some important secondary benefits once he has established a hedging program. As bankers are painfully aware, extremely volatile and unpredictable changes in a borrower's loan rates have sometimes created cash flow problems of sufficient magnitude to induce workout situations that endanger both the corporation and its banker. By using interest rate futures contracts—thus preventing these situations—the bank can be sure that loans made to the corporation are less likely to jeopardize the cash flow of the corporate borrower, and the bank can also encourage new customers to borrow funds.

The most important concern for a banker intending to use futures contracts to cover his interest rate risk is that there may be a difference between the change in the cost of funds borrowed to issue the loan and the change in the yield on the futures contract itself. Fortunately, there are some straightforward procedures for determining this risk. Table 1 (page 326) describes some historical risk experience. This table illustrates the extent to which the imperfect relationship between changes in Treasury bill futures yields and the three-month certificate of deposit rate will affect a hedge of a fixed rate loan. As the table shows, the risk implicit in this arrangement depends on the period over which the hedge is maintained. The longer that period, the greater the extent to which the futures position reduces the risk of borrowing in the CD market.

With a one-day hedge there is less than a 2 percent decline in risk, whereas with a hedge maintained for a month, the reduction becomes 80 percent. Table 1 also gives estimates of the size of the "hedge ratio," the ratio of dollar value of futures position to dollar value of borrowings which will minimize the risk implicit in the prime rate loan. As the table indicates, for a hedge maintained over a period as long as a month, the ratio is roughly 125 percent. That is, for every $1 million borrowed, $1,250,000 worth of futures contracts should be sold. But, with the cooperation of a CD dealer and a little ingenuity, the risk of an adverse change in the CD rate relative to the futures hedge can be eliminated. This could be done by using the Treasury bill futures contract, rather than another market rate, to determine the price of the CD.

If the bank set its borrowing rate using the futures market price, rather than a cash market price, and hedged its CD with a futures contract, the yield on the CD could be floated in tandem with market rates, because any increase in the cost of funds to the bank would be exactly offset by margin payments on the bank's futures position. With this change in bank debt management policy, a fixed rate loan could be funded by a fixed rate CD from the point of view of the bank, and a floating rate CD from the point of view of the dealer. The example described in Tables 9 and 10 illustrates how this procedure would work. Table 9 describes the bank's earnings on the loan (column 1), the interest cost of the CD sold to the dealer before margin earnings (column 2), and the hedge ratio (column 3) during the first ten days of December, 1979.

The loan is issued on December 3 at a fixed rate 250 points above the December Treasury bill futures yield and funded through a CD issued at a

TABLE 9

Interest Yields on Loan and Interest Cost of Floating Rate C Ds

Date		Loan Rate	C D Interest Cost	Hedge Ratio	Interest Cost Reduction Due to Hedge	Net Interest Cost
Dec.	3	13.92	12.92	.156	Entry	12.92
	4	13.92	12.92	.144	—	12.92
	5	13.92	12.97	.133	.05	12.92
	6	13.92	12.92	.122	—	12.92
	7	13.92	13.66	.111	.74	12.92
	10	13.92	13.36	.078	.44	12.92
	11	13.92	13.58	.067	.66	12.92
	12	13.92	13.65	.055	.73	12.92
	13	13.92	13.91	.044	.99	12.92
	14	13.92	13.72	.033	.80	12.92

150-point premium to the December futures contract, but floating with it on a day-to-day basis. The hedge ratio gives the ratio of futures positions to loan size (contracts per million) to reduce the risk. The ratio declines as hedges are lifted at the time the rollover is done.

The effect of the hedge maintained at the declining hedge ratio of the far right column of Table 9 is to reduce the floating rate CD to a fixed rate CD from the point of view of the bank. The spread between the loan and the CD is exactly 100 points—the yield on the loan is 13.92 percent; the cost of the CD, 12.92 percent. So from the point of view of the bank, a fixed rate loan is being financed by a fixed rate CD. From the point of view of the dealer, the yield on the CD is floating on an overnight basis.

Table 10 shows the earnings on the CD, assuming that the dealer financed the CD by borrowing through overnight repurchase agreements. As the table illustrates, on days when the dealer's borrowing rate rises due to increases in overnight market yields, the increase in cost is offset to a great extent by margin payments, so that the bank basically "passes through" the margin payments and calls to the dealer.

There are variations on this basic theme—turning the floating rate CD to a fixed rate CD with T-bill futures. Suppose that instead of floating the CD on a daily basis, the bank decided to revise the loan rate on a weekly basis, using Monday's settlement prices for T-bill futures. This would work to the dealer's benefit if he is interested in floating the CD rate less frequently than daily.

The bank could then set the loan rate 250 points above the T-bill futures price as before. The dealer would buy the CD at a 100-point premium as before, but adjust it only on a weekly basis. The dealer's results for the same two-week period would be as shown in Table 11 (page 336).

TABLE 10

Dealer's Interest Earnings and Costs

Date	C D Earnings	Overnight Repo Rate	Differences
Dec. 3	12.92	12.50	0.42
4	12.92	12.50	0.42
5	12.97	11.88	1.09
6	12.92	12.75	0.20
7	13.66	13.00	0.66
10	13.36	13.13	0.20
11	13.58	13.25	0.23
12	13.65	13.00	0.65
13	13.91	14.00	(0.09)
14	13.72	12.50	1.22
Average	13.35	12.85	0.50

TABLE 11

Dealer Earnings Synthetic C D II

Week Beginning Date	Loan Earnings	Cost of Funds	Difference
Dec. 3	12.92	12.50	.42
Dec.10	13.36	13.00	.36
Average	13.14	12.75	.39

Table 12 shows the net income from the loan funded by the CD as in the first example.

TABLE 12

Net Income Synthetic C D II

Week Beginning	Earnings on Loan	Cost of C D	Margin Earnings	Net Interest Cost	Hedge Ratio
Dec. 3	13.92	12.92	——	12.92	.078
Dec. 10	13.92	13.36	.44	12.92	

Thus, using the futures markets, both the bank and the dealer are "hedged." The bank is hedged because its costs of funds and its earnings are fixed. The dealer, on the other hand, is hedged by the bank's ability, using futures, to sell the dealer a CD that floats with T-bill futures prices on a day-to-day basis along with the dealer's cost of funds.

HEDGING IN EURO-OPERATIONS

One potential bank use of futures markets is in Eurodollar operations. Here futures can be used to take positions consistent with the bank's interest rate forecast. For example, a Eurodollar banker who believes that future spot rates will be higher than current rates would ordinarily sell longer-maturity accounts and buy shorter-maturity Eurodollar accounts, anticipating a capital gain as rates rise. But, for a number of reasons, the Eurodollar cash market is not a perfect vehicle for taking positions based on forecasts of interest rates. One reason is that it is a market characterized by limits on the amount of deposits one bank will be willing to place at another bank. That is, each bank has a credit line with every other bank, and in selling cash (buying deposits), banks will not go above the limits of their credit line to the other bank. As a result, the lesser names in the Euromarket have difficulty from time to time in selling their own time deposits, while the prime names in the Euromarket have trouble finding acceptable deposits of other banks. Hence, it can be difficult quickly to enter or balance an exposed position using the cash market. This situation, where credit limits between traders prevent them from otherwise mutually beneficial transactions, is typical of forward markets and has formed the basis for establishing other futures markets.

A futures market improves on a forward market by allowing traders to buy from and sell to one another without exposure to the credit risk of the parties with whom they trade. Using futures, the bank could offset positions it might have taken in the cash market without concern for the credit risk of the trader on the opposite side because the Exchange acts as a buyer to every seller and a seller to every buyer. So, although it is possible to hedge market risk in the Eurodollar cash market, it is much easier and safer to do so in the Treasury bill futures market.

Table 13 describes hedge ratios and the percentage of cash market risk exposure that the futures market offsets for Eurodollars. As the table indicates, the relationships between three-month Eurodollars and Treasury bill futures are similar to the corresponding relationships between domestic CDs and Treasury bill futures.

Table 13

**Hedge Performance of 90-Day T-Bill
Futures Contracts Against
Three-Month Eurodollar Offer Rates
(LIBOR)
June 1, 1978–May 30, 1980**

Time Period	Hedge Ratio	Percentage Reduction in Risk
Daily	.193	.028
Weekly	.947	.453
Monthly	1.313	.805

CONCLUSION

The intent of this chapter has been to illustrate a few basic ways in which banks can use futures markets to stabilize and improve their earnings, while concomitantly serving their corporate customers more effectively than they do today. There would seem to be little doubt that the skillful use of futures contracts can help banking institutions compete in a world of varied credit resources. Specifically, the use of futures should help to dissuade a bank's most creditworthy customers from shifting to the commercial paper market as a major source of credit.

As this chapter illustrates, the areas of bank operations that are presently the most logical candidates for using Treasury bill futures are (1) dealer operations, (2) liability management and loan policy, and (3) Euro-operations. The examples given for using the contracts in each of these areas are illustrative only. Many others could be provided, and there are undoubtedly hundreds of imaginative, innovative ways for using financial futures that have not yet been conceived. Though futures markets have provided a risk management mechanism to agriculture for more than a hundred years, they are a relatively new phenomenon to the financial community. Banks and other financial institutions are really only beginning to learn how to use them to manage their own risks, and to help customers manage their risks. As a consequence, we can expect major innovations to take place in this area of activity over the next decade or two. Banks which are postured to take advantage of those innovations (or, even more importantly, innovate ahead of their competitors) will be much more successful in the coming years than will those which fail to understand and master this new mechanism.

Though this chapter describes just three areas of bank operations where futures can now feasibly be used, that too should not be considered a managerial constraint. The three enumerated here are presently the most logical areas, but some banks are already discovering broader uses. Depending on how a particular bank is organized, and on the size and scope of its banking activities, one can certainly perceive the legitimate and profitable use of futures markets in many other areas of bank operations a decade from now. In this dynamic, rapidly changing industry—with new futures contracts emerging continually—there should be no constraints on sound managerial innovation.

A few years from now futures trading will be second nature to thousands of people in the banking world. Today, however, there is still much to learn about this newly available risk management mechanism.

Appendix

THE MODEL

The model specification is $CD = B_0 + B_1(TBF) + u_i$, where CD is changes in secondary market yields for three-month certificates of deposit, TBF is changes in the IMM's 90-day Treasury bill futures, and u_i is the random disturbance term. The significant t-statistic for the regression coefficient, B_1, indicates a direct relationship between the explanatory and dependent variables.

DESCRIPTION OF DATA

Using daily, weekly, and monthly data, this time-series analysis considers two periods: March 1, 1976, through May 30, 1980, and the shortened interval, June 1, 1978, through May 30, 1980. Trading in 90-day Treasury bills at the Chicago Mercantile Exchange was initiated in January, 1976. Since there is a start-up time associated with a new futures contract during which traders "test the water" and many potential users of the market do not as yet know of the existence of the contract, the shorter time period was studied to test whether over time there has been a shift in the overall relationship between T-bill futures and certificates of deposit.

All data series were retrieved from Data Resources, Inc. The 90-day secondary CD series is defined by DRI as "General market offering rates for the top seven U.S. commercial banks as perceived by the Bank of America."

By "gluing" together the settlement prices for nearby options present throughout the relevant time period, the Treasury bill futures data series was created. The nearby option was used, however, only until the first day of the delivery month. So, for example, as of March 1 the March contract month is not used, but the series switches to the June contract month.

Weekly changes were from last trading day of the week, usually changes in Friday-to-Friday settlement prices. Similarly, monthly data were from the last day of one month to the last day of the next month. Regressions relate to daily, weekly, or monthly rate changes in CD and T-bill futures contracts.

EMPIRICAL RESULTS

1976–1980. According to the t-statistics presented in Table 1 (page 000), in all cases TBF is significantly different from zero whereas all the decoy terms are not significantly different from zero.

The correlation coefficients suggest that on a short-term basis the degree of linear association between yield changes in T-bill futures and CDs is not high; however, as the length of time increases to a week and to a month, the correlation (and corresponding risk reduction) rises.

According to the R^2 for the regression, with daily changes 11.39% of the variation in the dependent variable is captured by the variation in the independent variable. Entering and exiting the futures market within the day translates to a 11.39% reduction in interest rate risk exposure. The R^2 rises to 44.05% when weekly data are used, and increases further to 77.58% using monthly intervals.

On a day-to-day basis the hedge ratio is roughly four to one: for every four cash three-month CDs issued, one T-bill futures contract should have been sold. On a week-by-week basis, the coefficient for the explanatory variable becomes about .8. Roughly five CDs would have been hedged with four T-bills. Finally, the coefficient for month-long hedges is about 1.2. In other words, according to the regressions, on a monthly basis every five CDs ought to be hedged with six T-bill futures contracts.

1978–1980. Comparison of the regression results from this shortened time period with those from the previous time interval confirms that in the second period a change in the relationship between yield changes in 90-day T-bill futures and 90-day CDs indeed has occurred. Over time, hedging CD interest rate exposure with T-bill futures has become a more effective strategy.

As was true for the last set of regressions, in all cases the t-statistics for the coefficients of the independent variable are significant while those for the constant term are insignificant. As evidenced by the daily, weekly, and monthly correlation matrices, in all instances relative to the 1976–1980 period the strength of the linear association between rate changes in T-bill futures and CDs for the 1978–1980 time period is greater.

According to the R^2 period of 1978–1980 as compared to 1976–1980, for all data frequencies a larger percentage of the variability in the dependent variable is explained by the variation in the independent variable. Previously, for example, on a day-by-day basis 11.39% of interest rate risk exposure was eliminated by hedging CDs with T-bill futures. Now, 11.95% of this exposure is removed. The hedger who remains in the futures market for monthly periods is afforded the opportunity to eliminate 82.28% of his exposure to interest rate risk, whereas during the 1976–1980 time period only 77.58% of this exposure was eliminated.

25

Unaudited Financial Statements Past and Present

Lenders today are required to make extremely difficult decisions regarding the allocation of credit to prospective borrowers. In order to make such decisions intelligently, lenders should take advantage of every available bit of information they can secure about their potential borrowers. The basic documents required in all but the smallest lending institutions include the financial statements of the borrower. Obviously, in the case of major credits, the lender will usually require a complete set of audited financial statements, including a balance sheet, statement of operations, statement of equity, and statement of changes in financial position, together with the related opinion of the independent accountant. But what about the situation in which either the size of the proposed loan or the potential borrower's financial condition is such that the cost of securing an independent audit is prohibitive? In terms of numbers of transactions, this situation probably occurs much more frequently than those in which audited financial statements are available. In such situations the lender must walk a delicate line between granting a loan based on insufficient information and allowing what may be the start of a long-lasting and highly rewarding banking relationship to go to a competitor.

Unaudited Financial Statements—Past Tense

Unaudited financial statements can be a significant help in an attempt to bridge the gap between inadequate financial information and that which is too costly.

The use of such statements and the extent of reliance to be placed on them must be tempered, however, by a realistic understanding of the conditions under which they were prepared and the extent of involvement of the outside accountant in their preparation. Prior to December, 1978, it was virtually impossible for the user of unaudited financial statements to determine for himself how much (or how little) work had been done by the independent accountant in their preparation, because the information which the accountant was allowed by professional standards to include in his report was extremely limited. This is the only form of opinion which was permitted:

The accompanying [list of financial statements covered] were not audited by us and accordingly we do not express an opinion on them.

[Accountant's signature and date]

The accountant was not permitted to enumerate any procedures he had performed during the course of his review or to give anything other than this rather uninformative disclaimer. Certainly, if he became aware of any information which would render the financial statements misleading or inaccurate in any material regard, he was obliged to insist upon their revision, and if they were not appropriately revised, he was required to set forth his reservations in his disclaimer. Further, if the client was unwilling to accept one of these alternatives, the accountant could not be associated with the financial statements and was prohibited from even typing or reproducing them.

This rather narrow scenario provided (and rightfully so) only the coldest of comfort to the users of such unaudited financial statements. As a practical matter, however, the preparation of many such statements had involved a great deal of time and effort on the part of the independent accountant. The participation of the independent accountant in the preparation of unaudited financial statements might have ranged from extracting the information from the client's books, arranging it in appropriate financial statement format, and tying it to the performance of selected verification procedures. The accountant may have relied almost entirely on representations of management or he may have performed limited audit procedures such as a review of the collectibility of accounts receivable, review of inventory pricing and cost accounting records, or an analysis of the client's compliance with the capitalization requirements of leases.

The extent to which these procedures were performed varied from client to client and accountant to accountant. An apparently not unreasonable assumption (although a perhaps somewhat idealistic one) made by the users of many such financial statements was that the accountant had become involved in the preparation of the unaudited financial statements to the extent required for him to obtain a reasonable level of assurance that they were not grossly inaccurate. From the standpoint of the users, however, there was one glaring deficiency with this approach. Many times they were unable to differentiate between those financial statements which had received the benefit of in-depth preparation procedures and those with which the accountant had had minimal involvement.

The New Era

In early 1979 much of the uncertainty on the part of the user regarding the extent of the independent accountant's involvement with unaudited financial statements was removed when the American Institute of Certified Public Accountants (AICPA) authorized the performance of a two-class approach to the preparation of unaudited financial statements in the first of a series of documents entitled *Statements on Standards for Accounting and Review Services* (SSARS). The SSARS relates only to *nonpublic* entities as defined in that document—basically, those entities whose securities are not traded in a public market or who have not filed with a regulatory agency in anticipation of a sale in a public market.

One of the types of service authorized by the SSARS, a compilation, closely parallels the minimum level of procedures which had been performed prior to issuance of SSARS 1, and the other, a review service, involves the application of more involved procedures which permit the accountant to provide limited assurance that the financial statements do not require material modification to be in conformity with generally accepted accounting principles. It is essential for a potential lender who may rely on unaudited financial statements to understand the nature and extent of procedures performed by an accountant during a compilation or review of such statements and how to recognize the difference.

Compilation of Financial Statements

The unaudited financial statement compilation is little more than management's representation of financial data on which the independent accountant provides no assurance. Although the accountant providing compilation services should have a working knowledge of the accounting principles and practices peculiar to his client's industry, as well as the nature of that client's business transactions, accounting records, and stated qualifications of its key accounting personnel, he is not obligated to perform any analytical procedures or to make direct inquiries of management regarding the financial data compiled. He may need, however, to make certain inquiries in order to obtain the data necessary to compile adequately the entity's financial statements. For example, inquiries may be necessary to determine the amount of bad debts and obsolete inventory for which management believes provision should be made. Also, inquiries as to the existence of contingent liabilities and significant subsequent events are appropriate.

The inquiries and procedures performed, if any, in a compilation of financial statements are a matter of the accountant's judgment. In tailoring the nature and scope of inquiries and procedures, he will consider the information to be used to compile the financial statements and the related records generated by the entity's accounting system. For example, if the accountant, based on his knowledge of the entity, is aware that the entity's personnel do not regularly perform bank reconciliations or subsidiary ledger to general ledger control account reconciliations, he should normally inquire as to whether these procedures have been performed for the period to be reported on. If inquiry discloses that these types of procedures have not been performed, the accountant ordinarily should request the entity's personnel to complete the necessary procedures.

The preceding discussion is not intended to imply that the accountant is required to make inquiries or perform other procedures to verify, corroborate, or review information supplied by the entity. However, because of the background understanding he may have of the entity's books, records, and accounting personnel as a result of his previous association with the client, the accountant may become aware that the information supplied by the entity may be incomplete or incorrect. It is in these circumstances that the accountant will normally obtain additional or revised information.

Current accounting literature permits the accountant, at management's request, to compile financial statements that omit substantially all disclosures, including the statement of changes in financial position, provided that (1) the omission of substantially all disclosures is clearly indicated in his report, and (2) the omission is not, to his knowledge, undertaken with the intention of misleading those who might reasonably be expected to use such financial statements. Additionally, an accountant performing a compilation is not required to be "independent" of his client, provided the lack of independence is disclosed in his report on the financial statements.

As discussed above, these requirements of the accounting profession related to a compilation of financial statements do not differ substantially from those which were encumbent upon accountants prior to the issuance of SSARS 1. The accountant's standard report resulting from a compilation engagement briefly describes his association with the financial information and should leave little doubt in the reader's mind as to the degree of assurance provided by the accountant's report, as in this example:

The accompanying [list of financial statements covered] have been compiled by us. A compilation is limited to presenting in the form of financial statements information that is the representation of management. We have *not audited or reviewed* the accompanying financial statements and, accordingly, *do not express an opinion* or any other form of assurance on them [emphasis added].

[Accountant's signature and date]

The accountant refers only to the compilation of financial information in his standard report and is not permitted to describe any of the supplementary procedures he *may* have performed incidental to that compilation. In other words, the ultimate users of the financial statements must assume that no audit or review procedures have been performed and would be wise to temper their reliance on the financial information accordingly.

Review of Financial Statements

For those lenders who require more assurance than that provided by a compilation of financial statements (which will probably be the situation in most cases) but who are not in a position to request their customers to engage the services of an independent accountant to perform a complete audit, because of either costs or time or other constraints, the concept of the financial statement review may provide a satisfactory alternative. Although presumably less reliable than audited financial statements, statements which have been subjected to review procedures provide the user with *limited assurance* that the financial information presented is in accordance with generally accepted accounting principles. In order to provide such assurance, the accountant (who is required to be "independent" of his client in a review engagement) performs certain procedures in addition to those performed in a compilation. Such additional procedures consist primarily of inquiries and analytical procedures and do not include most of the independent verification steps which are normally an integral part of a full-scope audit of financial statements.

To review financial statements, the accountant should possess or obtain an understanding of the entity's industry and business, and specialized accounting practices, if any. Understanding the entity's business will usually include a general understanding of the entity's organization, personnel, basic accounting records, its operating characteristics, and the nature of its assets, liabilities, revenues, and expenses. Such an understanding would also ordinarily include a general knowledge of the entity's production, distribution, and compensation methods, types of products and services, operating locations, and material transactions with related parties. An accountant's understanding of an entity's business is ordinarily obtained through experience with the entity or its industry and inquiry of the entity's personnel. Obviously, the most in-depth understanding of the client's operations will exist in those situations in which the accountant has a long-standing relationship with his client developed over a period of years.

It is incumbent upon the accountant to perform inquiry and analytical procedures in a review engagement. Briefly, such procedures and inquiries might include the following:

- Inquiries concerning the entity's accounting principles and practices and the methods followed in applying them
- Inquiries concerning the entity's procedures for recording, classifying,

and summarizing transactions, and accumulating information for disclosure in the financial statements

- Inquiries concerning actions taken at meetings of stockholders, the board of directors, committees of the board of directors, or comparable meetings that may affect the financial statements
- Inquiries of persons having responsibility for financial and accounting matters concerning (1) whether the financial statements have been prepared in conformity with generally accepted accounting principles consistently applied; (2) changes in the entity's business activities or accounting principles and practices; (3) matters as to which questions have arisen in the course of applying the foregoing procedures; and (4) events subsequent to the date of the financial statements that would have a material effect on the financial statements

The inquiries made by the accountant during his review are predicated on his judgment, considering the nature and materiality of financial statement amounts, as well as the likelihood of errors or misrepresentation of specific items. In essence, the accountant attempts to determine through his inquiries whether any unusual transactions have occurred and whether financial data are properly recorded, classified, and summarized in the accounting records. The accountant's procedures include:

- Reading the financial statements to consider, on the basis of information coming to the accountant's attention, whether the financial statements appear to conform with generally accepted accounting principles
- Obtaining reports from other accountants, if any, who have been engaged to audit or review the financial statements of significant components of the reporting entity, its subsidiaries, and other investees
- Analytical procedures designed to identify relationships and individual items that appear to be unusual. Analytical procedures should include (1) comparison of the financial statements with statements for comparable prior period(s), (2) comparison of the financial statements with anticipated results, if available (for example, budgets and forecasts), and (3) study of the relationships of the elements of the financial statements that would be expected to conform to a predictable pattern based on the entity's experience.

These review procedures may be modified or extended based upon knowledge obtained while performing them or as a result of problems encountered in previous relationships with the client. Procedures will normally be modified or extended when the accountant becomes aware that information coming to his attention is incorrect or incomplete; *or* when he believes that the client has not maintained certain aspects of his accounting system that are important to financial statement preparation.

Examples of situations in which the accountant might consider extending his procedures are:

- Subsidiary ledgers not reconciled to their related general ledger control accounts
- Accounts payable or other material payables not supported by a detail listing
- Bank accounts not reconciled
- Inventories not based upon physical count, reasonable gross profit percentage, perpetual records, or other reasonable basis

Inquiry and limited analytical and other procedures, effectively applied by an experienced professional, can be extremely productive in the review of financial statements; nevertheless, it is important that those who rely on such financial statements understand the limitations of these procedures, especially when, as is normally the case in a review, they are not supported by independent verifications of the representations of management. Assuming the answers received by the accountant in the course of making the necessary inquiries during a financial statement review "make sense" to him, he will have complied with his professional standards.

It should be evident that a review does not provide the same degree of assurance as does an audit. Whereas an audit includes independent verification of amounts in financial statements, a review generally consists of limited inquiry and analytical procedures designed only to identify those relationships or individual amounts that appear unusual and thus subject to error and further investigation.

Although the accountant's standard report for a review makes clear the distinction between audited and reviewed financial statements, a reading of this report, as contrasted with the compilation report set forth above, should also leave little doubt in the reader's mind as to their relative advantages and disadvantages. Following is the standard review report:

We have reviewed the [list of financial statements] in accordance with standards established by the American Institute of Certified Public Accountants. All information included in these financial statements is the representation of management.

A review consists principally of inquiries of company personnel and analytical procedures applied to financial data. It is *substantially less in scope than an examination in accordance with generally accepted auditing standards,* the objective of which is the expression of an opinion regarding the financial statements taken as a whole. Accordingly, *we do not express such an opinion* [emphasis added].

Based on our review, we are not aware of any material modifications that should be made to the accompanying financial statements in order for them to be in conformity with generally accepted accounting principles.

[Accountant's Signature and Date]

A review of financial statements may (or may not) bring to light material misstatements or errors in the financial information presented. However, financial statement readers must be aware that a review, similar to a compilation, is not performed in accordance with generally accepted auditing standards. Hence, the accountant does not express an opinion on the financial statements taken as a whole, and the reader has the somewhat cool comfort that the accountant, after performing limited procedures, is not aware of any material modifications required in order for the statements to conform with generally accepted accounting principles.

The following may be helpful in summarizing certain of the more significant differences between the various types of unaudited financial statements and those which have been subjected to an audit.

Condition	Unaudited Financial Statements		Audited Financial Statements
	Compilation	Review	
Type of assurance	None	Negative assurance on GAAP*	Opinion on fair presentation as to GAAP* and consistency
Procedures performed	None normally required	Inquiry and analytical procedures	Independent verification procedures in accordance with GAAS†
Accountant's independence	Not required (but must be disclosed, if not)	Required	Required

*Generally accepted accounting principles promulgated by authoritative accounting literature, including Financial Accounting Standards Board Opinions, Accounting Principles Board Options, and AICPA Accounting Research Bulletins.
†Generally accepted auditing standards as adopted by the AICPA.

Except in the case of compiled financial statements in which the issuer has elected to omit substantially all disclosures, as discussed earlier, unaudited financial statements, whether compiled or reviewed, as well as audited financial statements, are required to contain similar disclosures—those mandated by generally accepted accounting principles. Therefore, in theory at least, except for the accountant's report accompanying them, audited, reviewed, or compiled financial statements should appear the same. For example, each set of financial statements should contain a summary of significant accounting policies, "capital" leases (as defined in accounting literature) should be accounted for and disclosed appropriately, and commitments and contingent liabilities should be disclosed in the notes to the financial statements. As a practical matter, however, various surveys have been made from time to time which indicate that often unaudited financial statements do *not* contain many of the disclosures (and at times, appropriate accounting treatment) required by the body of authoritative accounting literature.

By this time the reader should have a fair understanding of the conceptual differences between audited and unaudited financial statements and an appreciation of the degree of outside involvement which distinguishes financial statements which have been reviewed from those that have been compiled. This knowledge is beneficial to a potential lender, however, only if he knows how to make use of it in his relationship with his customer. What can a lender do to make certain that he will receive the benefit he expects from the unaudited financial statements to be provided by his borrower and at the same time keep the borrower's cost at a reasonable level?

An Alternative Approach

The first step, obviously, is to make certain that all interested parties are in agreement as to the type of accountant's report to be issued on the financial statements and the work to be done by the outside accountant in their preparation. In order to achieve such a meeting of the minds, it is often helpful for the lender, the borrower, and the borrower's accountant to meet prior to the accountant beginning his work to discuss the relative merits of a compilation, a review, and an audit. At this time the lender should indicate his areas of primary concern (inventory, accounts receivable, etc.) with the financial statements and ascertain the nature and extent of procedures to be performed by the accountant in that area.

In the event such procedures are deemed to be insufficient for the lender's purposes, there are various alternatives which may be considered. The engagement may be upgraded (from a compilation to a review, or from a review to an audit) or the accountant may perform certain specified procedures on one or more specified elements, accounts, or items in the financial statements. In such a case the accountant will insist that all parties involved have a clear understanding of the procedures to be performed (normally by reducing the understanding to writing), distribution of the report so prepared will be restricted to the parties involved in the actual or proposed transaction, and financial statements of the entity will not be allowed to accompany the report on the specified procedures.

Upon completion of the procedures discussed above, the accountant should be able to issue a report similar to the following:

We have applied certain agreed-upon procedures, as discussed below, to accounting records of [name of company], as of [date], solely to assist you in connection with [purpose of engagement]. It is understood that this report is solely for your information and is not to be referred to or distributed to anyone not a member of [parties to proposed transaction] for any purpose. Our procedures and findings are as follows:
[Detailed discussion of procedures and findings]
Because the above procedures were not sufficient to constitute an examination made

in accordance with generally accepted auditing standards, we do not express an opinion on any of the specific accounts referred to above. In connection with the procedures referred to above, no matters came to our attention that caused us to believe that the [specified elements, accounts, or items] should be adjusted. Had we performed additional procedures or had we made an examination of the financial statements in accordance with generally accepted auditing standards, matters might have come to our attention that would have been reported to you. This report should not be associated with the financial statements of [name of company] for the year ended [date].

[Accountant's Signature and Date]

Following completion of the accountant's work in connection with one of the various types of unaudited financial statements, it may be beneficial for the lender to meet with the borrower and the accountant who prepared the financial statements in order to give the lender the opportunity to discuss the types of procedures performed by the accountant, his findings, and any other matters which may be of significance to the lender. The accountant will normally insist upon his client being present at such a meeting, and in those cases in which he is not present, he will insist that his client authorize him (preferably in writing) to participate. This procedure also gives the potential borrower the opportunity to make any commentary or supplemental explanation which may not be apparent from reading the financial statements.

CONCLUSION

The years ahead bring a need for education related to the preparation, presentation, and resulting reliance which can be placed on financial information with which independent accountants are associated. It is essential that both those who engage the services of independent accountants and those who are the ultimate users of the product of their efforts understand the types of procedures performed prior to reliance on either audited or unaudited information. Although many entities are required by outside investors, lenders, regulators, or other interested parties to have an examination performed in accordance with generally accepted auditing standards, in other circumstances it may not be prudent or practical to do so. (This is becoming particularly true with the increased emphasis by government, industry, and the professions on meeting the needs of "small business" enterprises.) Cost, degree of investor or creditor involvement in daily business operations, current economic conditions, and competency and reliability of in-house expertise are but a few of the criteria to be weighed in determining to what degree independent accountants should be involved in the preparation and presentation of financial information. No matter which approach is determined to best suit the needs of a particular business, it must be emphasized that the business community in general should become intimately familiar not only with the various types of financial statement services provided by independent accountants, but also the varying degree of reliance that can be placed on their final products.

26

Loan Loss Reserve Management and Unwise Lending Practices

The decade of the seventies proved to be a very unsettling one for many bankers. Not having been in banking during the depression period of 1929–40, most lending officials had become accustomed to the relative economic stability that prevailed for more than twenty years following the Korean War. Inflation was not a serious problem and interest rate fluctuations were relatively moderate. As a result, losses on commercial loans never became a significant problem for bankers. Indeed, bankers were mostly complacent concerning the risks inherent in their loan portfolios. Yet, this complacency was to dissipate quickly as commercial banks faced the more tumultuous economic environment of the 1970s. Loan losses soared at many institutions, while reserves were depleted. Loan loss accounting, a subject previously relegated only to theoretical discussion, suddenly became a concern for bank management. What was an adequate level of reserve? How could one measure the risk inherent in a loan portfolio? What lending practices could be adopted to reduce future loan losses? These and similar questions became the central topics of conversation among bankers and remain so currently. Indeed, even though the decade of the eighties commenced with a sharply lower level of actual loan loss experience, these questions remain relevant. Few if any economists are willing to characterize the outlook for the economy of the next ten years as one displaying stability. To the contrary, most expect a period of violent, oftentimes unpredictable change. It is within this context that this chapter will explore the questions of loan loss reserve management and unwise lending policies.

The Development of Loan Loss Accounting

Prior to 1969, losses on loans did not flow through the reported earnings statement. Rather, additions via recoveries and deductions via losses were directly credited to or debited from the loan loss reserve which itself had been established by transfers from the undivided profits account. Additional supplements to the loan loss reserve in excess of the transfer from undivided profits representing net charge-offs were possible under Internal Revenue Service guidelines in effect prior to 1969. Transfers from undivided profits were permissible until the loan loss reserve equaled 2.4 percent of average outstanding loans. The attraction to the banker was that for every dollar of retained income that was transferred to the reserve, one was allowed also to transfer the deferred taxes that theoretically had been paid on that income. In the accounting parlance of that time, the transfer from retained income became the contingency portion of the reserve while the tax savings became the deferred tax portion. The absolute size of the reserve was determined by Internal Revenue Service regulations and had no relation to actual or estimated loss experience.

Beginning in 1969, two significant changes were required in the accounting for loan losses. First, it was determined rather arbitrarily that what was considered the total reserve for loan losses (the tax reserve) as of December 31, 1968, would now be considered a valuation reserve. Additions to this reserve could now only be made by expense provisions taken above the line or by loan loss recoveries that would be credited to the reserve. All actual losses would be charged directly to the reserve. Second, the provisions for loan losses running through the income statement would be determined either by an average formula calculation or by the direct experience method. Since the latter method meant that provisions in any one year would have to equal net charge-offs sustained during that year, thereby leading to potential earnings volatility, most larger banks opted for the formula method, which allowed for a smoothing of the impact of loan losses. Basically, a bank would find the ratio of net charge-offs to average loans for the past four years as well as the current year. This ratio would then be applied to the level of loans currently outstanding to determine the provision that would be charged to the income statement. If the provision determined by the formula exceeded actual net charge-offs for the period, the valuation reserve would obviously rise, and vice versa.

The changes outlined above affected financial reporting books but not tax books. Revised Internal Revenue Service guidelines still allowed for transfers from retained earnings pursuant to a declining percentage schedule. To the extent these tax formulas allowed additions to the reserve in excess of those determined by formula for financial reporting purposes, the contingency and deferred tax portions of the reserve reemerged. From the viewpoint of financial reporting books, the contingency portion was created by transfers from retained earnings, while the deferred tax portion consisted of those taxes that theoretically would have been paid to increase the retained earnings account. It should be emphasized that while prior to 1976 banks showed one total reserve on the liability side of the balance sheet, only the valuation portion was available to absorb losses. The contingency and deferred tax portions, having arisen out of the difference between book and tax reporting, were not available to absorb losses. For balance sheet presentation subsequent to December 31, 1975, the loan loss reserve was removed from the liability side of the balance sheet. The valuation portion was netted as a contra asset against loans, while the contingency portion was returned to retained earnings and the deferred tax portion was transferred to other liabilities.

For the first few years following the introduction of the formula in 1969, loss experience was not appreciably different from the average figure determined by the calculation. Thus, provisions by and large (there were some substantial exceptions) equaled charge-offs, and the reserve level did not decline in absolute terms. Yet, few at the time took note of the fact that although the valuation reserve was being maintained, it was not growing in proportion to the loan portfolio. Indeed, inherent in the mathematics of the formula was the necessary condition that the valuation reserve would decline in relation to the loan portfolio as loans grew. The formula allowed for replenishment over time of reductions in the reserve due to losses but it did not allow for growth in the portfolio. Accordingly, it should not be surprising that as measured by the Keefe Bank Index, the valuation reserve as a percentage of loans declined from 2.2 percent in 1968 to 1.04 percent in 1973. This was indeed a substantial drop.

Only compounding the problem was the fact that the five-year averaging format contained a real vulnerability if the loss experience in the current year greatly exceeded the average. This was exactly what occured in 1974 and 1975 with the advent of a severe recession. Many banks experienced a tripling if not a quadrupling in losses compared to their historical average. The formula only called for an increase in provision that would cover 20 to 25 percent of the incremental losses, thereby resulting in a sharp decline in the valuation reserve. One hundred percent of the losses, of course, were directly charged against the valuation reserve as they were incurred. This forced many banks to take a "supplemental" provision in excess of the amount required by the formula in order to maintain a reasonable reserve. It should be noted that when the formula was devised in 1969, the calculation was supposed to represent the minimum that management would provide. There was nothing to prevent provisions in excess of the formula. Unfortunately, the minimum became the maximum, as virtually no major bank charged its income statement more than the formula required during the 1969–73 period.

As losses remained high through 1975 and into 1976, more and more banks were forced to abandon the formula and provide for losses more or less on an "as incurred" basis since reserve levels continued to be weak. Finally, in mid-1976, the Federal Reserve issued orders formally abolishing the formula method for loan loss accounting. Henceforth, banks were required to determine loan loss provisions based upon their judgment of what "would maintain an adequate reserve level to absorb the expected loan losses based upon management's knowledge of the bank's loan portfolio as presently evaluated." The formula was scrapped and replaced by judgment. Suddenly the onus was placed on management where, in fact, it had been all along even though few recognized this. The question then, of course, immediately became one of how to determine reserve adequacy.

The Determination of Reserve Adequacy

In the absence of the formula crutch, bankers were at somewhat of a loss in determining what was an adequate provision. As a starting point, one could always look at the current level of charge-offs. Presumably, over time, the provision would at least have to equal net charge-offs. But that position still does not address the question of reserve adequacy relative to the remaining loan portfolio. Clearly, there are credits within the portfolio where losses, while not currently identified in absolute terms, are very likely. If the reserve is not large enough to reflect this potential loss, then gross loans are overstated on the balance sheet.

It should be mentioned at the outset that there exists no foolproof method for measuring the adequacy of reserves. Any level arrived at will, by necessity, be a function of management judgment that can only be validated at some future date. It is easy in retrospect to analyze the adequacy of any particular level of reserve. Prospective analysis, however, is a much different matter. The following will represent comments on some methods that bankers in the past have employed to arrive at the determination of adequacy. As will be concluded, no absolute judgments on adequacy can ultimately be determined.

The simplest way to approach the question of comparative adequacy among banks might first be to measure the valuation reserve relative to total loans. All other factors being equal, the larger the reserve, the more adequate one might conclude it is. This argument, of course, assumes that on a comparative basis all bank portfolios contain the same level of inherent risk. Indeed, experience has shown that this is not true. Perhaps a more valid approach might be to "risk adjust" each bank portfolio, that is, recognize that differing types of loans have varying degrees of risk. Residential mortgage loans, for example, normally carry substantially less risk than industrial loans to "middle market" companies. Thus, a bank with a 0.8 percent reserve against a loan portfolio comprised 30 percent of mortgages may actually be more "adequate" than a bank with a 1.1 percent reserve against a portfolio totally comprised of commercial and industrial loans.

Another approach to the question of adequacy suggests that loss characteristics displayed by a loan portfolio in the past are a reliable proxy for estimating future prospects. Thus, a bank with a high historical loss experience might be expected to require a larger reserve than a bank with a lower loss experience. Interestingly, there appears to be a reasonable amount of validity to this position. If one examined the loss experience of the fifty largest banks in the U.S. for three periods—1966–69, 1974–76, and 1979–80—it could be shown that a fairly strong correlation exists. On balance, those banks that did relatively well in the earlier periods are continuing to do so currently, and vice versa. Yet, while some statistical evidence does exist to support this case, it must be remembered that the problem loan areas of yesterday are not necessarily going to be the same in the future. Take, for example, the case of a bank that historically maintained both a high-quality domestic commercial and industrial loan portfolio and a significant overseas governmental lending exposure. Since losses in both areas had been minimal in the past, is it reasonable to assume that the same condition would prevail in the future? One need only to look at the recent concern developing over loans to lesser-developed countries to answer that question. Driving forward by looking in the rear view mirror hardly seems an appropriate manner to arrive at judgments concerning the adequacy of current reserve levels.

A more constructive approach to determining reserve adequacy might be to access the reserve in relation to the prevailing level of problem assets within the portfolio. Following the loan problems of the 1974–76 period, the Securities and Exchange Commission required all bank holding companies to disclose the level of nonperforming assets, that is, assets that either are placed on a nonaccrual basis or where the original interest rate has been renegotiated. Included with these two categories would be foreclosed real estate taken in satisfaction of a previous loan. Why not simply compare the level of the reserve to the total of nonperforming assets? Or perhaps in a somewhat more sophisticated approach, why not arrive at management's best guess of what actual loss is inherent in the nonperforming asset total, subtract this "allocated" amount from the existing reserve, and then look at the remaining "unallocated" portion of the reserve in relation to the total loan portfolio.

This, in fact, is what the SEC was strongly pushing banking companies to disclose in the 1977–78 period. The SEC thought it would be helpful for investors to know the level of the "unallocated" reserve relative to total loans. As the SEC unfortunately found out, however, this neat theoretical exercise has substantial practical limitations. First, the determination of the level of problem assets is necessarily a function of judgment which, by definition, will vary greatly among banks. Once the total nonperforming asset figure had been determined, then management had to provide a second judgment—that of estimating the extent of loss within the problem asset portfolio. Again, no two managements can be expected to arrive at exactly the same conclusions, even assuming that they had identical problem loan portfolios. The final step, of course, was to deduct the expected loss from the existing reserve to arrive at the figure for the remaining "unallocated" reserve and then compare this level to the total loan portfolio.

While this entire process was a perfectly valid exercise for an individual bank to follow, it did not insure that results would be consistent among all banks; indeed, one could only expect results to be just the opposite. As such, was the SEC actually informing investors when it suggested that comparisons be made among banks on the basis of the extent of unallocated reserve to total loans? Without doubt, it was actually encouraging disclosure that had the exact opposite effect, that of misleading the investor. The fact that the SEC quietly dropped its nagging insistence on the review of the unallocated portion of the reserve should serve to attest to the problems in determining reserve adequacy following this method.

Thus, one can see that it is very difficult to arrive at any meaningful measure of reserve adequacy. This is exactly the conclusion alluded to earlier in this chapter. The problem with all of the methods discussed revolves around the fact that each effort to define adequacy was conceived of from a static viewpoint, whereas perhaps reserve adequacy is only understood in a dynamic sense. It is misleading to think of reserve adequacy at any one point in time. Rather, one must look to the evolving condition of the overall loan portfolio and assess it in terms of the valuation reserve that is constantly being replenished by a continuing stream of earnings. The question should not be, nor can it ever realistically be, one of looking at a given reserve level at a single point in time and measuring the adequacy of that reserve against losses that will be sustained over various periods in the future. All future potential losses which can only be estimated in the most imprecise manner should be viewed against the ongoing ability of a bank to provide for those losses.

It appears highly suspect that any bank can make the blanket statement that its valuation reserve at any one point is adequate to absorb what is by necessity an indeterminable amount of future loan losses. Rather, one would be much more comfortable with a statement to the effect that "given a continuing ability to produce earnings and assessing this ability in light of the existing level of reserves, it is felt that the combination of both factors should be adequate to absorb any reasonable estimate of potential loan losses." In other words, reserve adequacy is actually a function of the adequacy of the earnings stream that provides the replenishment of reserves to offset losses.

Take, for example, the year-end 1974 statements of the hundred largest American banks, in which each attested to the adequacy of its particular reserve level. Within twelve months, 18 of these banks were to report net charge-offs equaling or exceeding the year-end 1974 valuation reserve, while another ten were to sustain losses equal to at least 85 percent of the reserve. Can it be said in retrospect that the valuation reserves of these 28 banks were adequate? If one is only looking to the actual reserve, obviously these 28 banks did not have adequate reserves. Yet, it is important to note that only one of these 28 banks actually experienced negative earnings for 1975 and that 11 of the 28 banks actually experienced an increase in earnings even after providing for more than was charged-off. If at the end of 1974, 27 of these 28 banks made the statement that the existing reserve level in conjunction with the ongoing ability to generate earnings was adequate to absorb anticipated losses and leave a reasonable reserve for the next year, then such a statement would have been valid.

Reserves of and by themselves should never be segregated from the overall operations of the bank and represented as the measure of protection against inestimable future losses. No reserve may be adequate in that light. Yet, there is a seeming fixation exhibited by bankers, accountants, regulatory authorities, and investors to look at the level of the reserve, relative to the loan portfolio it should protect, without considering the underlying strength of earnings that would replenish the reserve. It is submitted that a bank having a valuation reserve equaling 1.5 percent of its loan portfolio but earning only 0.4 percent on its assets may well be in a significantly overall weakened position relative to another bank that might have a reserve of only 0.8 percent but earns 1 percent on its assets. Which bank would be in a superior position to maintain an adequate valuation reserve over time assuming similar loss experience? Obviously, it is the bank with the higher level of ongoing profitability and not the bank that currently has a higher absolute reserve. It is for this reason that reserve adequacy can only be viewed as a fluid concept defying any absolute definitions.

Actual Reserve Management in a Fluid Context

Much of the preceding has been somewhat theoretical and perhaps not terribly helpful for the controller of a bank who must decide each quarter the particular level of expense provision for loan losses and resulting valuation reserve. How exactly are loan loss expense provisions determined currently? The answer to this question may be somewhat surprising.

A review of the operating results for the major banks in the United States for the 1978–80 period seems to indicate two distinct practices. Over the entire period, it would seem that most banks have adopted a policy of providing an amount of expense sufficient to cover all losses incurred plus an amount to maintain the valuation reserve at a relatively constant percentage relationship to the total loan portfolio. In other words, there may be little management judgment at all in trying to assess the adequacy of the reserve. Instead, the decision may have been made to leave it at a reasonably constant level and deal with losses directly through the income statement. In such an instance, the reserve theoretically ceases to be a reserve, becoming instead a mere segregation of equity capital, except for the tax effects. Such a practice is not what a bank controller might indicate to the outside auditors as being his method for determining provisions. In reality, however, such practice indeed seems to be prevalent.

The other practice that can be observed from the operations of many major banks is a controversial one that relates more to the determination of provisions from one quarterly reporting period to the next rather than over a period of several years. In particular, there appears to be a growing trend toward changing the level of the provision in order to "smooth" short-term fluctuations in reported earnings. Increasingly as banks are faced with large unpredicted changes in the level of interest rates, earnings derived from net interest income and bond trading have become much more volatile. Given the penchant of investors for stability and growth, many bankers have found that the provision for loan losses is a very useful tool in the short run to smooth reported earnings. This practice has been witnessed on many occasions when bond trading, for example, was extremely strong. Such strength would often be accompanied by an unexplained increase in the provision for loan losses, only to be followed in the next quarter by a reduction. This type of practice has been particularly noticeable with some of the major money center banks whose exposure to rapidly changing interest rates is greater than many of the smaller regional banks.

Thus, one is left with a somewhat unsatisfactory answer to the question of how bankers currently determine the amount of provision for loan losses to arrive at an adequate level of reserve. In the long run, the most popular identifiable practice seems to be one of covering current losses and providing for the growth in the loan portfolio. In the short run, more and more banks seem to be turning to the provision as a method of reducing quarter-to-quarter fluctuations in reported earnings. Neither practice is likely to please the serious student of accounting, but this seems to be the only consistent explanation of what is currently happening.

Unwise Lending Practices

The decade of the 1970s provides the analyst with a tremendous field of study in determining what constituted unwise lending practices. Indeed, during the recession which began in 1974, substantial losses were experienced in all areas of lending by banks of all sizes. Regardless of whether or not one wanted to study consumer loan losses sustained by small regional banks, middle-market commercial and industrial losses sustained by larger regionals, international losses sustained by major money center banks, or real estate losses sustained by nearly all types of banks, explicit examples of each type of loan problem could be readily isolated and examined. For the purposes of this chapter, however, the intent will be somewhat more general in nature. If there are any general lessons to be derived from this period, they would have to involve both the problems of lending outside of one's natural market territory and the deleterious effects that can result from overconcentration with a given loan portfolio.

The concept of a natural marketplace is not a new thought that was developed after 1975. Rather, it has been discussed and implicitly followed by bankers for decades. In short, this concept suggests that each bank, depending upon its size, location, management talent, and financial resources has natural marketplaces or service territories that would be logical and prudent to serve. In the same vein, there exist other marketplaces that would neither be logical nor prudent for a given bank to serve. In attempting actually to define a natural marketplace for a single bank, certain extremes are obvious. For example, a small regional bank in Colorado would hardly be participating in its natural service territory were it to extend credit to Brazil or attempt to fund its operations in the Asia dollar market. In the same regard, lending to a major commercial real estate project in Florida with funds raised through brokered CDs from New York would also represent an extension beyond the natural marketplace of a small Colorado bank. Yet, consumer and small commercial loans to borrowers in close proximity to the head office of this bank would clearly be within the natural marketplace. Now, if one were trying to define the natural markets of a major New York City bank, perhaps they would be just the opposite of those of a small Colorado bank, that is, loans in Brazil and Florida might be fine but consumer loans in Colorado would be beyond the natural service territory.

The problem with lending outside of a bank's given market is simply the fact that the information necessary to make an informed credit judgment is oftentimes difficult, if not impossible, for the given bank to obtain and/or interpret. What can a small Colorado bank expect to know and understand about lending to the government of Brazil? Perhaps a New York City correspondent might make credit information on Brazil available to the Colorado bank, but who at the small bank would be capable of understanding it? Similarly, how can a Colorado bank be expected to perform the necessary on-site inspections of its Florida real estate loan? One could continue with the problems and limitations of lending beyond the natural market, but the point should be obvious. Lending on the basis of poor credit information by definition will invite a higher loss experience. This point unfortunately is not always appreciated until it is too late.

Several recent actual examples should serve to illustrate exactly what can happen. A $750 million bank in the East lost almost $2 million in an offshore tanker loan to a Greek shipper. What could this bank possibly have known about lending in the tanker market and lending to Greek shippers? A medium-sized New England bank lost $1 million on land loans in the Arizona desert. How can a northeastern bank expect to understand and monitor a raw land loan, the most risky of real estate loans, when it is located nearly 3,000 miles away? And finally, a $2 billion bank in the Midwest lost several million dollars advancing funds to a tiny bank in Panama. Why? The object lesson common to all these examples should be simple. Know your customer. Unfortunately, when a bank extends beyond what might reasonably be considered its natural marketplace, it becomes more difficult to abide by that maxim.

The second general concept that resulted in substantial losses in the 1974–76 period related to concentration within a given loan portfolio. The idea of diversifying risk is a well-accepted principle in both banking and insurance. A sometimes overlooked point, however, is that in failing to realize what the ultimate collateral might be in a given loan, substantial inadvertent concentrations might be built into the total loan portfolio. Perhaps the most dramatic illustration of this point can be found in the banking industry's involvement with real estate investment trusts (REITs). Exposure to REITs in most cases was first obtained by granting backup lines to the commercial paper being issued by these trusts. Unfortunately, in all too many instances, the decision to grant the line was not made in the real estate lending division but rather in the financial industry or some related division. The loan was not to a finance company but rather to a real estate company. This realization became painfully clear as the lines were subsequently drawn down and eventually foreclosed upon. At this point many banks suddenly realized that their exposure to real estate was substantially greater than had been originally thought. In the same vein a major money center bank in early 1970 extended nearly a legal lending limit loan to an entertainment park, classifying the loan under travel and entertainment. As the fortunes of the park declined, this bank, in contemplation of foreclosure, suddenly realized that what it actually had was not a travel and entertainment division credit at all, but rather a real estate credit, for that is exactly what it would have received upon foreclosure. Fortunately, the outlook for the park improved and foreclosure was never required. One could continue with numerous examples but the point should now be clear. Failure to realize the ultimate collateral one is holding only masks inadvertent massive concentrations within a loan portfolio, particularly in the real estate area. This lesson was painfully learned during the 1970s.

CONCLUSION

The conclusion of this chapter, by necessity, is a tentative one. In reviewing the development of loan loss reserve management, it can be shown that one has moved from purely tax considerations prior to 1969 to a formula basis, which was subsequently abolished, to judgment, which in turn has largely been relegated to concerns of constant reserve levels and interim earnings management. The simple absolutes one can be comfortable with do not exist in the concept of reserve adequacy. Ultimately, the concept of adequacy must relate to the overall earnings strength of the institution. It is a bank's level of profitability over time, not the level of the reserve at any point in time, that must be understood. Lending beyond a bank's natural marketplace and undue loan concentrations will only serve to reduce that profitability.

Lending to U.S. Multinational Corporations

A U.S. multinational corporation may be defined as a major firm, included in the list of the Fortune 500 large industrial companies, where a substantial portion, 25 percent or more, of production, sales, and/or earnings is the result of foreign operations.

Moreover, a U.S. multinational usually is cash rich and as a consequence has only nominal requirements for bank credit in the United States. What funds that are needed domestically tend to be obtained in the commercial paper market. Notwithstanding this, practically every U.S. multinational corporation has substantial credit commitments from major U.S. banks—either revolving credits or commercial paper backup lines. These facilities can be utilized in the event a need for funds in the United States develops. In sharp contrast, nearly every U.S. multinational corporation has widely diversified and in many instances substantial credit and financing needs abroad to service overseas operations.

The typical U.S. multinational corporation has a strong consolidated balance sheet and enjoys excellent earnings and substantial cash flows. Managements are skilled, and financial staffs are professional and highly sophisticated.

The structure of the finance or treasury function varies widely. In some firms the function is highly centralized, with large staffs at corporate headquarters. Occasionally this structure is aided by regional finance officers of the corporation stationed at strategic spots overseas but reporting on a direct line to corporate headquarters. At the other extreme, the finance and treasury function is widely disbursed, with relatively autonomous corporate officers managing the finances of the local overseas branch and/or subsidiary. Under this latter decentralized arrangement, corporate treasury officers at headquarters have only nominal knowledge of day-to-day activities, monitoring and maintaining control over only the aggregate consolidated treasury operations.

Regardless of the structure of the finance or treasury function at corporate headquarters, however, most U.S. multinational corporations tend to select their bankers by the extent to which the bank serves the worldwide needs of the corporation. Accordingly, the objective—servicing the overseas financing needs of a multinational corporation—is facilitated by the extent of the overseas network of installations of the bank and by its ability and willingness to assume foreign country risk. Thus, banks which have extensive installations abroad enjoy a competitive advantage. Moreover, to exploit both, that is, to service most efficiently the multinational corporation's total financing needs as well as to utilize most advantageously the overseas offices and installations, most major U.S. banks have established separate multinational corporate banking units.

While the organizational arrangement varies, usually the worldwide credit responsibility for a particular multinational account is assigned to one individual. It is the responsibility of the account officer, assisted by the required support staff, to service the credit and noncredit (cash management and foreign exchange exposure management, for example) needs of the multinational corporation, not only at headquarters in the United States but across the country and abroad as well. This requires a thorough knowledge of the company, its organization and structure, products, manufacturing, distribution, and sales, not to mention financial and operating results. Points of personal contact in the multinational corporation by the banker are many and cover a wide spectrum of activities as well as geography. The objective of the account officer is to determine the credit and noncredit needs of the company, both in the United States and abroad. Most efforts include the preparation of a marketing strategy outline for each individual corporation. Its preparation includes market intelligence garnered at the multinational's corporate headquarters as well as from the corporation's installations and offices overseas. The need for close communication between the account officer and his counterparts abroad is apparent if the relationship is to be developed and strengthened. Independent surveys of corporate financial officers, incidentally, reveal a very strong preference for this type of financial servicing of accounts.

The overseas financial needs of the corporation change over time and as the fortunes of the corporation shift in any particular market as conditions change. Typically, however, lending to the U.S. multinational corporations in the United States does not differ from the ordinary corporate short-term commercial and/or term lending and is covered elsewhere in this text. However, the more common need of the U.S. multinational corporation is for funds overseas to finance a local need. The needs and borrowing capabilities of the local installation, not to mention conditions peculiar to the location, vary widely.

The Multicurrency Line of Credit

Perhaps the most versatile and comprehensive financial instrument used by U.S. multinationals is the multicurrency line of credit. Ordinarily, it is granted to the parent corporation and is available to it and/or to the overseas installations or subsidiaries. At the time the commitment is extended, usually for one year with a stated expiration date, the total may be subdivided into various amounts of named foreign currencies available to the respective overseas installations of the multinational corporation. An alternative arrangement is to delay, naming the installation or subsidiary and the currency and amounts until the need arises. In these situations the commitment states that amounts will be determined and allocated under the overall line when the need arises. The purpose of the credit typically would be to finance the usual corporate needs, but it also may include letters of credit and acceptances. The multicurrency line permits the chief financial officer or treasurer to combine into one commitment a facility that provides him with control yet considerable flexibility. The banker finds it a useful marketing technique as it facilitates and helps insure the participation of the bank in satisfying some of the multinational firm's overseas financial requirements. It also strengthens the position of the account relationship officer at the bank's head office with his counterparts serving the account at the bank's overseas installations. Funds extended under the commitment are under the guarantee of the parent multinational corporation.

An alternative arrangement, depending on circumstances, would have the obligor for funds advanced under the commitment be a subsidiary or affiliate of the multinational corporation and located in a foreign country.

The credit now takes on an added dimension, namely, an international risk, for the bank must determine not only the creditworthiness of the borrower but also the capability of the country involved to generate the foreign exchange—U.S. dollars—to permit the repayment of the debt at maturity. The analysis of country risk and the responsibility for determining the amount of risk acceptable to the bank (that is, the amount of credit the bank will extend to borrowers in the country under review) usually is not undertaken by the corporate relationship officer but by other bank staff. The general topic of country risk is treated elsewhere in this text. The lending officer responsible for the corporate relationship would be obliged to analyze the creditworthiness and capability of the subsidiary. Obviously, in some instances, the balance sheet, profit performance, and cash flow of the subsidiary or affiliate may not warrant the extension of the credit requested. In that instance the banker may suggest that the parent corporation inject additional capital into the subsidiary in order to strengthen the balance sheet. Alternative arrangements are possible. The banker may request collateral or a guarantee, or a comfort letter from the parent corporation. (A comfort letter is an informal assurance by the parent corporation to the bank and designed to persuade the bank to extend funds to the subsidiary by suggesting to the bank that it will not incur any loss.)

The multicurrency line, similar to most credit commitments, usually is for a stated period of time, ordinarily a year. Moreover, a credit commitment fee is paid, usually ½ percent per annum, either payable by means of a deposit balance requirement or remitted periodically. Though the compensation arrangement varies widely, most credit commitments carry some required balance arrangement either expressly stated or agreed upon verbally between the banker responsible for the relationship and the finance officer or treasurer of the corporation.

The Revolving Credit Agreement

The revolving credit agreement, as the title suggests, involves an arrangement covering an extended period—five years, for example—whereby the banker agrees to make available to the corporation (or its subsidiary or affiliate) a named dollar total. Moreover, the funds may be advanced and repaid, but the total remains available into the future. Funds may be advanced at stated named intervals or the credit may provide that the credit will be utilized as required. In short, the revolving credit agreement may be a lengthy document, the terms and conditions of which may be whatever the banker and client agree to make them.

Frequently a multinational corporation may have very substantial needs for funds which far exceed the lending capacity of any private bank. In this instance the corporation may approach a number of banks and invite them collectively to participate in a revolving credit, appointing one bank to act as manager of the syndicate.

Project Finance Loan

Recently U.S. multinational corporations have undertaken major investments in foreign countries that involve the development and construction of an entire industrial, mining, or refining complex. Often these projects may cost $500 million to $1.5 billion or more and are so vast that construction extends over a number of years with several additional years required before the project generates sufficient cash flow to permit any debt repayment. (This type of financing is not unlike the typical domestic term loan described elsewhere in this text.) Arranging the financing of such projects often is undertaken by an international bank which will manage the syndication, with several others also taking substantial participations and acting as co-managers of the financing. Documentation of the financing or loan agreement often includes independent engineering and accounting reviews and appraisals submitted in support of the project and the anticipated cash flows. Terms of the financing usually provide for funds to be advanced over a period of years as construction proceeds. Moreover, repayment of the loan often is delayed until production is sufficient to generate the required cash flow.

In sharp contrast to the revolving credit and term loans of the U.S. multinational corporations which run for extended periods—five to ten years at times—"transaction" or "money market loans" were spawned by market conditions in 1980. These loans are of very short maturity—one day to 30 days —with most borrowings averaging 7 to 15 days at rates priced fractionally above money market rates but below the prime. This has been a phenomenon peculiar to a period of rapidly fluctuating rates at high levels. Presumably, when short-term interest rates drop to more moderate levels and stabilize, such transaction loans are not likely to be as readily available.

In short, the bank financing arrangements of multinational corporations and the major international commercial banks tend to be limited only by the creative capabilities of the participants—the bankers and the chief financial officers of the corporations and their staffs. The borrowers typically are among the most creditworthy, and the sums required often are very large. These two factors make them exceedingly attractive to the major international commercial banks. The resulting competitive drama that occurs in the marketplace is readily evident and understandable.

The arrangements outlined above should not suggest that borrowing by a U.S. multinational and its subsidiaries and affiliates is limited to these. U.S. commercial banks and their branches and installations abroad extend credit either for short-term or for extended periods, in dollars or in foreign currencies, as available and required. In these instances, the procedures and practices described elsewhere in this text would apply and prevail.

28

Loans to Foreign Governments

Lending to foreign governments or their agencies is apt to be viewed with apprehension by bankers contemplating such ventures for the first time. Although understandable, it is a mistake, usually born of fear of the unknown and often fed by several faulty assumptions. In this chapter we hope to diminish anxiety by examining those inhibiting assumptions and charting some of the landmarks that can guide the newcomer to transnational finance successfully into the territory of foreign lending. There are profits to be made from this type of finance. Equally important, there are rewards to both the lender and the borrower—inherent in the process of assisting development and strengthening the bonds of international financial community. As Spaceship Earth hurtles toward the twenty-first century, transnational business will become—perhaps must become—everyday business for full-service financial institutions.

One error is to assume that "a loan is a loan is a loan," that what works in New Orleans will work in New Delhi. Conversely, it is equally erroneous to assume that business across the border—any border—is so different that the traditional verities of domestic finance get lost in translation and simply do not apply. Often after being pulled in opposite directions by these two wrong assumptions, the prospective lender retreats from the dilemma by deciding that home is happier and engaging in foreign lending is more trouble than it's worth.

Each assumption is a partial truth. Doing business abroad is different. It is more complex than doing business in your own backyard. But it is equally true that the canons of prudent banking practice form the foundation of international finance and are applicable throughout the world.

The classic tools of risk and repayment evaluations—signing up the customer and the territory, asking the right questions, getting the right answers, and tracking the inevitably shifting circumstances—do not change simply because a credit is being negotiated in another country.

At the same time, subtleties of indigenous law, culture, custom, and practice must be weighed in the negotiation and lending process. There are more differences than language in another country, and the successful venturer abroad always approaches such differences with respect and close attention to preparatory homework. Make haste slowly, sensitively, and confidently.

Once these realities of transnational finance are recognized and accepted, you will discover reasons in abundance to search out customers and markets beyond your home base. Demand abounds, creating infinite opportunities. Need encourages attractive pricing. Earning potential is substantial—so much so that you will find competitors at each elbow. Also, opportunities deriving from this category of credit are not limited to developing new customers and markets across the border. Often other and equally substantial earnings may arise from your bank's in-place, in-house ability to provide services to new and existing domestic customers involved in transnational business.

Lending to foreign governments and government entities promotes diversification of loan portfolios. It is another profitable outlet for funds. Moreover as account officers become familiar with the country, its needs and business community, opportunities for new lending, commercial and governmental, will be discovered.

Yields from foreign lending are profitable. Though fluctuating from time to time, yields have been attractive. While there has been some decline in recent times, this is more a reflection of increasing competition rather than lessening potential. Also, when bank portfolios approach saturation of a particular country, the yield level rises, thus creating new opportunities.

It should also be recognized that the risk factor is necessarily diminished by the desire of the borrowing country to maintain access to external credit. Such access is of paramount importance to governments. Thus, most countries continue to meet debt obligations and thereby mitigate risk to the lender.

It is apparent that lending to foreign governments or their chartered companies offers a number of attractions to full service banks. How then does a lender approach such an enterprise?

Such lending must be analyzed from two perspectives: The prospective lender must evaluate the strengths and weaknesses of the borrowing country, and it must evaluate its own abilities to carry the loan through term.

A Look at the Borrower

In analyzing the borrowing country, it is helpful to apply the time-honored three C test, examining character, capacity, and capital. Though many of the facets to be examined are difficult to quantify and many are uncomfortably but necessarily subjective, this approach allows a prudent lender to assess a mix of complex variables within a generally valid framework. It is a hard fact of life that decisions are based on probability and can never be made with benefit of all the facts. However, these criteria allow the lender to fit available facts into coherent relationships and thus reach a rational lending decision.

CHARACTER

It is, of course, difficult to profile a country's character; the variables are manifold and inherently imprecise. However, the following analysis will point up criteria that will permit reasonable lending judgments.

A primary element of character as applied to a government is political stability. The ability of a country's political system to permit peaceful internal successions, deal effectively with its internal problems, and maintain acceptable relations with neighboring and other countries over a long period of time is a mark of functioning, stable governmental process. In assessing this factor, the lender should not allow personal prejudices or mere differences to cloud his vision. Stability is a function of many processes, paramount among which are effectiveness of governmental policy and actions, the potential for social unrest of major proportions, and the effect of external factors.

An effective government maintains itself over a significant period of time with a minimum of internal dislocation. It must be able to generate and implement policies to deal effectively with the unique economic, social, and political exigencies which it may face. These include changing economic, financial, social, and political conditions; energy needs; development of a well-functioning economy; sensible utilization of existing resources; and proper attention to the needs and aspirations of its people.

One mark of how effectively a particular governmental system operates is its *ability to resolve internal conflicts* with little political or economic disruption.

Almost every nation contains influential groups such as labor, religious, racial, and ethnic segments, and other special or single-interest associations whose political aims or philosophies are diverse and perhaps different from those of the government in power. The ability to cope with and accommodate such groups while maintaining a reasonable degree of their support is a hallmark of stability. Failure to resolve conflicts that may arise can lead to serious discord, manifested by strikes, political strife, slowdowns, and other dislocations. Such events, if not successfully negotiated or resolved, may ultimately injure the economy and the ability to generate foreign exchange for the repayment of debt. Moreover, the ability to repay external debt can be adversely affected by the necessity of diverting funds to remedy social and economic disorders.

The *potential for social unrest* is an allied factor which the prospective lender must plug into the loan equation. There are of course wide variations between countries because of substantial ethnic or political differences, traditions of violence, and other divisive situations. Consequently, a careful evaluation must be made of the potential for major attacks on, or resistance to, the existing government and its policies and practices. Strikes in key industries, student unrest, ethnic and racial militancy and strength, and religious opposition are some of the factors that must be noted. Some countries have a history of internal discord that has been kept under control by strong government action. If such opposition groups unite, expand their support, or intensify disruptive activities, the continuance of the existing government may become tenuous. Such a situation would inevitably alter debt repayment ability.

A tradition of *orderly succession* is of signal importance in country character evaluation. The ability of a nation's political system to change governments is important for the prospective lender to consider. History abounds with examples of one-man and oligarchic regimes replaced by chaos or uncertainty because of the absence of succession procedures accepted by parties to the process and the populace. Without a history of comparatively tranquil governmental progression, any country's stability is precarious and its financial relations uncertain—to the possible detriment of the lender.

External factors necessarily impinge upon the prospective lender's analysis. Even though a particular government is keeping its house in order, its relationships with its neighbors or the designs and ambitions of its neighbors may directly affect stability.

The country's internal political and social environment, natural resources, geographical position, and proximity to other politically unstable nations may all determine the extent to which the country is vulnerable to outside interference. Such vulnerability may result in direct attack from an external source or subversion, both of which impair the ability to pursue projected economic development and repayment of debt. The existence of an actual or imagined threat will directly influence the amount of defense expenditures. Substantial increases in defense spending may, of course, interfere with projected economic development and seriously alter repayment schedules. However, it should be recognized that in some instances supposed or actual outside threats tend to unify and strengthen support for the existing government.

From a more positive perspective, good *relations with other nations and membership in regional alliances* tend to bolster the "stability index" of a country. Close relationships with other nations can promote mutually advantageous trade in needed goods, receipt of aid, technical assistance, and other benefits. Strong military alliances may increase the nation's security and possibly result in decreased military expenditures, thus freeing funds for development projects that further strengthen the country's economic base and conceivably decrease internal discord.

Membership in productive regional economic and military alliances is a factor to which the lender should in most cases react positively. Such regional associations as the Andean Pact and others are well-intentioned attempts to foster economic development of individual countries in certain areas by careful, concerted planning. Also, such alliances, often based upon cultural ties as well as geographical proximity and recognition of shared economic goals, tend to minimize the possibility of military action between the signatory nations.

The country's *relations with the United States* should be a key item in the character evaluation. The local attitudes about U.S. banks can range from general goodwill to resentment and hostility. In addition, unless there has been a long-standing, mutually beneficial relationship, such attitudes may quickly shift in response to other international tensions and pressures reflecting the debtor country's relations with the United States and response to U.S. policy. Obviously, such attitudes may influence the decision to repay or repudiate debt. A country involved in significant trade with the United States would be unlikely to jeopardize that relationship unnecessarily. On the other side of the ledger, if past relations with the United States have not been handled well and perceivable animus against the United States exists, the lender should proceed with caution.

As noted above, the assessment of the character of a country is largely subjective and rife with intangibles that defy neat classification. The analysis depends greatly upon the reliability of information sources. If a bank has experienced personnel domiciled in the country or visiting it frequently, it can benefit from their knowledge of conditions and personal familiarity with members of the government and business communities. Without such sources, the problem is more difficult. Research utilizing various public and private resources provides the alert banker with enough information to decide if a country's character, in conjunction with information detailed later in this chapter, warrants the issuance of funds.

CAPACITY

Stability, discussed as an important index of character, also necessarily influences capacity to service debt. Other factors must be included in the measurement of capacity. In addition to assessing the solidity of the country's economic base, one should also be aware of variations in capacity determined by the type of loan being made.

The International Monetary Fund's Annual Report on trade and exchange restrictions lists actual defaults and payment arrears as indicators of respective debt servicing abilities, along with other valuable information. Three principal sets of circumstances are noted as broad indications of a country's debt service capacity.

High external liquidity is of paramount importance in capacity analysis. A country with low external indebtedness, ample reserves, and a positive external cash flow will have greater ability to service external debt than a country suffering from low liquidity.

Domestic policy is also a consideration. For example, a country pursuing highly expansionary economic policies is more likely to encounter debt service problems than a nation following a more restrained, measured economic program. Thus an examination of the prospective borrowing country's budget and modes of financing should have a high priority in capacity analysis.

The *structural variables* of a nation's economy are also worthy of serious consideration. A well-diversified and balanced economy naturally will be more resilient and better able to withstand the shock of unforeseen adverse domestic or foreign events. Its debt servicing capacity will tend to be superior to that of an economy which is narrowly based, heavily dependent upon foreign sources for essential supplies, and thus possessing limited scope for sudden adjustments to changing circumstances.

There are other elements in capacity evaluation that must be recognized. Normally, because of its nature, complexity, and size, a nation will not get out of debt in the classical banking sense. The degree of indebtedness varies among nations classified as young or mature debtor nations and mature creditor nations. After all, a country is an on-going, evolving entity, and its capacity will normally increase as it grows and moves from one classification to another.

Proper use of credit is one factor affecting such evolution and growth. Credit from external sources is an obvious benefit provided the funds are used for purposes that will enhance and increase the viability of the economy. Because of this, particularly with less developed nations, it is extremely important that they maintain credit access to external markets. These markets are volatile and react quickly to news of internal strife, political unrest, and adverse economic events. Such negative reactions not only affect the ability to borrow but the cost of borrowing as well. Notable increases in total borrowing costs may seriously hinder further development. For such reasons, a nation tends to protect its credit reputation as a valuable asset. Also, the skill and acumen of a nation's leaders are an important element of capacity.

Prospective lenders should also look closely at the natural resources of a country. Whatever the resources are—metals, timber, oil, coal—they are sources of repayment because they are easily converted to foreign exchange. The manner in which revenues from such resources are utilized is important to the lender. Many developing countries are wisely using funds derived from natural resources to expand and strengthen their respective economics. This, of course, increases capacity.

Unfortunately, some less developed nations are almost completely dependent upon a single crop or other resource to generate foreign earnings from exports. As a consequence, their economies are exposed to cyclical price fluctuations in the world market. Such countries therefore have limited flexibility in responding to adversity, which can negatively affect their capacity to repay.

Another critical measure of capacity is determined by the nature of the loan. Lending to foreign nations can involve various government entities. The borrowing entity and the purpose of the loan affect capacity. Government-owned corporations are, perhaps, the most common borrower. The purpose for which loan funds will be used deserves critical study.

1. Loans to enable the corporation to marshall and export basic resources or commodities. A loan of this type can be viewed as self-liquidating inasmuch as the ultimate purchaser pays against documents. The main risk to the lender lies in the ability of the corporation to process, collect, and ship the exports. Internal dislocation would affect such loans.

2. Loans for the purpose of importing oil, foodstuffs, or other basic commodities. Loans to corporations charged with this function are relatively low risk. Because of the need for such imports, it is in the best interests of the government to see that these loans are paid promptly as agreed.

3. Loans to a corporation chartered for the express purpose of developing a specific project. If all goes well, the development of such projects should increase capacity to repay because they generate foreign exchange or allow substitution for imports. A lender must make a careful decision as to whether the projects merit free-standing status or whether a government guarantee is needed. When a guarantee is not offered but government support is implied, the lender must make an extremely careful analysis.

4. Loans to a corporation involved in mining, manufacturing, or service industries. Ordinarily, such loans can be analyzed as one would evaluate a loan to any other corporate entity. The need for a government guarantee must be assessed. With almost all loans to government-owned corporations, the legal aspects must be fully explored. In some countries, for example, corporations such as these are prevented from going into bankruptcy.

There are two other common forms of foreign lending. The first is loans to development banks. Such banks are normally chartered to promote developmental activities within the country. As such, these loans are usually properly viewed as a government risk. The second form consists of loans to the central government or to the country's central bank. These loans are ordinarily for more general purposes such as rectifying balance of payments deficits, further development of the country's infrastructures, such as schools and hospitals. Such loans are generally of longer maturity and require a different type of analysis than loans to government-owned corporations.

CAPITAL

In a strict accounting sense, it is virtually impossible to list all of a nation's assets and liabilities and subsequently arrive at a net worth figure. However, though the information is diverse, the assessments often subjective, and many intangibles enter the evaluation, a judgment can be made about a country's capital.

Perhaps the greatest asset that a country possesses is its people. Significant investment that a nation has made in its educational system normally results in a well-trained work force familiar with technology and able to work productively in the economic environment of the country. In addition, as amorphous and ill-defined as it is, the general attitude of the populace must be noted. Also, tribal, religious, and language divisions among the people should be weighed in the lender's thinking. In this regard, a lender should not become victimized by his own personal assumptions; a pejorative judgment should not flow from the mere fact of difference. An objective view is the *sine qua non* of a fair and effective evaluation.

Natural resources in abundance rank high in assessing a country's capital. Conversely, a poorly endowed nation often faces severe economic disadvantages, not the least of which is the inability to generate sufficient income for repayment. In such instances, the lender should make a careful distinction between general purpose loans and those secured by exports. The latter type of loan will ordinarily be retired from sources outside the exporting country.

A country's overall investment in its total economic base is a key criterion in measuring capital. With a broad and diversified economic matrix, a country is better able to withstand economic shocks. Production facilities generate wealth for the country either as sources of foreign exchange or as import substitution, thereby diminishing the need for foreign exchange. A country with a balanced developmental plan, geared to produce goods eventually in sufficient quantity to meet local market needs, merits lending support. However, if such production facilities are uneconomic to the point of needing protection against free-world markets, the lender and the country as well should examine other modes of development and assistance.

A country's foreign reserve position is another important factor in evaluating capital. Similar to "cash and due from banks" on a balance sheet, a good foreign reserve position cushions adversity by covering imports of vital supplies.

While the asset items noted above may provide a broad estimate of a country's capital, the assessment must be refined and quantified. Just as certain ratios can assist in analyzing trends in a corporation, so can they help determine a nation's creditworthiness. Inasmuch as the lender's main concern is the country's debt service capacity, the ratios that increase that capacity should be noted.

1. International reserves over imports. An increase in this ratio is indicative of the country's external liquidity. It measures the country's reserve cushion compared to potential demand for input payments. It is often referred to as the input coverage ratio.

2. Debt service over exports. This, too, is an indicator of the country's external liquidity position. This is the classical debt service ratio and is widely used to assess debt service capacity, particularly when the ratio decreases.

3. Government surplus over government revenues. Increases in this ratio are helpful in indicating the government's fiscal policy. A high surplus is normally associated with a strong ability to service debt; large deficits in relation to revenues would, of course, point toward diminished debt servicing ability.

4. Bank net claims on government over the sum of the country's net foreign assets plus total domestic credit. Increases in this ratio should be carefully monitored as an indicator of possible debt servicing problems. This situation would likely occur if the government has heavily borrowed from the banking sector in relation to the country's entire monetary sector as represented by the sum of its net foreign assets (official plus banking sector) and its total domestic credit extended. This ratio is a good indicator of the government's financing policy.

5. Exports over gross domestic product (GDP). Increases in this ratio reflect favorably on the country's debt servicing ability.

6. Domestic per capita GDP over U.S. per capita GDP. In this ratio, the U.S. GDP is used as a scale factor to adjust for secular trends. Increases in this ratio suggest improving ability to service debt. A country with a high per capita GDP is in a better position to overcome unforeseen difficulties.

As with any ratios, those noted above should be examined over a period of time sufficient to allow trends to emerge. When used carefully and in conjunction with other assets making up a country's capital, they can be of immense help to the lender.

Having assessed a country's character, capacity, and capital, the prospective lender may be in a position to decide to grant a loan. However, before doing so, the lending institution must consider whether or not it is able to extend credit, whether the credit should be extended, and how much it should be. The legal implications affecting such loans must also be analyzed.

A Look at the Lender

Most lending to foreign governments involves large loans with long tenors. It is therefore a venture requiring a careful assessment of the strengths, weaknesses, and goals of the prospective lending bank. This type of lending requires a sustainable long-term commitment.

A primary requirement is that the lending bank have sufficient knowledge of the borrowing country, or convenient access to such information.

The lending bank must have the particular skills to carry the venture through to successful fruition. This might require project financing skills and the ability to marshall export agency credits from the appropriate exporting countries.

Because most international credits are syndicated, the lender should be able to examine intelligently the qualifications of the lead bank. Does it have a successful track record in organizing, administering, and placing previous syndications? The lead bank selected must also have the expertise to be able to give counsel on the external markets and handle the negotiation and documentation.

More specifically the lending bank must ask itself some tough questions: Does it have the ability to fund the loan at the agreed upon price over term? Has a portfolio examination been conducted with particular regard to tenor, currency, earnings, and other financings of a similar nature? For example, are there too many loans to different countries that rely upon exporting the same commodity for repayment? Has the level of existing debt been analyzed in relation to lending exposure? Does the loan comply with bank policy? Is it the type of loan the bank wants to make?

If the answers to these questions are right and the other requirements have been met, the lending bank is now in a position to consider how much credit it is willing to commit to a given country. A country limit must be determined.

The first consideration to be examined in determining a country limit is Regulation K. The aggregation of credits to government entities as defined by the "means and purpose" test of the Comptroller of the Currency must not exceed 10 percent of capital and surplus.

However, because few banks would be willing to commit this ceiling in many countries, the lending bank must impose its own country limit that is coincident with the bank's lending objectives. Typically, the limit includes loans to government entities along with all loans that constitute transfer risk outstanding. Transfer risk is defined as any credit for which repayment of the loan will be in a currency other than the currency indigenous to the borrower, the borrower's country, or to the lender's domiciling unit.

There are additional criteria which may be used in establishing a country limit. These could include a percentage of a country's GDP, a percentage of the country's total debt, a percentage of all U.S. bank claims in a country, or an amount based upon the lender's previously established risk rating system. Outer limits should be set for each country.

A Look at the Law

In conjunction with the other aspects of lending to a foreign country that have been discussed, applicable laws must be considered. The issue of which court of law prevails is critical. Until recently it was accepted practice for loan agreements to specify that either U.S. or United Kingdom law would pertain should disputes arise. This situation has changed. Countries have challenged this practice, and some have passed legislation requiring arbitration or adjudication of disputes under their respective laws. While this can be viewed as a normal expression of national pride, it does pose another factor to be examined closely by the lending bank. This trend will probably continue and, because of competition, will likely be accepted. It is merely another element among many in which the lending bank must develop expertise. And, of course, which law prevails is still usually subject to negotiation.

Another factor of the legal environment of foreign lending pertains to loan syndication and the responsibilities of the lead or agent bank. The loan syndication agreement should delineate the relationship between the agent and participating banks, and the duties and responsibilities of the agent acting as a representative for the other lenders. While the agreement attempts to place certain limits on the agent's obligations and liabilities, including accounting and reporting functions, other duties and responsibilities may be implied or imposed by law regardless of the terms of the agreement.

Implied responsibilities require that the agent exercise the same care on behalf of the member lenders as it would on its own behalf. Further, under certain circumstances, the agent may be required to make reasonable and appropriate recommendations to other members of the syndication.

Additionally, there are agent responsibilities required by law. The agent must avoid any possible or actual conflict of interest. This precludes any action favoring its direct credits to the borrower or its portion of the syndicated credit. The agent may not take security for its own account. The conflict of interest requirement necessarily hinders the agent's serving as financial advisor to the borrower or assuming the role of indenture trustee.

The agent is required to disclose all pertinent information to all member banks. This includes even information given in confidence by the borrower—a condition which could possibly be illegal in certain countries. Also, this provision extends to include information possessed by any of the agent bank's branches or offices throughout the world.

The agent also is forbidden from acting in its own self-interest or in the interest of another syndication to the detriment of members of the original syndication.

A FINAL LOOK

From the preceding discussion of many of the aspects associated with lending to foreign governments, it may appear to be a forbidding prospect to the lender considering it for the first time. Such lending is a complex enterprise. The nature and number of the variables in the lending venture may seem to confound rational decision-making. It may seem, simply enough, not worth the trouble.

Difficulties abound, but so do opportunities. With proper attention to traditional prudent banking practice, careful assessment of the borrower and the lending bank as well, and experienced legal counsel, foreign governmental lending can be a profitable and natural extension of a bank's activities. It will require significant commitments of time, personnel, and, above all, judicious and tough-minded thought. It is worth the effort because of profits to be earned, experience to be gained, and growth for the lending bank.

29

Credit Extension to Foreign Banks

The international business of most U.S. banks well into the period after World War II was concentrated mainly in dealing with foreign banks. Their foreign exposure was primarily to banks and generally for the purpose of financing short-term trade transactions. There were a number of notable exceptions, one being the role played by J. P. Morgan & Co., one of the predecessor institutions of Morgan Guaranty, in the financing and supplying of Great Britain and France during the early years of World War I. In addition, J. P. Morgan was prominent during the latter part of the nineteenth century and up to the passage of the Banking Act of 1933 in originating and underwriting foreign government and foreign corporate bonds. There was a surge of overseas activity including the rapid expansion of foreign branches by leading U.S. banks in the late 1920s, but credit overextension, poor lending techniques, and declining world raw material prices produced some sharp financial losses and a retreat by American banks from the foreign scene.

After World War II, American business began to expand abroad. In response, U.S. banks across the country broadened their international banking capabilities and expertise. This growth was given added impetus through the imposition of U.S. foreign exchange controls in 1963, when U.S. banks were forced to build up their overseas resources in order to continue to service their international clients. Simultaneously, there began the tremendous expansion of the Eurocurrency market, which now has its counterpart in the Asian dollar market.

The amount of foreign credit extended by U.S. banks and their overseas branches and subsidiaries has grown enormously in this period. The number of U.S. bank participants has also expanded, and it is estimated that some 400 commercial banks in the United States are engaged to some degree in international business. The ranks of borrowers have also grown, and in addition to foreign banks now encompass a high percentage of borrowings by foreign corporations, both public and private, by official and nonofficial government agencies, and by governments themselves. The terms and structures of these credits have evolved from the simple short-term advance to highly complex syndicated loans.

Business with foreign banks continues to rank as of key importance with U.S. international banks. In terms of foreign credit exposure, foreign banks are the most important group as a whole for United States commercial banks. The periodic country exposure lending survey prepared by the Federal Reserve Board, the Office of the Comptroller of the Currency, and the Federal Deposit Insurance Corporation indicates that as of December 31, 1979, business with other banks accounted for the largest amount of foreign claims by the 130 U.S. banks surveyed, including their foreign offices. Cross-border and cross-currency claims for these banks totaled $246 billion, of which $136 billion was on banks, $67 billion on the private nonbank sector, and $43 billion on the public sector. These figures do not include unused guidance lines and advised lines as discussed below, nor the exposure of those U.S. banks lending abroad but not canvassed in the survey.

The Market

The American correspondent banker surveying his overseas market will find that although there are literally thousands of banks in the world, only a relatively few are engaged in operations outside their own borders and even fewer are active participants in the international credit markets. The 1978–79 edition of *The Bankers' Almanac and Year Book,* one of the best reference works on the subject, lists more than 1,600 banks outside of the United States which do an international business. These are mainly commercial banks, but are also in other important categories such as the English merchant banks, the savings and cooperative banks in Germany, the Swiss private investment banks, and the Japanese trust and banking corporations, and their counterparts in other countries of the world. Among the commercial banks, one normally counts government-owned banks such as those in France and Italy, whose business is identical in most respects to the nongovernmental competition in the United States, Great Britain, and Japan.

With respect to size, *The American Banker* annually publishes listings of the 500 largest banks in the world. The survey of December 31, 1979, shows that 405 of the 500 largest banks ranked in terms of deposits, were outside of the United States. It is this relatively small grouping of institutions which by and large account for the major share of credit extended by U.S. banks to the overseas banking industry.

Distinguishing Characteristics

Each U.S. bank dealing with foreign banks will, of course, have to determine for itself what policies and what practices and procedures will govern the extension of credit to its overseas correspondents, and there is no blueprint of the right way to go. Nevertheless, the business of lending to foreign banks as it has evolved over the years has developed certain characteristics which distinguish it from the corporate and public lending sectors. These can be identified as follows:

1. Active relationships between correspondent banks generally involve the principle of reciprocity including a mutual willingness to extend credit facilities. For example, U.S. banks with branches abroad will depend on the banks in the host country for a certain percentage of their local currency funding needs. These foreign banks in turn will look to their principal U.S. correspondents to help fund branches and subsidiaries they may operate in the U.S. Similarly, Euro-redeposit operations and foreign exchange trading imply the presence of reciprocal credit arrangements between the participants.

2. Credit facilities in favor of other banks are normally short-term up to one year and are usually made on an unsecured basis. The short-term is primarily due to the reluctance of banks to finance their own competition by providing longer-term credits, unsecured because of the assumed superior creditworthiness of banks.

3. Lines of credit to support traditional financings, such as trade transactions (for example, by letters of credit or acceptances), are more often than not formally advised in writing to the beneficiary bank and are subject to review, generally on an annual basis. They are usually not formal commitments and therefore do not irrevocably bind the bank granting the credit.

On the other hand, lines of credit which authorize the traders of banks to place short-term deposits with other banks and to deal with them in foreign exchange are normally not advised either in writing or verbally to the partner banks but are normally set up on an internal basis on the records of banks. These facilities are often referred to as guidance lines.

4. The extension of credit by one bank to another in the interbank market is essentially done at cost with no or very little margin of profit. As a matter of fact, the banking system as a whole cannot make a profit with banks trading among themselves. They must make their profits from the final borrowers, such as corporations, governments, and individuals. Put another way, the

interbank market is a transmission mechanism from the ultimate provider of funds to the ultimate customer rather than a pure lending market. Of course, credits arranged between banks outside of the interbank market, such as overdraft facilities and term credits as discussed in more detail below, are priced with a margin and are more analogous to corporate-type loans.

5. The lending of funds by banks to businesses and individuals in the form of advances or overdrafts is usually classified as loans among a bank's risk assets. On the other hand, such credits as between banks normally take the form of deposits and are classified as such, rather than as loans. There is generally no difference between loans and deposits as far as credit risk is concerned. (The only exception is that in a few countries, including Australia, deposits in commercial banks are guarantied by the central bank, whereas loans to the same commercial banks are not.) However, for certain regulatory purposes, discussed in more detail below, it may make a difference whether the transaction constitutes a loan or a deposit.

Sources of Credit Information

Of key importance in correspondent relationships involving the extension of credit is a regular schedule of calls on foreign correspondents supplemented by their visits to the United States to develop relative credit information. One of the basic principles of sound credit analysis, whoever the borrower, is to satisfy oneself as to the expertise and caliber of management. However, this judgment factor is perhaps even more important when analyzing foreign banks, particularly in those countries that do not have broad disclosure requirements and where an analysis of public financial information may not be too meaningful.

Additional information is provided by outside sources, including reports by credit agencies such as Dun & Bradstreet or its counterparts which operate in many areas of the world. Further would be reports from other U.S. banks. In this regard U.S. banks guided by the Robert Morris Associates' code of ethics traditionally have been willing to exchange credit information on foreign bank clients, giving an indication of the type and size of credit facilities. However, in recent years U.S. banks, particularly the money center banks, have become much more reluctant to exchange meaningful information because of competitive reasons. Information received from banks overseas is also generally not too revealing and such reports normally do not telegraph incipient problems.

Often a better source of outside information on a foreign bank is the foreign exchange and money traders, who, because their activity requires daily contact with the market, are more sensitive to "problem" banks.

The final source of credit information is the financial statements of foreign banks. The advantages and pitfalls in analyzing such statements are discussed below. It is important to appreciate in this regard that bank supervisory and regulatory climates differ widely in the countries of the world, so each country has to be understood in its own right. Thus, many countries have laws which purport to regulate bank action, but do little to ensure compliance. Many countries furthermore do little in the way of detailed on-site examination of the actual operations of their banks. It is necessary, therefore, to know such things as the skills and influence of the central bank and other regulatory agencies and how professionally and effectively they operate. Obviously, knowing how much the authorities actually monitor bank performance can be reassuring about their soundness. Also one must judge how committed the central bank is to act as a lender of last resort and to be responsible for the health and stability of the banks within its system.

Analysis of Financial Statements

The quality of credit information varies from country to country. For example, in many countries the establishment of hidden reserves is a perfectly acceptable and even encouraged practice to even out a bank's earnings over a period of time. However, the practice does, of course, distort balance sheets and profit and loss statements. Although few hard facts and figures are available, indirect evidence suggests that it is not uncommon for banks in some countries to understate capital by one-quarter to one-half of the actual amount. It is also interesting to observe that in recent years a number of major international banks have been able to absorb large foreign exchange and other losses without impairing their stated capital or injuring their dividend pay-out record.

Another problem in analyzing the financial statements of banks lies in the fact that it is often difficult, if not impossible, to test the validity of balance sheet asset values, particularly in the key loan and investment accounts. In such cases, even when a bank's statement shows a satisfactory balance between various asset and liability accounts, the credit officer should exercise caution because that bank's capital can be wiped out by poor asset quality or imprudent risk concentration. Needless to say, bank financial statements which are independently audited, where auditing standards are of high quality and truly independent, should reassure such officers more than those which are not.

Accepting the fact that different accounting practices and procedures are observed from country to country, it is nevertheless useful formally to spread the financial statements of foreign banks and develop appropriate ratios to measure the liquidity, solvency, capital adequacy, and earnings strength of the institutions. A comparison of such ratios particularly for banks within the same country operating under the same rules and regulations can be instructive. Thus, if the ratios for one bank are markedly weaker than those of its peer institutions, it can alert the analyst to the presence of a possible problem.

Dozens of ratios can be calculated, and in principle those used for the purpose of analyzing domestic U.S. banks would also be applicable for international purposes. In principle, the more detailed the analysis, the more useful and informative the conclusions as to the strength and viability of the bank in question. In practice, however, a great many foreign banks of the world do not provide a great deal of line-by-line statement and earnings information. Nevertheless, it should normally be possible to derive the following key ratios from the financial statements of most banks:

- Profitability: return on assets, return on equity, and net income growth
- Capital adequacy: equity to assets and loans to equity
- Liquidity: loans as percent of assets and deposits as percent of assets

These ratios will normally be calculated initially for a period back at least three years and then kept on a current basis.

In addition to ratio information, financial statements may reveal much else of importance. For example, they tell how big the bank in question is, the kind of growth it has experienced, the types of business in which it is engaged (from the distribution and types of asset and liability accounts), and the types of change a bank has undergone relative to previous periods (as different asset and liability accounts become more or less prominent). For example, a loan breakdown showing mortgages and fixed advances secured by mortgages gives clues about that bank's position in the construction finance business. A substantial investment account tells the observer that a bank has a major equity position. The existence of different types of liability accounts provides insights into deposit sources, volatility and rate risk.

Other Key Credit Considerations

Often as important for the credit officer in analyzing correspondent banks is to develop information *not* revealed by the financial statements. Illustrative of the kinds of subjects that might be raised are the following:

Bank Ownership. The banker should try to determine the amount of loans to and investments in affiliated businesses of his correspondent. Many banks' financial difficulties are caused by the business problems of an owner and the companies which he owns compounded by substantial intercompany loans or investments. The failure of a prominent private bank in Geneva in 1977 comes to mind. Furthermore, the directors of a bank should be checked for their corporate affiliations. If these affiliations are substantial compared to the size of the bank, consideration should be given to asking the bank whether it lends to these organizations. This is particularly important with smaller or regional banks where management is often involved in local commercial enterprises. There are several examples in recent international bank experience to illustrate this point.

Diversification of Loan Portfolio. It is useful to know the legal limits restricting a bank's loans to one customer or group of customers. If there are none, it would be helpful to find out if the bank in question has imposed its own house limit on loans. If a bank's portfolio is not diversified, the questions should be raised: Does it specialize in any one area? Does it reflect the business of the local market or does it reflect the bank's preference for certain industries?

Liability Management. Also important to risk appraisal is understanding the nature of the sources of funds on which a bank relies to finance its loan and investment portfolio and the volatility and term of such funds.

Investment Portfolio. Is the bank being analyzed a dealer or an investor? That is to say, does it trade and hold positions for its own account or does it merely act as broker between buyers and sellers? If acting as investor, how is its ability to invest restricted by the banking system in which it operates? To what extent do its investment policies when compared with its liability structure create concentration risks?

Attitudes Toward Risk. This caption refers to a bank's sensitivity to risk and to seeing the kind of business that it accepts or refuses and exploring with the bank its lending and operating practices. The development of such information will also help to decide whether senior management has enough information to control the bank. In addition, there are a number of areas in bank operations which can involve substantial risk but which may not show up directly on financial statements. Examples would be foreign exchange trading positions and trust and fiduciary operations.

As a practical matter, it is unlikely that answers can always be developed on all of the above areas of each correspondent's business activities, but the more information that can be obtained, the more comfortable a bank's management will be with any particular credit relationship.

Types of Credit

The credit extended by U.S. banks to their foreign correspondents can be divided broadly into the following categories:

1. Traditional facilities
2. Treasury facilities
3. Temporary overdraft lines
4. Nostro accounts
5. Reciprocal agreements
6. Operating lines
7. Guarantees
8. Advances

Traditional Facilities. As noted, a U.S. bank's international engagements are historically rooted in the financing of short-term trade financings. The techniques have not changed basically and continue to be centered in the letter of credit and related financing of payments under letters of credit by the creation of acceptances or the granting of advances. There are many variations in such facilities. In a typical agreement, the U.S. bank will advise its foreign correspondent that it holds a line of credit available whereby it will confirm letters of credit of the correspondent up to a specified dollar amount for a specified period to cover exports from the United States or between third countries. The agreement may further provide that the U.S. correspondent will accept drafts drawn on it which may then be discounted in the market. It may also provide for advances to the foreign correspondent to finance payments under letters of credit.

The above form of credit line is normally established on an unsecured basis except for the protection that may be provided to the U.S. bank by its having title to the underlying goods through the endorsement of the shipping documents in its favor. The terms and conditions will generally be advised in writing and will be subject to review on a periodic basis at the option of the U.S. bank.

Treasury Facilities. This category broadly encompasses those internal guidance lines set up by U.S. banks to permit their traders to deal in foreign exchange as well as in the domestic and the international money markets. More recently, they might also include lines for trading in gold.

In the foreign exchange area, the lines are primarily to establish limits up to which a trader of the U.S. bank is permitted to deal in forward foreign exchange contracts with any one foreign bank. The authority is usually restricted to contracts with a maturity of up to one year but may be longer with special permission. Some banks may also set limits for spot trading.

In the money market area, treasury facilities establish limits up to which a trader may place Eurocurrency or domestic currency deposits with foreign banks in the international or domestic markets. Eurocurrency deposits are by definition deposits placed with a foreign correspondent in a currency other than that of the country where the correspondent is located. Domestic deposits are by definition deposits placed with a correspondent in his own currency. An example of the first would be a dollar deposit placed by a London branch of a U.S. bank with a Luxembourg subsidiary of a German bank. An example of the latter would be a deutsche mark deposit placed by a branch of a U.S. bank in Germany with a local German bank.

Overdraft Lines. These may or may not be advised to a correspondent but are normally intended to cover very short-term overdrafts resulting from payments made to the debit of a correspondent bank's account before the receipt of covering funds. In the normal course of events, a correspondent will be controlling its payments and providing sufficient funds to keep its account in credit. At times, however, such as when there is a payment under a letter of credit, the correspondent may only be advised of the transaction after the fact, and during the period it is arranging to cover a payment it may run a temporary overdraft.

Nostro Accounts. In order to execute payments in foreign currencies for account of its customers and also in order to settle foreign exchange, redeposit, and other operations, a U.S. bank will have to maintain foreign currency accounts in the principal trading currencies. U.S. banks will thus open Deutsche mark accounts with one or more of their German correspondents, French franc accounts with their French correspondents, etc. These are referred to as nostro accounts, that is to say, "our accounts." The credit exposure of the U.S. banks in the opening of the account is represented by the balances they keep on deposit at any one time. It also may be recognized by way of an internal guidance line setting the maximum amount that may be maintained in such accounts at any one time along with an indication of what is the desired average target balance. In fact, however, most U.S. banks probably do not separately document this type of credit exposure, but rather include it among treasury facilities.

Reciprocal Agreements. These are specialized standby agreements between a U.S. bank and its foreign correspondents. They are designed primarily to provide reciprocal funding arrangements which can be used in the event normal market channels are closed to either partner. They are particularly common between banks which maintain branch or other foreign operations in one another's countries, whereby, a U.S. bank will guarantee dollar availability to its correspondent in return for a commitment of local currency availability. A U.S. bank may, therefore, arrange to commit a dollar standby in favor of the American branch of a German bank in return for a similar commitment from the German bank to establish a deutsche mark standby in favor of the German branch of the U.S. bank. Similarly, such agreements may be tailored by U.S. banks to commit the availability of Eurodollar deposits, again in return for local currency commitments.

The agreements themselves under such reciprocals are usually drawn up with as close to the identical wording as possible and similar terms and conditions to reflect the reciprocal nature of these agreements. They are priced at floating rates.

A variation of this category of credit is agreements between two banks providing for the actual reciprocal placing of deposits with one another for longer periods of time up to five years or more, rather than being one of a standby nature.

Operating Lines. These are guidance lines set up internally by some U.S. banks to permit their operating departments to process transactions up to stated limits which may result in credit exposure without referring them to a loaning officer. They are usually for a very short duration, the most common being the so-called "daylight" overdraft lines, which authorize payment clerks to execute dollar payments to the debit of a foreign correspondent's account before covering funds have been received. Such operating lines are established internally to facilitate the money transfer operations of a bank and reflect the expectation that such overdrafts will be covered in the course of the day's business. Of course, the risk is that this may not happen and a true overdraft will result, carrying over into the next day's business. At any time such daylight overdrafts may be very sizeable, particularly if the U.S. bank is acting as a clearing agent for the foreign correspondent.

Guarantees. A U.S. bank will be creating a credit exposure when it accepts the guarantee of a foreign correspondent in order to induce it to extend some form of credit accommodation to a third party. It may take many forms but perhaps the most common is to respond to a foreign correspondent's request to grant credit to one of its clients under protection of a bank guarantee. Examples are the so-called impact loans, arranged and guaranteed by Japanese banks, to Japanese corporations for capital expansion purposes.

Advances. A foreign correspondent may often be invited to make proposals for a credit transaction involving short- to medium-term advances under neither a line nor a commitment but simply on an offering basis. In such cases, each proposal is dealt with separately and the U.S. correspondent can on each occasion decide whether its own position and interests permit it to agree to a proposal. If so, the advance may be booked as a one-shot transaction. For example, it may be a $1 million six-month advance to finance a shipment of wheat.

This category would also include loans to a foreign bank for relending to its customer. Examples are the Resolution 63 loans of the Banco Central do Brazil, which permit Brazilian banks to borrow from their correspondents in hard currencies on specified terms for relending to local clients in cruzeiros for working capital purposes.

Similarly in many countries, but particularly those in eastern Europe, loans to governments and government agencies are not made directly but rather through their specialized foreign trade bank. Thus a U.S. bank doing business in Romania will invariably be dealing only with the Romanian Bank for Foreign Trade and not the ultimate beneficiaries. The credit under such arrangements will often be for a medium term and have many characteristics of a corporate loan, including appropriate loan language and documentation.

It also has become more common for U.S. banks to grant term loans to selected foreign banks for their own capital purposes.

Undoubtedly, many other variations of the advance have been concluded between U.S. banks and their foreign correspondents. The point worth noting is that the extension of credit between international banks is evolving from the almost exclusive simple short-term credit to a greater willingness to negotiate more intricate longer-term forms of financing.

Loans versus Deposits

As noted above, credit extended to banks, foreign or domestic, although sometimes classified as a loan, is generally included among the deposit categories. While, as also noted, there is generally no difference in the credit risk arising out of loans or deposits to banks, for certain regulatory purposes arbitrary distinctions are drawn between loans and deposits. In considering risk assets for the purpose of measuring capital adequacy, Federal Reserve examiners include loans to banks, but not deposits. Similarly, under the Federal Reserve Act and the National Banking Act there are no limits on deposits by member banks (including national banks) with foreign banks, whereas these acts do impose limits on loans. New York State banks in turn are subject to separate legal limits for loans and deposits, and other states may also provide separate legal limits.

There are no hard and fast rules for determining whether a transaction is a loan or deposit although, generally, how the parties treat and book the transaction may be regarded as determinative. On the other hand, where a transaction has clearly the earmarks of customary loan documentation, for example, merely calling the transaction a deposit would not necessarily make it such for regulatory purposes.

Country Risk, Exposure, and Limits

In extending credit to a foreign bank, the risk of course is not only the bank itself but also as with other foreign loans the risk of doing business in the country where the borrower is located. This is generally identified as country risk, and a 1977 report on the subject prepared by the International Committee of the Association of Reserve City Bankers defined it as "a spectrum of risks arising from the economic, social and political environments of a given foreign country (including government policies framed in response to trends in these environments) having potential favorable or adverse consequences for foreigners' debt and/or equity investments in that country. . . . These risks are incurred as a result of corporate activities undertaken in a foreign country and are distinct from considerations relating to a given entity's creditworthiness."

A full discussion of this concept is beyond the scope of this chapter, but as applied to the extension of credit to foreign banks, it in essence recognizes that claims on banks in any one country may become uncollectible in whole or in part not because of the inability or the unwillingness on the part of these banks to pay their debts but because of circumstances beyond their control. Examples of such events are a rescheduling of foreign debts, moratoriums, foreign exchange controls, and inconvertibility decrees.

Related to the subject of country risk, but as a distinct concept, is the exercise of quantifying the total amount of assets actually and potentially at risk in each country of the world where a U.S. bank does business. The term "country exposure" is generally applied to this process and is defined in the report referred to above by the ARCB as "a term of measurement which refers to the volume of assets held and off-balance sheet items considered to be subject to the country risk of a given country." In theory this is a simple concept. However, to put it into practice is a much more difficult matter and involves myriad judgments on individual credit facilities with no one uniform exposure system in place for all U.S. banks. The only generalization that might be made is that most banks, with a number of notable exceptions, treat unguaranteed risk assets as exposure to the country where the borrower resides.

One of these exceptions in the handling of country exposure, particularly pertinent to this chapter, pertains to the treatment accorded to credits extended to branches of foreign banks. Thus some U.S. banks treat an unsecured claim on the branch of another bank in a foreign country as country exposure to the parent bank and not as exposure in the country where the branch is located. For example, if a deposit is placed with the Tokyo branch of a French bank, the deposit would under this system be counted as French country exposure, as that is where the head office of the depository bank is located, and not as Japanese exposure. The principle underlying this practice is that every credit facility and risk asset should be placed in the country which best reflects the location of the unit having ultimate *legal* responsibility for repayment of the obligation.

The drawback of allocating risk to the parent bank rather than to its foreign branch to whom the credit has actually been extended is that it does not take into account the possibility that the government of the foreign country may prevent such a branch from meeting its obligations, for example, by way of foreign exchange controls, an event outside of the control of the parent bank. Should the parent bank nevertheless be obligated to make good on the credit? The answer is not clear, either legally or morally. Some banks, including Morgan Guaranty, attempt to control this type of risk by having two measures of exposure, one based on the legal principle of allocation and the second on what might be called the "sovereign risk" principle of allocation. In the second category of exposure would be placed all outstandings subject to possible loss if there is a Castro-like catastrophe in a specific country resulting in the expropriation of assets and the institution of exchange controls prohibiting the cross-border transfer of funds.

Each bank must decide for itself how to solve the difficult problems which arise in allocating and measuring country exposure, particularly with respect to banks in such cases as touched upon above. It is evident that there is no one perfect answer and that there will probably always be a degree of distortion and imperfection in whatever system is constructed. In any event, once a decision has been made on the design of a bank's country exposure system, management normally will wish to establish a maximum amount of credit exposure it will be prepared to accept for each country where it does business. These are generally referred to as "country limits." As already noted, credit facilities to banks will normally account for a substantial share of these limits for most of the countries of the world. Morgan Guaranty includes under such exposure all of the types of facilities described in an earlier paragraph, both used and unused, including forward foreign exchange lines. The latter for exposure purposes are counted by some banks at 10 percent of the line, while others use higher percentages. The principle of not including such lines at one hundred percent of face amount is based on the expectation that even if a contractual partner in a foreign exchange contract fails to perform on maturity, the contract can be unwound in the spot market with no more than a 10 percent loss of principal. It may be questioned whether in the world of floating exchange rates a 10 percent factor is sufficiently high.

The question of what is an appropriate limit for any given country is one that will be answered differently by different banks depending on their size, experience, and judgment of risk. Each bank will develop its own form of quantitative analysis and its own series of economic indicators to control and limit its country exposure as it may define that term. There is a growing literature on the techniques and principles underlying country analysis. It is sufficient to note here that they vary from the simple to the highly complex and may include a whole spectrum of inputs from balance of payments calculations to considerations of a country's domestic fiscal and monetary policies to the structuring of many more or less detailed ratios. While appreciating that such analytical exercises contribute importantly to the processes of setting country limits, it should be recognized nevertheless that setting country limits is a highly judgmental matter and, although bankers may not like to admit it, a great deal of intuition goes into arriving at what is an appropriate limit for any one country of the world.

BIBLIOGRAPHY

"Country Exposure, Country Limits and Lending to LDC's," by A. Bruce Brackenridge, *The Journal of Commercial Bank Lending,* July, 1977, pages 3–13.

Country Exposure Measurement and Reporting Practices of Member Banks, Association of Reserve City Bankers, March, 1977.

"International Bank Lending: A Guided Tour Through the Data," Federal Reserve Bank of New York, *Quarterly Review,* Autumn, 1978, pages 39–46.

Lending in International Commercial Banking, by T.H. Donaldson, The MacMillan Press Ltd., London, 1979. Available in the United States through Halstead Press, a subsidiary of John Wiley and Sons, Inc., New York.

Offshore Lending by U.S. Commercial Banks, F. John Mathis, editor, copyright 1975 by Bankers' Association for Foreign Trade and Robert Morris Associates.

Preparing a Bank's Written International Lending Policy, copyright 1977 by Robert Morris Associates and Bankers' Association for Foreign Trade.

30

Lending to Foreign Companies

Lending to foreign local companies has become an increasingly important aspect of international banking. Large money center banks, through either their local branches, representative offices, headquarters, or affiliate banks, are actively pursuing loans to indigenous companies. Regional banks have also been vigorous in this marketplace, following the pattern of the money center banks and providing a source of funds for syndicated loans to the international private sector.

What has been the experience? Generally speaking, except for some specific areas where loans were related to property or shipping, the experience has been favorable. Statistical evidence from large money center banks suggests that bad debts associated with international operations are consistently lower than the domestic experience. However, the international lender should not be lulled into the belief that international lending is safer than domestic lending, nor should he forgo profitable loans out of fear that international lending is more risky as well as less profitable than domestic lending.

As in the case of loans made to domestic borrowers, there is no substitute for a complete and thorough credit analysis of the prospective international borrower. Many of the lending criteria discussed in other chapters of this book apply to making loans to local foreign companies. As there are many similarities, so too are there significant differences. Generally these additional factors encompass a comprehensive understanding of the host country and its political, social, and economic strengths and weaknesses, in addition to differences in accounting and legal practices.

An example of an actual large international loan may best serve to illustrate many of the factors, subsequently elaborated upon in this chapter, that an international lender is required to analyze.

Established in 1892, MEXPAP, Inc., was a profitable but stodgy company in a capital-intensive industry. The host country, considered to be one of the most advanced of the developing countries, had a history of political, social, and economic stability. MEXPAP had enjoyed an important market franchise and had controlled a significant share of the market. Its market share, however, had been declining over several years since no new major incremental capital investment had taken place. The company's plant and equipment had been reasonably well maintained, but was old and technology was second or third generation.

MEXPAP was a fully integrated producer. Raw material sources were owned by the company, and almost all of its material needs were supplied locally. The local market was growing and the prospective demand for its products was very strong inasmuch as national demand exceeded national production.

Perceiving a profitable opportunity, one of the host country's most important financial institutions had recently increased its investment, becoming the controlling owner in this publicly traded company. Its intent was to revitalize MEXPAP's plant, management, and other operating aspects. Operating management was changed and an aggressive ten-year investment program was developed and initiated. Since local financing was not sufficient, international loans and supplier credits were obtained from U.S. and European banking sources to complement local borrowings. Cash flow loans exceeding $100 million were extended to MEXPAP for plant expansion based on the company's forecasts and historical profitability. Employing over 4,000 workers, MEXPAP was considered to be one of the better credit risks in the host country's private sector. Yet four years later, unable to pay interest, faced with over $137 million in dollar debt, a devalued currency, and massive asset write-offs, MEXPAP faced certain bankruptcy.

There are many credit considerations touched on in the case of MEXPAP. Some are credit considerations applicable to lending irrespective of domestic or international considerations. An examination of the general aspects of international lending and later how they relate to the case of MEXPAP in particular may be helpful to focus the scope of this chapter. The discussion will principally relate to a U.S. lender making a loan in dollars to a foreign company whose base currency is not dollars. The reader should be cautioned that all considerations which should be taken into account in an international loan are not necessarily referred to in this discussion.

Consideration: Cross-Currency Risk

In most cases where a domestic lender makes a loan to a foreign borrower, the loan is denominated in the currency of the lender. In some of the developed countries, large international banks do make loans denominated in local currency, but in the aggregate most international loans are dollar denominated. When the borrower's obligation to pay is denominated in dollars and his cash resources are fundamentally the currency of the host country, a cross-currency or foreign exchange risk arises. Sometimes this risk is referred to as country risk. There are two factors which are implied in the discussion of cross-currency risk: (1) the effect of the borrower's country's political, social, and economic factors on the ability of the borrower to repay the loan; and (2) transfer risk.

Although it is not the intent of this chapter to discuss in detail the questions raised as to country risk, a reasonable understanding of the key issues affecting a country's creditworthiness is essential in order properly to assess the creditworthiness of a particular borrower. The international lender should be aware of the foreign country's economic team and the influence and effectiveness of the central bank; the impact of the economic/financial team on political leadership; and the ability of political leadership to implement decisions. Other key factors regarding the host country might be:

1. Its relations with the International Monetary Fund, World Bank, and the international commercial banking community; and a willingness to provide the latter with economic and other financial information

2. Its natural resource base, including effects of past development strategies and its ability to make use of its natural resource base

3. Its human resource base: education level, demographic characteristics, and entrepreneurial capacity

4. Its financial resource base, including past success in stimulating domestic savings, developing local financial markets, and reducing the relative importance of foreign capital in aggregate domestic investment

5. Its export diversification, by commodity and region

6. Its outlook for domestic political stability—in the sense of the likelihood that future political change will be orderly, with fundamental economic policies unchanged.

The transfer risk arises when there is a potential for exchange controls or currency fluctuations as between the local currency and the currency borrowed. Foreign exchange risks are dynamic, that is, foreign exchange risks associated with international transactions come not only from the existence of different national monies, but also from the variations over time of their relative values.

The lender must accept the threat of loss from exchange rate variations as an unfavorable risk when he undertakes to make loans to a company in a currency other than that of the host country. Many lenders are under the false assumption that because the loan is extended in the lender's base currency, the foreign exchange risk is to the borrower. On the contrary, one might argue that the lender has as much of a foreign exchange risk as the borrower. For example, suppose company X borrows currency Y from Bank Y. Due to economic, social, or political factors, the host country where company X operates decides that it cannot make foreign exchange (currency Y) available to company X to pay Bank Y. This decision is made in spite of the fact that company X has sufficient local currency, and, may I add, the desire to pay Bank Y. Another common foreign exchange risk that a lender assumes, even though his loan is in his own base currency, is the risk of devaluation. For example, company X borrows currency Y from Bank Y. Company X then converts currency Y at the current rate of exchange for the local currency of company X. Obviously, the risk here, other factors remaining equal, is the potential that the exchange rate between the two currencies over time will materially change. In the event the local currency of company X has devalued as to currency Y, company X may not have sufficient local currency to retire the loan in currency Y. In both cases, the lender may not receive repayment of his loan at the time, place, and/or currency agreed.

When a major devaluation occurs, such as happened in Mexico in 1976 where the exchange rate went from U.S. $1 = pesos 12.50 to U.S. $1 = pesos 22.50 (almost 100 percent devaluation of the Mexican peso), there was little the international lending community could do. In this instance, Mexican companies with major dollar obligations were faced with the fact that, in terms of Mexcan pesos, their debt had virtually doubled overnight, and unfortunately, their cash flow in terms of pesos was the same.

Once the lender has thoroughly analyzed a specific country's economic, political, and social trends to determine the probability of exchange controls and/or currency fluctuations, the lender might consider these additional factors that may alter the cross-currency risk:

COUNTRY FACTORS

1. To what extent is there a forward foreign exchange market, that is, a market whereby the borrower or lender could enter into a forward foreign exchange contract specifying a fixed rate of exchange between the currency borrowed and the local currency, for delivery at a specific date in the future?

2. To what extent can the foreign exchange risk be insured with governmental agencies such as the Foreign Credit Insurance Corporation (FCIA), or export-import banks, both in the United States and in other major developed countries?

BORROWER FACTORS

1. To what extent does the borrower earn foreign exchange by exporting its products? Will these foreign exchange earnings be available to repay the loans?

2. To what extent is the borrower dependent upon its raw materials from nonlocal sources? And to what extent is the borrower dependent upon a raw material whose price is quoted in nonlocal currency (for example, certain metals and oil products)?

3. To what extent is the borrower free to increase its prices to offset any devaluation of its base currency? To what extent is the borrower's debt coverage in excess of normal acceptable coverages?

A common practice among some analysts, either as an attempt to standardize the analysis or to comply with policy, is translating currencies into the currency of the lender, then using the lender's currency to make the analysis. This practice can lead to gross errors and misinformation, even when done with sophistication, and should be avoided. Fundamentally, a borrower should be analyzed using its own currency, with the objective of determining the borrower's ability to generate local currency in sufficient amounts to purchase the required foreign currency, at a forecasted exchange rate.

Consideration: Accounting Principles and Practices

The general accounting principles and practices of the borrower's country reflected in the borrower's financial statements can mislead the international lender accustomed to other principles and practices. These differences in accounting principles and practices should be fully understood by the international lender. For example, in many countries, consolidated financial statements are not prepared. The lack of consolidated statements may conceal many important facts and grossly understate or overstate the assets of the borrower. An international lender should be careful to discriminate between a consolidated statement, that is, a statement wherein all intercompany transactions are eliminated, and a combined statement, that is, a statement wherein only the principal intercompany accounts (principally investment accounts) are eliminated. Many times the latter is supplied by the borrower in response to a lender's need to look at the "big picture." For example, many times an international borrower is a holding company and the holding company's financial statements can be materially misleading due to non-arm's-length transactions and controlling the timing of dividend payments by subsidiaries.

International accounting practices regarding depreciation, amortization, bad debt provisions, inventory valuations, etc. may be heavily influenced by tax considerations rather than matching costs and revenues. The use of reserves to even out swings in earnings or the lack of adequate reserves are characteristics of accounting principles and practices in many countries. Or with important financial ramifications, sometimes local accounting practices do not require the company to create reserves for pensions and similar indirect labor contingencies. This unstated and unfunded contingency may be quite large, particularly if the company has been in existence for many years. Some foreign accounting practices do not require disclosure of subsequent events after the company's fiscal year end, thus eliminating important facts that might materially alter the financial position of the company after the close of the statement. Practices and principles associated with inflation accounting are also vastly different from country to country. Some countries commonly allow a revaluation of a company's fixed assets on a form of price level accounting, while other countries use appraisal accounting. Foreign exchange losses and gains can have a material impact on the representation of the financial statements in the international lending arena (where many loans create a cross-currency exposure).

Not only do different accounting practices and principles complicate competent analysis, they occasionally make customary financial covenants meaningless. An international lender should insure that the loan documentation identify any changes to local accounting principles and practices so that covenants are meaningful and functional.

The international lender should not accept statements audited (even by a reputable firm) at face value. Unlike the protective and punitive powers of the Securities and Exchange Commission in the United States, many foreign countries do not impose strict rules and penalties as to the reporting requirements of publicly traded companies. However, the fact that accounting principles and practices might differ and that audited statements are not customary should not diminish the importance of obtaining audited statements. Any corporate borrower who is sufficiently large and sophisticated to borrow in the international community should be capable of providing audited statements. Furthermore, an international lender should not be so bashful that he neglects to make a thorough investigation of the auditor. Generally, large international accounting firms have associate offices in most developed or developing countries. Nevertheless, the lender should not hesitate to investigate the reputation of a particular accounting firm with his local counsel or correspondent bank.

Consideration: Legal Aspects

Major areas of concern to the international lender are legal aspects and loan documentation. Fundamentally, the challenge to a lender and his legal counsel is to assure that risks identified by the lender and lawyer as being significant for that particular country and borrower remain adequately covered. Obviously the documentation should place the lender in the best posture to obtain a judgment and to collect on that judgment in the event of default. For example, too often in preparing loan documentation, counsel focuses primarily on the ability to bring suit against a borrower in a specific jurisdiction, without regard to the anticipated location of the borrower's assets, the difficulties likely to be encountered in enforcing a foreign judgment in the courts of the borrower's country, or, lastly, the possible value of bringing suit initially in the courts of the borrower's country.

Some additional legal suggestions for the international lender might be:

1. Examine with the help of U.S. and local foreign counsel the likelihood of ever bringing suit against the borrower in the courts of the borrower's country. The relative length of the court calendars in the two countries, the relative cost of litigation in the two countries, the difficulty in enforcing a U.S. judgment in the courts of the borrower's country, and the likelihood of finding assets of the borrower outside of his country are all factors to be taken into account. The key issue, of course, in deciding whether to bring suit in the courts of the borrower's country, is the objectiveness and predictability of the local courts. If the courts pass this test (and more of them will than one might initially predict), one is likely to find that the local law is more creditor-oriented than U.S. law and it certainly is easier to base one's case on local law rather than having to prove foreign law. Involve local foreign counsel in the drafting process to assure that the documentation, to the extent feasible, incorporates helpful terminology and concepts to facilitate local court action (for example, have the borrower agree to a "domicile" in the jurisdiction of his country where the best judges are likely to be found).

   a. Where available, have local foreign counsel advise on the preparation of documentation permitting executive action, that is, legal action enabling prejudgment attachment of borrower's or guarantor's assets. In many countries executive action can be sought based on a promissory note containing an unconditional promise to pay an amount of money determinable from the face of the note. The note should stand on its own, independent of the loan agreement.

   b. Use a dual-language note, that is, a note that has the complete text in both borrower's and lender's own language.

   c. If there is a possibility that suit will be initiated against the borrower in the courts of the borrower's country, consider with U.S. and local counsel the advisability of a choice of law clause protecting the normal election of U.S. law, but permitting suit to be brought in the courts of the borrower's country based on the laws of that country rather than U.S. law.

   d. Use local foregin counsel to obtain and review documents evidencing authority of borrower to enter into transactions which are customary in that country rather than, or in addition to, the customary forms used by the foreign lender.

   e. An agreed-upon translation of the documents which, when, executed
   will assure that the language of the documents made available to the
   courts will be what the parties agreed to. At a minimum, the language
   to be used for the official documents should be agreed to.

   2. If a credit is denominated in dollars but is made available in various
currencies, any necessary exchange control permit will normally be issued
assuming repayment in dollars. Either before initial drawdown or before first
drawdown in a new currency other than dollars, the borrower must be required
to obtain exchange control permits needed to protect the lender from the
exchange risk associated with multicurrency loans.
   3. Avoid where possible the use of "comfort" or "awareness" letters. Such
documents are not guaranties.
   4. Be specific in the documentation. Responsibilities of the parties as to
withholding taxes, reserves, and other similar matters, when not covered, can
make a profitable loan into a loser simply by the stroke of a pen in some
government official's hand.

   Although most cash flow (non-trade related) loans to foreign countries are
made on an unsecured basis, there are many loan situations where security is
taken as a secondary source of repayment. Here the international lender should
be aware that, generally speaking, simple procedures to perfect security (like
the filing of UCC-1 forms in the United States) do not exist, and in fact in some
countries effective non-possessory security interests (for example, in inventory)
are extremely difficult to perfect. Additionally, the cost both in legal documentation, registration, policing, and control of the collateral may far outweigh the
benefits to be derived from the security in question. In international lending,
particularly as it relates to short- or medium-term non-trade related financing,
a common "solution" to the problem of security interest has been the negative
pledge clause (for example, the borrower agrees not to pledge any of its assets
to secure any other creditor) and pari passu clause (for example, the lender
agrees that the borrower can grant security for other indebtedness provided
the borrower secures the indebtedness due the lender "equally and ratably").
These clauses, of course, provide little comfort if the borrower breeches them
when stretched thin financially.
   These clauses pose additional weaknesses in the international context. In
some foreign countries local lenders have preference as to collections over
foreign lenders. In other countries it is common practice for a borrower to sign
documents that do not appear to be security agreements, but give a lender the
right to take specifically defined collateral at any time he wishes.
   Many times the form of the clause in the legal documentation is critical
as to its effect as a default. The courts might not accept the breach of a
covenant not within the control of the borrower (for example, a negative
pledge clause as it relates to entities other than the borrower, if included as
a covenant rather than an event of default). Due to the diversity of countries

and their legal structures, there are obviously numerous legal traps that need the careful scrutiny of the international lender before he makes the loan.

Even after the international lender becomes proficient in his analysis of balance of payments, cross-currency risk, and legal and accounting differences, there are still other credit considerations or business judgments that might confront him. Many considerations are similar to those related to domestic lending, but often there are subtle differences.

Other Considerations

OWNERSHIP

Knowledge regarding ownership is the key to extending any credit, and such knowledge becomes critical in the international context. Today "one-man shows" or closely held family companies are common international borrowers. An international lender should not be seduced into lending to a company or family group based on name, business, or political connections. Because of the close business and political circles in many foreign countries, however, it is important that ownership be well respected in both arenas. An international lender should also be cognizant of conflicts of interest. It is not unusual for a local financial institution, which also might be a lender, to own equity in the borrowing company. In such circumstances, the analysis might question the extent to which the local financial institution is prepared to support the company and what role it has played in previous problem circumstances where it played a dual role as lender and owner.

OTHER LENDERS

The international lender should be fully aware of the other financial institutions lending to the borrower in question. Lenders should be cautious of a foreign company that relies heavily on brokers to place its paper, or companies that seek unusual sources of financing. In the event a problem occurs, a cohesive lender group is essential. The international lender should be aware that, should a problem arise, a unified international lending group may not be possible, due to a variety of factors including communications among the lenders, different laws governing the lenders, and funding of the respective loans.

Remember that in most foreign countries the reason companies are borrowing in the international marketplace is because of the small indigenous capital markets. Therefore, the international lender should recognize that the foreign borrower cannot generally find local currency borrowings in good times, let alone when there is a financial crisis. As local capital markets become more sophisticated, there may be opportunities to make participating loans with local financial institutions. Many times these institutions can provide valuable assistance in dealing with governmental entities or handling other essential aspects where a foreigner may not be as adept or welcome.

The international lender should do his own homework and make his own decision. Naively playing follow the leader may have disastrous consequences in international lending.

GOVERNMENT INVOLVEMENT

An international lender cannot ignore the fact that in most foreign countries government plays an active role in day-to-day activities of the borrower. Often government may own equity in the borrower, or may be the borrower's principal source of raw material or may compete directly with the borrower through a state-controlled company. The borrower might be in an industry where there are price controls or other government-imposed restrictions. Generally speaking, a government's position is to foster employment, and these policies may be detrimental to the borrower when the government-controlled competition is more interested in creating jobs than profits. The international lender should also consider the type of business the borrower is in so as to determine the priority of the industry to the government's short- and long-term interests. An international lender should be aware of the host government's attitude toward foreign loans, including (but not limited to) the purpose and the terms of the credit. Some foreign countries require a registration of the parties to the loan and the terms thereof. In other foreign countries government authorities have used "verbal persuasion" to discourage loans to specific industries or for speculative purposes.

HUMAN RESOURCES

Both the competency of the borrower's management and the discipline of its labor force must be thoroughly analyzed before making any loan. In developing countries one cannot even assume that the large companies have management depth or sophisticated accounting and management reporting systems. There are still many large publicly traded companies who appear to have sophisticated management, but are really closely held and managed corporations. In rapidly growing economies there is considerable lack of upper echelon and middle management. Thus, as a result, many foreign borrowers have one or two strong managers, with other key management positions filled with unseasoned executives. One of the areas that require close scrutiny in these companies is the area of financial systems and controls. One of the effects of rapid growth, coupled with inflation, is to demonstrate strong earnings. These earnings may tend to camouflage serious accounting and management control problems.

It is vital that the international lender be aware of the labor situation of his foreign borrowers. Because of strong labor laws and political consequences, reducing a labor force can be extremely problematical in foreign countries. Some foreign countries have fragmented unions while others have separate unions that operate under a common banner and monolithic leadership. The lender should be aware of the borrower's union affiliation, the discipline of its labor force, and the flexibility that the foreign borrower might have to increase or decrease his labor requirements.

TECHNOLOGY

An international lender should assess of the basic technology used by his borrower and the borrower's access to new technology. In some foreign countries, there may be restrictions on obtaining external technology or other foreign investment limitations. Related to the question of technology is the state of the borrower's productive plant and equipment. The age of equipment is not necessarily indicative of an inefficient plant; older equipment does, nevertheless, require significant maintenance, and the availability of spare parts, particularly in foreign countries, may present problems.

RAW MATERIAL SOURCE

It is not uncommon for a foreign borrower to be significantly dependent on raw materials whose source is not indigenous to the borrower's country. The lender should analyze the reliability of the raw material source, the mode of transporting the raw material, and the host government's open or closed border policy as to the importation of the raw material in question. If the raw material is sourced locally, it is not uncommon to have only one source, and questions regarding its quality and availability must be thoroughly reviewed.

PURPOSE

One of the key elements in making any loan is to determine the exact purpose of the loan. The catch-all phrases "for working capital" or "plant expansion" do not go far enough. In many of the less developed and developing countries reliance on short-term capital for long-term financing requirements is prevalent. Obviously, this situation can cause severe balance sheet distortions as well as affecting a foreign borrower's ability to roll over large volumes of short-term financing.

SUMMARY

Now, let us go back to the case of MEXPAP. How many "international considerations" can be identified? For example:

1. *Cross-Currency Risk:* MEXPAP. derived 100 percent of its sales and revenues in a devaluated local currency, yet over 90 percent of its liabilities were denominated in dollars.

2. *Accounting Principles and Practices:* MEXPAP had customarily provided its lenders combined interim statements and consolidated year-end statements. Interim statements did not reflect the fact that MEXPAP's subsidiaries were out of control. Much to the lenders' chagrin, at the pinnacle of MEXPAP's financial crisis, the lenders were informed that the company's balance sheet did not reflect substantial contingent liabilities for labor pensions and related costs. Of course, such a situation would not be complete without mentioning a complete lack of accounting practices and controls and poor auditing standards found in the company.

3. *Legal Aspects:* MEXPAP's lenders' loan documentation was poorly organized, signatures were missing or unauthorized signatures appeared, promissory notes were not completed, and, in some cases, loan documentation had been misfiled. Of the twenty-one lenders to MEXPAP, eight were local banks with over 35 percent of the loans. These banks enjoyed a preferrential position for the collections of their loans, vis-a-vis the other lenders, even though all the lenders had been considered "unsecured" lenders.

4. *Ownership:* MEXPAP was publicly traded but effectively controlled by one of the local lenders in the lending group—an obvious potential for conflict of interest.

5. *Lending Group:* MEXPAP had foreign lenders from the United States, England, France, and Italy as well as loans from the Export-Import Banks of the United States, England, and France. Finding a method to put all lenders, both local and foreign, on an equal basis was the most difficult problem in the restructuring of the company's indebtedness

6. *Government Involvement:* MEXPAP was an important company in an important industry. The scenario of bankruptcy and liquidation presented untenable political considerations. A significant portion of MEXPAP's products had price controls and one of MEXPAP's major competitors was state-controlled.

7. *Human Resources:* MEXPAP was an old company and through the years had yielded to too many union demands. Labor productivity was low compared with the competition, and the labor union's attitude was combative. Nonunionized management had also become complacent.

8. *Technology:* MEXPAP's equipment was outdated and its competitors, principally subsidiaries of large multinational companies, had efficient productive means to bring new products to the market.

9. *Purpose:* In the case of MEXPAP, the lenders were careless in defining the exact purpose of the loans. This error was compounded in that a loan structure was established that was inappropriate. When a major external financial crisis came, the ability of MEXPAP to roll over large amounts of short-term loans became impossible.

It has been the intent of this writer to demonstrate that the risks of international lending can be analyzed and mitigated by a prudent lender. Along with the application of common sense the risks associated with international lending, like domestic lending, are reduced if (1) there is a thorough analysis and comprehension of the credit; (2) credit standards are set, then maintained; and (3) competent counsel is used for the preparation and review of all loan documentation.

NOTE: I am indebted to Michael L. Owen, Vice President and Associate General Counsel of Bank of America, for his invaluable assistance relative to the legal aspects of international lending referred to in this chapter.

R.P.S.

31

Syndication of International Loans

The practice of syndicating the risk of lending goes back at least as far as fourteenth-century Italy, where banking partnerships were formed to finance single ventures. Indeed, syndicating risk is so central to the lending function that the practice probably existed among the banks of Babylon 33 centuries ago.

During the 1970s the syndication of international lending developed dramatically in size and significance. The advent of the Eurocurrency market in the late 1960s combined with the development of the floating-interest-rate loan led to a surge of international lending. This activity was based in London, where most of the major banks of the world established offices to participate in it. The growth of the London market, in turn, made possible the raising of unheard of sums, through the vehicle of the medium-term syndicated Eurocurrency loan. The syndicated Eurocurrency loan has become the single most important financing vehicle in the world today.

The original model for syndicated Eurocurrency loans was the multibank floating-rate term loan, which had been highly developed in the early 1960s in the United States. Similarly, the reasons for the creation and development of syndicated Eurocurrency loans are closely related to the origins of multibank lending: (1) the increasing size of individual loans; (2) the desire to spread risks; (3) the attractiveness of management fees; and (4) the desire to form profitable working relationships with other banks. The basic features of the multibank United States term loan were easily adapted to the conditions of the Eurocurrency market in the mid-sixties, and the new Eurocurrency vehicle has flourished ever since.

Virtually any kind of international risk can be syndicated, including bankers' acceptance facilities, export credits, risks under letters of credit, and performance bonds. Even short-term advances to correspondent banks overseas have been syndicated. However, by far the most common syndication vehicle, and the one to be discussed in this chapter, is the medium-term Eurocurrency loan. It has the following characteristics: the maturity is 3 to 15 years, often with amortization during the latter half of the term; the interest rate is normally quoted as a spread over the London interbank offered rate (LIBOR) and adjusted at predetermined intervals (normally 3 to 6 months); and there is a lead bank or syndicate manager (or group of managers) which negotiates the terms of the loan with the borrower (maturity, amortization, interest rate, covenants, etc.) and incorporates them into a loan agreement, and sells participations in the loan to a number of other banks.

The Eurocurrency Market

The market for Eurocurrency syndicated loans is centered in London, where there is a great concentration of institutions, skills, and communication facilities which makes it possible to bring borrowers and lenders together efficiently from every corner of the world. During the last few years subcenters of the Eurocurrency market have developed in Singapore, Hong Kong, Bahrain, and Luxembourg, but the focal point continues to be London.

The Eurocurrency market is essentially a market in deposits among banks located outside of the country in whose currency the deposits are denominated. For example, a Eurodollar is most generally defined as a U.S. dollar account held in a bank (including a branch of a United States bank) located outside of the United States. Similarly a Euro deutschemark is a deutschemark account held in a bank located outside of Germany, and a Euro Swiss franc is a Swiss franc account held in a bank outside of Switzerland. By far the most common unit in the Eurocurrency market is the Eurodollar, which constitutes about 70 percent of the market.

The Eurocurrency market has grown with remarkable speed during the 1970s, with its size estimated at $600 billion in December, 1979, as against $65 billion in 1970. From 1968 to 1978 the number of banks in London authorized to deal in Eurocurrencies increased from 175 to 363. This impressive expansion does not reflect the large increase in representative offices, investment banks, loan brokers, law and accounting firms, and other entities, which add substance and skill to the London market. Of the present total of 363 banks, approximately 60 are American owned. Within the total, banks from about 90 countries are represented.

The Three Parties to the Syndication

There are three parties to any loan syndication: the borrower, the syndicate manager or leader, and the participating or lending banks. We shall view the syndication process from the perspective of each.

THE BORROWER

The borrower is interested in having his financing needs met in a convenient, flexible, and economical manner. That is his immediate interest.

The borrower also has a long-term interest in maintaining and improving his credit standing in world financial markets. This means that the borrower should weigh the reputation and professionalism of the syndicate manager against the apparent short-term advantage of a lower rate proposed by a less professional manager.

THE SYNDICATE MANAGER (OR MANAGEMENT GROUP)

The syndicate manager negotiates the terms of the loan with the borrower and obtains from him a mandate to syndicate the loan. The manager prepares the basic information memorandum, which analyzes the financial condition of the borrower and the text of the loan agreement, sells participations in the loan to other banks, and oversees the implementation of the loan agreement. In recent years there has been a tendency for a group of banks to form a management group to share underwriting responsibility and to divide among themselves the functions of a syndicate manager. Syndicate managers are often the major commercial banks of the industrialized world, although smaller syndicates are not infrequently led by investment banks, consortium banks, or other specialized institutions.

It should be noted that, while the syndicate manager performs most of the functions of a conventional broker or agent, he is also an active participant in the negotiation and implementation of the loan and therefore he carries considerably more responsibility than merely that of a middleman. In most cases (with the exception of investment banks) the syndicate manager holds a significant part of the loan in his own portfolio. His loyalty is owed equally to the borrower and to the participating banks, and he must balance delicately the interests of both parties. If a loan develops problems, a conflict of interest can easily arise.

THE PARTICIPATING BANKS (LENDERS)

The banks taking participations in a Eurocurrency credit make their independent credit decisions based on the information provided by the syndicate manager and other information available to them. Although the participating banks may rely to a certain extent on the integrity and reputation of the syndicate manager, it is clearly understood that they fully accept the credit risk of the borrower. Participating banks are often regional or medium-sized banks from the major industrialized countries of the world, although banks from OPEC countries have recently become more active in this business.

Agreeing on the Mandate

The successful syndicate manager of an institution is skilled at identifying a creditworthy borrower whose needs can best be met by a syndicated Eurocurrency loan, and then making a marketable and acceptable offer to the borrower. Following negotiation of the basic terms of the loan, the prospective syndicate manager normally submits a written offer to the borrower which, when accepted, constitutes a mandate from the borrower to organize the syndicate along the lines specified. When formulating the offer, the prospective syndicate manager must give careful consideration to the marketability of the loan. Lenders are under constant pressure to reduce spreads and otherwise liberalize lending terms, and the syndicate manager must bid aggressively to obtain the mandate. However, if he is too aggressive, he will not be able to syndicate the loan. During recent years competition for mandates has become fierce, and this fact, combined with the high liquidity of the Eurocurrency market, has driven spreads down to historic lows.

In approaching the problems of fixing the price (that is, the spread over LIBOR) of a loan, it is important that the syndicate manager help the borrower see his position in the market relative to other borrowers. It is also important to compare for the borrower alternative methods of finance, such as fixed-rate medium-term loans, floating-rate notes, bond issues, private placements, and other methods.

The particular spread a borrower is able to command is influenced by the following five factors:

1. His credit rating
2. The acceptability of his country in the syndication market
3. The availability of other loans in the market for that country
4. The frequency with which he has come to the market before
5. Market trends (that is, which way spreads and rates are moving)

One critical factor for the borrower to remember is that the difference in spreads is not nearly so great as the fluctuations which can take place in the absolute level of the London interbank offered rate. For the period from 1969 to 1979, the six-month Eurodollar LIBOR rate ranged from below 6 percent to over 19 percent. A spread of one-half percent may sound wonderful, but when placed on top of a 19 percent LIBOR, it can be a crushing burden.

Fixed-rate loans are not very common in the medium-term Eurocurrency market due to the fact that the majority of the interbank deposit business is done for periods of less than one year. Most bank lenders are not prepared to take the rate exposure necessary to make an attractive fixed-rate offer.

Once the price has been fixed and the mandate obtained, the syndicate manager must work with the borrower to develop the terms of the lending contract which will meet the needs of the borrower and satisfy the requirements of the market.

During recent years, there has been a tendency for loan agreements to become increasingly complex. In addition to specifying terms, conditions, and drawdown details, the following clauses are normally also included:

Conditions Precedent. This section lists all data required to be supplied by the borrower and legal advisers, prior to drawing.

Representations and Warranties. A series of undertakings by the borrower to the lenders. These are normally intended to assume that the borrower has obtained the necessary authorizations and consents, but can cover other matters such as taxes.

Changes in Circumstances. This covers any changes (such as local taxation) affecting the borrower or the banks so that the cost of funding may be increased. It protects the banks by placing the onus of recompense on the borrower.

Events of Default. This section prescribes events such as nonpayment of interest or material adverse change, which will allow the lenders to declare the loan in default. Such a declaration will normally enable lenders to accelerate the loan and take other action to protect their interests.

Cross Default. This enables the lenders to declare a default and take action to protect their claims in the event the borrower is in default of other loan agreements.

Sovereign Immunity Waiver. This protects the lenders against the borrower claiming sovereign immunity from judicial proceedings.

Agent. This section details the responsibilities of the agent in relation to the borrower and lenders. It often prescribes voting procedures to be used in the event problems develop.

Jurisdiction. This establishes the country of jurisdiction for settlement of disputes, which in most instances is the United Kingdom or the United States.

Negative Pledge. This clause prevents the borrower from pledging assets to other creditors.

Use of Proceeds. This restricts the borrower to using the funds provided for a specific project or purpose.

It is impossible for the loan agreement to cover every contingency which might arise in a syndicated loan. However, accountants, maritime specialists, appraisers, trustees, petroleum specialists, and others can assist in adjusting the text to fit the needs of a particular loan.

Not infrequently, the purpose of the loan is ill-defined. Many governments which have raised loans in the market have borrowed for general budgetary purposes or general balance of payments support, and many corporations for general corporate purposes. Although this is not necessarily bad, it should be considered carefully when making a credit decision. Recent loans to some developing countries, irrespective of the stated purpose, have in fact been raised to refinance existing debt. Above all, the capacity of the borrower to service the loan must be rigorously examined so that the repayment schedule represents a realistic and practical possibility.

Implementing the Mandate

Once the terms of the loan agreement have been worked out, the syndicate manager (or management group) must address himself to syndicating the loan. Generally speaking, there are three basic methods for marketing loans in the London market.

The first is the *best-effort syndicate,* in which the manager indicates to the borrower that he will be prepared to offer the loan to the market under a certain set of terms and conditions. If the loan is not successfully sold, the offer will be withdrawn from the market and the borrower will have to seek funds elsewhere. Investment banks often come to the market in this way because of their inability to make firm commitments of funds. During recent years, the pure best-effort method has been less frequently used, and some investment banks have phased out of the syndicated Eurocurrency loan business, primarily because of their inability to commit funds from their own resources.

The second method is the *firm-commitment syndicate,* in which the manager gives the borrower a firm commitment to arrange a specified amount under a certain set of terms and conditions. If the offer is not successfully sold, the manager will take the full amount of the loan into his own portfolio. During the past few years, it has become quite common for the syndicate manager to commit firmly for one amount and offer to increase that amount on a best-effort basis.

The third method is the *club syndicate,* in which a syndicate is arranged by a limited group of banks each undertaking to hold its share of the loan. Normally, club syndicates are for smaller amounts, say, $30 to $80 million, and have the advantage of assuring the borrower that the loan will be firmly and immediately placed. Recently club syndicates have been used to raise somewhat larger amounts, some reaching the $300 million range.

There are many variations and combinations of these three basic methods of arranging a Eurocurrency syndicated loan. In some cases syndicates of only a few banks can be arranged and kept confidential. This can be of value to the borrower wishing to maintain a low profile in the market.

SELECTION OF PARTICIPANTS

When a syndicate manager selects the initial group of participating banks to whom he will offer participations, a number of basic factors must be considered: the size of the loan which is to be syndicated; the reception the loan will meet in the market place; the banks which have been active subscribers in the leader's prior syndicates; and the preferences of the borrower. The borrower, because of past relationships and location, often has a list of banks he would like included. In large syndications the number of banks selected may well exceed 500.

Once the marketing strategy is developed and a list of suitable participants is drawn up, the syndicate manager prepares and circulates to the potential participants two basic documents, the offering telex and the information memorandum.

The Offering Telex. This is a key document that is normally sent to a large number of banks summarizing the most important features of the loan, including the name of the borrower, amount of the loan, maturity, interest rate, repayment schedule, drawdown schedule, commitment fees, participation fees, purpose of the loan, prepayment conditions, and any other pertinent information on the loan or borrower. It is a direct offering to be accepted or declined by the prospective lending bank.

The Information Memorandum. This memorandum, often in the form of a printed brochure, gives a full description of the loan and the borrower, including the basic terms and conditions as set out in the offering telex. It normally contains the history, background, and detailed financial data on the borrower, a country report and statistics (if a state borrower), purpose of the loan or project, cash flow projections, and other information. The material provided in the information memorandum should originate from the borrower or government officials, and the source should be clearly indicated. Normally a strong waiver of responsibility by the manager is included at the front of the memorandum.

It is important to stress at this point that credit analysis is the responsibility of the prospective lender, who should not rely entirely on the contents of the information memorandum nor the presence of a number of big-name banks in the management group.

During the selling process the managers will be required to answer many questions regarding the loan and its documentation, and they are expected to respond as fully as possible. One bank in the management group is responsible for "keeping the book" on the syndication. This involves maintaining a record of all banks contacted and of the responses received.

Sometimes, the amount subscribed by the participants exceeds the expectation of the syndicate manager. In such cases the manager will either reduce the share of each participant or approach the borrower to increase the total amount of the loan. From the manager's point of view, the latter is the preferable course since it normally means a higher management fee.

Once the amount of the total loan and share of each participant is firmly agreed, the final loan agreement is prepared and a signing ceremony is arranged. It is not unusual that some of the terms of the original agreement are modified during the syndication process as a result of suggestions, or demands, from potential participants or their attorneys. All participating banks are represented at the signing ceremony, and normally each bank becomes a legal party to the loan agreement.

About the time of the signing ceremony, the syndicate manager arranges for a tombstone advertisement in the financial press announcing the conclusion of the loan. The following points of information can be determined from a tombstone and are keyed to the numbered sections in Figure 1.

Points 1, 2, and 3 identify the borrower, the amount of the loan, and the term, respectively. The term is sometimes stated explicitly (as in this case), whereas in others it is simply indicated as medium-term or short-term.

The management group is listed in the section bracketed by point 4. It is this group that has received the mandate from the borrower and has determined the syndication strategy.

The co-managers, shown by point 5, are those banks which have committed for a substantial amount and will receive a higher front-end fee. However, they normally have very little to do with the management of the syndicate.

Perhaps the most interesting is point 6, which lists the banks providing the funds. It is possible to measure the worldwide reception which the borrower receives by looking at the tombstone. In many cases a borrower would like to have maximum exposure, and it is often an advantage for lenders to have worldwide placement.

Point 7 shows the agent bank which will have a particular responsibility in the servicing of the loan agreement.

FEES

There are four basic types of fees paid by the borrower under a Eurocurrency credit:

1. *Commitment.* This fee, which is normally in the range of one-quarter to one-half percent is paid on a per annum basis on the undrawn portion of the loan.

2. *Management.* This is the total fee paid by the borrower to the lead manager and/or the management group. It is negotiated in each case and

Figure 1

May 1980   This announcement appears
                                                                     as a matter of record only

BANK OF GREECE ————————————1
US $ 550,000,000 ———————————2
Eight Year Loan ———————————————3

managed by

AMSTERDAM-ROTTERDAM BANK N.V.   BANK OF MONTREAL
BANKERS TRUST INTERNATIONAL LIMITED   BANQUE NATIONALE DE PARIS
CHASE MERCHANT BANKING GROUP   CREDIT LYONNAIS
DEUTSCHE BANK   THE FUJI BANK, LIMITED
COMPAGNIE FINANCIERE LUXEMBOURG   NATIONAL BANK OF CANADA
LLOYDS BANK INTERNATIONAL LIMITED   WESTDEUTSCHE LANDESBANK
SOCIETE GENERALE   GIROZENTRALE   4

ALLIED IRISH INVESTMENT BANK LIMITED   ASSOCIATED JAPANESE BANK
BANQUE EUROPEENNE DE CREDIT (BEC)   (INTERNATIONAL) LIMITED
CREDIT COMMERCIAL DE FRANCE   CAISSE NATIONALE DE CREDIT AGRICOLE
SOCIETE GENERALE DE BANQUE S.A.   EUROPEAN ARAB BANK GROUP
– BANQUE BELGE LIMITED   UNION BANK OF SWITZERLAND

co-managed by

BANQUE DE L'INDOCHINE ET DE SUEZ   BARCLAYS BANK INTERNATIONAL LIMITED
GULF RIYAD BANK E.C.   HESSISCHE LANDESBANK – GIROZENTRALE –
HYPOBANK INTERNATIONAL S.A.   LONDON & CONTINENTAL BANKERS LIMITED   5
ORION BANK LIMITED   TORONTO DOMINION BANK

provided by

Amsterdam-Rotterdam Bank N.V.   Banque Nordeurope S.A.   Morgan Grenfell & Co.
Allied Irish Investment Bank   Barclays Bank International   Limited
Limited   Limited   National Bank of Canada
Associated Japanese Bank (International) BfG Luxemburg   National Bank of North America
Limited   Caisse Nationale de Credit Agricole Nederlandse Credietbank (Overseas) nv
Banco de Bilbao S.A.   Canadian Imperial Bank   Österreichische Länderbank
London Branch   of Commerce (International) S.A. Aktiengesellschaft
Bank of Ireland   The Chase Manhattan Bank, N.A.   Orion Bank
Bank of Montreal   Credit Commercial de France   Limited
Bank of Montreal International   Credit Lyonnais   Slavenburg Overseas Banking Corporation
Limited   Daiwa Europe N.V.   (Netherlands Antilles)   6
Bank of New Zealand   Deutsche Bank   Societe Generale
The Bank of Nova Scotia Channel Islands Compagnie Financiere Luxembourg Société Générale de Banque S.A.
Limited   European Arab Bank Group   Sofis
Bankers Trust Company   The Fuji Bank,   Limited
Banque Belge   Limited   Swiss Bank Corporation (Luxembourg)
Limited   Grindlay Brandts   Limited
Banque Commerciale pour   Limited   Toronto Dominion Bank
l'Europe du Nord (Eurobank)   Gulf Riyad Bank E.C.   Trade Development Bank Overseas Inc.,
Banque Europeenne de Credit (BEC)   Hessische Landesbank – Girozentrale – Panama
Banque de l'Indochine et de Suez   Hypobank International S.A.   UBAF-ARAB American Bank
Banque Francaise du Commerce Exterieur IBJ Finanz AG   Union Bank of Switzerland
Banque Generale du Luxembourg S.A.   Lloyds Bank International   WestLB International S.A.
Banque Nationale de Grece (France)   Limited   Williams, Glyn & Co
Banque Nationale de Paris   London & Continental Bankers   Yamaichi International (Nederland) N.V.
                                      Limited

Agent
BANK OF MONTREAL ———————————7

ranges from ½ to to 2 percent flat and is normally paid at the time the loan agreement is signed. Allocation of fees among co-managers and participants takes place after deduction of the *praecipium,* which is the portion set aside for the lead manager or management group as compensation for their work in putting the syndicate together. A special allocation may be made to the agent bank for its services.

3. *Co-Manager.* "Co-manager" is normally a euphemism for a large participant, and the co-management fee, which is normally larger than the participation fee, is to compensate for agreeing to underwrite a fairly large portion of the loan.

4. *Participation.* This front-end fee, which is similar to but smaller than the co-manager's fee, is paid to the participating banks in proportion to the size of their individual commitments. The amounts normally range from $\frac{1}{16}$ to ½ percent. Participations below a minimum amount, say, $2 million, normally do not attract any fee.

Information on the commitment and participation fees is usually set forth in the offering telex and is widely known, whereas information on management and co-management fees is generally not made available to syndicate participants or the public.

SERVICING THE LOAN

Servicing the loan is the responsibility of the agent bank, which may or may not be the lead manager. When a loan is led by a management group, the agent bank is normally a member of the group. In addition to handling the operational aspects of the loan such as rate fixing, collecting interest, and paying and receiving principal, the agent is also expected to maintain a close relationship with the borrower to obtain current and authoritative information on the financial situation of the borrower and keep the participants informed with respect to any significant changes. Normally, the agent bank does not have the right to renegotiate and must obtain the concurrence of most or all of the participating banks before it can waive an event of default or renegotiate a covenant in the loan agreement.

Problem Areas

Generally speaking, the syndicated loan business has developed and expanded without any particular problems since the great majority of loans has been serviced properly by the borrower and there have been relatively few instances of default. However, during 1974 and 1975 serious problems arose with respect to some syndicated loans, particularly shipping loans and loans to real estate investment trusts in the United States. Once a situation of default arises, a host of legal and policy issues tend to develop between the syndicate manager and the participants, and sometimes between the participants. There can be major conflicts of interest. Sometimes the participants will claim that the manager has not performed his function properly, possibly by not providing the syndicate with enough information, or by taking insufficient action to collect the loan. Sometimes smaller participating banks refuse to cooperate with any group effort in the hope of being bought out. The exact legal responsibilities of the syndicate manager are by no means clear and are not likely to be defined until after there has been a series of specific court decisions, which will entail years of litigation.

The developments in connection with Iran, particularly in freezing of Iranian assets by U.S. banks, have uncorked a series of legal problems which will also take years to sort out. For example, can an American bank, as a syndicate manager, declare an event of default when the payment of interest was prevented by the U.S. government freeze order? Or, can that same bank use frozen Iranian assets to offset its claim against the government of Iran, and not apply these funds proportionately to claims of other banks participating in the syndicate? With banks from many countries participating in the one syndicate, and with each having a different political, legal, and financial relationship with Iran, the legal ramifications are considerable.

Future Trends

Looking ahead, it seems likely that the rate of growth of the market for syndicated Eurocurrency loans will decline somewhat. This will result partly from a more vigorous pursuit of restrictive monetary policies in the major countries and partly as a consequence of the deteriorated terms of lending which, as assets become more scarce, will cause banks in some countries to focus more attention on domestic lending. Finally, as the loan service burden of major borrowing countries continues to increase, the appetite of lenders for more loans to those countries can be expected to decline.

In the future, other market centers may expand and become more formidable competitors to London. Already sizeable loans are being raised in Singapore, Hong Kong, Bahrain, Luxembourg, and elsewhere. Some syndicated loans, while funded with Eurocurrencies and booked in London, are actually arranged in the United States, France, Germany, and elsewhere.

As more transactions are arranged away from London and various regional centers acquire more familiarity and expertise in Eurocurrency lending techniques, the process of decentralization seems likely to continue. Events such as the reopening of New York to foreign borrowers and the accumulation of vast amounts of liquid funds in the hands of Middle East oil producers may accelerate the trend away from London. For the foreseeable future, however, other offshore lending centers will probably remain satellites of the London market for the simple reason that no other center is likely to have a comparable array of international banking institutions and financial talent and expertise.

One factor that could result in a general curtailment in the market would be a concerted action by the monetary authorities of the major countries to "control" the Eurocurrency market. There has recently been a great deal of discussion of this, particularly in the United States and Germany and among bank regulatory authorities. British authorities, however, are strongly against most of the control suggestions which have been advanced and they are generally supported by their colleagues in Luxembourg. One area that does seem to have a wide measure of support is the movement to harmonize capital ratios. Agreement in this area is likely to be difficult and slow, but the movement toward more restrictive capital ratios will probably have the effect of slowing down the growth of the Eurocurrency market.

Although the history of the Eurocurrency market is replete with predictions of its ultimate demise, it has demonstrated remarkable resilience and vigor, even in the most difficult of times. In fact, it seems to prosper in adversity. When domestic capital markets have been hemmed in by restrictions and undermined by a lack of confidence, the Euromarket has often stood out as a deep, reliable, and flexible source of capital. Given the enormous capital requirements to be faced in the years ahead, it seems reasonable to predict that the Eurocurrency market will supply a major portion of these requirements and that the syndicated Eurocurrency loan will remain as the principal lending vehicle.

Index